THIRD EDITION

KOVELS'
DEPRESSION GLASS & AMERICAN DINNERWARE PRICE LIST

Ralph and Terry Kovel

Crown Publishers, Inc.
New York

Published by Crown Publishers, Inc., 201 East 50th Street,
New York, New York 10022
Manufactured in the United States of America

LIBRARY OF CONGRESS
Library of Congress Cataloging-in-Publication Data
Kovel, Ralph M.
[Depression glass & American dinnerware price list]
Kovels' depression glass & American dinnerware price list/Ralph and Terry Kovel.—3rd ed.
p. cm.
Rev. ed. of: The Kovels' illustrated price guide to depression glass and American dinnerware. 2nd ed. c1983.
Bibliography: p.
1. Depression glass—Catalogs. 2. Ceramic tableware—United States—History—20th century—Catalogs. I. Kovel, Terry H. II. Kovel, Ralph M. Kovels' Illustrated price guide to depression glass and American dinnerware. III. Title. IV. Title: Depression glass & American dinnerware price list. V. Title: Depression glass and American dinnerware price list. VI. Title: Kovels' depression glass and American dinnerware price list.
NK5439.D44K68 1988
738.2'0973'07509—dc19
ISBN 0-517-56865-9 (pbk.)
Design by Deborah Kerner

10 9 8 7 6 5 4 3

CONTENTS

DEPRESSION GLASS

AMERICAN DINNERWARE

ACKNOWLEDGMENTS

We want to thank the following companies and collectors who knowingly or unknowingly helped us to find pictures and prices for this book.

A–Z Antiques; Edith M. Ackerman; Agora; Herbert Allgood; Betty J. Anonby; Anita's Attic; Barbara Balin; Edna Barnes; Howard & Elly Barnett; Dwayne Bastian; Ginger Berry; Dennis Bialek; Florianna Bieros; Tom Bloom; Roselyn A. Blum; Maxine Bolt; Ida Bonner; Rebecca Brandenburg; Elaine Brede; Neida Brewer; Shirley Brodowski; Tammy Brooks; Betty Brown; Ed Burleson; Esther Butler; C & L Collectibles; C & M Glass Shop; Cameo Antiques; O. L. Cannon; P. Carlson; Sharon Carter; Carolyn Cator; Sandy & Pauline Cheshire; Carol & Len Chrzanowski; Churchmouse Antiques; Angelana Clark; Collector's Corner; Collectors Store; Terry Collings; Country Hicks Antiques; D and M Collectibles; Velma Dahl; Dan and Bill's Antiques; Darrels'; Mary C. Davis; Deer Trail Antiques; Martha DeLeo; Deborah Disanto and Michael Smondrowski; Tom Dowling; John & Rebekah Duffus; Arlene O'Green Dunn; Fancy That Antiques & Uniques; Ruth Farrington; Jon Feir; Fenner's Antiques; James Fletcher; Dan Fortney; Rodney G. Fulton; Priscilla Gimple; Glass Cellar; Glas Haus; Norma Goff; Joe Graber; Mark & Carol Graham; Joyce Gulmise; Don Hall; Eva Hansen; Evelyn Hidinger; Mark Hoaglin; Hoques Antiques & Curios; Helen Howell; Mrs. Lyle Irwin; Jaegers; Jan-tiques; Jenkins Antiques; Jolena Antiques; Evelyn Wilson Jones; Wanda Jones; K.C.'s Glass Cupboard; Hildegard Lary; Connie Leggett; Sharon Leiby; Angel & Joan Lopez; Ellie Lowenstein; Virginia Lucas; Debbie Maggard; Pam Manley; Maxine's Antiques; Jean Mayes; Joe McDonald; Dorothy Meyer; Milkweed Antiques; Doris W. Miller; Dorraine Modisett; Moore's Antiques; Morris Antiques; Ruth E. Mullett; Madonna M. Mumper; Christine Nagy; Nancy's Antiques; Barbara Nanney; Betty Newbound; Olde Loved Things; Christine Olson; L. Orbach; Shirley A. Patterson; Rae Patrick; Edward P. Paul & Co.; Alice B. Paulus; Neva Pearson; Robert Pierce; E. L. Pillow; Popkorn; Marie Pytel; John E. Rainka, Jr.; Linda Ricketts; Richard Riegel; Robert W. Riley; Marie A. Roberts; Robinson Sales; Shirley A. Robinson; Eileen Rodgers; Sharon Rummery; Dan Russo; Gwen Sandberg; Judy Sansale; Roselle Schliefman; Elizabeth Scott; Georgia Seibel; Kathy Small; Leslie Steven Silver; Mary Stacey; M. Steelman; Sugar Hill Antiques; Summer Kitchen Antiques; T & J's Yesteryear Collectibles; Tatiana's Collection; Robert Taylor; Susie Thompson; Janice Thran; Dave Tjarks; TMS Glassware; Ron Todd; Turners Antiques; Donna Upham; Mrs. C. W. Usey; Leni Vargo; R. Walker; Treva D. Weymer; Margaret & Kenn Whitmyer; Faith Wong's Collectors Junction; Mary Ann Woodard; Diane Worrell; Allen Wutke; Delmer H. Youngen.

Special thanks go to: Wolf's Gallery; Western Reserve Depression Glass Club; Nora Koch, editor of *Depression Glass Daze,* for providing information on reproduction glass which regularly appears in that newspaper; the many authors whose books helped us with our research and who are listed in the bibliographies; Crown Publishers, especially Ann Cahn, Deborah Kerner, and Milton Wackerow; Jeffrey Clark for the line drawings of patterns; and the many people on our staff who typed, collated, proofed, and did the other jobs that help us look like experts.

DEPRESSION GLASS

DEPRESSION GLASS

Introduction

Clear and pastel-colored glassware in matching sets became popular about 1925. The Fostoria Glass Company of Fostoria, Ohio, made the first of these glass sets, which included dinner plates, coffee cups, and other pieces to be used at a dinner table. The glassware was expensive and its popularity led to similar pieces being made by other companies that were able to produce a less expensive glass.

Inexpensive glass was made by a method called tank molding: silica sand, soda ash, and limestone were heated, and the molten glass mixture was passed through pipes to an automated pressing mold. Patterns were acid-etched or tooled into the mold so the finished glassware had a design. The pressing process made a glass that often had flaws or bubbles, so the decorations were often lacy in appearance to help hide the flaws.

During the late 1960s, interest in the inexpensive pastel glass led to several books, and the term "Depression glass" came into general use, even though the glassware was made before, during, and after the Depression. The name has gradually come to include other glassware made from 1925 through the 1970s. This price list includes the lacy types, the pseudo-sandwich glass patterns, the hobnail variations, the solid-colored wares of ruby, cobalt, or green, and the many opaque glass patterns. In the past few years another term, "elegant glassware of the Depression," has come to be used. This refers to the better-quality glass made at the

---

Particular patterns can be found by using either the Depression Glass or American Dinnerware main listings, both of which are arranged alphabetically. Depression Glass begins on page 7 and American Dinnerware on page 123. There is no index of pattern names in this book as it would only duplicate the main listings. However, we have compiled lists of known Depression glass and American Dinnerware patterns along with information on manufacturers, dates, alternate names, and descriptions. These can be found at the end of each section.

same time. There is much overlap between these types of glass, and the exact name to use for a pattern may be in doubt. Because of this, we have listed Depression and some "elegant" patterns here. All of the pattern names are from original catalogs, Depression glass books, lists, or shows.

Depression glass designs can be divided into groups. The etched designs, for example, Adam or Cherry Blossom, were made first, from about 1925 to 1935. Pastel colors were used.

Raised designs, often with fruit and flower patterns, for example, Open Rose and Sharon, were made in the mid-1930s. Strong colors like cobalt blue or Royal Ruby, opaque glass pastels, and clear glass were popular.

Geometric wares, for example, Hobnail and Ribbon, were made during the late 1920s and again in the late 1930s and early 1940s. Simple outlines and bold colors predominated. Art Deco-influenced geometric designs include Imperial Octagon and United States Octagon.

Enameled or silk-screened patterns were developed during the 1940s. White enameled designs were added to the glass. Cobalt blue, Royal Ruby, and clear glass were the most popular colors that were decorated this way. Shirley Temple glasswares and Sailboats are two such enameled patterns.

A few patterns, Floral & Diamond Band for example, were made to resemble the pressed glass of the nineteenth century, particularly the Lacy Sandwich pattern made by the Sandwich, Massachusetts, glassworks. About ten such pseudo-Sandwich patterns were made and most of them were referred to as Sandwich in manufacturers' catalogs.

Depression glass utility wares were also made. The dishes were meant to be used in the kitchen and not on the table, for example, ice-box dishes, lemon reamers, canister sets.

Opaque glass was popular in the 1930s. Each of the colors was given a special name by the company that produced it, for example, Monax or Ivrene.

Opaque green glass was known by a variety of names. Jade green is a generic name used by many companies. Jade-ite was the green color used by Anchor Hocking; Jadite was a color of glass and a pattern of green kitchenware made by Jeannette Glass Company. To avoid unnecessary confusion, we have chosen to always spell the word "jadite" in this book. Delphite, an opaque blue glass, is sometimes spelled "delfite" in the ads, but we have chosen to always use the delphite spelling.

This book is not an in-depth study of Depression glass. The beginner who needs more information about patterns, manufacturers, color groups, or how and where to buy should see the Bibliography and club lists we have included.

Hundreds of patterns, many not listed in other price books, are included here. But if you wish to specialize in one pattern of Depression glass, there may be a book available that includes many colored photographs of your pattern. There may also be a book available with special information about the factory making your pattern. The best way to learn about Depression glass is to attend the regional and national shows devoted to glass. Your local newspaper or the collectors' publications listed in this book will print the dates and locations.

There is a list of reproductions and a list of known glass patterns and manufacturers following the last glass price entries.

This book is a price report. Prices are actual offerings in the marketplace. They are not an average. The high and low prices represent different sales. Prices reported are not those from garage or house sales or flea markets. They are only from dealers who understand the Depression glass market and who sell at shops, at shows, or through national advertising.

Information about American ceramic dinnerware and the prices for these pieces can be found in the second half of this book.

DEPRESSION GLASS *Bibliography*

Archer, Margaret and Douglas. *Imperial Glass.* Paducah, Kentucky: Collector Books, 1978.

Cambridge Glass Co. (catalog reprint). Privately printed, 1976 (P.O. Box 416, Cambridge, OH 43725).

Fine Handmade Table Glassware (catalog reprint). Privately printed, 1978 (P.O. Box 416, Cambridge, OH 43725).

Florence, Gene. *Collector's Encyclopedia of Depression Glass,* 8th edition. Paducah, Kentucky: Collector Books, 1987.

Florence, Gene. *Elegant Glassware of the Depression Era,* 3rd edition. Paducah, Kentucky: Collector Books, 1988.

Florence, Gene. *Kitchen Glassware of the Depression Years,* 2nd edition. Paducah, Kentucky: Collector Books, 1983.

Florence, Gene. *Pocket Guide to Depression Glass,* 5th edition. Paducah, Kentucky: Collector Books, 1987.

Florence, Gene. *Very Rare Glassware of the Depression Years.* Paducah, Kentucky: Collector Books, 1988.

Fountain, Mel. *Swankyswigs, with Price Guide.* Privately printed, 1979 (201 Alvena, Wichita, KS 67203).

Heacock, William. *Fenton Glass—The First Twenty-Five Years.* Privately printed, 1978 (P.O. Box 663, Marietta, OH 45750).

Hudgeons, Thomas E. III. *Official Price Guide to Depression Glass.* New York: House of Collectibles, 1985.

Klamkin, Marian. *Collector's Guide to Depression Glass.* New York: Hawthorn Books, 1973.

Kovel, Ralph and Terry. *Kovels' Antiques & Collectibles Price List,* 20th edition. New York: Crown Publishers, 1987.

Kovel, Ralph and Terry, *Kovels' Guide to Selling Your Antiques & Collectibles.* New York: Crown Publishers, 1987.

Kovel, Ralph and Terry. *Kovels' Know Your Collectibles.* New York: Crown Publishers, 1981.

Luckey, Carl F. *Identification & Value Guide to Depression Era Glassware,* 2nd edition. Florence, Alabama: Books Americana, 1986.

McGrain, Pat. *1981 Price Survey.* Privately printed, 1980 (Box 219, Frederick, MD 21701).

McGrain, Patrick, ed. *Fostoria—The Popular Years.* Privately printed, 1982 (Box 219, Frederick, MD 21701).

Schliesmann, Mark. *Price Survey,* 3rd edition. Privately printed, 1986 (Box 838-PS, Racine, WI 53403).

Stout, Sandra McPhee. *Depression Glass in Color.* Lombard, Illinois: Wallace-Homestead Book Co., 1970.

Stout, Sandra McPhee. *Depression Glass Number Two.* Lombard, Illinois: Wallace-Homestead Book Co., 1971.

Stout, Sandra McPhee. *Depression Glass III.* Lombard, Illinois: Wallace-Homestead Book Co., 1976.

Stout, Sandra McPhee. *Depression Glass Price Guide.* Lombard, Illinois: Wallace-Homestead Book Co., 1975.

Warner, Ian. *Swankyswigs, A Pattern Guide and Check List.* Privately printed, 1982 (Box 57, Otisville, MI 48463).

Weatherman, Hazel Marie. *Colored Glassware of the Depression Era.* Privately printed, 1970 (P.O. Box 4444, Springfield, MO 65804).

Weatherman, Hazel Marie. *Colored Glassware of the Depression Era. 2.* Privately printed, 1974 (P.O. Box 4444, Springfield, MO 65804).

Weatherman, Hazel Marie. *Decorated Tumbler.* Privately printed, 1978 (P.O. Box 4444, Springfield, MO 65804).

Weatherman, Hazel Marie. *Fostoria—Its First Fifty Years.* Privately printed, 1972 (P.O. Box 4444, Springfield, MO 65804).

Weatherman, Hazel Marie. *Price Guide to the Decorated Tumbler.* Privately printed, 1979 (P.O. Box 4444, Springfield, MO 65804).

Weiss, Jeffrey. *Cornerstone Collector's Guide to Glass.* New York: Simon & Schuster, 1981.

DEPRESSION GLASS
Clubs and Publications

CLUBS

Fenton Art Glass Collectors of America, Inc., *Butterfly Net* (newsletter), P.O. Box 384, Williamstown, WV 26187.

Fostoria Glass Society of America, Inc., *Facets of Fostoria* (newsletter), P.O. Box 826, Moundsville, WV 26041.

Heisey Collectors of America, *Heisey News* (newsletter), P.O. Box 27, Newark, OH 43055.

Michiana Association of Candlewick Collectors, MACC *Spyglass* (newsletter), 17370 Battles Road, South Bend, IN 46614.

National Cambridge Collectors, Inc., *Cambridge Crystal Ball* (newsletter), P.O. Box 416, Cambridge, OH 43725.

National Candlewick Collectors Club, *Candlewick Collector* (newsletter), 275 Milledge Terrace, Athens, GA 30606.

National Depression Glass Association, *News & Views* (newsletter), P.O. Box 11123, Springfield, MO 65808.

National Duncan Glass Society, *National Duncan Glass Journal* (newsletter), P.O. Box 965, Washington, PA 15301-0965.

National Imperial Glass Collectors Society, *Glasszette* (newsletter), P.O. Box 534, Bellaire, OH 43906.

National Milk Glass Collectors Society, *Opaque News* (newsletter), P.O. Box 402, Northfield, MN 55057.

National Reamer Collectors Association, NRCA *Quarterly Review* (newsletter), 2914 Bucknell Street, Bakersfield, CA 93305.

PUBLICATIONS

Antique Trader Weekly (newspaper), P.O. Box 1050, Dubuque, IA 52001.

Depression Glass Daze (newspaper), Box 57, Otisville, MI 48463.

Glass Collector's Digest (magazine), P.O. Box 553, Marietta, OH 45750.

Glass Review (magazine), P.O. Box 7188, Redlands, CA 92373.

Kovels on Antiques and Collectibles (newsletter), P.O. Box 22200, Beachwood, OH 44122.

Matching Services: China, Silver, Crystal (leaflet), Ralph and Terry Kovel (P.O. Box 22900, Beachwood, OH 44122).

DEPRESSION GLASS

Color Names

This is a list of some of the most confusing color names:

AMBER	Topaz, Golden Glow
BLUE GREEN	Ultramarine
CLEAR	Crystal
DEEP BLUE	Ritz blue, cobalt, dark blue, deep blue
GREEN	Springtime Green, emerald, Imperial Green, Forest Green, Nu-green
MEDIUM BLUE	Madonna
OPAQUE BLACK	Black
OPAQUE BLUE	Delphite
OPAQUE GREEN	Jadite
OPAQUE OFF-WHITE	Chinex, Clambroth, Cremax, Ivrene
OPAQUE WHITE	Milk white, Monax
PINK	Rose Marie, Rose, Rose Pink, Rose Tint, Rose Glow, Nu-rose, Wild Rose, Flamingo, Cheri-glo
PURPLE	Burgundy, amythyst
RED	Royal Ruby, Ruby Red, Carmen

A

Accordian Pleats, see Round Robin

Adam

Adam, sometimes called Chain Daisy or Fan & Feather, is a glass pattern made from 1932 to 1934 by the Jeannette Glass Company, Jeannette, Pennsylvania. Sets can be found in crystal, green, and pink. A few pieces are known in yellow, but this does not seem to have been a standard production color. Reproductions have been made in green and pink.

CRYSTAL

Ashtray, 4 1/2 In. 12.00

GREEN

Ashtray, 4 1/2 In. 8.00 To 15.00
Bowl, 4 3/4 In. 7.00 To 12.00
Bowl, 5 3/4 In. 21.00 To 40.00
Bowl, 7 3/4 In. 12.00 To 15.00
Bowl, 9 In. 30.00
Bowl, Oval, 10 In. 13.00
Cake Plate, Footed, 10 In. 14.00 To 18.50
Candleholder, 4 In., Pair 69.50
Creamer 11.00 To 13.00
Cup 13.00
Cup & Saucer 18.50 To 25.00
Pitcher, Square Base, 32 Oz., 8 In. 30.00 To 35.00
Plate, 6 In. 3.50
Plate, 7 3/4 In. 6.00 To 8.75
Plate, 8 In. 7.50
Plate, 9 In. 11.00 To 16.00
Plate, Grill, 9 In. 10.00 To 14.00
Platter, 11 3/4 In. 10.00 To 15.00
Relish, 2 Sections, 8 In. 10.00
Saucer 2.50 To 3.00
Sherbet, 3 In. 26.50 To 28.00
Sugar 7.50
Sugar, Cover 30.00 To 35.00
Tumbler, 4 1/2 In. 10.00 To 14.00
Tumbler, 5 1/2 In. 27.50 To 30.00
Vase, 7 1/2 In. 28.00 To 40.00

PINK

Ashtray, 4 1/2 In. 9.00
Bowl, 4 3/4 In. 8.00 To 10.00
Bowl, 5 3/4 In. 27.00
Bowl, 7 3/4 In. 11.00 To 18.00
Bowl, 9 In. 15.00 To 18.50
Bowl, Cover, 9 In. 33.00 To 37.00
Bowl, Oval, 10 In. 12.00 To 15.00
Butter, Cover 50.00 To 75.00
Cake Plate 10.00
Candleholder, 4 In., Pair 45.00 To 57.00
Candy Container, Cover 45.00 To 60.00
Creamer 9.00 To 15.00
Cup 15.00 To 19.75
Cup & Saucer 16.50 To 20.00
Pitcher, 32 Oz., 8 In. 19.00 To 23.00
Plate, 6 In. 3.00 To 6.00
Plate, 7 3/4 In. 5.50 To 12.50
Plate, 9 In. 10.00 To 16.00
Plate, Grill, 9 In. 8.00 To 15.50
Platter, 11 3/4 In. 9.00 To 12.00
Relish, 2 Sections 10.00 To 13.50
Salt & Pepper, 4 In. 38.00 To 55.00
Saltshaker 18.00
Saucer 2.00 To 3.50
Sherbet 13.00 To 18.00
Sugar & Creamer, Cover 27.00 To 35.00
Sugar, Cover 24.00 To 27.00
Tumbler, 4 1/2 In. 12.00 To 18.50
Tumbler, Footed, 5 1/2 In. 40.00
Vase, 7 1/2 In. 135.00 To 175.00

Akro Agate

Picture a marble cake with the irregular mixture of colors running through the batter. This is what Akro Agate is usually like, a marbleized mixture of colored glass. The Akro Agate Company, Clarksburg, West Virginia, originally made children's marbles. The marbleized dinnerware and other glass children's sets were made in many colors from 1932 to 1951.

BLUE

Cup, Child's 8.00 To 11.00
Pitcher, Water, Octagonal 11.00
Plate, Child's 11.00 To 14.00
Powder Box, Lady 50.00
Sugar & Creamer, Ivory Cover, Octagonal 20.00
Teapot, Child's, Interior Panel 20.00
Teapot, Child's, Stacked Disc 12.00
Teapot, Ivory Cover, Octagonal 8.00

GREEN

Creamer, Child's 20.00
Cup & Saucer, Child's 5.00 To 13.00
Cup & Saucer, Demitasse 9.50
Cup, Child's 3.00 To 15.00
Plate, Child's 1.50 To 5.00
Saucer, Child's 2.00
Sugar, Child's 20.00
Tea Set, Child's, 6 Piece 35.00

Tea Set, Child's, 8 Piece 30.00
Tea Set, Child's, 8 Piece, Box....45.00
Tea Set, Child's, 22 Piece....65.00 To 115.00
Tea Set, Child's, Stippled Band, 16 Piece....30.00
Teapot, Child's....20.00
Tumbler, Child's.... 6.50
Water Set, Child's, 5 Piece....15.00

IVORY

Creamer, Child's.... 5.00
Saucer, Child's.... 2.25
Tumbler, Child's.... 6.00

PINK

Plate, Child's.... 3.75
Saucer, Child's.... 5.00

PUMPKIN

Cup, Child's....15.00
Cup, Open Handle....20.00

PURPLE

Cup, Child's, Concentric Rib....35.00
Planter, Octagonal....12.00

RED

Plate, Child's, Interior Panel.... 7.00

TAN

Saucer.... 2.50

YELLOW

Saucer, Child's....3.00 To 8.00

Alice

An 8 1/2-inch plate, cup, and saucer were apparently the only pieces made in the Alice pattern. This 1940s pattern was made by the Anchor Hocking Glass Company, Lancaster, Ohio, in opaque white with a pink or blue border and in jadite. Other related sections in this book are Fire-King, Jadite, Jane-Ray, Square, Swirl Fire-King, and Turquoise Blue.

JADITE

Cup & Saucer....1.25 To 4.00
Saucer.... 1.00

PINK

Cup & Saucer.... 6.00

WHITE

Cup & Saucer.... 6.00
Plate, 9 In.... 8.50
Saucer.... 2.00

Alpine Caprice

Caprice and Alpine Caprice were made from the same molds. Alpine Caprice has a satin finish, Caprice is transparent. Alpine Caprice, made by the Cambridge Glass Company, Cambridge, Ohio, about 1936, was made in blue, crystal, and pink satin-finished glass.

Alpine Caprice, see also Caprice

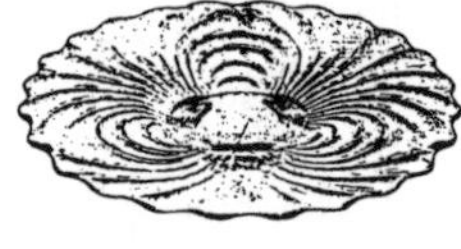

BLUE

Bowl, 2 Handles, 4-Footed, Oval, 11 In....50.00
Bowl, 2 Handles, Footed, Low, 6 In....18.00
Bowl, 4-Footed, 12 1/2 In....68.00
Bowl, 4-Footed, Cupped, 13 1/2 In....60.00
Candleholder, 7 In., Pair...50.00
Candlestick, Pair....75.00
Candy Dish, Cover, 4-Footed.... 100.00
Dish, Mayonnaise, Footed, Spoon....60.00
Finger Bowl....45.00

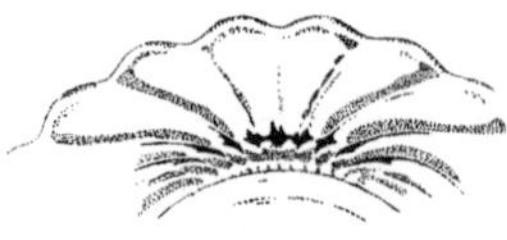

Plate, 14 In....50.00
Relish, 2 Sections....35.00
Relish, 3 Sections, 8 In. 20.00
Shaker Set, 3 Piece.... 125.00
Sugar....12.00

CRYSTAL

Ashtray, 4 In.... 7.00
Candleholder, 2-Light, Keyhole....27.00
Celery, 12 In....45.00
Plate, 3-Footed, 14 In. 40.00
Plate, 8 1/2 In....15.00
Relish, 2 Sections, 6 1/2 In....18.00
Relish, 3 Sections, 8 In. 30.00

PINK

Candleholder, 3-Light, Pair.... 195.00

American

American is a pattern made to resemble the pressed glass of an earlier time. It was introduced by Fostoria Glass, Moundsville, West Virginia, in 1915 and remained in production until the factory closed in 1986. Most pieces were made of clear, colorless glass known as crystal. A few pieces are known in amber, green, and milk glass. It is similar to Cube pattern, but after looking care-

fully, you will soon learn to tell the two patterns apart. Many pieces of American pattern were reproduced after 1987.

AMBER

Powder Jar, Cover......... 169.00

CRYSTAL

Ashtray, 2 1/4 In...........3.50 To 4.00
Ashtray, Hat Shape, 2 1/8 In........12.00 To 15.00
Ashtray, Hat Shape, 2 3/4 In....................15.00
Ashtray, Hat Shape, 4 In..........................34.00
Ashtray, Oval, 3 In.......... 6.00
Ashtray, Oval, 3 7/8 In. 9.00
Banana Boat, 8 1/2 In......14.00
Banana Boat, 12 In..........20.00
Basket..........................50.00
Basket, Reed Handle ... 85.00 To 90.00
Bonbon, 3-Footed, 7 In.............. 6.00 To 18.00
Bookends, Eagle............55.00
Bottle, Bitters................32.00
Bottle, Condiment, Stopper.................... 125.00
Bottle, Oil....................27.00
Bottle, Whiskey, 1/2 Pt. ...40.00
Bowl, 5 In....................10.00
Bowl, 8 1/2 In. 25.00
Bowl, 12 In. 50.00
Bowl, 13 In. .....35.00 To 45.00
Bowl, 2 Sections, 6 1/2 In.....................25.00
Bowl, 3 Handles, 5 In. 8.50
Bowl, 3-Footed, 10 1/2 In..................16.00
Bowl, 3-Footed, 7 In. 12.00
Bowl, 4 1/2 In.......... 9.00 To 12.00
Bowl, Console, 11 In. 30.00
Bowl, Console, Hat Center, 15 In...................... 123.00
Bowl, Cover, 5 In..............20.00 To 24.00
Bowl, Cover, 11 In..........40.00
Bowl, Cupped, 8 In. 45.00
Bowl, Footed, 16 In.........95.00
Bowl, Fruit, Footed, Hexagonal, 4 3/4 In...................... 8.00
Bowl, Handle, Square, 4 1/2 In...........7.00 To 8.50
Bowl, Lemon, Cover............35.00 To 45.00
Bowl, Nut, With Nutcracker & Picks.........................65.00
Bowl, Olive, Oval, 6 In.....12.50
Bowl, Oval, 3 3/4 In. 9.00
Bowl, Oval, 9 In............22.00 To 28.00
Bowl, Oval, 11 In.........95.00
Bowl, Oval, 11 1/4 In......60.00
Bowl, Oval, 11 3/4 In. ......32.00 To 38.00
Bowl, Pickle, Oval, 8 In.............12.00 To 14.00
Bowl, Rolled Edge, 11 1/2 In. ......34.00 To 47.50
Bowl, Tom & Jerry, 12 In...........80.00 To 100.00
Bowl, Tricornered, 3-Footed, 11 In........................12.00
Bowl, Vegetable, Oval, 2 Sections, 10 In. 30.00
Bowl, Vegetable, Oval, 9 In.........................25.00
Bowl, Wedding, Cover, 6 1/2 X 8 In..............75.00
Box, Pomade, 2 X 1 7/8 In............ 225.00
Box, Powder, 3 X 3 X 2 7/8 In. 150.00
Butter, Cover, 1 Lb.............70.00 To 90.00
Butter, Cover, 1/4 Lb...........30.00 To 33.00
Cake Plate, 12 In...........42.50
Cake Plate, Handle, 10 In............16.00 To 25.00
Cake Plate, Handles, 12 In........................40.00
Cake Plate, Metal Handle, 10 1/2 In..................25.00
Cake Stand, Square Pedestal, 10 In........................45.00
Candleholder, 3 In., Pair ... 18.00
Candleholder, 6 In., Pair ... 50.00
Candleholder, Square, 7 1/4 In....................95.00
Candy Container, Cover, 3 Sections.......53.00 To 75.00
Candy Container, Cover, Footed...........30.00 To 37.50
Celery, 6 In. 35.00
Celery, Oval, 10 In............13.50 To 17.00
Centerpiece, 9 1/2 In.........25.00 To 35.00
Centerpiece, 11 In...........60.00
Cheese & Cracker Set...............45.00 To 47.00
Cigarette Box, Cover............22.00 To 25.00
Coaster........................12.00
Compote, 5 1/4 X 9 1/2 In. 68.00
Compote, Cover, 5 In.......25.00
Compote, Cover, Footed, 9 In..........................32.00
Cookie Jar.................. 175.00
Cordial, Bourbon.......... 100.00
Creamer, 2 1/2 In............ 4.00
Creamer, 3 1/2 In...........12.00
Creamer, Individual..........3.00 To 6.50
Cruet, 7 Oz...................30.00
Cup & Saucer..... 8.00 To 12.00
Decanter, 24 Oz., 9 1/4 In.....................80.00

Decanter, Gin, Etched Stopper.............98.00
Decanter, Scotch, Etched Stopper.........85.00 To 100.00
Decanter, Whiskey.........45.00 To 90.00
Dish, Ice Cream, Oval, 13 1/2 In..................55.00
Dish, Mayonnaise, 3 Piece......................35.00
Dish, Sauce, Liner...........57.00
Goblet, 5 1/2 In. 8.00
Goblet, 6 7/8 Oz......... 8.00 To 12.50
Gravy Boat, Underplate 50.00
Ice Bucket, Metal Handle... 35.00 To 60.00
Ice Tub, Liner, 5 5/8 In.........34.00 To 45.00
Ice Tub, Liner, 6 1/2 In....50.00
Jar, Jam, Cover, 6 3/4 In.....................45.00
Jar, Pomade, 2 X 1 7/8 In............ 225.00
Lamp, Hurricane, 3 Piece.................... 155.00

Mustard, Cover............24.00 To 30.00
Napkin Ring.................. 6.00
Oyster Cocktail, 3 1/2 In.....................10.00
Picture, Frame...............10.00
Pitcher, 1 Pt., 5 3/8 In.........18.00 To 27.50
Pitcher, 1/2 Gal., 8 In......60.00
Pitcher, Ice Lip, 3 Pt., 6 1/2 In.........35.00 To 47.00
Plate, 6 In..................... 7.00
Plate, 7 In.................... 9.50
Plate, 7 1/2 In.... 7.00 To 10.00
Plate, 8 1/2 In......7.00 To 9.00
Plate, 9 In..................18.00
Plate, 9 1/2 In.........14.00 To 18.00
Plate, 10 1/2 In. 20.00
Plate, Crescent, 7 1/2 X 4 3/4 In. 38.00
Plate, Torte, 14 In...........35.00
Plate, Torte, 20 In...........90.00
Plate, Torte, Oval, 13 1/2 In...................65.00
Platter, Center Handle, Oval, 12 In.........................65.00
Platter, Oval, 12 In.............40.00 To 45.00
Punch Bowl, 18 In. 150.00
Punch Bowl, Base, 14 In..........125.00 To 155.00
Punch Set, Ladle, 8 Cups, 14 In. Bowl.............. 225.00
Relish, 2 Sections, Boat.............. 9.00 To 15.00
Relish, 3 Sections, Oval, 9 In.........................25.00
Relish, 3 Sections, Oval, 11 In.........................22.00
Rose Bowl, 3 1/2 In........16.00
Salt & Pepper, 3 1/2 In. ...20.00
Salt & Pepper, Tray, Individual...................20.00
Salt Dip, Individual 290.00
Saltshaker............6.00 To 8.00
Sandwich Server, Center Handle.............27.00
Sandwich Server, Handles, 12 In.........................30.00
Sherbet, Flat, 3 1/4 In....... 5.00
Sherbet, Footed, 3 1/4 In.....................10.00
Soup, Cream, Liner..........45.00
Strawholder, Cover........ 235.00
Sugar & Creamer, Individual..................10.00
Sugar & Creamer, Large....45.00
Sugar & Creamer, Small....25.00
Sugar & Creamer, Tray.....35.00
Sugar & Creamer, Tray, Individual...................22.00
Syrup, Glass Cover..........75.00
Syrup, Sani-Cut Server......55.00
Toothpick.....................22.50
Tray, 4 Sections, Square, 10 In........................35.00
Tray, 4 Sections, Square, 10 3/4 In..................85.00
Tray, 4 Sections, Square, 11 In.........................80.00
Tray, Center Handle, 12 In.........................30.00
Tray, Condiment........... 110.00
Tray, Handle, Oval, 10 In.........................40.00
Tray, Muffin, Turned Handles, 12 In.........................28.00
Tray, Oval, 10 1/2 In. 75.00
Tray, Square 125.00
Tumbler, 3 3/8 In.......... 8.00 To 12.00
Tumbler, 5 In................12.00
Tumbler, Flared, 4 1/8 In.....................12.50
Tumbler, Footed, 4 3/4 In.....................11.00
Tumbler, Footed, 5 1/2 In.....................14.00
Tumbler, Footed, 5 Oz. 10.00
Urn, Square, 6 In............25.00
Urn, Square, 7 1/2 In. 33.00
Vase, 4 1/2 In..............85.00
Vase, 8 1/2 In..............13.00
Vase, 10 In...................85.00
Vase, 12 In...................90.00
Vase, 20 In................ 295.00
Vase, Bud, Flared, 6 In.....10.00
Vase, Bud, Flared, 8 In.....20.00
Vase, Flared, 6 In. 23.00
Vase, Flared, 9 In. 40.00
Vase, Flared, 9 1/2 In.........85.00 To 95.00
Vase, Footed, Square, 9 In..........................30.00
Vase, Sterling Overlay, 6 In..........................30.00
Whiskey, 2 Oz.... 5.00 To 10.00

American Beauty, see English Hobnail

American Pioneer

Panels of hobnail-like protrusions and plain panels were used in the design of American Pioneer. It was made by Liberty Works, Egg Harbor, New Jersey, from 1931 to 1934. Crystal, green, and pink dishes are easily found. Amber is rare.

CRYSTAL

Bowl, Handles, 9 1/4 In.....................10.00
Creamer, 2 3/4 In...........12.00
Cup............................. 4.00
Cup & Saucer..... 8.00 To 10.00
Ice Bucket.....................20.00
Plate, 8 In..................... 5.00
Saucer................2.00 To 3.50
Sugar, 2 3/4 In..............11.00

GREEN

Bowl, Handles, 9 In.........25.00
Cup............................. 8.00
Cup & Saucer................12.00
Plate, 8 In...........6.00 To 7.50
Plate, Handles, 11 1/2 In..................11.50

If you move glass in cold weather be sure to let it sit at room temperature for several hours before you try unpacking it. The glass will break more easily if there is an abrupt temperature change.

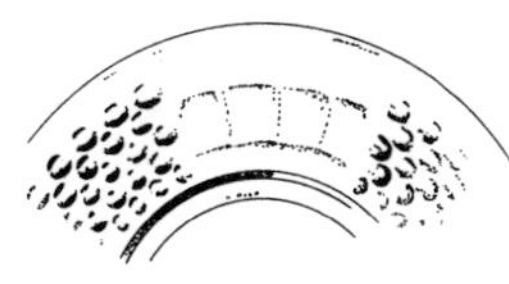

Saucer.......................... 3.75
Sugar, 2 3/4 In.............14.00

PINK

Creamer 12.00
Cup & Saucer 8.00
Ice Bucket, Handle ....35.00 To 40.00
Pitcher, Cover, 5 In.............75.00 To 80.00
Plate, 6 In..................... 3.00
Plate, 8 In..................... 5.00
Plate, 11 In.................... 8.00

American Sweetheart

In 1930 Macbeth-Evans Glass Company introduced American Sweetheart. At first it was made of pink glass, but soon other colors were added. The pattern continued in production until 1936. Blue, pink, red, cremax, and monax pieces were made. Sometimes a gold, platinum, green, pink, red, or smoky black trim was used on monax pieces. There is a center design on most plates, but some monax plates are found with plain centers. One of the rarest items in this pattern is the monax sugar bowl lid. The bowls are easy to find but the lids seem to have broken.

MONAX

Bowl, 6 In......... 8.00 To 12.00
Bowl, 9 In........32.00 To 47.00
Bowl, Cereal 12.00
Bowl, Console, 18 In. 350.00
Bowl, Vegetable, Oval, 11 In............36.00 To 45.00
Creamer ....5.00 To 8.50
Cup..................5.00 To 6.00
Cup & Saucer ..... 8.50 To 12.50
Plate, 6 In. ....2.50 To 3.50
Plate, 8 In. ....3.00 To 6.00
Plate, 9 3/4 In.........10.00 To 14.50
Plate, 10 1/4 In. .... 9.00 To 16.50
Plate, 9 In. 9.00
Plate, Chop, 11 In............. 9.00 To 13.50
Plate, Server, 12 In.............. 8.00 To 14.00
Platter, Oval, 13 In............35.00 To 38.00
Salt & Pepper........ 175.00 To 230.00
Saucer................1.00 To 2.00
Sherbet, Footed, 4 1/4 In.........11.00 To 17.00
Sugar & Creamer.........11.00 To 25.00
Sugar, Footed ....4.00 To 8.50
Tidbit, 2 Tiers 65.00

PINK

Bowl, 6 In......... 5.00 To 10.00
Bowl, 9 In........14.00 To 24.00
Bowl, Vegetable, Oval, 11 In............20.00 To 27.50
Creamer 10.50
Cup..................5.00 To 8.50
Cup & Saucer ..... 8.00 To 12.50
Pitcher, 60 Oz., 7 1/2 In.................. 365.00
Plate, 6 In. ....1.00 To 3.00
Plate, 6 1/2 In................ 2.00
Plate, 8 In. ....4.00 To 8.00
Plate, 9 3/4 In.........12.00 To 20.00
Plate, Chop, 11 In............ 8.50
Plate, Server, 12 In.............. 7.00 To 11.00
Platter, Oval, 13 In............14.50 To 20.00
Salt & Pepper............. 245.00
Saucer................1.50 To 3.00

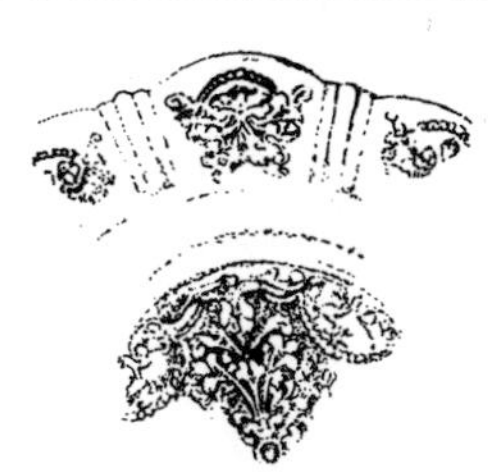

Sherbet, 3 3/4 In............12.50
Sherbet, 4 1/4 In.......... 6.00 To 10.00
Soup, Dish, 9 1/2 In.........25.00 To 29.50
Sugar & Creamer............22.00
Tumbler, 3 1/2 In.........30.00 To 40.00
Tumbler, 4 3/8 In. 34.00

RED

Plate, Server, 15 1/2 In................ 245.00
Sugar & Creamer.......... 190.00

Anniversary

Although pink Anniversary pattern was made from 1947 to 1949, it is still considered Depression glass by collectors. Crystal pieces are shown in a 1949 catalog. Later, amethyst and milk glass pieces were made. From 1970 to 1972 crystal and an iridescent carnival-glass-like amber color were used. The pattern was the product of the Jeannette Glass Company, Jeannette, Pennsylvania.

CRYSTAL

Bowl, 4 7/8 In. 4.00
Bowl, 7 3/8 In. 6.00
Bowl, 9 In..................... 8.00
Butter, Cover .... 22.50 To 26.00
Cake Plate, Metal Cover..... 8.00
Candleholder, 4 7/8 In., Pair 15.00
Candy Container, Footed ... 18.00
Compote, 3-Footed 6.00
Cup & Saucer ....2.50 To 5.00

Plate, 6 In. 1.25
Plate, Sandwich,
12 1/2 In. 5.00
Sherbet 7.00
Sugar & Creamer 5.00
Tidbit, 2 Tiers 8.00
Vase, 6 1/2 In. 8.00
Wall Pocket 20.00
Wine 8.00

IRIDESCENT

Cup & Saucer 2.50
Plate, 6 In. 1.25
Plate, 9 In. 2.50

PINK

Butter, Cover 45.00
Candy Container, Cover 27.00
Compote, 3-Footed 6.00
Wine 10.50

Apple Blossom, see Dogwood

Aunt Polly

U.S. Glass Company, a firm with factories in Indiana, Ohio, Pennsylvania, and West Virginia, made Aunt Polly glass. The pattern can be found in blue, green, and iridescent. Pink pieces have been reported. The pattern was made in the late 1920s.

BLUE

Bowl, 4 1/2 In. 10.00
Bowl, 8 In. .... 18.00 To 24.00
Compote, Handle 16.00
Creamer 30.00
Dish, Jelly, Handle, Footed,
5 1/4 In. 22.00
Pitcher, 48 Oz., 8 In. 110.00
Plate, 6 In. 3.00
Plate, 8 In. .... 7.50 To 15.00
Saltshaker 65.00
Sherbet .... 6.00 To 8.00
Sugar, Cover .... 95.00 To 115.00
Vase, Footed, 8 1/2 In. 28.00

GREEN

Bowl, 7 7/8 In. 25.00
Butter, Cover 200.00
Candy Container, Cover 42.00
Dish, Pickle, Handle 18.00
Plate, 6 In. 1.75
Sherbet 6.00
Sugar 15.00
Vase, Footed, 6 1/2 In. 15.00
Vase, Footed, 8 1/2 In. 28.00

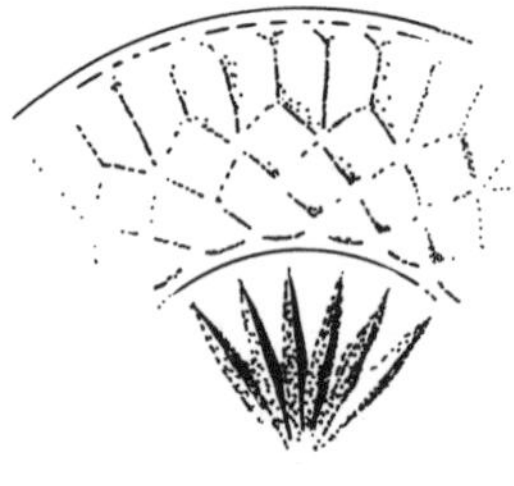

IRIDESCENT

Sherbet .... 5.00 To 7.00
Sherbet, Footed,
Underplate 10.00

Aurora, see Petalware

Avocado

Although the center fruit looks more like a pear, the pattern has been named Avocado. It was made originally from 1923 to 1933 by the Indiana Glass Company, Dunkirk, Indiana, in crystal, green, and pink. In 1973, a reproduction line of pitchers and tumblers appeared in amethyst, blue, frosted pink, green, and pink. In 1982, amber-colored creamers and sugars, cups and

saucers, plates and serving dishes were made. Pieces have also been made in red and yellow. The pattern is sometimes called Sweet Pear or No. 601.

CRYSTAL

Bowl, Oval, 2 Handles,
8 In. 10.00
Bowl, Salad, 7 1/2 In. 10.00
Compote, Footed 15.00

GREEN

Bowl, 1 Handle, 6 In. 16.50
Bowl, 2 Handles,
5 1/4 In. .... 15.00 To 20.00
Bowl, 7 1/2 In. 35.00
Bowl, Deep, 9 In. 85.00
Bowl, Footed, 6 1/4 In. 29.50
Bowl, Oval, 2 Handles,
8 In. 16.00
Cake Plate, Handle,
10 In. 32.00
Creamer .... 38.00 To 45.00
Cup 24.00
Dish, Pickle, Oval, 8 In. 20.00
Plate, 6 1/2 In. 8.00
Plate,
8 1/4 In. .... 15.00 To 18.50
Saucer 18.00
Sherbet .... 30.00 To 35.00
Soup, Dish, 7 1/2 In. 49.50

Sugar.............17.00 To 30.00
Sugar &
Creamer.........39.00 To 75.00

PINK

Bowl, Footed,
6 1/4 In.........12.00 To 19.50
Cup & Saucer................45.00
Plate, 6 3/4 In...............11.00

B

B Pattern, see Dogwood

Ballerina, see Cameo

Bamboo Optic

Bamboo Optic pattern was made by Liberty Works of Egg Harbor, New Jersey, about 1929. Pink and green luncheon sets and other pieces were made. The pattern resembles Octagon.

GREEN

Bowl, 4 In..................... 3.25
Bowl, 8 In..................... 7.25
Cup & Saucer................. 5.25
Plate, 6 1/4 In...............11.50
Plate, 8 1/4 In................ 3.75
Plate, 12 3/4 In. 12.00
Sherbet...............4.00 To 4.50

PINK

Cup & Saucer................. 6.00
Plate, 8 In. ....2.00 To 3.75

Banded Cherry, see Cherry Blossom

Banded Fine Rib, see Coronation

Banded Petalware, see Petalware

Banded Rainbow, see Ring

Banded Ribbon, see New Century

Banded Rings, see Ring

Baroque

Fostoria Glass Company of Moundsville, West Virginia, made Baroque, or No. 2496, from 1936 to 1966. The pattern was made in crystal, blue (azure), yellow (topaz), and green. The same molds were used to make other glass patterns decorated with etched designs.

BLUE

Bowl, Handle, Footed,
11 1/2 In...................45.00
Goblet, 4 1/4 In. 30.00
Plate, Torte, 14 In...........45.00
Rose Bowl, 3 3/4 In........35.00

CRYSTAL

Bowl, Rolled Edge,
11 In.........................27.00
Candleholder, 4 In., Pair...20.00
Cocktail, 3 In.................14.00
Cup & Saucer................12.00
Dish, Mayonnaise,
3 Piece.......................28.00
Plate, 7 1/2 In................ 8.00
Plate, 8 1/2 In................ 9.00
Sherbet, 5 Oz. .... 8.00 To 12.00
Sugar & Creamer,
Footed.......................20.00
Tumbler, 4 1/4 In. 18.00

YELLOW

Bowl, Flared,
12 In............25.00 To 43.00
Candleholder, 5 1/2 In.,
Pair..........................40.00
Compote, 6 1/2 In..........35.00
Cup & Saucer................14.50
Goblet, 4 1/4 In. 28.00
Ice Bucket....................50.00
Plate, 8 In. .... 8.25 To 10.00
Plate, Cracker, 11 In. 26.00
Plate, Torte, 14 In...........39.00
Relish, 3 Sections, 10 In....20.00

Sugar & Creamer, Footed........................28.00
Sugar & Creamer, Tray, Individual...................55.00
Vase, 8 In....................65.00

Basket, see No. 615

Beaded Block

Imperial Glass Company, Bellaire, Ohio, made Beaded Block from 1927 to the 1930s. It was made in amber, crystal, green, ice blue, pink, red, and vaseline. Frosted or iridescent pieces were also made, leading some collectors to name the pattern Frosted Block. Some iridescent pink pieces made recently have been found marked with the IG trademark used from 1951 to 1977.

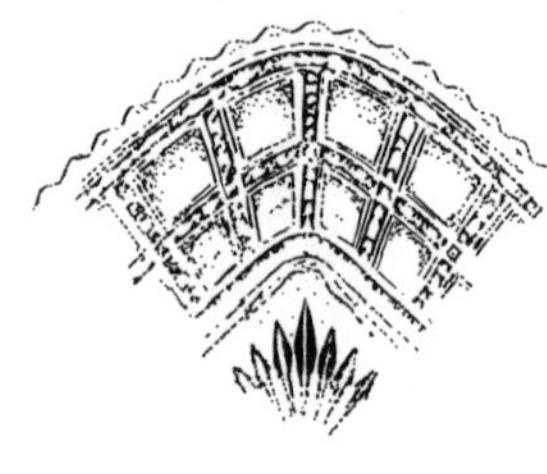

AMBER

Bowl, 5 3/8 In.............10.00
Bowl, Round, 6 1/4 In...... 7.50
Creamer......................12.50
Plate, 7 3/4 In................ 6.50
Soup, Cream.................18.00

GREEN

Bowl, 5 3/8 In.............. 9.50
Bowl, 7 In....................27.00
Bowl, 8 3/4 In.............12.50
Pitcher........................35.00
Plate, 6 In..................... 1.75
Plate, 7 3/4 In................ 5.75
Plate, 8 In..................... 3.00

ICE BLUE

Vase, 6 In....................14.00

IRIDESCENT

Celery, Oval, 8 1/2 In......16.00
Dish, Pickle..................16.00
Pitcher...................... 100.00

PINK

Bowl, Round, 4 1/2 In...... 8.00
Plate, 6 In..................... 2.50
Plate, 8 In..................... 4.50
Vase, Footed, 6 In...........12.00

VASELINE

Plate, 6 In..................... 2.00
Plate, 7 3/4 In......7.00 To 9.00
Plate, 8 In..................... 4.50
Sugar & Creamer............. 6.50
Vase, 6 In....................26.00

Berwick, see Boopie

Beverage With Sailboats, see White Ship

Big Rib, see Manhattan

Block, see Block Optic

Block Optic

Block Optic, sometimes called Block, was made from 1929 to 1933 by the Hocking Glass Company, Lancaster, Ohio. Slight variations in the design of some pieces, like creamers and sugars, show that the pattern was redesigned at times. Crystal, green, and pink pieces are common. Yellow examples are harder to find. Some pieces were made with a black stem or a black flat foot.

CRYSTAL

Candy Container, Footed, 6 1/4 In.....................25.00
Goblet, 5 3/4 In. 5.00
Ice Bucket..................... 8.50
Pitcher, 54 Oz., 8 1/2 In.....................12.00
Plate, 8 In..................... 2.50
Sherbet, 3 1/4 In............. 2.50
Sherbet, 4 3/4 In............. 4.00
Sugar, Rayed–Foot 4.00

GREEN

Bottle & Tumbler, Set...............35.00 To 50.00
Bowl, 4 1/4 In. 4.00
Bowl, 5 1/4 In. ....6.50 To 7.50
Bowl, 7 1/2 In. 19.75
Bowl, 8 1/2 In. 12.00
Butter, Cover ....30.00 To 37.00
Candleholder, Pair...........55.00
Candy Container, Cover, 6 1/4 In.....................40.00
Creamer, Cone Shape........ 7.00
Creamer, Flat.................. 7.00
Cup & Saucer..... 5.00 To 12.00
Goblet, 5 3/4 In.........15.00 To 22.00
Ice Bucket, Handle..........23.00 To 25.00
Mug...........................25.00
Pitcher, 54 Oz., 8 1/2 In.........19.50 To 32.50
Pitcher, 68 Oz., 7 5/8 In.........36.00 To 47.50
Pitcher, 80 Oz., 8 In........35.00
Plate, 6 In...........1.00 To 2.00
Plate, 8 In..................... 2.50
Plate, 9 In........11.50 To 12.50
Plate, 10 1/2 In.......10.00 To 12.50
Plate, Sandwich Server, Center Handle..........35.00 To 45.00
Plate, Sherbet....... 1.00 To 2.50
Salt & Pepper, Footed...........20.00 To 25.00
Salt & Pepper, Squat............30.00 To 38.00
Sherbet, 3 1/4 In............. 4.00
Sherbet, 4 3/4 In............. 9.00
Sherbet, Cone Shape, 3 In................2.00 To 4.50

Sugar & Creamer,
Cone Shape.................18.00
Sugar & Creamer,
Footed.......................13.00
Sugar,
Cone Shape........6.00 To 8.50
Sugar, Plain Handle.......... 5.00
Tumbler,
3 3/4 In.........10.00 To 13.00
Whiskey, 2 1/2 In...........14.00
Wine,
4 1/2 In.........16.50 To 22.00

PINK

Butter Tub.......65.00 To 75.00
Candy Container, Cover,
6 1/4 In.....................45.00
Creamer, Cone Shape........ 7.00
Cup & Saucer.......7.00 To 9.00
Goblet, 4 In..................20.00
Goblet, 5 3/4 In. 15.00
Pitcher, 54 Oz.,
8 1/2 In.....................28.00
Plate, 6 In...........1.00 To 2.50
Plate, 8 In...........2.00 To 3.00
Plate, Sandwich Server,
Center Handle..............25.00
Salt & Pepper................25.00
Sandwich Server, Center
Handle..........26.00 To 32.00
Sherbet, 3 1/4 In............ 4.75
Sherbet, 4 3/4 In............ 8.00
Sugar & Creamer............20.00
Sugar & Creamer,
Footed.......................12.00
Sugar, Tall..................... 5.00
Tumbler, 3 7/8 In. 10.00
Tumbler, 5 In................ 8.75
Whiskey, 1 Oz. 35.00
Wine,
4 1/2 In.........18.00 To 22.00

YELLOW

Candy Container, Cover,
2 1/4 In.....................29.00
Candy Container, Cover,
6 1/4 In.....................45.00
Creamer, Cone Shape........ 9.50
Creamer, Round............. 7.50
Cup..................4.00 To 5.00
Plate, 6 In...........1.00 To 2.00
Plate, 8 In...........3.00 To 4.50
Sherbet, 3 1/4 In............ 5.00
Sherbet, 4 3/4 In...........12.50

Sugar &
Creamer.......... 8.50 To 14.00
Sugar, Cone Shape........... 9.50
Sugar, Round................. 7.00

Boopie

With a name like Boopie, it must have some other attraction. This Anchor Hocking pattern was made in the late 1940s and 1950s. Only glasses of various sizes are known, including the 3 1/2-ounce, 4-ounce, 6-ounce, and 9-ounce. The pattern came in crystal, forest green, and royal ruby.

CRYSTAL

Sherbet, Footed............... 2.00
Tumbler, Footed,
3 1/2 In...................... 2.00
Tumbler, Footed,
3 7/8 In...................... 1.25
Tumbler, Footed,
4 1/2 In...................... 1.25
Tumbler, Footed,
5 1/2 In...................... 4.50
Wine........................... 1.25

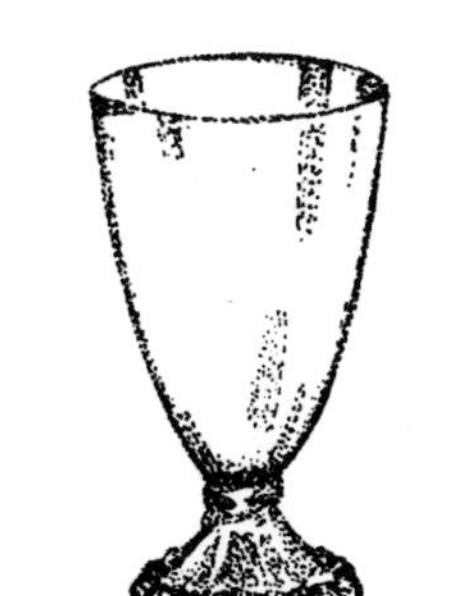

GREEN

Sherbet, Footed............... 5.00
Tumbler, Footed,
3 1/2 In...................... 4.00
Tumbler, Footed,
6 In................5.00 To 5.50

ROYAL RUBY

Sherbet, 4 In........4.75 To 8.00
Tumbler, Footed,
5 1/2 In...................... 6.00

Bouquet & Lattice, see Normandie

Bowknot

The Bowknot pattern remains a mystery. The manufacturer is still unidentified. The swags and bows of the pattern were mold-etched. There does not seem to be a full dinner set of this pattern. Only the 7-inch plate, cup, sherbet, two sizes of bowls, and two types of 10-ounce tumblers have been found. Green pieces are found easily. The pattern was also made in crystal.

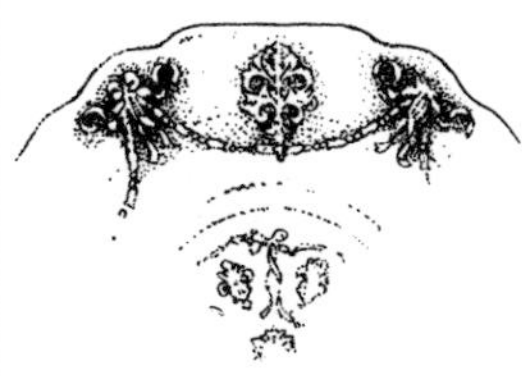

CRYSTAL

Plate, 7 In..................... 7.00
Tumbler, 5 In................11.00

GREEN

Cup...................5.00 To 8.50
Plate, 7 In...........6.50 To 7.00
Tumbler, Footed,
5 In..............9.00 To 12.00

Bridal Bouquet, see No. 615

Bubble

Names of Depression glass patterns can be depressingly confusing. Bubble is also known as Bullseye, the original name given by Anchor Hocking Glass Company, or as Provincial, the 1960s name. Bubble was made in many colors, originally in crystal, pale blue, and pink. Dark green was issued in 1954. Later, milk white and ruby red were made. Recently, yellow pieces have been seen, possibly made in the 1950s. Reproductions have appeared in the 1980s in green, jadite, pink, and royal ruby. They usually have an anchor mark on the bottom.

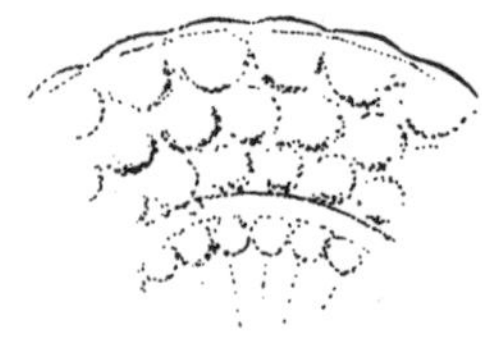

BLUE

Bowl, 4 In........ 6.00 To 10.50
Bowl, 4 1/2 In. ....4.50 To 7.00
Bowl, 5 1/4 In. ....5.00 To 8.50
Bowl, 8 3/8 In. ....7.00 To 9.00
Creamer ....15.00 To 21.50
Cup....................2.00 To 4.00
Cup & Saucer ....2.50 To 6.50
Plate, 6 3/4 In......1.00 To 2.50
Plate, 9 3/8 In......3.00 To 6.50
Plate, Grill, 9 3/8 In.......... 6.00 To 11.00
Platter, Oval, 12 In.............. 6.00 To 12.00
Saucer.................. .75 To 1.25
Soup, Dish, 7 3/4 In...........6.00 To 9.50
Sugar............... 9.75 To 17.50
Sugar & Creamer.........30.00 To 45.00

CRYSTAL

Bowl, 4 In..........2.00 To 3.50
Bowl, 4 1/2 In. ....1.75 To 3.00
Bowl, 5 1/4 In. 3.00
Bowl, 8 3/8 In. ....3.00 To 4.50
Bowl, 11 1/2 In.............15.00
Candleholder, Pair............ 8.00
Creamer ....3.50 To 6.50
Cup & Saucer ....1.50 To 3.50
Juice Set, 6 Piece............18.00
Plate, 6 3/4 In......1.75 To 2.00
Plate, 8 In....................12.00
Plate, 9 3/8 In......3.00 To 4.00
Sherbet......................... 1.00
Soup, Dish, 7 3/4 In......... 6.50
Sugar.................5.00 To 6.00
Tumbler, 4 In..... 4.50 To 11.50
Tumbler, 7 In................10.00

GREEN

Bowl, 4 1/2 In. ....2.00 To 5.00
Bowl, 5 1/4 In. 5.50
Bowl, 8 3/8 In. ....3.50 To 5.00
Creamer ....6.50 To 7.00
Cup & Saucer ....4.50 To 7.50
Plate, 9 3/8 In................ 5.00
Saucer.......................... 2.50
Sherbet..............4.00 To 4.50
Sugar.................6.00 To 7.00
Sugar & Creamer.........10.00 To 17.50
Sugar, Footed 6.00

RED

Bowl, 4 1/2 In. ....3.25 To 7.00
Bowl, 8 3/8 In. 7.50
Cup..................4.50 To 6.00
Cup & Saucer ....4.50 To 7.50
Pitcher, 64 Oz...........27.50 To 37.00
Plate, 9 3/8 In................ 4.00
Tumbler, 4 In.......5.00 To 6.50
Tumbler, 5 In..... 7.00 To 10.00
Tumbler, 6 In.......7.00 To 8.00
Tumbler, 7 In.... 10.00 To 15.00
Water Set, 7 Piece 75.00

WHITE

Bowl, 4 1/2 In. 1.50
Bowl, 8 1/4 In. 3.25
Creamer ....1.50 To 2.25
Sugar & Creamer............. 2.50

Bullseye, see Bubble

Burple

Burple is not a mistype but a real name used by the factory. Anchor Hocking Glass Company, Lancaster, Ohio, made crystal, forest green, and ruby red dessert sets in this pattern in the 1940s. There are also two sizes of bowls.

CRYSTAL

Bowl, 4 1/2 In. ....1.25 To 1.75
Bowl, 8 1/2 In. ....2.00 To 2.50
Tumbler, Footed, 4 1/2 In...................... 4.00
Tumbler, Footed, 5 7/8 In...................... 5.00

GREEN

Bowl, 4 1/2 In. ....1.50 To 1.75
Bowl, 8 1/2 In. ....2.00 To 4.50
Goblet, 6 In................... 6.00
Sherbet..............3.25 To 5.00
Tumbler, 6 1/2 In. 5.50
Tumbler, 6 5/8 In. 5.50
Tumbler, Crystal Base, 5 3/4 In...................... 5.00
Tumbler, Footed, 3 5/8 In...................... 3.50
Tumbler, Footed, 4 1/2 In...........3.00 To 4.00
Tumbler, Footed, 5 In. 4.50

Butterflies & Roses, see Flower Garden with Butterflies

Buttons & Bows, see Holiday

By Cracky

A strange cracked ice look to the glass must have inspired the name By Cracky for this pattern. It was made in the late 1920s by L.E. Smith Glass Company, Mt. Pleasant, Pennsylvania. Candleholders, flower frogs, 8-inch octagonal plates, and luncheon sets with sherbets were made. The luncheon set dish had several compartments. Amber, canary yellow, crystal, and green pieces were made. The pieces have an overall crackled pattern.

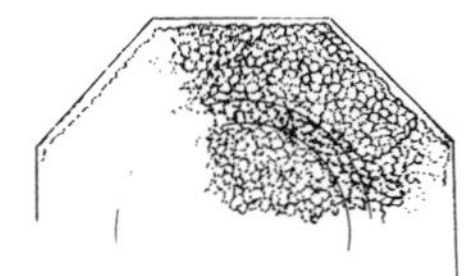

AMBER

Plate, 6 In. 1.50
Plate, 8 In. 2.50
Tray, 3 Sections.............. 2.00

CRYSTAL

Decanter....................... 9.50
Plate, Octagonal, 6 In........ 1.00
Plate, Octagonal, 8 In........ 1.75
Plate, Round, 7 In............ 1.50
Tray, 3 Sections.............. 3.00
Tumbler, 3 5/8 In. 2.00

GREEN

Plate, Octagonal, 6 In........ 2.00
Plate, Octagonal, 8 In........ 2.00
Plate, Round, 7 In............ 2.00
Tumbler 2.50

C

Cabbage Rose, see Sharon

Cabbage Rose With Single Arch, see Rosemary

Cameo

Cameo is understandably called Ballerina or Dancing Girl because the most identifiable feature of the etched pattern is the silhouette of the dancer. This pattern must have sold well when made by Hocking Glass Company from 1930 to 1934 because many different pieces were made, from dinner sets and servers, to cookie jars and lamps. The pattern was made in crystal with a platinum rim, and in green, pink, and yellow. In 1981 reproductions were made of both pink and green Cameo salt and pepper shakers. Childrens' dishes have been made in green, pink, and yellow but there were never any old Cameo childrens' dishes.

GREEN

Bottle, Whitehouse Vinegar.......... 12.00 To 15.00
Bowl, 5 1/2 In......... 17.00 To 20.00
Bowl, 7 1/4 In......... 24.00 To 37.00
Bowl, 8 1/4 In......... 22.00 To 24.00
Bowl, Vegetable, Oval, 10 In......................... 13.50
Butter, Cover 120.00
Cake Plate, Footed............ 8.50 To 16.00

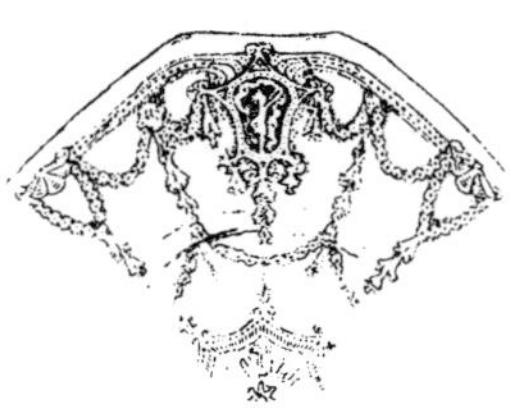

Candlestick, 4 In., Pair.............. 60.00 To 70.00
Candy Dish, Cover, 4 In.............. 35.00 To 37.50
Cookie Jar, Cover............ 30.00 To 35.00
Creamer, 3 1/4 In......... 10.00 To 16.50
Creamer, 4 1/4 In............ 9.50
Cup................. 7.00 To 11.00
Cup & Saucer .... 10.50 To 13.00
Decanter, Stopper.......... 77.00 To 88.00
Dish, Mayonnaise ..... 15.00 To 24.00
Goblet, 6 In...... 30.00 To 40.00
Jar, Jam, Cover...........80.00 To 122.50
Pitcher, 6 In...... 24.00 To 42.50
Pitcher, 8 1/2 In......... 32.50 To 40.00
Plate, 6 In. 1.25
Plate, 8 In. ....4.25 To 8.00
Plate, 9 1/2 In.... 6.50 To 14.00
Plate, 10 In........ 8.00 To 10.50
Plate, Closed Handles, 11 1/2 In........ 6.50 To 11.00
Plate, Grill .... 7.00 To 10.00
Plate, Grill, Closed Handle 40.00
Plate, Grill, Closed Handles.............47.50
Plate, Sandwich, 10 In. 9.00
Plate, Square, 8 1/2 In......... 25.00 To 38.00
Platter, 12 In..... 11.00 To 14.00
Powder Dish, Gold Trim 140.00
Relish, 3 Sections, Footed........... 15.00 To 19.00
Salt & Pepper .... 25.00 To 50.00
Saucer.......................... 6.00
Sherbet, 4 7/8 In......... 19.00 To 20.00
Soup, Dish .... 24.00 To 31.50
Sugar & Creamer, 3 1/4 In......... 19.50 To 22.00

Sugar & Creamer, 4 1/4 In....................24.00
Sugar, 3 1/4 In......... 7.00 To 11.50
Sugar, 4 1/4 In.........10.00 To 16.50
Tumbler, 3 3/4 In.........17.00 To 22.00
Tumbler, 4 In............15.00 To 18.00
Tumbler, 4 3/4 In. 20.00
Tumbler, 5 In............18.00 To 22.50
Tumbler, 5 1/4 In. 50.00
Tumbler, Footed, 3 Oz............35.00 To 38.00
Tumbler, Footed, 5 3/4 In.........40.00 To 50.00
Vase, 5 3/4 In..............85.00
Vase, 8 In. ....12.00 To 19.00
Wine, 4 In........40.00 To 45.00

PINK

Bowl, 5 1/2 In. 85.00
Bowl, 8 3/4 In. 125.00
Cup............................85.00
Goblet, 6 In.......... 110.00 To 175.00
Plate, 8 In. 45.00
Plate, 10 In..................30.00
Sherbet, 4 7/8 In.......... 175.00
Sugar..........................50.00
Wine, 4 In................. 175.00

YELLOW

Bowl, 5 1/2 In.........21.25 To 22.50
Bowl, Vegetable, Oval, 10 In............20.00 To 35.00
Candy Dish, Cover, 4 In....18.00
Creamer, 3 1/4 In......... 7.25 To 11.00
Cup..................5.00 To 9.00
Cup & Saucer ..... 6.00 To 14.00
Pitcher, 8 1/2 In. 35.00
Plate, 6 In. ....1.25 To 2.50
Plate, 8 In. ....7.50 To 9.00
Plate, 9 1/2 In.... 4.00 To 10.00
Plate, Grill ....3.50 To 7.00
Platter, 12 In.....25.00 To 40.00
Saucer........................ 2.25
Sherbet, 3 1/8 In...........22.75
Sugar.............. 8.00 To 10.00
Sugar & Creamer.........21.00 To 30.00
Tumbler, 4 In...............10.00
Tumbler, 5 In...............60.00
Tumbler, Footed, 5 In............. 10.00 To 15.00

Candlewick

Candlewick was made by Imperial Glass Company, Bellaire, Ohio, from 1937 to 1982. Many similar patterns have been made by other companies. The beaded edge is the only design. Although the glass was first made in crystal, it has also been produced in black, nut brown, sunshine yellow, ultra blue, and verde (green). Some pieces of crystal are decorated with gold. Pieces have been found in red, pink, lavender, and amber, and with fired–on gold, red, blue, or green beading. Some sets were made with etchings and hand–painted designs.

Candlewick

CRYSTAL

Ashtray, Heart Shape, 6 1/2 In....................12.00
Ashtray, Oblong, 4 1/2 In..................... 3.75
Ashtray, Square, 3 1/4 In..................... 5.00
Basket, 6 1/2 In.........23.00 To 27.50
Basket, 11 In................65.00
Bell, 4 In. 18.00
Bowl, 5 1/2 In. 8.00
Bowl, 6 In...................12.50
Bowl, 10 In. ....20.00 To 40.00
Bowl, 10 1/2 In.......25.00 To 35.00
Bowl, 2 Handles, 4 1/2 In........ 9.00 To 12.00
Bowl, 2 Handles, 6 In............. 9.00 To 10.00
Bowl, 2 Handles, 7 In. 11.00
Bowl, 2 Handles, 10 In.....14.00
Bowl, 3–Footed, 6 In. 30.00
Bowl, Cupped, 10 In........22.00
Bowl, Float, 12 In...........40.00
Bowl, Mayonnaise 25.00
Butter, Cover, Floral Etch 75.00
Butter, Cover, Oblong, 1/4 Lb..........20.00 To 21.00
Butter, Cover, Round, 5 1/2 In........22.50 To 25.00
Cake Plate, Footed, 11 In............55.00 To 75.00
Candleholder, 2–Light 18.00
Candleholder, Flower, 5 In..........................20.00
Candy Dish, Cover, 3 Sections.......55.00 To 70.00
Candy Dish, Cover, Footed..................... 135.00

Coaster, 4 In. ....3.75 To 7.00
Coaster, With Spoon Rest...........25.00
Compote, 8 In. 75.00
Cordial, 1 Oz...............30.00
Creamer 7.00
Cup............................ 9.00
Cup & Saucer ..... 6.50 To 12.00
Deviled Egg Plate............85.00 To 97.50
Goblet, 9 Oz..... 12.50 To 14.00
Jar, Marmalade, 3 Piece.........19.00 To 25.00
Jar, Marmalade, 4 Piece 28.00
Ladle, Mayonnaise............ 8.50
Lamp, Hurricane, 3 Piece.........88.00 To 90.00
Mirror, 4 1/2 In........75.00 To 85.00
Mustard Pot, Cover...........25.00 To 30.00

Pitcher, Beaded Handle, 80 Oz..........90.00 To 110.00
Pitcher, Manhattan, 40 Oz......... 170.00 To 175.00
Plate, 6 In...........3.75 To 6.00
Plate, 7 In..................... 5.75
Plate, 8 1/2 In................. 8.50
Plate, 10 In....... 18.00 To 24.00
Plate, 2 Handles, 5 1/2 In..................... 5.00
Plate, 2 Handles, 8 1/2 In....................15.00
Plate, 2 Handles, 10 In..... 17.00
Plate, 2 Handles, 12 In..... 20.00
Plate, Birthday 225.00
Plate, Canape, 6 In........... 9.00
Plate, Cupped Edge, 17 In..........................40.00
Punch Cup 7.00
Punch Set, Underplate, 12 Cups 175.00
Relish, 2 Sections, 6 1/2 In......... 6.00 To 12.00
Relish, 3 Sections, 10 In............60.00 To 68.00
Relish, 4 Sections, 8 1/2 In........ 15.00 To 25.00
Relish, 5 Sections, 13 1/2 In...................45.00
Salt & Pepper, Beaded, Bulbous, Footed.......................10.00
Salt & Pepper, Individual .... 9.50 To 12.50
Salt Dip, 2 In. ....5.50 To 7.00
Sauce Boat, Underplate ... 135.00
Saucer.......................... 5.50
Soup, Cream .....35.00 To 40.00
Sugar & Creamer, Individual .... 10.00 To 15.00
Tidbit, 2 Tiers ... 47.50 To 60.00
Tray, Center Handle, 10 1/2 In...................24.00
Tray, Center Handle, 11 1/2 In...................26.00
Tray, Lemon, Handle, 5 1/2 In.........27.00 To 30.00
Tumbler, Footed, 5 Oz..............6.00 To 8.50
Tumbler, Footed, 10 Oz...........10.00 To 14.00
Tumbler, Footed, 12 Oz............12.00 To 17.00
Vase, Bud, 5 3/4 In. 42.00
Vase, Ruffled, 8 In.......... 18.00
Vase, Straight Sides, 10 In.........................30.00
Wine 20.00

Cape Cod

Cape Cod was a pattern made by the Imperial Glass Company, Bellaire, Ohio, from 1932. It is usually found in crystal, but was also made in amber, azalea, light blue, cobalt blue, green, milk glass, and ruby. In 1978 the dinner set was reproduced. The cruet was reproduced in 1986 without the rayed bottom.

AMBER

Cruet.............17.00 To 20.00

BLUE

Sherbet.........................10.00

CRYSTAL

Ashtray, 4 In. 13.00
Basket, 11 In.................90.00
Bowl, 4 1/2 In. ....3.00 To 4.00
Bowl, 5 1/2 In. 5.00
Bowl, 2 Handles, 7 1/2 In.....................13.00
Bowl, Fruit, 6 In............. 6.00
Bowl, Vegetable, 10 In.....27.00
Butter, Cover 30.00
Cake Plate, 11 In............45.00
Cake Plate, Footed, 10 1/2 In.......35.00 To 45.00
Compote, 7 In. 39.00
Compote, Cover, 6 In.......65.00

Cordial, 1 1/2 Oz........10.00 To 20.00
Cruet..............15.00 To 35.00
Cup............................. 3.00
Cup & Saucer, Tea 17.00
Decanter, Rye.... 55.00 To 90.00
Dish, Sundae........5.00 To 6.50
Eggcup........................30.00
Epergne, 2 Piece..........90.00 To 95.00
Goblet, 11 Oz................. 8.00
Lamp, Hurricane.............98.00
Marmalade, Cover, Spoon........................28.00
Mayonnaise, Liner...........19.00
Mustard, 3 Piece..........17.00 To 26.00
Parfait, 6 Oz. 13.00
Pitcher, Ice Lip, 2 Qt. 85.00
Plate, 7 In..................... 4.50
Plate, 8 In...........4.00 To 6.00
Plate, 10 In...................16.00
Plate, 14 In...................35.00
Plate, Birthday, 13 In..... 175.00
Plate, Cupped, 14 In........20.00
Plate, Cupped, 16 In........37.00
Plate, Dinner, 10 In.........25.00
Punch Bowl, 12 1/2 In.....45.00
Punch Set, 15 Piece...... 160.00 To 225.00
Relish, 3 Sections, Oval, 9 1/2 In.........20.00 To 35.00
Relish, 4 Sections, 9 1/2 In.........15.00 To 35.00
Salt & Pepper, Individual ....17.00 To 25.00
Salt Dip.......................11.00
Sugar.......................... 7.50

To test the age of engraving on glass, place a white handkerchief on the inside. If the engraving is old, the lines will usually show up darker than the rest of the glass. New engraving has a bright powderlike surface.

Sugar & Creamer, Footed............ 9.00 To 16.00
Tumbler, 6 Oz................ 8.00
Tumbler, 7 Oz................ 6.00
Tumbler, 10 Oz............... 7.00
Tumbler, 12 Oz..... 6.00 To 9.00
Tumbler, Footed, 6 Oz................ 6.00 To 7.00
Vase, 10 In................... 49.00
Vase, Flip, 8 1/2 In......... 75.00
Whiskey, 2 1/2 In............ 8.00

RED

Goblet, Footed............... 15.00
Plate, 8 In................... 15.00

Caprice

Caprice was advertised in 1936 as the most popular crystal pattern in America. It was made until 1953. Over 200 pieces were made in the line. Frosted pieces were called Alpine Caprice, the name given by the maker, Cambridge Glass Company, Cambridge, Ohio. The sets were made in amber, amethyst, blue, cobalt blue, moonlight blue, crystal, emerald green, light green, pink, and milk glass. Reproductions are being made in cobalt and moonlight blue.

Caprice, see also Alpine Caprice

AMBER

Cup & Saucer................ 25.00
Vase, 5 In. 75.00

BLUE

Ashtray, 5 In..... 15.00 To 22.00
Ashtray, Shell, 3-Footed, 2 3/4 In...................... 7.00
Bonbon, 2 Handles, Square, 6 In.......................... 27.00
Bonbon, Footed, Square, 6 In.......................... 30.00
Bowl, 10 In. 65.00
Bowl, 2 Handles, Crimped, 11 In......................... 60.00

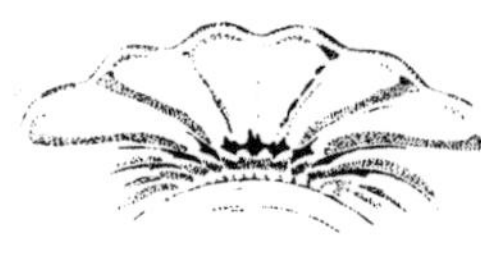

Bowl, 2 Handles, Footed, Oval, 11 In......................... 45.00
Bowl, 4-Footed, 12 1/2 In.................. 65.00
Candleholder, 3-Light 54.00
Candleholder, Prisms, 7 In., Pair.............. 45.00 To 65.00
Celery......................... 42.00
Cigarette Box, Cover, 2 1/4 X 3 1/2 In. 27.00
Coaster, 3 1/2 In......... 22.00 To 25.00
Compote, Footed, 7 In.............. 32.50 To 60.00
Cordial, 1 Oz................ 95.00
Cup & Saucer.... 30.00 To 35.00
Goblet, 10 Oz................ 40.00
Ice Bucket.................. 200.00
Jar, Jam, 2 Handles, 4 1/4 In......... 25.00 To 29.50
Mustard, Cover, 2 Oz..... 125.00
Pitcher, Ball, 32 Oz....... 235.00
Pitcher, Ball, 80 Oz......... 175.00 To 200.00
Plate, 8 1/2 In......... 18.50 To 20.00
Plate, 9 1/2 In.............. 90.00
Plate, 16 In................... 75.00
Plate, 4-Footed, 11 In............ 35.00 To 38.00
Plate, 4-Footed, 14 In. 65.00
Relish, 2 Sections, Handles, 6 1/2 In......... 22.00 To 30.00
Relish, 3 Sections, 8 In............. 27.00 To 35.00
Saucer................ 5.00 To 7.00
Sherbet, Low..... 22.50 To 27.50
Sherbet, Tall 25.00
Sugar & Creamer, Large .... 42.00 To 55.00
Sugar, Individual .... 12.00 To 15.00
Sugar, Large...... 20.00 To 24.00
Sugar, Medium 17.00
Tumbler, 9 Oz............... 35.00
Tumbler, 12 Oz............. 30.00
Tumbler, Footed, 5 Oz. ... 24.00
Tumbler, Footed, 12 Oz.... 55.00
Vase, 3 1/2 In............ 125.00
Vase, 4 1/2 In............ 150.00

CRYSTAL

Ashtray, 3 In................ 10.00
Ashtray, 4 In.................. 5.00
Ashtray, Shell, 2 3/4 In......... 5.00 To 10.00
Bonbon, 2 Handles, Square, 6 In.......................... 10.00
Bonbon, 6 In................. 18.00
Bonbon, Footed, 6 In. 4.00
Bowl, 4-Footed, 11 In...... 28.00
Bowl, 4-Footed, 13 In...... 28.00
Candleholder, 2 1/2 In., Pair.......................... 18.00
Candleholder, 3-Light, Pair.............. 50.00 To 65.00
Candleholder, Prisms, 7 In., Pair.......................... 22.00
Candy Container, Cover, 3-Footed........ 28.00 To 47.00
Champagne....... 13.00 To 20.00
Cigarette Box, Cover, 2 1/4 X 3 1/2 In......... 15.00 To 25.00
Coaster........................ 15.00
Compote, Footed, 7 In............. 15.00 To 25.00
Console Set, 3-Light Candleholders..... 75.00

Cruet, 3 Oz.................. 12.00
Cup............................ 7.00
Cup & Saucer..... 8.50 To 14.00
Dish, Pickle, 9 In............. 15.00 To 20.00
Ice Bucket, Tongs........... 40.00
Plate, 6 1/2 In................ 8.00
Plate, 7 1/2 In...... 4.00 To 7.50
Plate, 8 1/2 In.... 8.00 To 15.00
Plate, 9 1/2 In......... 25.00 To 32.50
Plate, 14 In.................. 20.00
Plate, 4-Footed, 11 In. 28.00
Plate, Lemon, Handles, 6 1/2 In..................... 12.00
Relish, 2 Sections, 6 1/2 In....... 10.00 To 15.00
Relish, 3 Sections, 8 In. 9.00

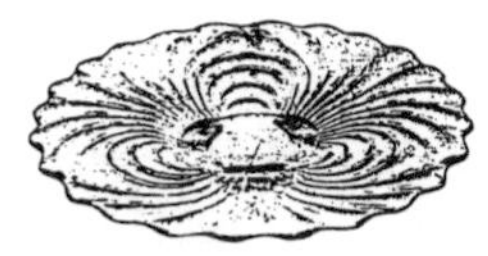

Relish, 3 Sections, 12 In.... 20.00
Salt & Pepper, Individual... 20.00
Sherbet, Tall, 6 Oz.......... 12.00
Sugar & Creamer, Individual....... 18.00 To 21.00
Sugar & Creamer, Large.... 21.00
Sugar, Individual ... 7.00 To 9.00
Sugar, Large.................. 12.00
Tumbler, 5 Oz............... 12.50
Tumbler, 12 Oz.............. 12.00
Tumbler, Footed, 10 Oz........... 11.00 To 20.00
Tumbler, Footed, 12 Oz.... 25.00

PINK

Candleholder, 3-Light 195.00
Cup & Saucer .... 28.00 To 38.00
Plate, 8 1/2 In......... 14.00 To 27.00
Relish, 3 Sections, 8 In. 50.00
Saucer................ 4.00 To 6.00
Sherbet, Tall 30.00
Sugar, Creamer & Tray, Individual................... 75.00

Caribbean

The rippled design of Caribbean is slick and modern in appearance and has attracted many collectors. It was made by Duncan and Miller Glass Company, Pittsburgh, Pennsylvania, from 1936 to 1955. Sets were made of crystal, amber, blue, and red glass. The Duncan and Miller catalogs identify the line as No. 112.

BLUE

Bowl, 8 1/2 In. 95.00
Bowl, Oval, 10 3/4 In...... 75.00
Candy Container, Cover, Footed....................... 35.00
Champagne.................. 28.00
Cheese & Cracker Set............... 30.00 To 40.00
Compote...................... 45.00
Console, 12 In. 55.00
Cup & Saucer 12.50
Finger Bowl, 4 1/2 In...... 45.00
Plate, 7 1/2 In.............. 14.00
Punch Set, Round, 17 Piece.................. 225.00
Relish, 5 Sections, 13 In.... 95.00
Sherbet, Low..... 35.00 To 45.00
Sugar & Creamer........... 38.00
Tumbler, Footed, 5 3/8 In..................... 60.00
Vase, 7 1/4 In............ 110.00
Vase, Ruffled, 5 3/4 In..... 22.50
Vase, Scalloped, 9 In........ 65.00

CRYSTAL

Bowl, Oval, Handles, 10 3/4 In.................. 30.00
Bowl, Salad, 9 In. 30.00
Candy Container, Cover 45.00
Plate, 8 1/2 In.............. 12.00
Punch Set, Red Handle, 15 Piece.................. 175.00
Sugar & Creamer........... 14.00

Century

Century pattern was made by Fostoria Glass Company from 1926 until 1986. It is a plain pattern with a slightly rippled rim. Full dinner sets were made.

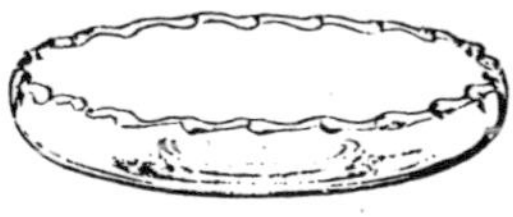

CRYSTAL

Bowl, Flared, 10 3/4 In.... 35.00
Bowl, Flared, 12 In. 20.00

Bowl, Footed, Triangular, 7 1/8 In..................... 12.00
Bowl, Salad, 8 1/2 In....... 25.00
Compote, 4 3/8 In.......... 15.00
Cruet.......................... 35.00
Ice Bucket.................... 48.00
Mayonnaise Set, 3 Piece.... 25.00
Mustard Pot, Cover, Footed, 6 In.......................... 25.00
Oyster Cocktail, 4 1/2 Oz.................... 10.00
Pitcher, 6 1/8 In. 45.00
Pitcher, 7 1/8 In. 85.00
Plate, Crescent, 7 1/2 In.................... 20.00
Relish, 3 Sections............ 25.00
Saucer.......................... 4.00
Sherbet, 4 1/2 In........... 8.00 To 9.50
Tray, Utility, Handle, 9 1/8 In.................... 18.00

Chain Daisy, see Adam

Chantilly

As late as the 1960s the Jeannette Glass Company, Jeannette, Pennsylvania, made a pattern called Chantilly which is collected by Depression glass buffs. It was made in crystal and pink.

CRYSTAL

Bowl, Flared, 4-Footed, 12 In........................ 26.00
Cake Plate, Tab Handle, 13 1/2 In.................. 28.00
Candy Container, Cover, 3-Footed.................... 75.00
Console....................... 45.00
Creamer 12.00
Cruet, Stopper, Pair 100.00
Goblet, 10 Oz............... 20.00
Relish, 3 Sections, 9 In. 19.00

Salt & Pepper.... 16.00 To 30.00
Saltshaker......... 12.00 To 13.00
Sherbet, Low..... 22.50 To 25.00
Sugar & Creamer............ 25.00
Sugar & Creamer, Sterling Base.... 33.00 To 55.00
Sugar, Scalloped, Individual................... 12.00

Cherry, see Cherry Blossom

Cherry Blossom

Cherry Blossom is one of the most popular Depression glass patterns. It has been called Banded Cherry, Cherry, or Paneled Cherry Blossom by some collectors. The pattern was made by the Jeannette Glass Company, Jeannette, Pennsylvania, from 1930 to 1939. Full dinner sets and serving pieces were made in a wide range of colors. Pieces were made in crystal, delphite (opaque blue), green, jadite (opaque green), and pink. Many reproductions of Cherry Blossom pieces have been made and sold in recent years.

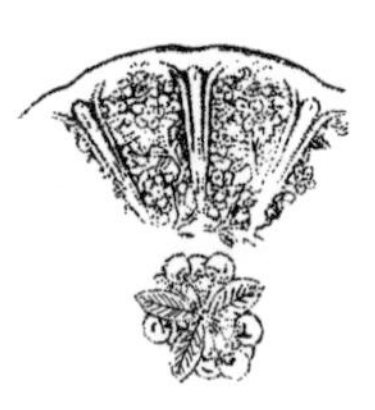

CRYSTAL

Bowl, 2 Handles, 9 In. 18.00
Cup & Saucer................ 95.00
Dinner Set, Child's, 14 Piece.................. 160.00

DELPHITE

Bowl, 2 Handles, 9 In............. 12.00 To 16.00
Bowl, 8 1/2 In........ 18.00 To 35.00
Bowl, 9 In.................... 22.00
Creamer .... 12.50 To 18.00
Creamer, Child's............. 25.00
Cup & Saucer................ 17.50
Cup & Saucer, Child's........... 27.00 To 29.00
Cup, Child's.................. 22.00
Dinner Set, Child's, 14 Piece.................. 195.00
Pitcher, Footed, 36 Oz., 8 In............60.00 To 100.00
Plate, 6 In..................... 7.00
Plate, 9 In......... 9.50 To 12.00
Plate, Child's, 6 In................6.00 To 8.25
Sandwich Tray, 10 1/2 In....... 12.50 To 18.00
Saucer.......................... 3.50
Saucer, Child's ...... 2.00 To 4.00
Sugar.............. 13.00 To 15.50
Sugar & Creamer......... 25.00 To 30.00
Sugar & Creamer, Child's....................... 25.00
Tray, Sandwich, 10 1/2 In....... 12.50 To 18.00
Tumbler, Footed, 8 Oz., 4 1/2 In..................... 13.00

GREEN

Bowl, 2 Handles, 9 In............. 10.00 To 20.00
Bowl, 3-Footed, 10 1/2 In....... 53.00 To 60.00
Bowl, 4 3/4 In.......... 8.00 To 11.00
Bowl, 8 1/2 In......... 18.00 To 23.00
Bowl, Vegetable, Oval, 9 In............. 20.00 To 25.00
Butter, Cover .... 55.00 To 90.00
Cake Plate, 10 1/4 In....... 13.00 To 20.00
Coaster............ 6.00 To 11.00
Creamer .... 10.00 To 20.00
Cup & Saucer.... 13.00 To 20.00
Mug, 7 Oz..... 135.00 To 150.00
Pitcher, 42 Oz., 8 In............. 31.00 To 45.00
Pitcher, Footed, 36 Oz., 8 In............. 35.00 To 37.50
Plate, 6 In. .... 4.00 To 5.50
Plate, 7 In. .... 11.00 To 15.00
Plate, 9 In.................... 12.00
Plate, Grill, 9 In............. 13.00 To 18.00
Plate, Sherbet................. 9.00

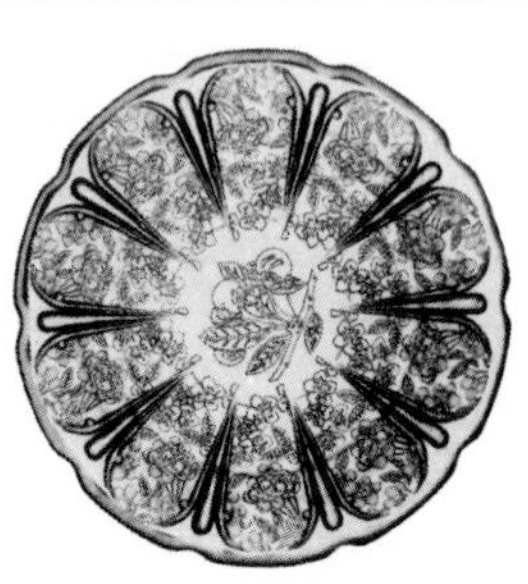

Platter, Divided, 13 In...... 35.00
Platter, Oval, 11 In............. 20.00 To 28.00
Platter, Oval, 13 In.......... 30.00
Saucer................ 2.50 To 3.00
Sherbet............. 8.75 To 13.00
Soup, Dish .... 35.00 To 37.00
Sugar................. 5.50 To 9.00
Sugar & Creamer, Cover........... 30.00 To 32.50
Sugar, Cover 22.00
Tray, Sandwich, 10 1/2 In.................... 9.00
Tumbler, 4 Oz., 3 1/2 In..................... 13.50
Tumbler, 9 Oz., 4 1/4 In......... 13.00 To 17.00
Tumbler, 12 Oz., 5 In. 40.00
Tumbler, Footed, 4 Oz., 3 3/4 In......... 10.00 To 14.00
Tumbler, Footed, 8 Oz., 4 1/2 In..................... 28.00
Tumbler, Footed, 9 Oz., 4 1/2 In......... 19.00 To 30.00

PINK

Bowl, 2 Handles, 9 In. 9.50
Bowl, 3-Footed, 10 1/2 In....... 32.00 To 35.00
Bowl, 4 3/4 In.......... 7.00 To 12.50
Bowl, 5 3/4 In......... 16.00 To 18.00
Bowl, 8 1/2 In......... 12.00 To 25.00
Bowl, Oval, 9 In............. 15.00 To 30.00
Bowl, Round, 8 1/2 In..... 15.00
Cake Plate, Footed 22.00
Coaster............. 7.50 To 12.00
Creamer 7.50
Cup............................ 8.50
Cup & Saucer .... 12.00 To 18.50

Cup & Saucer, Child's 20.00
Mug, 7 Oz..... 110.00 To 175.00
Pitcher, 42 Oz., 8 In........ 30.00
Pitcher, Footed, 36 Oz.,
8 In.......................... 35.00
Plate, 6 In........... 2.50 To 7.00
Plate, 7 In........ 10.50 To 14.50
Plate, 9 In......... 8.50 To 20.00
Plate, Child's,
6 In................. 5.50 To 7.00
Plate, Grill,
9 In.............. 15.50 To 17.00
Platter, 13 In..... 24.00 To 35.00
Platter, Divided, 13 In...... 28.00
Platter, Oval,
11 In............. 14.00 To 24.50
Saucer................ 1.75 To 5.00
Saucer, Child's 2.75
Sherbet............ 7.00 To 13.00
Soup, Dish .... 32.50 To 47.50
Sugar & Creamer, Cover ... 32.00
Sugar, Cover 20.00
Tray, Sandwich,
10 1/2 In....... 10.00 To 18.00
Tumbler, 4 Oz.,
3 1/2 In.......... 9.00 To 12.00
Tumbler, 9 Oz.,
4 1/4 In..................... 12.00
Tumbler, 12 Oz.,
5 In.............. 32.00 To 40.00
Tumbler, Footed, 4 Oz.,
3 3/4 In...................... 8.50
Tumbler, Footed, 8 Oz.,
4 1/2 In..................... 18.00
Tumbler, Footed, 9 Oz.,
4 1/2 In......... 19.00 To 25.00

Cherry-Berry

Two similar patterns, Cherry-Berry and Strawberry, can be confusing. If the fruit pictured is a cherry, then the pattern is called Cherry-Berry. If the strawberry is used, then the pattern has that name. The dishes were made by the U.S. Glass Company in the early 1930s in amber, crystal, green, and pink.

Cherry-Berry, see also Strawberry

GREEN

Bowl,
7 1/2 In......... 12.00 To 15.00
Compote.......... 12.00 To 15.00
Sherbet......................... 5.00
Sugar, Large.................. 25.00

PINK

Plate, 6 In...................... 4.50
Sugar & Creamer........... 40.00

Chinex Classic

Chinex Classic and Cremax are very similar patterns made by Macbeth-Evans Division of Corning Glass Works from about 1938 to 1942. Chinex and Cremax are both words with two meanings. Each is the name of a pattern and the name of a color used for other patterns. Chinex is ivory-colored, Cremax is a bit whiter. Chinex Classic, the dinnerware pattern, has a piecrust edge, and just inside the edge is an elongated feathered scroll. It may or may not have a decal-decorated center and colored edging. The Cremax pattern has just the piecrust edge. The decals used on Chinex Classic are either floral designs or brown-toned scenics.

Chinex Classic, see also Cremax

IVORY WITH DECAL

Bowl, 9 In.................... 18.00
Cup.................. 3.00 To 4.50
Cup & Saucer 4.75
Plate, 6 1/4 In...... 3.00 To 4.50
Plate, 11 1/2 In. ... 8.00 To 9.25

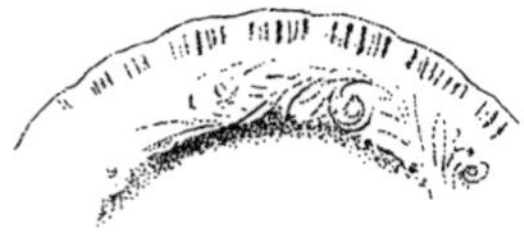

Saucer.......................... 2.00
Sherbet........... 10.50 To 13.50
Sugar........................... 9.25

IVORY

Bowl, 5 3/4 In. 5.50
Butter, Cover 55.00
Creamer 5.25
Cup & Saucer .... 4.50 To 6.00
Plate, 9 3/4 In...... 3.00 To 8.00
Plate, 11 1/2 In. 5.00
Plate, Blue Border,
10 In.......................... 6.00
Sugar........................... 5.25
Sugar & Creamer........... 12.00

Chintz

Several companies made a glass named Chintz. To identify the pieces of Chintz pattern, remember the design is named for the etched pattern, not the shape, of the glass. Fostoria Glass Company made Baroque, a glass shape that included molded fleur-de-lis-shaped handles and ridges. This glass blank was then etched with design No. 338 and then sold as Chintz pattern. The etched design pictures branches of leaves and flowers. It was also used on some vases and other pieces that were not Baroque blanks. Only crystal pieces were made. Pieces were made from 1940 to 1972. To

confuse this even more, the company made other etched designs (Navarre) on the Baroque blanks. Another Chintz pattern was made by A. H. Heisey Company from 1931 to 1938. It was an etched design of butterflies and encircled flowers. This Chintz pattern was made in crystal, green (Moongleam), orchid (Alexandrite, a glass that turned from blue to purple depending on the lighting source), pink (Flamingo), and yellow (Sahara). Pieces listed in this book are for Fostoria Chintz.

CRYSTAL

Candleholder, 2-Light, Pair 50.00
Compote 35.00
Creamer 7.00
Cruet 50.00
Goblet, 4 Oz. ..... 20.00 To 24.50
Goblet, 7 5/8 In. .... 15.00 To 25.00
Ice Bucket, Tongs 95.00
Jar, Jelly, Cover 65.00
Mayonnaise, 3 Piece 52.50
Oyster Cocktail, 3 3/8 In. 16.00
Pitcher, 9 1/2 In. 19.00
Plate, 7 1/2 In. .... 12.00 To 15.00
Plate, 9 1/2 In. 37.50
Relish, 3 Sections, 10 1/2 In. 30.00
Sherbet, 4 3/8 In. 16.00
Sugar & Creamer .... 28.00 To 35.00
Tray, Sandwich, Center Handle, 11 In. 32.00
Tumbler, 5 Oz. .... 19.00 To 20.00
Tumbler, 13 Oz. 24.00
Wine, 5 3/8 In. 22.00

Christmas Candy Ribbon, **see Christmas Candy**

Christmas Candy

Christmas Candy, sometimes called Christmas Candy Ribbon, was made by the Indiana Glass Company, Dunkirk, Indiana, in 1937. The pattern, apparently only made in luncheon sets, was made in crystal, a light green called seafoam green, a bright blue called teal blue, and dark emerald green.

CRYSTAL

Cup 4.00
Cup & Saucer .... 4.00 To 5.50
Plate, 8 1/4 In. 5.00
Sugar 3.75

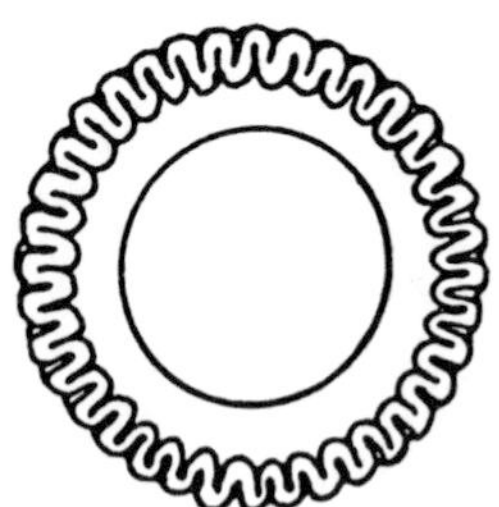

Sugar & Creamer .... 12.00 To 14.00

TEAL BLUE

Dish, Soup 20.00
Plate, 9 In. 20.00
Saucer 3.50

Circle

Circles ring the Circle pattern made by Hocking Glass Company, Lancaster, Ohio, in the 1930s. It is often found in green, but is less available in crystal and pink.

CRYSTAL

Goblet, Green Stem, 8 Oz. 8.50
Sherbet, Green Stem 4.50
Tumbler, 4 Oz. 2.50
Wine, 4 1/2 In. 4.00
Wine, Green Stem, 4 1/2 In. 5.50

GREEN

Bowl, 4 1/2 In. 4.00
Bowl, 5 1/2 In. 6.50
Cup .... 2.00 To 3.00
Cup & Saucer .... 3.00 To 5.50
Goblet, 8 Oz. .... 7.00 To 8.75

Go outside and try to read your house numbers from the street. If you can't read them, get new, larger ones. Police responding to an emergency must be able to see the numbers in your address.

Pitcher, 80 Oz. 14.00
Plate, 6 In. .... 1.25 To 2.00
Plate, 8 1/4 In. 7.00
Sherbet, 3 1/8 In. .... 2.50 To 4.50
Sherbet, 4 3/4 In. .... 4.00 To 5.75
Sugar & Creamer 18.00
Tumbler, 8 Oz. ...... 4.00 To 6.00

PINK

Creamer 7.25
Cup 2.00
Plate, 8 1/4 In. 5.50
Plate, 9 1/2 In. 10.00

Circular Ribs, see Circle

Classic, see Chinex Classic

Cleo

In 1930 the Cambridge Glass Company, Cambridge, Ohio, introduced an etched pattern called Cleo. Many pieces are marked with the Cambridge C in a triangle. Sets were made in amber, blue, crystal, green, pink, and yellow.

AMBER

Bowl, 10 In. 18.00
Ice Bucket, Tongs 60.00

BLUE

Basket, 11 In. 75.00
Bonbon, 5 1/2 In. 35.00
Candy Container 50.00
Console 40.00

GREEN

Candleholder, Pair 45.00
Cup 18.00
Cup & Saucer 24.00
Ice Bucket 50.00

PINK

Candleholder, 4 In. 20.00
Candy Container, Cover 80.00
Creamer 18.00
Cup & Saucer 35.00
Ice Bucket, Tongs 85.00

Cloverleaf

Three-leaf clovers form part of the border of Cloverleaf pattern made by Hazel-Atlas Glass Company from 1930 to 1936. It was made in black, crystal, green, pink, and topaz.

BLACK

Ashtray, 4 In. .... 50.00 To 52.50
Creamer .... 8.75 To 12.00
Cup .... 8.00 To 12.00
Cup & Saucer .... 10.00 To 14.50
Plate, 8 In. .... 9.00 To 10.50
Salt & Pepper 47.00
Saucer .... 2.00 To 2.75
Sherbet .... 12.00 To 13.00
Sugar .... 8.75 To 12.50
Sugar & Creamer .... 16.00 To 23.00

CRYSTAL

Cup 3.00
Cup & Saucer 5.00
Plate, 8 In. 3.75
Saucer 1.50
Sherbet 4.00
Tumbler, 3 3/4 In. 25.00

GREEN

Bowl, 4 In. .... 10.00 To 13.50
Bowl, 5 In. .... 13.00 To 15.00
Bowl, 7 In. .... 20.00 To 30.00
Bowl, 8 In. 35.00
Candy Container, Cover .... 32.00 To 45.00
Creamer .... 5.25 To 12.00
Cup .... 4.00 To 8.00
Cup & Saucer .... 6.00 To 8.00
Plate, 6 In. .... 2.50 To 5.00
Plate, 8 In. .... 2.75 To 5.50
Plate, Grill .... 13.00 To 16.00
Salt & Pepper .... 18.00 To 28.00
Saucer .... 1.50 To 3.00
Sherbet .... 3.00 To 6.50
Sugar .... 6.50 To 8.00
Sugar & Creamer 15.00
Tumbler, 9 Oz., 4 In. .... 25.00 To 30.00
Tumbler, Footed, 10 Oz., 5 3/4 In. .... 14.00 To 18.00

PINK

Bowl, 4 In. 10.00
Candy Container, Cover 80.00
Cup .... 4.00 To 5.00
Cup & Saucer .... 5.00 To 6.00
Plate, 8 In. 4.25
Saucer .... 1.50 To 2.00
Sherbet .... 3.00 To 5.00

TOPAZ

Plate, Grill 16.50
Sugar 7.50
Tumbler, 10 Oz. 20.00

Colonial

Sometimes this pattern is called Knife & Fork, although Colonial is the more common name. It was made by Hocking Glass Company, Lancaster, Ohio, from 1934 to 1938. Colors include crystal, green, opaque white, and pink.

CRYSTAL

Butter........................30.00
Cocktail, 4 Oz.......6.50 To 8.00
Cordial, 3 3/4 In.......... 4.00 To 10.00
Cup...................4.00 To 4.50
Sugar.................5.00 To 5.50
Whiskey, 2 1/2 In............ 3.00
Wine, 4 1/2 In.......... 4.00 To 10.00

GREEN

Bowl, 4 1/2 In. .....5.50 To 7.50
Bowl, 9 In........12.00 To 18.00
Butter, Cover ....34.00 To 47.50
Claret, 5 1/4 In.........15.00 To 20.00
Cocktail, 4 Oz....13.00 To 21.50
Cordial, 3 3/4 In.........16.00 To 22.00
Creamer 13.00
Cup............................ 7.00
Cup & Saucer 12.50
Goblet, 5 3/4 In.........16.50 To 22.50
Plate, 6 In..................... 3.00
Plate, 8 1/2 In................ 4.50
Plate, 10 In.......35.00 To 48.00
Plate, Grill ....15.00 To 21.00
Platter, 12 In.................15.00
Saucer.......................... 1.50
Soup, Cream .....22.00 To 32.00
Soup, Dish ....22.00 To 45.00
Spooner..........65.00 To 110.00
Sugar & Creamer.........17.50 To 36.50
Tumbler, 5 Oz., 3 In.............14.00 To 23.50
Tumbler, 15 Oz.............67.50
Tumbler, Footed, 5 Oz., 4 In.........................14.00
Tumbler, Footed, 8 Oz., 3 1/4 In....................12.50
Tumbler, Footed, 10 Oz., 5 1/4 In.........36.00 To 38.00
Whiskey ....10.75 To 13.00
Wine, 4 1/2 In. 17.00

PINK

Bowl, 5 1/2 In. 40.00
Bowl, Vegetable, 10 In.............. 7.00 To 15.00
Creamer ....24.00 To 25.00
Cup & Saucer .... 10.50 To 11.00
Goblet, 3 Oz., 4 In.............10.00 To 12.75
Goblet, 8 1/2 Oz., 5 3/4 In.....................15.00
Pitcher, 54 Oz., 7 In........29.00
Pitcher, 68 Oz., 7 3/4 In.........29.50 To 50.00
Plate, 6 In..................... 3.00
Plate, 8 1/2 In......5.00 To 5.50
Plate, 10 In.......15.00 To 23.00
Plate, Grill .... 7.00 To 14.00
Platter, Oval, 12 In............10.00 To 25.00
Salt & Pepper 110.00
Saltshaker.........35.00 To 58.00
Saucer.......................... 3.50
Sherbet, 3 In. 11.75
Soup, Dish ....22.00 To 32.50
Spooner..........78.00 To 110.00
Tumbler, 9 Oz., 4 In................7.50 To 9.50
Tumbler, 12 Oz.............33.00
Tumbler, Footed, 10 Oz., 5 1/4 In.....................15.00
Whiskey, 2 1/2 In...........4.50 To 6.00

WHITE

Cup............................ 5.50
Cup & Saucer 8.00
Plate, 8 1/2 In............... 5.00
Plate, 10 In................... 9.75

Colonial Block

A small set of dishes, mostly serving pieces, was made in Colonial Block pattern by Hazel–Atlas Glass Company, a firm with factories in Ohio, Pennsylvania, and West Virginia. The dishes were made in the 1930s in green and pink and in white in the 1950s.

GREEN

Bowl, 4 In..................... 4.50
Bowl, 7 In....................10.00
Butter, Cover 34.00
Candy Container, Cover...........16.00 To 28.00
Creamer 4.00
Goblet ....7.00 To 8.50
Sugar.................6.00 To 8.00
Sugar & Creamer...........13.00

PINK

Bowl, 4 In..................... 4.50
Bowl, 7 In....................10.00
Sugar.................6.00 To 6.50

WHITE

Creamer 6.00
Sugar................4.00 To 5.00

Colonial Fluted

Federal Glass Company made Colonial Fluted pattern from 1928 to 1933. It was made in crystal and green.

CRYSTAL

Sherbet........................22.00

GREEN

Bowl, 4 In. .... 4.00 To 4.50
Bowl, 6 In. .... 5.00 To 6.00
Bowl, 7 1/2 In. .... 4.50 To 8.50
Creamer 4.50
Plate, 6 In. .... 1.50 To 2.00
Plate, 8 In. .... 3.00 To 3.75
Saucer 1.00
Sherbet 4.50
Sugar & Creamer 10.00
Sugar & Creamer, Cover ... 15.00

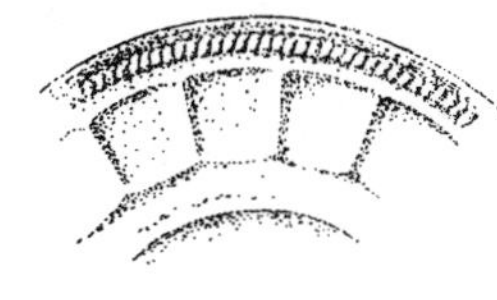

Colony

Colony is a pattern that has also been called Elongated Honeycomb or Hexagon Triple Band because of the features in the molding. It was made by Hazel-Atlas Glass Company in the 1930s in crystal, green, and pink. Another pattern, also named Colony, was made by Fostoria Glass Company.

CRYSTAL

Bonbon, 3-Footed,
7 In. .... 15.00 To 18.00
Bowl, 10 In. 37.00
Bowl, 11 In. 28.00
Bowl, 2 Handles,
4 3/4 In. 15.00
Bowl, Footed, Oval,
11 In. 37.00
Bowl, Oval, 2 Sections,
10 1/2 In. 35.00
Box, Cigarette, Cover 35.00
Butter, Cover, 1/4 Lb. 55.00
Cake Plate,
10 In. .... 16.00 To 21.00
Cake Plate, Footed,
12 In. .... 30.00 To 50.00
Candleholder, 3 1/2 In.,
Pair 20.00

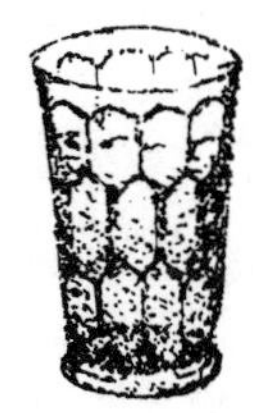

Candleholder, Double,
Pair 30.00
Candy Container,
Cover .... 27.00 To 32.50
Cheese & Cracker Set 45.00
Cocktail, 4 Oz. ..... 7.00 To 12.50
Creamer, 3 7/8 In. 8.50
Cruet .... 28.00 To 45.00
Cup 5.00
Cup & Saucer ..... 8.50 To 10.00
Dish, Lemon, 6 1/2 In. 12.00
Goblet, 9 Oz.,
3 7/8 In. .... 9.00 To 12.00
Jar, Jelly .... 32.50 To 35.00
Oyster Cocktail,
3 3/8 In. .... 9.00 To 12.50
Pitcher, 16 Oz. 32.00
Pitcher, 2 Qt.,
7 3/4 In. ..... 100.00 To 125.00
Plate, 6 In. 3.50
Plate, 8 In. 9.50
Plate, 9 In. .... 14.00 To 15.00
Plate, Footed, 12 In. 55.00
Plate, Torte, 13 In. 25.00
Platter, 12 In. 24.00
Platter, 12 1/2 In. 30.00
Powder Jar 79.00
Relish, 3 Sections,
10 1/2 In. ...... 13.00 To 19.00
Salt & Pepper,
3 5/8 In. .... 10.00 To 17.50
Saucer 2.00
Sherbet .... 4.00 To 10.00
Soup, Cream 25.00
Sugar .... 6.00 To 8.50
Sugar &
Creamer .... 12.50 To 18.00
Tumbler, 5 Oz.,
3 5/8 In. 12.50
Tumbler, 9 Oz.,
3 7/8 In. 16.00
Tumbler, Footed, 5 Oz.,
4 1/2 In. .... 6.50 To 10.00
Tumbler, Footed, 12 Oz.,
5 3/4 In. .... 10.00 To 15.00
Vase, Cupped,
7 In. .... 35.00 To 45.00
Vase, Flared, 7 1/2 In. 45.00
Vase, Flared, Footed,
7 1/2 In. 32.50
Wine, 4 1/4 In. 17.50

PINK

Bowl, 6 In. 30.00

Columbia

Columbia pattern can be found in crystal but is rare in pink. It was made by Federal Glass Company, Columbus, Ohio, from 1938 to 1942.

CRYSTAL

Bowl, 5 In. .... 6.75 To 11.50
Bowl,
8 1/2 In. .... 6.50 To 12.50
Bowl,
10 1/2 In. .... 8.50 To 12.50
Butter, Cover .... 11.00 To 14.00
Chop Plate,
11 3/4 In. .... 5.50 To 7.00
Cup .... 3.00 To 3.50
Cup & Saucer .... 3.75 To 6.00
Plate, 6 In. .... .50 To 2.00
Plate, 9 1/2 In. ..... 3.50 To 4.25
Soup, Dish .... 8.50 To 12.50

Coronation

Coronation was made by Anchor Hocking Glass Company, Lancaster, Ohio, from 1936 to 1940. Most pieces are crystal or pink, but there are also dark green and ruby red sets. The pattern is

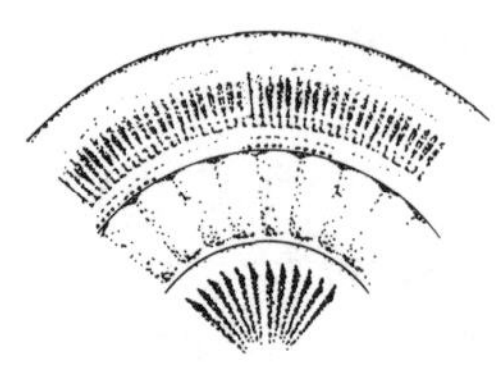

sometimes called Banded Fine Rib or Saxon. Some of the pieces are confused with those in Lace Edge pattern.

CRYSTAL

Bowl, 4 1/4 In. 4.00

PINK

Berry Set, 6 Piece 12.00
Bowl, 4 1/4 In. 2.00
Bowl, 8 In. 7.00
Cup .... 3.50 To 5.00
Cup & Saucer .... 2.50 To 5.50
Plate, 6 In. .... 1.00 To 2.00
Plate, 8 1/2 In. ..... 2.50 To 3.50
Saucer 2.00
Sherbet .... 2.50 To 4.50
Tumbler 7.50

RED

Berry Set, 7 Piece 25.00
Bowl, 4 1/4 In. .... 2.50 To 5.50
Bowl, 6 1/2 In. .... 6.75 To 7.75
Bowl, 8 In. .... 10.00 To 12.00

GREEN

Creamer, Child's 6.00
Cup, Child's 5.00
Goblet, 4 1/2 In. 4.00
Plate, 8 In. .... 2.00 To 2.50
Plate, 9 In. 3.50
Saucer, Child's 1.50
Sugar, Child's 6.00
Tumbler, 5 1/2 In. 5.00

YELLOW

Plate, 8 In. 1.50
Sherbet 3.00

Craquel

Craquel was made by the United States Glass Company in 1924. It has an overall stippled finish. Pieces were made in crystal with green trim and in blue and yellow.

Cremax

Cremax and Chinex Classic are confusing patterns. There is an added piece of molded design next to the fluted rim trim on Chinex Classic. Also the name Cremax and Chinex refer to colors as well as patterns. Cremax, made by Macbeth-Evans Division of Corning Glass Works, was popular in the late 1930s to the early 1940s. It is a cream-colored opaque glass, sometimes decorated with floral or brown-tinted decals or with a colored rim.

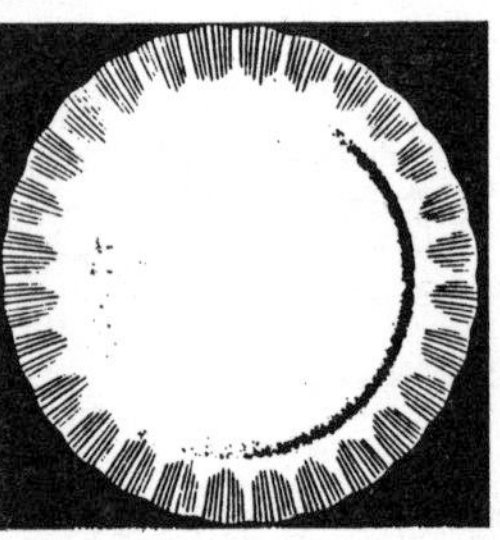

Cremax, see also Chinex Classic

CREAM-COLORED WITH BLUE DECAL

Cup & Saucer 4.50
Plate, 6 1/4 In. 2.50
Plate, 9 In. 5.00
Plate, Sandwich, 11 1/2 In. 8.00

CREAM-COLORED

Cup 3.25
Cup & Saucer, Green Border 4.00
Plate, 6 1/4 In. 1.25
Plate, 9 3/4 In. 3.25
Plate, Pink Border, 6 1/4 In. 1.50
Plate, Pink Border, 9 3/4 In. 3.50
Plate, Yellow Border, 9 3/4 In. 3.50
Saucer 1.25

Criss Cross, see X Design

Cube, see Cubist

Cubist

Cubist, or Cube, molded with the expected rectangular and diamond pattern, was made by Jeannette Glass Company from 1929 to 1933. It was made in amber, blue, canary yellow, crystal, green, pink, ultramarine, and white. It has been made recently in amber, opaque white, and avocado.

CRYSTAL

Bowl, 4 1/2 In. 3.00
Bowl, 6 1/2 In. 4.50
Plate, 8 In. 2.75
Powder Jar, Cover 8.00
Saucer 2.50
Sherbet 8.00
Sugar & Creamer, 2 In. .... 1.25 To 1.50

Don't brag about the value of your collection to strangers. It might lead to extra interest by the local burglary groups.

GREEN

Bowl, 4 1/2 In. 4.00
Butter, Cover .... 30.00 To 45.00
Candy Container,
Cover .... 17.00 To 23.00
Coaster .... 4.50 To 5.00
Creamer, 3 In. ...... 5.00 To 7.00
Cup 5.00
Cup & Saucer .... 6.00 To 7.50
Pitcher, 45 Oz.,
8 3/4 In. ..... 135.00 To 175.00
Plate, 6 In. .... 1.50 To 2.50
Plate, 8 In. .... 2.00 To 4.75
Salt & Pepper .... 20.00 To 28.00
Saltshaker .... 6.25 To 10.00
Saucer 2.50
Sherbet .... 5.00 To 8.00
Sugar, 3 In. 5.00
Sugar, Cover, 3 In. 14.50
Tumbler, 9 Oz., 4 In. 35.00

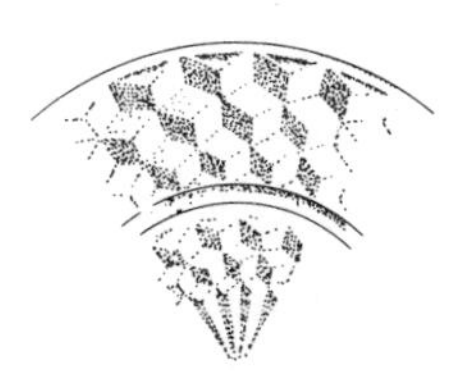

PINK

Bowl, 4 1/2 In. .... 3.00 To 5.25
Bowl, 6 1/2 In. .... 5.00 To 8.50
Butter, Cover .... 30.00 To 55.00
Candy Container,
Cover .... 16.00 To 20.00
Coaster .... 3.00 To 5.00
Cup & Saucer 6.00
Pitcher, 45 Oz.,
8 3/4 In. 122.50
Plate, 6 In. .... 1.50 To 4.00
Plate, 8 In. .... 3.00 To 3.25
Powder Jar,
Cover .... 10.00 To 13.00
Salt & Pepper 20.00
Saucer 2.50
Sherbet .... 3.00 To 6.00
Sugar & Creamer, 3 In. 15.00
Sugar, 2 In. 2.75
Sugar, 3 In. 3.25

D

Daisy, see No. 620

Daisy Petals, see Petalware

Dancing Girl, see Cameo

Decagon

Decagon, named for its 10-sided outline, was made by the Cambridge Glass Company of Cambridge, Ohio. The pattern, dating from the 1930s, was made in amber, dark blue (cobalt), light blue (Moonlight), green, pink, and red.

AMBER

Creamer 8.00
Cup & Saucer 4.50
Dish,
Mayonnaise ..... 18.00 To 23.00
Ice Bucket 22.00
Plate, 8 1/2 In. 4.00
Sandwich Server, Handle ... 15.00
Sugar & Creamer 4.50

COBALT

Cup & Saucer 12.00
Dish, Pickle, 9 In. 20.00
Goblet, 9 Oz. 20.00
Ice Bucket 42.00
Plate, 2 Handles, 11 In. 36.00
Plate, 7 1/2 In. 8.00
Plate, 9 1/2 In. 28.00
Sugar & Creamer,
Footed 25.00
Sugar,
Lightning Bolt Handles 7.00
Tumbler, Footed, 5 Oz. ... 13.00
Tumbler, Footed, 10 Oz. ... 15.00

GREEN

Bowl, Flat Rim, 5 1/2 In. ... 9.00
Bowl, Flat Rim, 6 In. 16.00
Bowl, Oval, 9 1/4 In. 27.00
Cup & Saucer 5.50
Plate, 8 1/2 In. ..... 4.00 To 6.75
Platter, Oval, 15 In. 60.00
Soup, Cream, Footed 9.00
Sugar 10.00
Sugar & Creamer 15.00
Wine 15.00

PINK

Bowl, Flat Rim, 5 3/4 In. 10.00
Ice Bucket 35.00
Plate, 8 1/4 In. 7.00
Plate, Grill, 10 In. 17.00

Della Robbia

Della Robbia is a heavy glass with raised pears and apples as part of the design. It was made by the Westmoreland Glass Company, Grapeville, Pennsylvania, from the 1920s to the 1940s. The pattern was made in crystal, Roselin, green, and amber. Crystal pieces often have fruit stained in natural colors.

CRYSTAL

Bowl, Handle, 8 In. 20.00
Compote 19.00 To 25.00
Plate, 10 1/2 In. 10.00
Salt & Pepper 25.00 To 45.00
Sugar & Creamer 24.00

Diamond, see Windsor

Diamond Pattern, see Miss America

Diamond Quilted

Imperial Glass Company, Bellaire, Ohio, made Diamond Quilted, sometimes called Flat Diamond in the 1920s and early 1930s. It was made in amber, black, blue, crystal, green, pink, and red. Dinner sets, luncheon

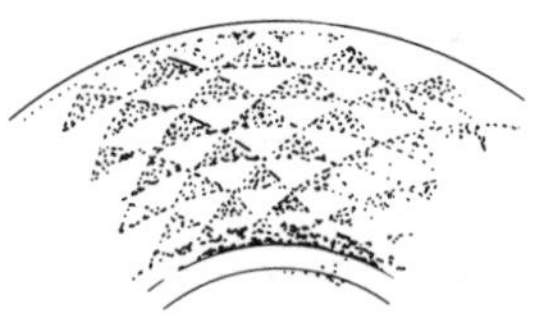

sets, and serving pieces, including a large punch bowl, were made; but not all items were made in all colors.

AMBER

Bowl, 7 In. 7.50
Candleholder, Pair 20.00
Dish, Mayonnaise, 3 Piece 35.00
Sherbet 6.00

BLACK

Creamer 12.50
Cup 10.00
Plate, 6 In. 6.00
Plate, 8 In. 9.00
Sugar & Creamer 25.00

BLUE

Bowl, 7 In. 12.00
Candleholder, 2 1/2 In., Pair 22.00
Creamer 12.50
Plate, 8 In. 9.00 To 12.75
Sherbet 10.00
Sugar 12.75
Sugar & Creamer 19.00

GREEN

Bowl, 7 In. 6.00 To 7.75
Candleholder, Flat, Pair 14.00
Creamer 9.25
Plate, 6 In. 2.00 To 2.50
Plate, 8 In. 3.00 To 4.75
Sherbet 4.00 To 6.50
Sugar 5.00 To 9.25

Sugar & Creamer 9.00 To 14.00

PINK

Bowl, 7 In. 6.00 To 8.50
Bowl, Handle, 5 1/2 In. 5.50 To 7.50
Candleholder 5.00
Creamer 3.00 To 8.75
Cup 3.75 To 6.00
Plate, 6 In. 3.50
Plate, 8 In. 2.50 To 5.50
Plate, 8 1/2 In. 4.75
Sherbet 4.00
Soup, Cream 6.00
Sugar 4.00 To 8.75
Sugar & Creamer 12.00

Diana

Diana is one of the many Depression glass patterns with swirls in the glass, which often causes confusion. Federal Glass Company, Columbus, Ohio, made this pattern, sometimes called Swirled Sharp Rib, from 1937 to 1941. It was made in amber, crystal, green, and pink. A pink bowl was reproduced in 1987.

AMBER

Bowl, 9 In. 6.00
Bowl, Console, 11 In. 6.00 To 8.00
Bowl, Scalloped Edge, 12 In. 9.00
Candy Container 25.00
Creamer 3.00
Cup & Saucer 5.00 To 7.00
Plate, 6 In. 2.00
Plate, 9 1/2 In. 6.50
Plate, 11 3/4 In. 5.00 To 7.00
Salt & Pepper 58.00
Soup, Cream, 5 1/2 In. 7.00

Sugar.......................... 3.00
Sugar & Creamer............ 16.00

CRYSTAL

Ashtray......................... 4.00
Bonbon, 2 Handles, 7 In.......................... 15.00
Bowl, 5 In...................... 2.00
Bowl, 9 In........... 5.00 To 6.00
Bowl, 11 In..................... 7.00
Bowl, Scalloped Edge, 12 In.......................... 5.00
Cake Set, 9 Piece............ 25.00
Candleholder................. 20.00
Candy Container, Cover 10.00
Child's Set, With Rack...... 40.00
Coaster, 3 1/2 In............. 2.00
Compote...................... 85.00
Creamer 3.00
Cruet.......................... 65.00
Cup & Saucer 3.50
Cup & Saucer, Child's 10.00
Cup & Saucer, Demitasse .... 4.00 To 5.00
Dish, Mayonnaise, 2 Sections................... 28.00
Jar, Jam, Cover 75.00
Pitcher, Ball, 80 Oz. 185.00
Plate, 6 In..................... 1.00
Plate, 8 1/2 In............... 15.00
Plate, 9 1/2 In................ 4.00
Platter.......................... 5.00
Relish, 5 Sections, 10 In............ 50.00 To 55.00
Relish, 5 Sections, 12 In.... 32.00
Saucer................ 1.00 To 2.00
Saucer, Child's 3.00
Sherbet....................... 10.00
Soup, Cream, 5 1/2 In........... 3.00 To 6.00
Sugar.......................... 3.50
Sugar & Creamer............ 6.00
Sugar & Creamer, Frosted 10.00
Tumbler, 4 1/8 In......... 12.00 To 12.50
Wine.......................... 29.50

GREEN

Cup & Saucer 4.00
Plate, 8 In..................... 3.00

PINK

Bowl, 5 In........... 2.50 To 5.00
Bowl, 9 In........... 6.00 To 7.00
Candy Container, Cover........... 18.00 To 25.00
Coaster, 3 1/2 In............ 3.00
Cup.................. 3.00 To 4.00
Plate, 6 In.......... 1.00 To 2.50
Plate, 9 1/2 In................ 6.00
Saucer............... 1.50 To 2.00
Saucer, Child's 10.00
Tumbler, 4 1/8 In......... 13.00 To 15.00

Dogwood

Dogwood is decorated with a strange flower that has been given many names. Collectors have called this pattern Apple Blossom, B pattern, Magnolia, or Wildrose. It was made from 1929 to about 1934 by Macbeth-Evans Glass Company. It is found in cremax, crystal, green, monax, pink, red, and yellow. Some pieces were made with such thin walls the factory redesigned the molds to make the pieces thicker.

CREMAX

Bowl, 6 1/2 In. 14.00
Bowl, 10 1/4 In............ 75.00
Bowl, 8 1/2 In. 42.50
Cake Plate, 13 In......... 125.00

CRYSTAL

Bowl, Footed, 11 In......... 68.00
Butter, Cover 90.00
Candleholder, Single Key, Pair 50.00
Dish, Mayonnaise, Spoon... 58.00
Plate, 8 In.................... 3.00
Relish 16.00
Salt & Pepper 28.00
Sugar, Thin, 2 1/2 In........ 7.00
Vase, 5 1/2 In.............. 15.00

GREEN

Bowl, 5 1/2 In. 7.00
Bowl, 10 1/2 In............ 80.00
Bowl, Console, 12 1/2 In.................. 33.00
Cake Plate, 13 In............ 45.00 To 75.00
Candy Container, Cover 85.00
Creamer 35.00
Cup & Saucer .... 15.00 To 20.00
Cup, Demitasse 15.00
Pitcher, 80 Oz., 8 In.......... 385.00 To 450.00

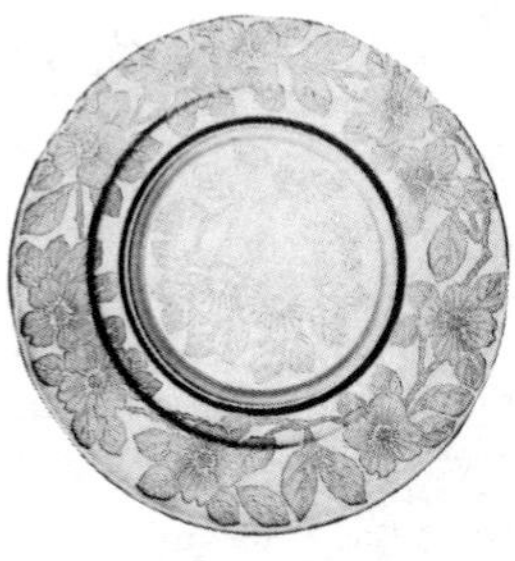

Plate, 6 In.......... 4.00 To 6.50
Plate, 8 In.......... 3.50 To 6.00
Plate, Grill, 10 1/2 In....... 8.00
Plate, Server, 2 Handles, 12 1/2 In.................. 45.00
Relish, 3 Sections............ 25.00
Saucer................ 3.00 To 5.00
Tumbler, 11 Oz., 4 3/4 In......... 65.00 To 75.00

MONAX

Plate, Server, 12 In............ 18.00 To 24.00

PINK

Ashtray, Square 7.00
Basket, 6 In. 30.00
Bowl, 5 1/2 In......... 11.50 To 18.00
Bowl, 8 1/2 In......... 30.00 To 40.00
Cake Plate, 13 In............ 60.00 To 75.00
Cheese & Cracker Set....... 32.00
Creamer, Thick, 3 1/4 In..................... 13.00
Creamer, Thin, 2 1/2 In.......... 8.00 To 12.50
Cruet........................ 350.00

Cup & Saucer, Thick .... 10.00 To 14.00
Cup & Saucer, Thin .... 9.00 To 16.00
Pitcher, 80 Oz., 8 In. .... 105.00 To 120.00
Plate, 6 In. .... 3.00 To 5.50
Plate, 8 In. .... 3.00 To 5.00
Plate, 9 1/4 In. .... 14.00 To 20.00
Plate, 10 1/2 In. ...... 13.50 To 16.50
Plate, Grill, 10 1/2 In. .... 9.75 To 15.00
Plate, Server, 12 In. .... 18.00 To 23.00
Platter, Oval, 12 In. 225.00
Relish, 2 Sections 25.00
Saucer .... 2.00 To 5.00
Sherbet .... 15.00 To 20.00
Sugar & Creamer, Thick 24.00
Sugar & Creamer, Thin .... 20.50 To 24.00
Sugar Shaker 150.00
Sugar, Thick, 3 1/4 In. .... 7.50 To 12.00
Sugar, Thin, 2 1/2 In. 9.00
Tumbler, 4 In. .... 25.00 To 30.00
Tumbler, 4 3/4 In. 32.50
Tumbler, 5 In. 35.00

Doric

Doric was made by Jeannette Glass Company, Jeannette, Pennsylvania, from 1935 to 1938. The molded pattern has also inspired another name for the pattern, Snowflake. It was made in delphite, green, pink, and yellow. A few white pieces may have been made.

DELPHITE

Bowl, 4 1/2 In. 4.75
Candy Container, 3 Sections 3.75
Creamer 7.00
Salt & Pepper 17.50
Sherbet .... 3.50 To 8.00

GREEN

Bowl, 4 1/2 In. .... 4.00 To 6.50
Bowl, 5 1/2 In. 20.00
Butter, Cover 57.00
Cake Plate, 10 In. .... 11.50 To 15.25
Candy Container, 3 Sections 6.50
Candy Container, Cover, 8 In. .... 22.00 To 31.00
Coaster, 3 In. 13.50
Creamer, 4 In. .... 7.50 To 10.50
Cup 6.00
Cup & Saucer .... 9.00 To 10.50
Pitcher, 6 In. ..... 25.00 To 33.00
Plate, 6 In. .... 2.50 To 3.25
Plate, 7 In. .... 10.00 To 15.00
Plate, 9 In. 12.25
Plate, Grill, 9 In. 10.00
Platter, Oval, 12 In. .... 12.00 To 13.00
Relish, 4 X 4 In. 6.00
Relish, 4 X 8 In. 10.00
Salt & Pepper .... 24.00 To 32.50
Saucer 2.00
Sherbet .... 7.00 To 10.00
Sugar & Creamer 19.00
Sugar, Cover ..... 28.50 To 32.00
Tray, Handle, 10 In. 12.00

PINK

Bowl, 4 1/2 In. .... 4.50 To 5.00
Bowl, 5 1/2 In. 20.00
Bowl, 8 1/4 In. 11.00
Bowl, Oval, 9 In. 12.00
Cake Plate, 10 In. 12.00
Cake Plate, 12 3/4 In. 20.00
Candy Container, 3 Sections 3.75
Candy Container, Cover, 8 In. .... 22.00 To 29.00
Creamer .... 7.00 To 9.50
Cup 10.00
Cup & Saucer .... 7.00 To 8.00
Pitcher, 6 In. ..... 25.00 To 30.00
Plate, 9 In. .... 6.50 To 10.00
Plate, 10 1/2 In. 8.00
Plate, Grill, 9 In. 7.00
Relish, 4 Piece ... 22.00 To 26.00
Relish, 4 X 4 In. 4.00
Relish, 4 X 8 In. 6.00
Salt & Pepper .... 20.00 To 28.00
Saucer 2.00
Sherbet .... 4.00 To 7.50
Sugar 8.50
Sugar & Creamer 32.50
Sugar, Cover 16.50
Tray, 8 X 8 In. ... 8.00 To 11.50
Tray, Handles, 10 In. 10.50
Tumbler, 4 1/2 In. 30.00
Tumbler, Footed, 4 In. 26.00

Doric & Pansy

The snowflake-like design of Doric alternates with squares holding pansies, so, of course, the pattern is named Doric & Pansy. It, too, was made by Jeannette Glass Company, but only in 1937 and 1938. It was made in crystal, pink, and ultramarine. The ultramarine varied in color from green to blue. A set of child's dishes called Pretty Polly Party Dishes was made in this pattern.

CRYSTAL

Cup 6.00
Cup & Saucer 8.25

PINK

Child's Set, 14 Piece ...... 145.00 To 190.00
Creamer, Child's 22.50
Cup & Saucer, Child's 32.50
Plate, 6 In. 4.00
Plate, Child's 16.00
Saucer, Child's ...... 2.00 To 3.00

ULTRAMARINE

Butter, Cover .... 395.00 To 475.00
Cup & Saucer .... 13.50 To 16.00
Plate, 6 In. .... 6.00 To 8.50
Plate, 9 In. .... 15.00 To 20.00
Plate, Child's .... 6.00 To 8.50
Salt & Pepper .... 300.00 To 400.00

Saucer................2.50 To 6.00
Saucer, Child's......3.50 To 5.00
Sugar............80.00 To 200.00
Sugar & Creamer...... 135.00 To 200.00
Sugar, Child's................28.00
Tray, 2 Handles, 10 In............13.00 To 14.00
Tumbler......................35.00
Tumbler, 4 1/2 In. 35.00

Doric With Pansy, see Doric & Pansy

Double Shield, see Mt. Pleasant

Double Swirl, see Swirl

Drape & Tassel, see Princess

Dutch, see Windmill

Dutch Rose, see Rosemary

E

Early American, see Princess Feather

Early American Hobnail, see Hobnail

Early American Rock Crystal, see Rock Crystal

Elongated Honeycomb, see Colony

English Hobnail

Westmoreland Glass Company, Grapeville, Pennsylvania, made English Hobnail pattern from the 1920s through the 1970s. It was made in amber, blue, cobalt, crystal, green, pink, red, and turquoise. There is much variation in the shading. Red English Hobnail has been made in the 1980s, a darker amber in the 1960s. Red and pink reproductions have been made since 1980.

English Hobnail, see also Miss America

AMBER

Bowl, 8 In...................16.00
Salt Dip, Footed........... 7.00 To 10.00
Tidbit, 2 Tiers..............45.00

BLUE

Candleholder, 3 1/2 In., Pair..........................37.50
Claret.........................18.00
Cup...............18.00 To 22.50
Goblet, 6 1/4 In. 26.00
Lamp, 8 In................. 100.00
Plate, 8 In. 11.00
Plate, 10 In..................30.00
Salt Dip, Footed..........10.00 To 12.00
Sherbet...........18.00 To 25.00
Sugar, Footed...............22.50

CRYSTAL

Bowl, 4 In..........4.00 To 5.50
Bowl, 5 In.................... 6.50
Bowl, 6 In.................... 9.00
Bowl, Console Set, Rolled Edge...............83.00
Bowl, Footed, 2 Handles, 8 In.........................30.00
Bowl, Rolled Edge, 11 In........................43.00
Butter, Silver Cover.........60.00
Candy Container, Cover, Cone Shape..... 15.00 To 22.00
Champagne..................10.00
Coaster, 5 1/2 In............ 3.75
Condiment Set, Child's......60.00

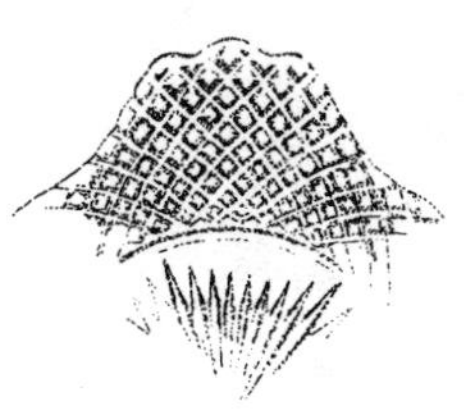

Cordial......................... 6.00
Creamer, Flat.................. 7.50
Creamer, Footed.............. 7.50
Cruet..........................25.00
Cup............................. 3.00
Cup & Saucer................. 6.00
Cup & Saucer, Black Bottom...............10.00
Eggcup........... 12.00 To 18.50
Goblet, 4 Oz.................. 6.00
Goblet, 6 In.................. 8.00
Jar, Jam, Cover..............25.00
Lamp..........................37.00
Plate, 6 In.................... 2.75
Plate, 8 1/2 In................ 5.00
Plate, Server, Black Bottom...............22.00
Punch Bowl, Base & Underplate....... 500.00
Relish, 5 Sections, Jar Center, Chrome Lid.................50.00
Salt & Pepper................30.00
Salt & Pepper, Silver Tops..................40.00
Salt Dip, Footed........... 5.00 To 10.00
Saucer.......................... 5.00
Sherbet..............4.00 To 7.50
Soup, Cream........3.00 To 7.00
Sugar, Footed................ 7.50
Tumbler, Footed, 5 3/4 In...................... 9.00
Wine, 3 1/2 In......... 8.00 To 12.00

GREEN

Bottle, Cologne..............25.00
Bowl, 8 In....................28.00
Bowl, Footed, 2 Handles, 8 In..........................37.00
Candy Container, Cone Shape.................42.00
Candy Container, Cover, 3-Footed....................45.00
Goblet, 4 Oz.................15.00
Lamp, Small..................65.00

Plate, 8 1/2 In. 8.00
Salt Dip, Footed 12.00
Vase 88.50

PINK

Candleholder, 8 1/2 In., Pair 42.50
Jar, Jam, Metal Cover 22.00
Lamp, Oil, 6 3/4 In. 65.00
Plate, 6 In. 3.00
Plate, 8 In. .... 6.00 To 7.00
Salt & Pepper 58.00
Salt Dip, Footed 12.00
Saltshaker 25.00
Sherbet 11.50
Vase, 7 1/2 In. 40.00

Fairfax

Fairfax was made by Fostoria Glass Company, Fostoria, Ohio, from 1927 to 1944. The name Fairfax refers to a glass blank and to an etching pattern. The same glass blanks were used for other etched designs including June, Trojan, and Versailles. The undecorated blank, also known as No. 2375, is popular with collectors. The same shapes were used to make other patterns with etched designs. The glass was made in amber, black, blue, green, orchid, pink, ruby, and topaz.

AMBER

Ashtray 6.00
Bonbon, Cover, Footed 45.00
Bowl, 5 In. .... 4.50 To 9.50
Bowl, 9 In. 13.00
Bowl, Vegetable, Oval, 10 In. 35.00
Bowl, Vegetable, Round, 9 In. 35.00
Butter, Cover 63.00
Candleholder, 3 In., Pair 16.00
Candy Container, 4 1/2 In. 20.00
Coaster 5.00
Compote, 7 1/2 In. 15.00
Cup & Saucer, Demitasse 15.00
Cup & Saucer, Flat 12.00
Cup & Saucer, Footed .... 4.00 To 6.00
Cup, Footed .... 2.50 To 5.00
Ice Bucket .... 25.00 To 30.00
Plate, 6 In. .... 3.00 To 5.00
Plate, 7 1/2 In. .... 3.00 To 4.50
Plate, 9 1/2 In. 12.50
Plate, 10 1/4 In. 29.50
Plate, 12 In. 40.00
Platter, 15 1/2 In. 75.00
Relish, 8 1/2 In. 6.00
Relish, 11 1/2 In. 9.50
Sauce Boat, Liner 44.00
Soup, Cream .... 8.50 To 11.00
Sugar & Creamer, Flat 25.00
Sugar & Creamer, Footed 15.00
Sugar, Flat, 3 1/2 In. 6.00
Sugar, Footed 5.50

BLUE

Baker, 10 1/2 In. 38.00
Bouillon, Saucer 17.00
Bowl, 4 1/2 In. 7.00
Bowl, Vegetable, Oval, 9 In. 45.00
Candy Container, Cover 75.00
Celery 22.50
Champagne .... 12.50 To 30.00
Cigarette Box, Cover, Large 26.00
Coaster 5.00
Compote, 7 In. .... 35.00 To 45.00
Console Set, 3 Piece 40.00
Creamer, Large 11.25
Cup & Saucer .... 9.00 To 12.50
Cup & Saucer, Demitasse .... 22.00 To 25.00
Cup, Demitasse 16.00
Dish, Mayonnaise, 3 Piece 85.00
Oyster Cocktail .... 12.50 To 18.00
Parfait, 5 1/4 In. 18.00
Plate, 7 1/2 In. 5.00
Plate, 8 1/2 In. 7.00
Plate, 9 1/2 In. 17.50
Plate, 10 1/4 In. 10.00
Plate, 12 In. 4.00
Plate, Server, Center Handle, 10 In. 25.00
Platter, 10 1/2 In. 20.00
Platter, 15 In. .... 48.00 To 50.00
Platter, Oval, 12 In. .... 30.00 To 47.50
Relish, 2 Sections, 8 1/2 In. .... 9.00 To 14.50
Relish, 3 Sections, 11 1/2 In. 13.00
Salt & Pepper 75.00

Don't keep identification on your key ring. If it is lost, it is an invitation for burglars to visit.

Don't put your name on your mailbox, front door mat, or screen door. It helps burglars find your phone number, then find out when you are away.

Sauce Boat, Underplate.....85.00
Sherbet,
4 1/4 In.........11.00 To 17.00
Sugar &
Creamer.........22.00 To 50.00
Tumbler, Footed,
4 1/2 In....................25.00
Tumbler, Footed,
5 1/2 In....................18.00
Tumbler, Footed, 6 In......25.00
Wine, 5 1/4 In.............23.00

CRYSTAL

Cup & Saucer.......4.50 To 6.00
Plate, 7 1/2 In................3.00

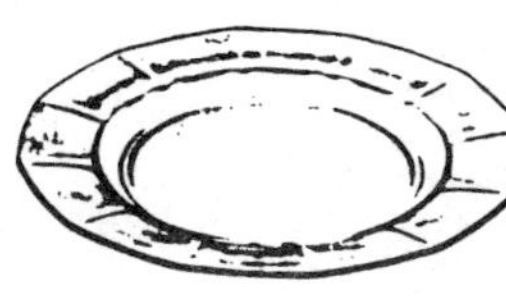

GREEN

Bouillon, Footed..............7.00
Bowl, 6 In....................9.00
Bowl, Vegetable, Oval,
10 1/4 In..................20.00
Butter, Cover....75.00 To 85.00
Candy Container, 3 Sections,
Cover........................35.00
Celery, 11 1/2 In...........11.00
Champagne...................20.00
Coaster.........................3.75
Compote,
7 In.............11.00 To 15.00
Creamer,
3 1/2 In...........7.00 To 7.50
Cup & Saucer.......4.50 To 7.50
Dish, Mayonnaise,
2 Piece......................32.00
Pitcher.........105.00 To 125.00
Plate, 6 In..........2.00 To 3.50
Plate, 7 In..........4.00 To 5.00
Plate, 8 In....................4.00
Plate,
9 1/2 In.........11.00 To 12.50
Plate, 10 1/4 In............12.00
Platter, 12 1/2 In...........18.50
Platter, 15 In................45.00
Relish, 2 Sections,
11 1/2 In..................11.00
Salt & Pepper................55.00
Sauce Boat...................27.00

Soup, Cream.................11.00
Sugar &
Creamer.........15.50 To 18.50
Sugar, 3 1/2 In.....6.00 To 7.50
Wine..........................32.50

ORCHID

Bowl, 6 In...................15.00
Cup & Saucer, Demitasse...18.00
Plate, 7 1/2 In...............4.50

PINK

Baker, Oval, 10 1/2 In.....25.00
Bouillon, Saucer............12.50
Butter, Cover................85.00
Champagne.......19.50 To 24.00
Cheese & Cracker Set.......15.00
Compote, 7 In...............25.00
Creamer, Footed..............6.00
Cup............................6.00
Cup & Saucer.....6.00 To 10.00
Cup, Demitasse...............9.00
Fruit Bowl, 5 In.............9.50
Oyster Cocktail..............18.00
Pitcher......................195.00
Plate, 6 In....................3.00
Plate, 7 1/2 In......4.00 To 4.75
Plate, 8 3/4 In................8.00
Plate,
9 1/2 In.........12.50 To 15.00
Relish,
2 Sections.......11.00 To 14.00
Salt & Pepper, Footed......35.00
Saltshaker, Footed, Large...25.00
Saucer.........................2.00
Sherbet, Low.................17.00
Sugar, Flat....................8.50
Sugar, Footed................12.50
Sweetmeat, 6 In..............9.00
Tray, Center Handle,
10 1/4 In.......15.00 To 20.00
Tumbler, 4 1/2 In...........24.00

TOPAZ

Butter, Cover................52.00

YELLOW

Bouillon, Saucer............12.00
Champagne...................14.00
Creamer, Footed..............7.50
Cup & Saucer.......5.00 To 5.75
Cup & Saucer, Demitasse...11.00
Dish, Lemon.................10.00
Dish, Mayonnaise...........20.00

Goblet,
8 1/4 In.........17.50 To 25.00
Oyster Cocktail...............9.00
Pail, Whipped Cream.......27.50
Parfait.........................18.00
Plate, 6 In....................3.00
Plate, 7 1/2 In................3.50
Platter, 15 1/2 In...........65.00
Salt & Pepper,
Original Tops...............60.00
Sauce Boat....................30.00
Saucer.........................1.00
Sugar &
Creamer.........15.00 To 18.00
Whiskey, 2 1/2 Oz..........20.00

Fan & Feather, see Adam

Fine Rib, see Homespun

Fire-King

Fire-King or Fire-King Oven Glass, Fire-King Oven Ware, and Fire-King Dinnerware were all made by Anchor Hocking Company, Lancaster, Ohio, from 1942 through the 1960s. Fire-King oven glass is a transparent, pale blue glassware with a lacy decoration. A matching dinnerware set is called Philbe. It was made in crystal and pale blue. Philbe is listed under its own name in this book. Fire-King Oven Ware is an opaque glass made by Anchor Hocking in the 1950s. It was made in blue, jadite, pink, and white, or ivory with gold or colored trim. Some mixing bowls and kitchen sets were made with tulips or red kitchen objects pictured on the sides. Fire-King Dinnerware sets were made in

patterns named Alice, Jadite, Jane-Ray, Square, Swirl Fire-King, and Turquoise Blue. These are listed in this book in their own sections.

Fire-King Dinnerware, see Alice; Jadite; Jane-Ray; Philbe; Square; Swirl Fire-King; and Turquoise Blue

BLUE

Baker, 1 Pt. 3.00
Baker, 1 1/2 Qt. 6.00
Baker, Cover, 10 Oz. 6.50
Bowl Set, 6 7/8, 8 3/8 & 10 1/8 In., 3 Piece 26.00
Bowl, 5 3/8 In. .....5.00 To 8.00
Bowl, Measuring, 16 Oz. 13.00
Bowl, Mixing, 6 7/8 In. .... 7.00 To 9.00
Bowl, Mixing, 8 3/8 In. 10.00
Bowl, Mixing, 10 1/8 In. 12.00
Cake Pan, 8 3/4 In. 9.00
Casserole, Knob Lid, 1 Pt. 6.00
Casserole, Knob Lid, 1 1/2 Qt. .... 7.00 To 12.00
Casserole, Knob Lid, 2 Qt. 9.00
Cup, Custard 1.75
Cup, Custard, 5 Oz. 2.50
Custard, 4 In. 1.00
Custard, 8 In. 2.50
Hot Plate, Tab Handle 8.50
Jar, Refrigerator, Cover, 4 1/2 X 5 In. 7.00
Loaf Pan, 9 1/8 In. .... 7.00 To 12.00
Measuring Cup, 1 Lip 9.00
Nurser, 4 Oz. .... 5.00 To 6.00
Nurser, 8 Oz. 13.00
Percolator Top 3.00
Pie Plate, 8 3/8 In. .... 4.50 To 6.00
Pie Plate, 9 In. .... 4.50 To 7.00
Pie Plate, 9 5/8 In. 8.00
Pie Plate, Individual, 4 3/8 In. 7.50
Pie Plate, Juice Saver, 10 3/8 In. 47.00
Roaster, Cover, 10 3/8 In. ...... 40.00 To 60.00
Utility Pan, 5 X 11 In. 8.00

CASSEROLE

Cover, 4 X 5 In. 6.00

CRYSTAL

Percolator, 2 1/8 In. 1.50

WHITE

Bowl, Mixing, Flower Design, 3 Piece 15.00
Bowl, Mixing, Fruit Design, 3 Piece 22.00
Bowl, Pink Flower, 5 In. 4.00
Bowl, Pink Flower, 6 In. 5.00
Bowl, Pink Flower, 8 1/2 In. 7.00
Casserole, Fruits, Cover, 4 X 8 In. 6.00
Casserole, Pink Flower, 8 1/4 In. 8.00
Grease Jar, Cover, Tulip 15.00
Loaf Pan, Pink Flower 8.00
Salt & Pepper, Tulip 8.50

Flanders

Flanders dinnerware was made by the United States Glass Company, at the Tiffin, Ohio, plant from 1914 to 1935. It was made in crystal and in pink or yellow (Mandarin) with crystal trim.

CRYSTAL

Champagne 15.00
Cordial 55.00
Goblet, 4 Oz. 15.00

Goblet, 7 3/4 In. .... 17.00 To 17.50
Plate, 10 1/2 In. 35.00
Tumbler, Footed, 12 Oz. .... 19.50 To 24.00

PINK

Champagne 25.00
Compote, Footed 65.00
Cordial 75.00
Cup & Saucer 60.00
Decanter, Stopper 285.00
Goblet, 4 Oz. 40.00
Goblet, 8 1/4 In. 27.50
Goblet, Crystal Trim, 4 Oz. 15.00
Oyster Cocktail 35.00
Parfait 40.00
Pitcher, Cover 225.00
Plate, 6 In. 12.50
Plate, 9 1/2 In. 50.00
Wine .... 35.00 To 55.00

Flat Diamond, see Diamond Quilted

Floragold

The iridescent marigold color of carnival glass was copied in this 1950s pattern made by Jeannette Glass Company, Jeannette, Pennsylvania. The pattern is called Floragold or Louisa, the name of the original carnival glass pattern that was copied. Pieces were made in crystal, iridescent, ice blue, shell pink, and reddish yellow.

CRYSTAL

Ashtray, 4 In. .... 2.00 To 4.50
Bowl, 5 1/2 In. 17.50
Bowl, Fruit, Ruffled, 12 In. 6.50
Bowl, Ruffled, 5 1/2 In. 3.00
Bowl, Ruffled, 9 1/2 In. .... 5.00 To 6.50
Bowl, Salad, 9 1/2 In. 25.00
Bowl, Square, 4 1/2 In. .... 3.00 To 4.00
Butter, Cover, Round .... 32.00 To 37.50

Butter, Oblong,
1/4 Lb.......... 11.50 To 15.00
Candleholder, Pair........... 35.00
Candy Container, 4-Footed,
5 1/4 In........... 4.00 To 5.00
Candy Container, Cover,
6 3/4 In..................... 25.00
Creamer .... 4.75 To 5.50
Cup.................. 3.00 To 4.50
Cup & Saucer ..... 7.00 To 12.00
Pitcher,
64 Oz........... 16.00 To 22.50
Plate,
8 1/2 In......... 14.50 To 16.00
Plate, 13 1/2 In. 12.00
Plate, Indented,
13 1/2 In.................. 22.00
Platter,
11 1/4 In....... 11.00 To 14.00
Salt & Pepper,
Plastic Tops..... 25.00 To 45.00
Sherbet.............. 6.50 To 8.00
Sugar & Creamer 9.00
Sugar, Cover ..... 12.50 To 18.00
Tumbler, Footed, 10 Oz..... 9.00
Tumbler, Footed, 15 Oz.... 15.00

IRIDESCENT

Bowl, 5 1/2 In. 22.50
Bowl, 9 1/2 In. .... 5.00 To 8.00
Bowl, Ruffled,
9 1/2 In........... 3.00 To 5.00
Bowl, Square, 4 1/2 In...... 3.00
Bowl, Square, 8 1/2 In...... 7.00
Butter, Cover, Round....... 35.00
Candy Container, 4-Footed,
5 1/4 In........... 3.00 To 5.00
Creamer .... 4.00 To 6.00
Cup.................. 2.00 To 4.50
Cup & Saucer 8.00
Pitcher, 64 Oz. 20.00
Plate, 5 3/4 In............... 3.00
Plate, 8 1/2 In.............. 17.50
Plate,
13 1/2 In....... 14.00 To 15.00
Salt & Pepper 24.50
Sherbet............... 5.00 To 8.00
Sugar, Cover ..... 10.00 To 15.00
Tumbler, Footed, 10 Oz..... 9.00
Tumbler, Footed, 15 Oz.... 55.00

PINK

Butter, Cover, Round....... 30.00
Candleholder, Pair........... 37.50
Cup & Saucer 9.00
Salt & Pepper 25.00

Floral

Poinsettia blossoms are the decorations on Floral pattern made by Jeannette Glass Company from 1931 to 1935. The pattern was made in amber, crystal, delphite, green, jadite, pink, red, and yellow.

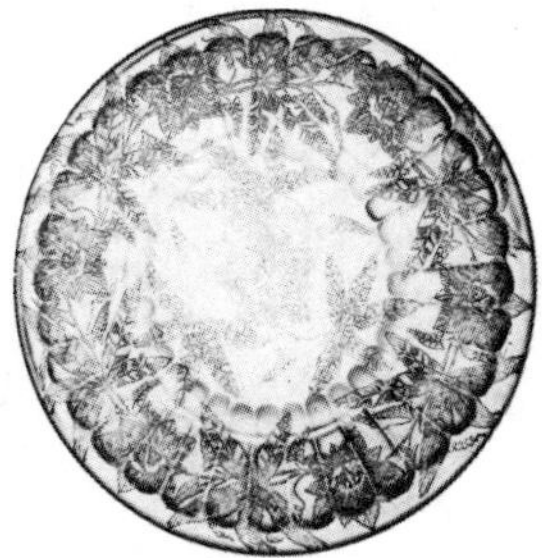

CRYSTAL

Pitcher, 32 Oz., 8 In........ 25.00

GREEN

Bowl, 4 In......... 8.00 To 16.50
Bowl,
7 1/2 In.......... 7.00 To 15.00
Bowl, Cover,
8 In............. 22.50 To 33.00
Bowl, Oval, 9 In............ 10.00
Bowl, Vegetable, Oval,
9 In......................... 11.00
Butter, Cover .... 65.00 To 67.50
Candleholder, 4 In.,
Pair .... 53.00 To 72.50
Candy Container,
Cover........... 22.00 To 32.00
Coaster............... 6.00 To 8.00
Creamer .... 7.50 To 9.50
Cup................ 9.00 To 10.00
Cup & Saucer .... 12.00 To 15.00
Pitcher,
5 1/2 In...... 375.00 To 450.00
Pitcher, 8 In...... 20.00 To 26.00
Plate, 6 In. .... 2.50 To 4.00
Plate, 8 In. .... 6.00 To 9.00
Plate, 9 In. .... 9.00 To 10.00
Platter, 10 3/4 In. 18.00
Platter, Oval, 10 3/4 In. ... 11.00
Refrigerator Dish, Cover,
5 In......................... 30.00
Relish,
2 Sections .... 8.00 To 11.00
Salt & Pepper, Footed,
4 In............. 29.00 To 38.00
Saucer................ 5.00 To 8.00
Sherbet............... 8.75 To 9.50
Soup, Cream 375.00
Sugar & Creamer, Cover ... 27.00
Sugar, Cover ..... 14.00 To 21.00
Tray, Square, 6 In. 10.00
Tumbler, 9 Oz.,
4 1/2 In.................. 150.00
Tumbler, Footed, 5 Oz.,
4 In......................... 14.00
Tumbler, Footed, 7 Oz.,
4 3/4 In......... 13.00 To 14.00
Tumbler, Footed, 9 Oz.,
5 1/4 In......... 28.00 To 30.00
Vase, 6 7/8 In............ 425.00

PINK

Bowl, 4 In......... 7.50 To 13.00
Bowl,
7 1/2 In.......... 8.00 To 15.00
Bowl, Cover,
8 In............. 20.00 To 24.00
Bowl, Oval,
9 In.............. 9.00 To 11.00
Butter, Cover .... 57.50 To 60.00
Candleholder, 4 In., Pair ... 50.00
Candy Container,
Cover........... 25.00 To 35.00
Coaster............ 5.50 To 10.00
Creamer .... 7.00 To 9.00
Cup.................. 6.00 To 8.00
Cup & Saucer .... 11.00 To 13.00
Pitcher, 48 Oz.,
10 1/4 In.... 150.00 To 175.00
Pitcher, Footed, 32 Oz.,
8 In............. 20.00 To 21.00
Plate, 6 In. .... 3.00 To 5.00
Plate, 8 In. .... 5.00 To 6.00
Plate, 9 In. .... 8.50 To 13.00

Platter,
10 3/4 In. .... 8.00 To 16.00
Relish,
2 Sections .... 7.00 To 12.50
Salt & Pepper,
6 In. .... 28.00 To 30.00
Salt & Pepper, Footed,
4 In. .... 28.00 To 35.00
Saucer .... 4.50 To 5.00
Sherbet .... 7.00 To 10.00
Sugar & Creamer 20.00
Sugar, Cover ..... 16.00 To 18.00
Tray, Handles,
6 In. .... 9.50 To 17.00
Tumbler, Footed, 5 Oz.,
4 In. .... 7.50 To 13.00
Tumbler, Footed, 7 Oz.,
4 3/4 In. .... 10.00 To 12.50
Tumbler, Footed, 9 Oz.,
5 1/4 In. .... 27.00 To 28.00

Floral & Diamond Band

Floral & Diamond Band was made by the U.S. Glass Company in the 1920s. It features a large center flower and pressed diamond bands of edging. The pattern was made in black, crystal, green, and pink. Some pieces are iridescent marigold color and are considered carnival glass, called Mayflower by the collectors.

CRYSTAL

Pitcher, 42 Oz., 8 In. 75.00

GREEN

Bowl, 8 In. 7.00
Bowl, Handle, 5 3/4 In. 6.00
Butter, Cover 80.00
Pitcher, 42 Oz.,
8 In. .... 55.00 To 85.00
Sherbet .... 2.00 To 5.50
Sugar & Creamer 10.00
Sugar, Small .... 4.50 To 5.00
Tumbler, 4 In. 6.00
Tumbler, 5 In. 8.00

PINK

Pitcher, 42 Oz.,
8 In. .... 58.00 To 60.00
Sherbet .... 4.00 To 5.00

Floral Rim, see Vitrock

Florentine No.1

Florentine No. 1, also called Poppy No. 1, is neither Florentine in appearance nor decorated with recognizable poppies. The plates are hexagonal, differentiating them from Florentine No. 2. The pattern was made by the Hazel-Atlas Glass Company from 1932 to 1935 in cobalt blue, crystal, green, pink, and yellow.

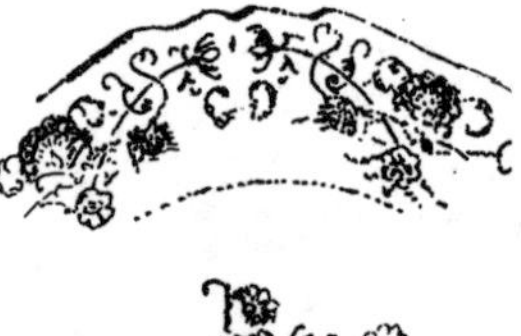

COBALT BLUE

5 In. 16.00
Creamer, Ruffled 42.50
Pitcher, Footed,
6 1/2 In. 495.00

CRYSTAL

Bowl, 5 In. 6.00
Cup 5.00
Cup & Saucer 6.00
Pitcher,
7 1/2 In. .... 30.00 To 42.00
Plate, 6 In. 3.00
Plate, 8 1/2 In. 4.50
Plate, 10 In. 7.50
Salt & Pepper .... 22.00 To 29.00
Saucer 3.00
Sherbet .... 4.00 To 4.75
Sugar .... 7.00 To 8.00
Sugar & Creamer 15.00

GREEN

Bowl, 5 In. .... 8.00 To 12.00
Bowl, Cover,
9 1/2 In. .... 22.00 To 37.00
Butter, Cover .... 80.00 To 95.00
Creamer .... 5.00 To 10.50
Cup .... 5.00 To 6.00
Pitcher, Footed,
6 1/2 In. .... 30.00 To 40.00
Plate, 6 In. 2.50
Plate, 8 1/2 In. ..... 5.50 To 6.50
Plate, 10 In. .... 8.50 To 12.00
Plate, Grill .... 7.00 To 14.50
Platter,
11 1/2 In. .... 9.25 To 18.00
Salt & Pepper,
Footed .... 27.00 To 32.00
Saltshaker 17.50
Saucer 2.00
Sherbet, Footed ..... 4.00 To 7.00

Soup, Cream 8.50
Sugar & Creamer,
Cover............ 32.00 To 35.00
Sugar, Cover ..... 17.50 To 25.75
Tumbler, 5 1/4 In. 9.25
Tumbler, Footed,
3 3/4 In.......... 9.25 To 11.50

PINK

Bowl, 5 In......... 6.00 To 11.00
Butter, Cover 58.00
Creamer .... 7.50 To 10.00
Creamer, Ruffled 21.50
Cup............................. 6.00
Cup & Saucer 8.00
Pitcher, 7 1/2 In. 80.00
Plate, 8 1/2 In................ 7.00
Plate, 10 In................... 14.00
Salt & Pepper 44.00
Saucer................ 2.00 To 2.50
Sherbet............. 7.75 To 10.50
Sugar & Creamer,
Cover............ 16.00 To 25.00
Sugar & Creamer,
Ruffled 40.00
Sugar, Cover ..... 19.00 To 21.00
Sugar, Ruffled 21.50
Tumbler, Footed,
5 1/4 In..................... 20.00

YELLOW

Cup................... 6.25 To 7.00
Cup & Saucer 10.00
Pitcher, 6 1/2 In. 43.00
Pitcher, 7 1/2 In. 140.00
Pitcher, Footed,
6 1/2 In..................... 35.00
Plate, 6 In. 3.00
Plate, 10 In................... 11.00
Salt & Pepper 32.00
Sherbet............. 7.50 To 10.00
Soup, Cream 14.00
Sugar................ 8.00 To 9.00
Sugar & Creamer, Cover ... 25.00
Tumbler, Footed,
4 3/4 In..................... 12.00

Florentine No.2

Florentine No. 2, sometimes called Poppy No. 2 or Oriental Poppy, was also made by Hazel–Atlas Glass Company from 1932 to 1935. It has round plates instead of the hexagonal pieces of Florentine No. 1. It was made in amber, cobalt, crystal, green, ice blue, and pink.

AMBER

Ashtray, 3 3/4 In............. 5.00
Bowl,
4 1/2 In.......... 8.50 To 10.50
Bowl, 6 In.................... 29.00
Bowl, 8 In........ 17.00 To 25.00
Bowl, Vegetable, Cover,
9 In.......................... 39.00
Butter,
Cover.......... 75.00 To 125.00
Candleholder, Pair........... 40.00
Candy Container,
Cover........... 75.00 To 99.00
Creamer .... 7.50 To 10.00
Cup, Custard 68.00
Gravy Boat,
Underplate...... 45.00 To 70.00
Pitcher, 7 1/2 In. 100.00
Plate, 6 In. .... 2.00 To 4.00
Plate, 8 1/2 In...... 3.00 To 7.50
Plate, 10 In........ 7.50 To 12.50
Plate, Grill .... 6.00 To 12.00
Plate, Indented,
6 /14 In..................... 18.00
Platter, 11 In...... 8.75 To 13.50
Relish,
3 Sections .... 14.00 To 18.00
Salt & Pepper .... 30.00 To 45.00
Saucer................ 1.50 To 3.00
Sherbet........... 40.00 To 55.00
Soup, Cream ..... 11.00 To 15.00
Sugar & Creamer,
Cover............ 25.00 To 30.00
Sugar, Cover ..... 20.00 To 23.00
Tray, Condiment............. 67.50
Tumbler,
3 1/2 In......... 22.50 To 45.00
Tumbler, 4 In.... 12.00 To 14.50
Tumbler, 5 In.... 30.00 To 42.50
Tumbler, Footed,
3 1/4 In.......... 5.50 To 10.00
Tumbler, Footed,
4 In.............. 6.00 To 14.50
Tumbler, Footed,
4 1/2 In......... 20.00 To 26.50

CRYSTAL

Candy Container,
Cover............ 50.00 To 75.00
Coaster, 3 1/4 In............. 7.50
Compote, Ruffled,
3 1/2 In.......... 8.00 To 12.50
Creamer 7.00
Cup............................. 4.00
Cup & Saucer .... 6.00 To 7.50
Cup, Custard 22.00
Pitcher,
7 1/2 In......... 30.00 To 40.00
Plate, 6 In. 1.50
Plate, 8 1/2 In...... 3.00 To 6.00
Plate, 10 In..................... 6.00
Platter, 11 In.................. 8.50
Salt & Pepper 25.00
Saucer.......................... 1.00
Sherbet............... 3.00 To 6.00
Soup, Cream .... 4.00 To 8.00
Sugar................. 4.50 To 5.00
Sugar & Creamer 8.00
Tumbler, 4 In....... 7.00 To 9.00
Tumbler, 5 In.... 10.00 To 18.00
Tumbler, Footed,
3 1/4 In...................... 6.00
Tumbler, Footed, 4 In. 6.00
Tumbler, Footed,
4 1/2 In..................... 10.00
Vase, 6 In. 15.00

GREEN

Bowl,
4 1/2 In.......... 6.00 To 10.00

Bowl, 6 In. 10.00
Bowl, 8 In. 12.00
Bowl, Cover, Oval, 9 In. 25.00 To 38.00
Butter, Cover 75.00 To 79.00
Candleholder, Pair 35.00
Candy Container, Cover 65.00 To 100.00
Coaster, 3 1/4 In. 7.50
Coaster, 3 3/4 In. 11.50
Coaster, 5 1/2 In. 12.00
Creamer 5.00 To 8.00
Cup 4.00 To 9.00
Cup & Saucer 6.00 To 9.00
Cup, Custard 70.00
Pitcher, Footed, 7 1/2 In. 22.00
Plate, 6 In. 1.75 To 3.50
Plate, 8 1/2 In. 3.00 To 8.50
Plate, 10 In. 7.00 To 8.75
Relish, 3 Sections 9.00
Salt & Pepper 27.00 To 32.50
Saltshaker 12.00 To 17.50
Saucer 2.00 To 3.50
Sherbet 3.50 To 8.00
Soup, Cream 4.75 To 9.50
Sugar 5.00 To 6.00
Sugar & Creamer 9.00
Tumbler, 3 1/2 In. 9.00
Tumbler, 4 In. 7.50 To 10.00
Tumbler, 5 In. 18.00 To 33.75
Tumbler, Footed, 3 1/4 In. 9.00 To 10.00
Tumbler, Footed, 4 1/2 In. 8.50 To 18.00
Vase, 6 In. 22.00

ICE BLUE

Compote, Ruffled 40.00
Soup, Cream, 5 In. 30.00
Tumbler, 4 In. 50.00

PINK

Candy Container, Cover 75.00
Compote, Ruffled, 3 1/2 In. 6.00 To 9.00
Relish, 3 Sections 14.00 To 15.00
Soup, Cream 6.00 To 9.00
Sugar, Cover 13.00 To 14.00
Tumbler, 4 In. 8.50

Flower, see Princess Feather

Flower & Leaf Bind, see Indiana Custard

Flower Basket, see No. 615

Flower Garden With Butterflies

There really is a butterfly hiding in the flower on this U.S. Glass Company pattern called Flower Garden with Butterflies, Butterflies and Roses, Flower Garden, or Wildrose with Apple Blossom. It was made in the late 1920s in a variety of colors including amber, black, blue, canary yellow, crystal, green, and pink.

AMBER

Ashtray 125.00 To 200.00
Plate, 8 In. 17.50
Tray, Oval, 10 In. 65.00

BLACK

Bowl, 9 In. 210.00
Candlesticks, 8 In. 225.00

Plate 100.00
Vase, 2 Handles, 10 In. 300.00

BLUE

Ashtray 125.00 To 200.00
Tray, Rectangular, 11 3/4 In. 75.00

CANARY YELLOW

Candy Container, Heart 500.00
Compote, 4 X 43/4 In. 40.00
Plate, 7 In. 22.50 To 25.00
Tray, Rectangular 75.00

GREEN

Ashtray 100.00 To 200.00
Candleholder, 8 In., Pair 45.00
Creamer 125.00
Cup & Saucer 75.00 To 125.00
Dresser Set, 3 Piece 275.00
Jar, Powder, Cover, Footed, 6 1/4 In. 55.00
Luncheon Set, 14 Piece 350.00
Plate, 8 In. 20.00 To 24.00
Salt & Pepper 28.00
Sandwich Server 75.00
Saucer 20.00 To 25.00
Sugar & Creamer 245.00
Tray, Rectangular, 11 3/4 In. 50.00
Vase, 6 1/4 In. 175.00
Vase, 10 1/2 In. 175.00

PINK

Ashtray 200.00
Candy Container, Cone Shape, 7 In. 115.00
Compote, 3 In. 30.00
Compote, 7 1/4 In. 50.00
Creamer 125.00
Plate, 8 In. 15.00
Saucer 20.00
Tray, Oval, 10 In. 42.50 To 65.00
Vase, 6 1/4 In. 150.00
Vase, 10 1/2 In. 100.00
Vase, Footed, 10 1/2 In. 80.00

Flower Rim, see Vitrock

Forest Green

There is no need to picture Forest Green in a black-and-white drawing because it is the color that identifies the pattern. Anchor Hocking Glass Company, Lancaster, Ohio, made this very plain pattern from 1950 to 1957. Other patterns were also made in this same deep green color, but these are known by the pattern name.

Ashtray............... 2.50 To 3.00
Bowl, 4 3/4 In. ..... 3.00 To 5.00
Bowl, 6 In........... 5.00 To 6.50
Bowl, 7 3/8 In. 10.00
Condiment Set, 4 Piece..... 40.00
Creamer .... 4.00 To 4.50
Cup............................ 1.25
Cup & Saucer .... 3.00 To 3.50
Cup & Saucer,
Square .... 3.00 To 3.50
Cup, Square 2.25
Pitcher,
22 Oz........... 11.00 To 20.00
Pitcher, 3 Qt. .... 18.00 To 20.00
Plate, 6 3/4 In................ 1.75
Plate, 8 3/8 In...... 3.00 To 5.00
Punch Bowl 18.00
Punch Cup 1.50
Saucer............... 1.00 To 2.00
Sugar................ 4.00 To 6.00
Sugar & Creamer ... 4.00 To 9.00
Tumbler, 10 Oz..... 2.00 To 4.00
Vase, 6 3/8 In...... 3.50 To 8.00
Vase, 9 In. 10.00

Fortune

Anchor Hocking made Fortune pattern in 1937 and 1938. The

simple design was made in crystal or pink.

CRYSTAL

Tumbler, 3 1/2 In. 4.00
Tumbler, 4 In................. 5.00

PINK

Bowl, Rolled Edge,
5 1/4 In..................... 4.00
Candy Container, Cover 15.00
Cup............................ 3.00
Tumbler, 4 In................. 4.00

Fostoria, see American

Frosted Block, see Beaded Block

Fruits

Pears, grapes, apples, and other fruits are displayed in small bunches on the pieces of Fruits pattern. Hazel-Atlas and several other companies made this pattern about 1931 to 1933. Pieces are known in crystal, green, pink, and iridized finish.

GREEN

Cup.................. 3.00 To 4.50
Cup & Saucer 5.50
Plate, 8 In. .... 3.25 To 4.00
Saucer............... 1.50 To 2.00
Sherbet........................ 5.00
Tumbler, 5 In............... 22.50

PINK

Bowl, 5 In................... 11.00
Plate, 8 In. 4.00
Tumbler, 4 In....... 6.00 To 7.00
Tumbler, 5 In............... 22.00

G

Georgian

Georgian, also known as Lovebirds, was made by the Federal Glass Company, Columbus, Ohio, from 1931 to 1935. The pattern shows alternating sections with birds in one, a basket of flowers in the next. It was made in crystal and green. Notice that it is mold-etched and in no way resembles the Fenton glass pattern called Georgian, listed in this book as Georgian Fenton.

Decorate with the neighborhood burglar in mind. Large windows can be made less attractive to intruders if you put plants on shelves across the window. Decorative shelves and grilles are made for this. Of course, be sure you can open the windows in case of fire.

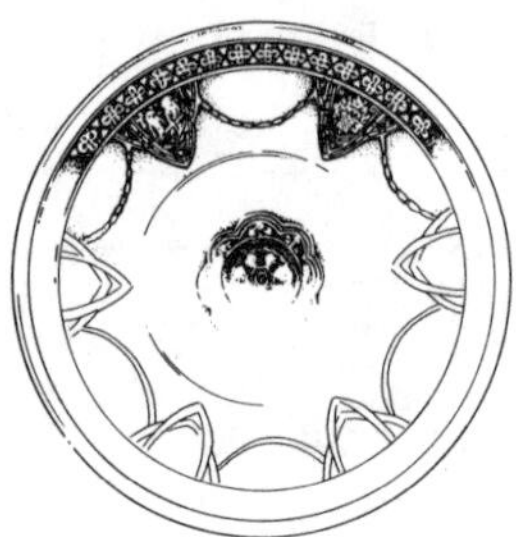

CRYSTAL

Bowl, 4 1/2 In. 2.50
Bowl, 5 3/4 In. 10.00
Bowl, 7 1/2 In. 35.00
Creamer, 3 In. 8.00
Cup & Saucer 6.00
Plate, 6 In. 1.50
Plate, 8 In. 4.00
Sherbet 7.00
Tumbler, 4 In. 8.00

GREEN

Bowl, 4 1/2 In. .....3.00 To 7.00
Bowl,
5 3/4 In.......... 8.50 To 14.00
Bowl,
6 1/2 In......... 15.00 To 45.00
Bowl,
7 1/2 In......... 42.00 To 51.25
Bowl, Vegetable, Oval,
9 In............. 42.00 To 45.00
Butter, Cover 70.00
Creamer, 3 In....... 6.50 To 7.50
Cup.................. 7.00 To 8.00
Cup & Saucer 10.50
Plate, 6 In. .... 2.00 To 3.00
Plate, 8 In. .... 4.00 To 8.00
Plate, 9 1/4 In.............. 18.00
Plate, Center Design,
9 1/4 In...................... 9.50
Platter, 11 1/2 In. 27.00
Sherbet.............. 4.50 To 9.50
Sugar & Creamer,
4 In............. 15.00 To 30.00
Sugar & Creamer, Cover,
3 In.......................... 35.00
Sugar, 3 In. .... 5.00 To 6.50
Sugar, 4 In. .... 6.00 To 7.50
Tumbler, 4 In.... 28.50 To 42.00

Georgian Fenton

Fenton Glass Company made this Georgian pattern tableware from about 1930. It came in many colors, some pale but many in the popular dark shades. Look for amber, black, cobalt blue, crystal,

green, pink, ruby, and topaz. It is very different from the Georgian or Lovebirds pattern made by the Federal Glass Company.

AMBER

Cup & Saucer 7.50
Goblet, 5 1/2 In. 3.50
Sherbet, Stem, 4 1/8 In. 5.00

COBALT BLUE

Bowl, 4 1/2 In. 5.00
Goblet, 5 1/2 In. 5.00
Tumbler, 4 In. 3.00

PINK

Goblet, 5 1/2 In. 3.00
Plate, 9 In. 4.00
Tumbler, 4 In. 3.50

RUBY

Sugar & Creamer 24.00
Tumbler, 8 Oz. 15.00
Tumbler, 12 Oz. 8.00

Gladiola, see Royal Lace

Gloria

Gloria is an etched glass pattern made by Cambridge Glass Company about 1930. It is similar to the Tiffin pattern called Flanders. Gloria was made in amber, crystal, emerald green, green, heatherbloom (pink-purple), pink, and yellow. Full dinner sets were made as well as serving pieces, vases, and candlesticks.

AMBER

Bowl, 6 In., Square 15.00
Compote, Cheese,
11 1/2 In. 25.00
Compote, Footed, 6 In...... 32.00
Compote, Tall, 7 In. 45.00

If photographing antiques for insurance records, use a Polaroid camera. There will be no negatives and no one else has to see your treasures.

Cup & Saucer 35.00
Pitcher, Ball, 80 Oz. 175.00
Plate, 8 1/2 In. 15.00
Plate, 14 In. 50.00
Sherbet, Low, 6 Oz. 12.00
Vase, 11 In. 75.00

CRYSTAL

Bowl, Square, 5 In. 10.00
Bowl, Tab Handle, 9 In. ... 20.50
Candleholder, Pair 75.00
Candlestick, 6 In., Pair 35.00
Compote, Tall, 7 In. 35.00
Creamer, Footed 12.00
Goblet, 9 Oz. 12.00
Plate, 8 1/2 In. 9.00
Plate, 14 In. 30.00
Salt & Pepper 25.00
Tumbler, 12 Oz. 15.00

GREEN

Bowl, 6 In., Square 15.00
Cocktail Shaker 155.00
Compote, Footed, 6 In. 32.00
Goblet, 8 Oz. 25.00
Goblet, 9 Oz. 25.00
Mayonnaise, Liner, Ladle ... 50.00
Pitcher, Ball, 80 Oz. 175.00
Plate, 6 In. 8.50
Plate, 8 1/2 In. 14.00
Plate, 14 In. 50.00
Relish, 5 Sections, 12 In. ... 45.00
Sherbet, Low, 6 Oz. 12.00
Tumbler, Footed, 8 Oz. 20.00
Vase, 11 In. 75.00

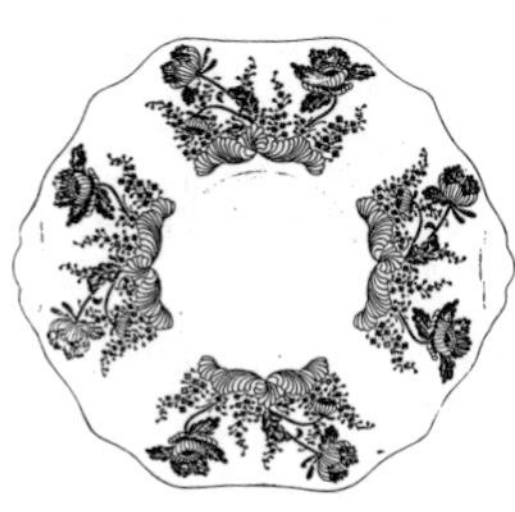

PINK

Bowl, Tab Handle, 9 In. ... 42.50
Candlestick, 6 In., Pair 70.00
Cocktail Shaker 155.00
Cup & Saucer 35.00
Goblet, 8 Oz. 25.00
Plate, 6 In. 8.50
Plate, 8 1/2 In. 14.00
Salt & Pepper 55.00
Tumbler, Footed, 5 Oz. 18.00
Tumbler, Footed, 8 Oz. 20.00

YELLOW

Bowl, Square, 5 In. 15.00
Compote, Cheese, 11 1/2 In. 25.00
Cordial 65.00
Creamer, Footed 17.00
Goblet, 9 Oz. 25.00
Mayonnaise, Liner, Ladle ... 50.00
Plate, Tab Handle, 10 In. 30.00
Relish, 5 Sections, 12 In. ... 45.00

Grape

Grape design is sometimes confused with the pattern known as Woolworth. Both have grapes in the pattern. Grape was made by Standard Glass Manufacturing Company, Lancaster, Ohio, in the 1930s. Full dinnerware sets were made in green, rose, and topaz.

Grape, see also Woolworth

H

Hairpin, see Newport

Hammered Band

The octagonal plate and serving pieces of this set of dishes are edged with a border that gave the name Hammered Band to the design. It was made by the L.E. Smith Glass Company, Mt. Pleasant, Pennsylvania, in the early 1930s. The pattern was made in amethyst, black, green, and pink. The pattern is sometimes called Melba or Pebbled Band.

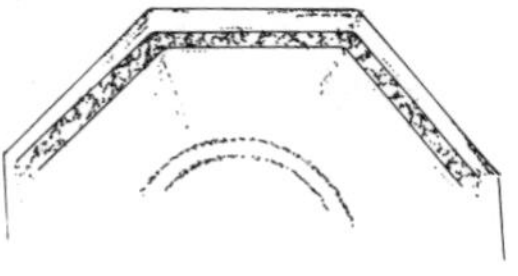

AMETHYST

Plate, 6 In. 1.50
Sugar 7.00
Tumbler, Footed, 4 1/4 In. 4.50

GREEN

Bowl, 5 In. 3.50
Plate, 9 In. 3.50
Saucer 1.00

PINK

Bowl, Ruffled, 10 In. 7.00
Plate 8 In. 3.00
Saucer 1.00
Sugar 7.50

Hanging Basket, see No. 615

Harp

The pattern name Harp describes the small lyre-shaped instruments that are included on the borders of these pieces of glass. This Jeannette Glass Company pattern was made from 1954 to 1957. Pieces are found in crystal, crystal with gold trim, light blue, and pink.

CRYSTAL

Ashtray .... 1.00 To 3.00
Ashtray,
Gold Trim .... 2.00 To 3.50
Cake Plate .... 10.00 To 15.00
Cup .... 4.00 To 5.00
Cup & Saucer 6.00
Plate, 7 In. 4.50
Tray,
2 Handles .... 12.00 To 18.00
Vase, 6 In. .... 8.00 To 8.75

Heritage

Federal Glass Company, Columbus, Ohio, made Heritage in the 1930s through the 1960s. Evidently the serving pieces were made in blue, light green, and pink, but the plates and dinnerware pieces were made only in crystal. Amber and crystal reproduction bowls were made in 1987.

CRYSTAL

Bowl, 5 In. .... 4.00 To 4.25
Bowl,
10 1/2 In. .... 6.00 To 10.00

Cup .... 2.50 To 6.00
Cup & Saucer .... 3.00 To 6.00
Plate, 8 In. .... 3.00 To 6.00
Plate, 9 1/4 In. ..... 4.00 To 8.00
Plate, 12 In. .... 6.50 To 8.50
Saucer .... 1.00 To 1.50
Sugar .... 8.00 To 12.50
Sugar & Creamer 17.00

Hex Optic, see Hexagon Optic

Hexagon Optic

Hexagon Optic, also called Honeycomb or Hex Optic, really does have an accurate, descriptive name. Pink or green sets of kitchenware were made in this pattern by Jeannette Glass Company, Jeannette, Pennsylvania, from 1928 to 1932. In the years near 1960 some iridized sets and some blue-green pieces were made.

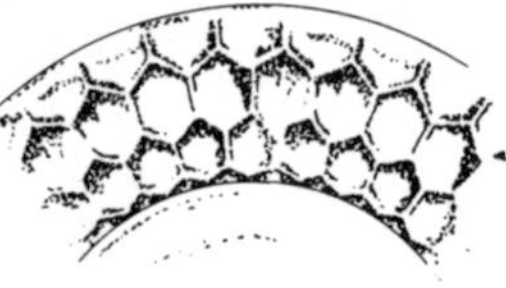

GREEN

Ice Bucket 18.00
Plate, 8 In. .... 2.50 To 4.00
Reamer Bucket 8.00
Saucer 1.00
Sherbet 3.00

IRIDESCENT

Water Set, Box, 7 Piece 25.00

PINK

Creamer 3.00
Cup & Saucer,
Solid Handle 5.00
Ice Bucket 20.00
Mixing Bowl, 7 1/4 In. 10.00
Plate, 8 In. .... 2.50 To 4.00
Saltshaker .... 7.00 To 10.00
Sugar 5.00
Tumbler, 3 3/4 In. 3.50

Hexagon Triple Band, see Colony

Hinge, see Patrician

Hobnail

Hobnail is the name of this pattern, although many similar patterns have been made with the hobbed decorations. Hocking Glass Company, Lancaster, Ohio, made this pattern from 1934 to 1936. It was made in crystal or pink. Some pieces were made with red rims or black feet.

Hobnail, see also Moonstone

CRYSTAL

Cup .... 1.75 To 2.00
Cup & Saucer 4.00
Decanter,
Stopper .... 12.00 To 15.00
Goblet, Footed, 5 Oz. 4.00
Pitcher, 10 Oz. 16.00
Plate, 8 1/2 In. ..... 2.50 To 3.00
Punch Cup 4.00
Saucer 1.00
Tumbler, 5 Oz. ..... 2.50 To 2.75

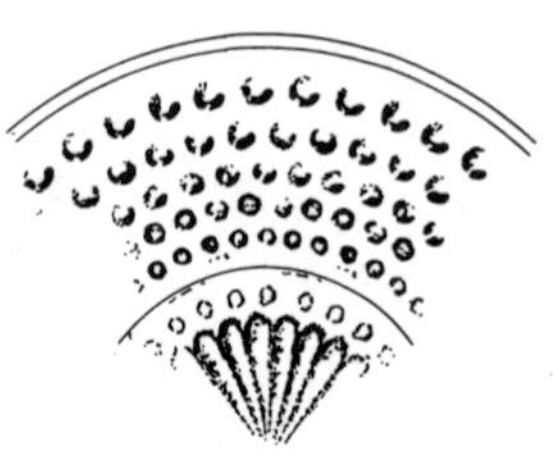

Tumbler, Footed,
3 1/2 In. 4.00 To 4.50
Tumbler, Red Trim,
4 3/4 In. 3.50
Water Set, Red Trim,
9 Piece 40.00
Whiskey 3.00

PINK

Cup 6.00
Cup & Saucer 2.50 To 4.50
Plate, 6 In. 1.75 To 3.00
Plate, 8 1/2 In. 5.00
Sherbet 2.00 To 5.00
Tumbler, Footed,
3 1/2 Oz. 15.00

Holiday

Holiday is one of the later Depression glass patterns. It was made from 1947 through 1949 by Jeannette Glass Company. The pattern is found in dinnerware sets of crystal, iridescent, and pink. A few pieces of opaque shell pink were made. The pattern is sometimes also called Buttons & Bows or Russian.

CRYSTAL

Plate, Chop 67.50

PINK

Bowl, 5 1/8 In. 5.00 To 7.50
Bowl,
8 1/2 In. 12.50 To 13.00
Bowl, Oval,
9 1/2 In. 10.00 To 15.00
Butter, Cover 25.00 To 35.00
Cake Plate, 3-Footed 55.00
Candleholder, Pair 53.00
Creamer 4.50

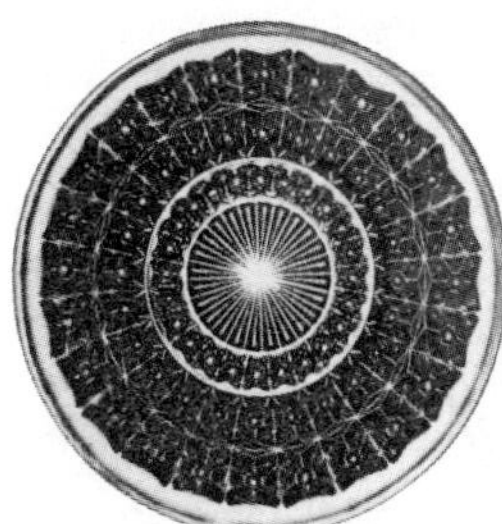

Cup 3.25 To 5.00
Cup & Saucer 6.00 To 12.00
Pitcher,
4 3/4 In. 40.00 To 48.00
Pitcher,
6 3/4 In. 20.00 To 35.00
Plate, 6 In. 2.00 To 4.50
Plate, 9 In. 7.00
Plate, 13 3/4 In. 45.00
Plate, 9 In. 14.00
Platter,
11 3/8 In. 8.00 To 12.50
Saucer 2.75 To 3.00
Sherbet 4.00 To 8.50
Soup, Dish 22.00 To 32.50
Sugar & Creamer,
Cover 18.00 To 22.00
Sugar, Cover 10.00 To 18.00
Tray, Sandwich,
10 1/2 In. 9.00 To 10.00
Tumbler, 4 In. 14.00 To 20.00
Tumbler, Footed,
4 In. 20.00 To 28.00
Tumbler, Footed,
6 In. 60.00 To 65.00

Homespun

Homespun, often called Fine Rib, is a cause of confusion. Several writers have presented different views about whether this is really one pattern or two. We prefer to call all of these pieces Homespun because that is the way most collectors use the name. Jeannette Glass Company made crystal, light blue, and pink pieces in this pattern in 1939 and 1940. Hazel-Atlas made other pieces in crystal and cobalt blue.

CRYSTAL

Bowl, 5 In. 5.00
Cup & Saucer 10.00 To 12.00
Cup & Saucer, Child's 15.00
Pitcher, 96 Oz. 17.50
Plate, 9 1/4 In. 8.00
Platter, 13 In. 5.50
Saucer, Child's 2.50
Sugar, Cover 10.00
Tumbler, 5 1/4 In. 15.00

PINK

Ashtray 7.00
Bowl, 5 In. 12.50
Bowl, 8 1/4 In. 10.00
Bowl, Handles, 4 1/2 In. 5.00
Butter, Cover 25.00
Creamer 4.00
Cup & Saucer, Child's 23.00
Plate, 6 In. 1.25 To 3.00
Plate, 9 1/4 In. 7.25 To 9.50
Plate, Child's 9.50
Platter, 13 In. 6.25 To 11.00
Saucer 2.00
Sherbet 4.50 To 7.50
Sugar 3.00 To 8.00
Teapot, Cover, Child's 70.00
Tumbler, 4 In. 8.50
Tumbler, 5 1/4 In. 19.00
Tumbler, Footed,
4 In. 3.00 To 4.00
Tumbler, Footed,
6 1/2 In. 10.00 To 22.00

Honeycomb, see Hexagon Optic

Horizontal Fine Rib, see Manhattan

Horizontal Rounded Big Rib, see Manhattan

Horizontal Sharp Big Rib, see Manhattan

Horseshoe, see No. 612

I

Indiana Custard

The design makes the old name Flower & Leaf Band clear, but the collectors prefer to call this pattern Indiana Custard. It is an opaque glassware of custard color and ivory made by the Indiana Glass Company. The sets were made from the 1930s to the 1950s. Some pieces have bands that are decorated with pastel colors or decal designs. The same pattern was made of milk glass in 1957. It was called Orange Blossom.

IVORY

Bowl, 4 7/8 In. ....4.00 To 8.00
Bowl, 6 In....................13.00
Bowl, 8 3/4 In. 30.00
Bowl, Vegetable, Oval, 9 1/2 In....................19.00
Butter, Cover ....35.00 To 55.00
Creamer ....10.75 To 15.00
Cup...........................29.00
Cup & Saucer ....31.00 To 34.00
Plate, 6 In.................... 3.50
Plate, 7 1/2 In................ 8.00
Plate, 8 7/8 In.... 7.50 To 10.00
Plate, 9 3/4 In.........16.00 To 18.00
Platter, Oval .....20.00 To 24.00
Saucer................4.50 To 5.00
Sugar.......................... 7.00
Sugar, Cover .....12.00 To 22.00

Iris & Herringbone, see Iris

Iris

The design of Iris is unusually bold for Depression glass. Molded representations of stalks of irises fill the center of a ribbed plate. Other pieces in the pattern show fewer irises, but the flower is predominant. Edges of pieces may be ruffled or beaded. It was made by Jeannette Glass Company, Jeannette, Pennsylvania, from 1928 to 1932 and then again in the 1950s and 1970s. Early pieces were made in crystal, iridescent, and pink; later pieces were made in blue-green or reddish yellow. The pattern is also called Iris & Herringbone. Reproduction candy vases have been made in a variety of colors since 1977.

CRYSTAL

Bowl, 9 1/2 In. 5.50
Bowl, Beaded, 4 1/2 In.......... 6.50 To 34.25
Bowl, Beaded, 8 In.............45.00 To 70.00
Bowl, Ruffled, 5 In...............3.00 To 6.50
Bowl, Ruffled, 8 In. 6.00

Bowl, Ruffled, 9 1/2 In......... 7.00 To 12.00
Bowl, Ruffled, 11 In..............6.50 To 9.00
Bowl, Ruffled, 11 1/2 In.... 8.00
Bowl, Straight, 11 In............26.00 To 37.50
Butter, Cover ....17.00 To 37.50
Candleholder, Pair..............17.25 To 23.00
Candy Container, Cover...........60.00 To 95.00
Coaster........................36.00
Creamer ....5.50 To 7.50
Cup............................ 8.00
Cup & Saucer ....11.00 To 13.75
Cup & Saucer, Demitasse ....60.00 To 65.00

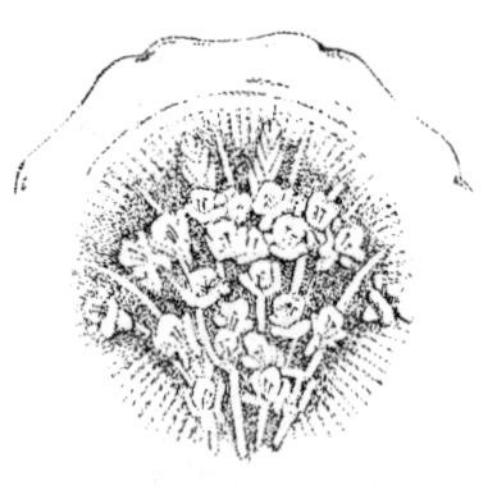

Cup, Demitasse ....17.00 To 25.00
Goblet, 4 1/4 In.........12.00 To 16.00
Goblet, 4 Oz., 5 3/4 In.........14.50 To 16.00
Goblet, 8 Oz., 5 3/4 In.........12.00 To 16.00
Lampshade, Frosted ....25.00 To 27.00
Nut Set ....25.00 To 45.00
Pitcher, Footed, 9 1/2 In.........14.00 To 27.50
Plate, 5 1/2 In................ 6.00
Plate, 8 In. 35.00
Plate, 9 In. ....28.00 To 32.00
Saucer................3.00 To 7.00
Sherbet, Footed, 2 1/2 In.........13.00 To 14.00
Sherbet, Footed, 4 In.............. 8.00 To 12.00
Soup, Dish, 7 1/2 In.........62.00 To 75.00
Sugar & Creamer.........14.00 To 25.00
Sugar, Cover .....10.00 To 14.50

Tumbler, 4 In. 46.00
Tumbler, Footed,
6 In. . . . . 6.00 To 14.00
Tumbler, Footed,
7 In. . . . . 12.50 To 14.00
Vase, 9 In. . . . . . . 10.00 To 15.00
Wine, 4 In. . . . . . . 10.50 To 15.00
Wine,
4 1/2 In. . . . . 10.00 To 11.00

IRIDESCENT

Bowl, 5 In. 4.75
Bowl, Beaded, 4 1/2 In. 6.00
Bowl, Beaded, 8 In. 20.00
Bowl, Ruffled,
11 In. . . . . 4.00 To 9.00
Butter, Cover . . . . 23.00 To 27.50
Creamer . . . . 6.00 To 7.00
Cup. . . . . 3.50 To 7.50
Cup & Saucer 11.00
Pitcher, Footed,
9 1/2 In. . . . . 26.50 To 32.50
Plate, 5 In. 4.00
Plate, 9 In. 16.50
Plate,
11 3/4 In. . . . . . . 10.00 To 12.50
Saucer. 3.00
Sherbet, Footed,
2 1/2 In. . . . . 4.25 To 9.50
Soup, Dish, 7 1/2 In. 15.00
Sugar, Cover 10.50
Tumbler, Footed,
6 In. . . . . 7.50 To 11.00
Vase, 9 In. . . . . . . 11.00 To 14.00

RED-YELLOW

Bowl, Beaded 9.50
Butter, Cover 42.50
Cup & Saucer 16.00
Goblet, 6 In. 14.00
Pitcher 33.00
Saucer. 5.00
Sugar. 14.00
Vase, 9 In. 25.00

Ivex, see Chinex Classic; Cremax

J

Jadite

Jadite is a color as well as a pattern. Kitchenware was made in jadite from 1936 to 1938 by Jeannette Glass Company. A matching set of dinnerware in the same green glass was called Jane-Ray. These pieces are listed in their own section. All of the pieces of kitchenware made of jadite were also made of a blue glass called delphite, but it is incorrect to call any but the green dishes by the name Jadite. For more information about related patterns and colors, see Alice, Fire-King, Jane-Ray, Philbe, Square, Swirl Fire-King, and Turquoise Blue in this book.

GREEN

Bowl, 4 1/4 In. 3.50
Bowl, 5 In. . . . . 3.00 To 7.00
Bowl, 6 In. . . . . 6.00 To 10.00
Bowl, 7 1/2 In. 12.00
Bowl, 8 In. 3.00
Bowl, Cover, 9 In. 10.00
Bowl, Oval, 7 In. 12.00
Bowl, Spout, 4 In. 8.00
Bowl, Spout,
7 In. . . . . 7.00 To 9.00
Butter, Cover 26.00
Canister, 4 Piece. 55.00
Canister, Coffee,
Square Metal Lid. 35.00
Canister, Tea,
Square Floral Lid. 25.00
Container, Cover, 10 Oz. 8.00
Container, Cover, 32 Oz. . . . 12.00
Drip Jar, Cover 16.00
Eggcup. . . . . 6.00 To 7.50
Measure, Flower Base,
16 Oz. 18.00
Measuring Cup Set,
4 Piece 35.00
Measuring Cup, 1/2 Cup. . . 10.00
Measuring Cup, 1/3 Cup. . . . 8.00
Measuring Cup, 1/4 Cup. . . . 6.00
Mixing Bowl, 6 In. 12.00
Mixing Bowl, 9 In. 18.00
Mixing Bowl, Large & Small,
2 Piece 25.00
Range Set, 4 Piece 40.00
Reamer, Large 35.00
Refrigerator, Cover,
8 1/2 X 4 1/2 In. 15.00
Refrigerator, Cover, Square,
4 1/4 In. 9.00
Salt & Pepper 13.00
Saltshaker, Ribbed 6.00
Shaker, Allspice 6.50
Shaker, Flour 8.00
Shaker, Spice 15.00
Sugar. 12.00
Sugar & Creamer, Round. . . . 4.00
Sugar, Cover 5.00
Tea Jar, Metal Cover,
Round 28.00
Towel Bar 25.00

Jane-Ray

A plain dinnerware set with ribbed edge was made of jadite from 1945 to 1963 by Anchor Hocking Glass Company, Lancaster, Ohio. It is called Jane-Ray. The matching kitchenware sets of the same green glass are called Jadite. Other related sections in this book are Alice,

If you are moving, be sure to get special insurance coverage for damage to your antiques.

Fire-King, Philbe, Square, Swirl Fire-King, and Turquoise Blue.

JADITE

Bowl, 5 In. 2.00
Bowl, 6 In. 3.75
Bowl, 7 1/2 In. 4.50
Bowl, 8 1/4 In. 5.00
Bowl, 9 In. 10.00
Creamer .... 1.00 To 4.00
Cup 2.00
Cup & Saucer 2.25
Eggcup, Double 4.50
Mug 2.50
Plate, 9 In. 1.50
Plate, 7 In. 3.50
Plate, 9 In. 3.50
Plate, 10 In. 5.50
Platter, Oval 5.00
Saucer .... .50 To 2.00
Soup, Dish, 7 5/8 In. .... 4.50 To 6.00
Sugar & Creamer, Cover 5.00
Sugar, Cover 4.00

Jubilee

In the early 1930s the Lancaster Glass Company, Lancaster, Ohio, made this dinnerware decorated with etched flowers. It was made in a yellow shade, called topaz, and in pink. Collectors will find many similar patterns. The original Lancaster Jubilee had twelve petals on the flower.

YELLOW

Creamer 16.50
Cup 12.00
Cup & Saucer .... 13.00 To 15.00
Goblet, 6 In. 20.00
Luncheon Set, 29 Piece 175.00
Plate, 7 In. .... 5.00 To 7.00
Plate, 8 3/4 In. .... 7.00 To 10.00
Plate, Mayonnaise 35.00
Saucer 1.50
Sugar .... 10.00 To 16.50
Sugar & Creamer 30.00
Tray, 2 Handles, 11 In. 27.00
Tray, Center Handle 25.00
Vase, 12 In. 150.00

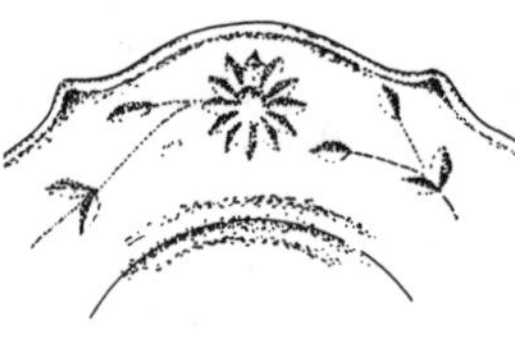

June

June is one of very few patterns that can be dated with some accuracy from the color. Fostoria Glass Company, Fostoria, Ohio, made full dinnerware sets but changed the color. From 1928 to 1944 the glass was azure, green, or rose. Crystal was made from 1928 to 1952. If your set is topaz, it dates from 1929 to 1938. Gold-tinted glass was made from 1938 to 1944. Pieces made of color with crystal stems or bases were made only from 1931 to 1944. Reproductions have been made in blue, crystal, pink, and yellow.

BLUE

Ashtray 40.00
Bowl, 6 In. 60.00
Bowl, Handles, 10 In. 85.00
Bowl, Lemon 32.50
Bowl, Vegetable, Oval, 9 In. 95.00
Bowl, Whipped Cream 40.00
Candleholder, Scroll, 5 In., Pair 95.00
Candy Container, Cover, 3 Sections .... 225.00 To 250.00
Celery, 11 In. .... 67.00 To 75.00
Champagne, 6 In. 37.50
Compote, 7 In. 95.00
Creamer, Large 35.00
Cup & Saucer .... 35.00 To 47.50
Dish, Mayonnaise, Ladle 45.00
Finger Bowl 24.00
Goblet, 5 1/4 In. 45.00
Goblet, 8 1/4 In. 47.50
Grapefruit, Footed 60.00
Ice Bucket, Handle 125.00
Plate, 6 In. 9.50
Plate, 7 1/2 In. 12.50
Plate, 8 3/4 In. .... 8.00 To 15.00
Plate, 9 1/2 In. 35.00
Plate, 10 1/4 In. 85.00
Plate, Server, Center Handle, 11 In. .... 75.00 To 95.00
Platter, 12 In. 125.00
Platter, 15 In. 225.00
Relish, 2 Sections, 8 1/2 In. .... 45.00 To 60.00
Salt & Pepper 220.00
Saucer 12.50
Saucer, Demitasse 25.00
Server, Center Handle, 11 In. 75.00
Soup, Cream, Liner 58.00
Sugar & Creamer, Individual 195.00
Sugar Pail .... 195.00 To 235.00
Sugar, Cover 65.00
Tumbler, 4 1/2 In. 48.00
Tumbler, Footed, 6 In. 42.00
Vase, 8 In. 195.00
Vase, Fan, Footed, 8 1/2 In. 275.00
Wine, 5 1/2 In. 55.00

CRYSTAL

Ashtray 35.00
Baker, 9 1/2 In. 39.00
Bowl, 5 In. 20.00
Bowl, Vegetable, Oval, 9 1/2 In. 55.00
Candleholder, 3 In. 18.00
Celery, 11 In. 35.00
Champagne, 6 In. .... 18.00 To 22.00
Claret, 6 In. .... 32.50 To 37.50
Cordial, 4 In. 55.00
Creamer 8.50
Creamer, Large 20.00
Cup & Saucer .... 17.00 To 22.00
Cup & Saucer, Demitasse 35.00
Cup, Demitasse 25.00

Goblet, 4 Oz. 27.00
Goblet, 8 1/4 In. 19.00 To 25.50
Oyster Cocktail 22.00
Parfait, 5 1/4 In. 35.00
Pitcher 165.00 To 200.00
Plate, 7 1/2 In. 8.00
Plate, 9 1/2 In. 17.50
Plate, 10 1/4 In. 29.50
Platter, 12 In. 55.00
Salt & Pepper 65.00
Saltshaker 37.50
Sherbet, 4 1/4 In. 20.00
Sugar & Creamer, Cover 75.00
Sugar & Creamer, Individual 95.00
Sugar, Cover, Large 90.00
Tray, Handles, 10 1/4 In. 35.00
Tumbler, 4 1/2 In. 27.50
Tumbler, Footed, 6 In. 21.50
Whiskey, 2 1/2 In. 35.00
Wine, 5 1/2 In. 19.75 To 37.50

PINK

Bonbon 39.50
Bouillon, Underplate 60.00
Bowl, 6 In. 45.00
Candleholder, 5 In., Pair 95.00
Candy Container, Cover 175.00 To 200.00
Champagne, 6 In. 33.50 To 37.50
Claret, 6 In. 65.00
Compote, 7 In. 75.00
Creamer, Large 35.00
Cup & Saucer 38.00 To 60.00
Dish, Mayonnaise, Ladle 100.00
Goblet, 5 1/4 In. 47.50
Goblet, 8 1/4 In. 42.50
Grapefruit Liner 65.00
Plate, 7 1/2 In. 6.00 To 8.00
Plate, 8 3/4 In. 15.00
Plate, 10 1/4 In. 75.00
Salt 45.00
Sauce Boat, Underplate, Spoon 100.00
Sherbet, 4 1/4 In. 30.00
Sugar Pail 235.00
Sugar, Cover 190.00
Tumbler, 5 1/4 In. 35.00
Vase, 8 In. 250.00
Vase, Fan, Footed, 8 1/2 In. 200.00

YELLOW

Ashtray 28.00 To 38.00
Baker, 9 1/2 In. 56.00
Bouillon 22.50
Bowl, 2 Handles, 9 In. 75.00
Bowl, 5 In. 22.00
Bowl, Console, 11 In. 20.00
Bowl, Console, 12 In. 40.00
Bowl, Vegetable, Oval, 9 1/2 In. 75.00

Candleholder, 2 In., Pair 34.00
Candleholder, 3 In. 18.00
Candleholder, 5 In., Pair 65.00
Candy Container, 3-Footed, Cover 175.00
Celery, 11 1/2 In. 38.00 To 47.50
Champagne, 6 In. 21.00
Claret, 6 In. 35.00 To 50.00
Compote 30.00
Cordial, 4 In. 75.00 To 95.00
Creamer, Large 27.50
Cruet, Stopper 395.00
Cup & Saucer 20.00 To 25.00
Cup & Saucer, Demitasse 60.00
Cup, Demitasse 25.00
Dish, Mayonnaise, 3 Piece 125.00
Dish, Mint, 4 1/2 In. 40.00
Finger Bowl 22.00
Goblet, 5 1/4 In. 35.00
Goblet, 8 1/4 In. 25.00
Jar, Jam, Footed, 7 In. 30.00
Parfait 40.00
Pitcher 395.00
Plate, 6 In. 6.00
Plate, 7 1/2 In. 5.00 To 8.00
Plate, 8 3/4 In. 12.50
Plate, 9 1/2 In. 22.50
Plate, 10 1/4 In. 40.00 To 47.50
Platter, 12 In. 55.00 To 75.00
Relish, 2 Sections, 8 3/4 In. 35.00
Salt & Pepper, Footed 145.00
Sherbet, 4 1/4 In. 18.00 To 25.00
Sugar & Creamer, Cover 235.00
Sugar & Creamer, Individual 82.00
Sugar, Individual 45.00
Tray, Center Handle, 11 In. 55.00
Tumbler, 4 1/2 In. 29.50
Tumbler, Footed, 5 1/4 In. 18.50
Tumbler, Footed, 6 In. 23.75 To 29.50
Vase, 8 In. 150.00
Wine, 5 1/2 In. 28.00 To 44.00

Knife & Fork, see Colonial

Lace Edge

To add to the confusion in the marketplace, this pattern, which is most often called Lace Edge, has been called Loop, Open Lace, or Open Scallop. The pieces themselves are often confused with other similar patterns, and cups or tumblers may be mixed

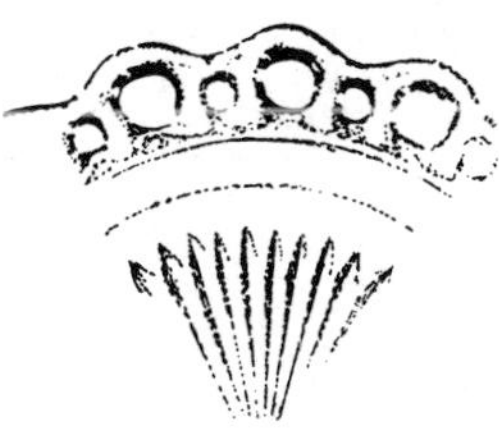

If you are the victim of a theft, be sure to give the police complete information about your antiques. You should have a good description, a photograph, and any known identifying marks.

up with Queen Mary or Coronation. Most of the pieces of Lace Edge were made of pink, although crystal is also found. It was made by Hocking Glass Company, Lancaster, Ohio, from 1935 to 1938.

Lace Edge, see also Coronation

CRYSTAL

Bowl,
6 3/8 In.......... 7.50 To 11.00
Butter, Cover 40.00
Candy Container, Ribbed,
Cover........................40.00
Console, 3-Footed......... 125.00
Plate, 8 3/4 In.... 8.00 To 11.00
Platter, Oval, 13 In..........11.00
Relish, 3 Sections,
7 1/2 In.....................50.00
Sugar & Creamer............30.00
Tumbler, Footed, 5 In. 45.00

PINK

Bowl, 3-Footed,
10 1/2 In....................85.00
Bowl,
6 3/8 In......... 10.00 To 12.00
Bowl, 7 3/4 In. 18.00
Bowl, 8 1/4 In. 10.00
Bowl, 9 1/2 In. 12.25
Bowl, Ribbed, 7 3/4 In. ...25.00
Bowl, Ribbed,
9 1/2 In......... 10.00 To 14.50
Butter, Cover .... 25.00 To 38.00
Candleholder...... 8.00 To 10.00
Candy Container.............10.00
Console, 3-Footed......... 125.00
Cookie Jar,
Cover........... 42.00 To 50.00
Creamer 15.00
Cup............... 14.00 To 16.00
Cup & Saucer .... 20.00 To 27.50
Custard Cup..................22.00
Flower Bowl,
Crystal Frog..... 16.50 To 33.00
Plate,
7 1/4 In......... 12.00 To 12.50
Plate, 8 In. 11.00
Plate,
8 3/4 In......... 10.00 To 12.00
Plate,
10 1/2 In. ...... 11.50 To 18.00
Plate, Grill,
10 1/2 In. ...... 10.00 To 16.00
Platter, 12 3/4 In. 15.00
Platter, 5 Sections,
12 3/4 In. ...... 13.00 To 15.00
Platter, Oval, 12 3/4 In. ...17.00
Relish, 3 Sections,
7 1/2 In....... 37.00 To 48.00
Relish, 3 Sections,
10 1/2 In. 13.50
Saucer................ 4.50 To 6.00
Sherbet, Footed..............50.00
Sugar............. 12.50 To 15.00
Sugar & Creamer............28.00
Tumbler,
4 1/2 In......... 7.50 To 10.00
Tumbler, Footed,
5 In............. 40.00 To 45.00

Lacy Daisy, see No. 618

Laurel

Opaque glass was used by McKee Glass Company, Jeannette, Pennsylvania, to make Laurel dinnerware. The pattern, with a raised band of flowers and leaves as the only decoration, was sometimes called Raspberry

Band. A few pieces have decals of a dog in the center, and that group is called Scottie Dog. The dinnerware was made of French Ivory, jade green, powder blue, or white opal. A child's set was made with a colored rim.

GREEN

Bowl, 5 In. 3.00
Bowl, 6 In. 20.00
Bowl, 9 In. 6.00
Bowl, 11 In. ..... 15.00 To 25.00
Cheese, Dish,
Cover............ 29.00 To 45.00
Creamer, Tall 7.00
Cup............................ 4.00
Cup & Saucer .... 6.00 To 9.00
Plate, 6 In. 5.00
Plate, 7 1/2 In................ 3.00
Plate, 9 1/8 In...... 4.50 To 7.00
Plate, Grill, 9 1/8 In......... 5.00
Platter, Oval,
10 3/4 In. .... 3.00 To 10.00
Sherbet............ 5.75 To 10.00
Sugar & Creamer............18.00
Sugar, Tall..................... 7.00

IVORY

Bowl, 5 In........... 3.00 To 4.50
Bowl, 6 In........... 5.00 To 6.00
Bowl, 9 In. 12.00
Bowl, 11 In. ..... 17.00 To 25.00
Bowl, Vegetable, Oval,
9 3/4 In........ 10.00 To 13.00
Candleholder, 4 In., Pair ...18.00
Cheese Dish,
Cover........... 32.00 To 47.50
Creamer, Child's.............18.50
Creamer, Low 9.50
Creamer, Tall 7.00
Cup............................ 5.00
Cup & Saucer 7.00
Plate, 6 In. 3.75
Plate, 7 1/2 In................ 5.00
Plate, 9 1/8 In...... 4.00 To 4.50
Plate, Child's, Red Edge..... 9.00

Plate, Grill ....4.50 To 6.50
Platter, Oval, 10 3/4 In....... 15.00 To 16.50
Salt & Pepper................32.00
Saucer........................... 2.50
Saucer, Child's, Red Edge... 7.00
Sherbet............ 7.00 To 10.00
Sugar & Creamer......... 12.00 To 12.50
Sugar, Tall..................... 7.00

WHITE

Sugar........................... 6.00

Lily Medallion, see American Sweetheart

Lincoln Drape, see Princess

Lincoln Inn

Lincoln Inn was made by the Fenton Glass Company, Williamstown, West Virginia, in 1928. The ridged dinnerware sets were made of amber, amethyst, black, light blue, cobalt, crystal, green, jadite (opaque green), pink, and red. A recent copy of the Lincoln Inn pitcher was made by Fenton Glass Company in iridized carnival glass.

COBALT

Cup & Saucer................14.00
Goblet, 6 In..................25.00
Nut Dish 14.00
Parfait, 5 In. 27.50
Plate, 6 In..................... 4.50
Sherbet, 4 3/4 In...........18.00
Tumbler, Footed, 5 Oz. ...18.00
Tumbler, Footed, 9 Oz. ...20.00
Tumbler, Footed, 12 Oz....22.00
Vase, 12 In................ 175.00

CRYSTAL

Sherbet........................ 4.00

GREEN

Sherbet........................14.50

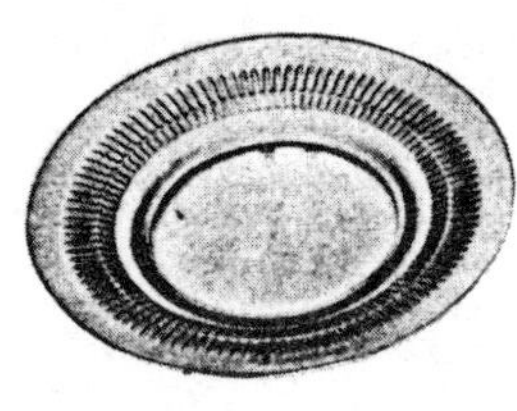

PINK

Creamer 10.00
Cup............................. 6.00
Plate, 8 In. ....3.00 To 7.00
Plate, 12 In................... 8.00
Saucer.......................... 2.00

RED

Compote......................75.00
Cup & Saucer .... 13.00 To 15.00
Goblet .... 12.50 To 25.00
Plate, 6 In..................... 5.25
Plate, 8 In..................... 6.00
Plate, 12 In...................14.00
Sherbet........... 12.00 To 18.00
Sugar & Creamer...........75.00
Tumbler, Footed, 5 In. 22.50

Line 994, see Popeye & Olive

Little Hostess, see Moderntone Little Hostess Party Set

Loop, see Lace Edge

Lorain, see No. 615

Louisa, see Floragold

Lovebirds, see Georgian

Lydia Ray, see New Century

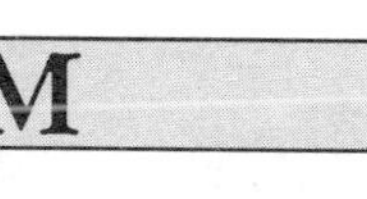

MacHOB

MacHOB is the name devised for the Macbeth–Evans pattern made with a hobnail design. This pattern was made from 1928 of crystal, monax, or pink.

CRYSTAL

Ice Tea Set, 7 Piece.........40.00
Tumbler, 4 In................. 4.00
Water Set, Pitcher, 6 Tumblers 28.00

MONAX

Tumbler, 12 Oz.............. 6.00

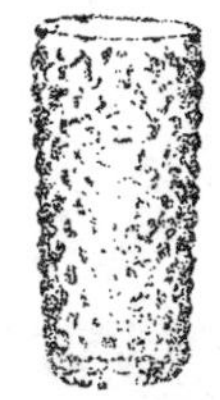

Madrid

Madrid has probably had more publicity than any other Depression glass pattern. It was originally made by the Federal Glass Company, Columbus, Ohio, from 1932 to 1939. It was made of amber, blue, crystal, green, and pink. In 1976 Federal Glass reworked the molds and made full sets of amber glass called Recollections. These can be identified by a small 76 worked into the pattern. In 1982 crystal pieces of Recollection were made. In more recent years blue, pink, and crystal pieces have been reproduced by the Indiana Glass Company.

AMBER

Bowl, 5 In...........3.25 To 5.00
Bowl, 7 In......... 8.00 To 11.00
Bowl, 8 In....................12.00
Bowl, 9 3/8 In. 13.00
Bowl, Vegetable, Oval, 10 In............ 10.00 To 13.00
Butter, Cover 60.00
Cake Plate, 11 1/4 In........ 9.00

Candleholder, 2 1/2 In., Pair 13.50
Compote, 11 In. 11.50
Console, 11 In. .... 10.00 To 12.50
Cookie Jar 32.50
Creamer 5.00
Cup .... 3.00 To 8.00
Cup & Saucer .... 4.00 To 9.75
Jar, Jam, 7 In. .... 9.00 To 19.00
Jell-O Mold, 2 1/8 In. .... 4.50 To 9.00
Pitcher, 5 1/2 In. .... 25.00 To 35.00
Pitcher, 8 1/2 In. .... 39.00 To 55.00
Pitcher, Ice Lip, 8 1/2 In. 40.00
Pitcher, Square, 8 In. .... 20.00 To 35.00

Plate, 6 In. .... 2.00 To 6.00
Plate, 7 1/2 In. .... 2.50 To 8.00
Plate, 8 7/8 In. 4.00
Plate, 9 In. .... 4.50 To 6.00
Plate, 10 1/2 In. .... 24.00 To 35.00
Plate, Grill, 10 1/2 In. .... 5.25 To 9.75
Platter, Oval, 11 1/2 In. .... 8.00 To 12.00
Relish, 4 Sections, 10 1/4 In. .... 7.00 To 12.00
Salt & Pepper .... 25.00 To 37.50
Salt & Pepper, Footed .... 45.00 To 55.00
Saltshaker 15.00
Saucer .... 1.25 To 2.00
Sherbet 8.00
Sherbet, Cone 3.25
Soup, Cream, 4 3/4 In. .... 7.25 To 10.00
Soup, Dish, 7 In. .... 8.00 To 9.50
Sugar .... 4.00 To 6.50
Sugar & Creamer, Cover .... 25.00 To 37.50
Sugar, Cover .... 25.00 To 32.50
Tumbler, 3 7/8 In. 12.00
Tumbler, 4 In. 9.00
Tumbler, 4 1/4 In. .... 8.00 To 15.00
Tumbler, 5 1/2 In. .... 13.00 To 22.00
Tumbler, Footed, 4 In. .... 9.00 To 17.00
Tumbler, Footed, 5 1/2 In. 14.00

BLUE

Bowl, Vegetable, Oval, 10 In. 24.00
Cup & Saucer 12.50
Pitcher, Square, 8 In. .... 125.00 To 140.00
Plate, 7 1/2 In. 18.00
Plate, 9 In. 16.00
Platter, Oval, 11 1/2 In. 28.00
Saltshaker 60.00
Tumbler, 4 In. 28.00
Tumbler, 4 1/4 In. 25.00
Tumbler, 5 In. 28.00

CRYSTAL

Butter 12.00
Cookie Jar 37.00
Cup & Saucer 8.00
Plate, 8 7/8 In. 4.00
Sherbet 4.00
Sugar & Creamer 15.00

GREEN

Bowl, 5 In. 8.75
Bowl, 8 In. .... 15.00 To 17.50
Bowl, Vegetable, Oval, 10 In. 14.00
Butter, Cover 65.00
Coaster 32.00
Creamer .... 6.00 To 12.50
Cup 5.50
Cup & Saucer 9.00
Pitcher, 8 1/2 In. 150.00
Pitcher, Square, 8 In. .... 97.50 To 105.00
Plate, 6 In. .... 2.00 To 6.00
Plate, 7 1/2 In. 9.00
Plate, 8 7/8 In. 7.50
Plate, 10 1/2 In. .... 22.00 To 30.00
Plate, Grill, 10 1/2 In. .... 11.00 To 13.50
Platter, Oval, 11 1/2 In. .... 12.50 To 14.00
Salt & Pepper 55.00
Salt & Pepper, Footed .... 60.00 To 75.00
Saucer 3.00
Sherbet .... 5.50 To 9.75
Soup, Dish, 7 In. 15.00
Sugar .... 7.00 To 15.00
Sugar & Creamer .... 16.00 To 25.00
Sugar, Cover .... 40.00 To 50.00
Tumbler, 4 1/4 In. .... 16.00 To 22.50
Tumbler, 5 1/2 In. .... 28.00 To 32.50
Tumbler, Footed, 5 1/2 In. 24.50

PINK

Bowl, 5 In. .... 4.50 To 7.00
Bowl, 9 3/8 In. .... 15.00 To 25.00
Console, Low, 11 In. 7.00
Cup & Saucer 6.50
Relish, 10 1/4 In. 7.50
Tumbler, 4 1/4 In. 10.00

Magnolia, see Dogwood

Manhattan

Manhattan is another modern-looking pattern with a design made of molded circles. It was made by Anchor Hocking Glass Company from 1938 to 1941 in crystal and pink. A few green and red pieces are also known. The pattern has been called many names, such as Horizontal Fine Rib, Horizontal Ribbed, Horizontal Rounded Big Rib, Horizontal Sharp Big Rib, and Ribbed.

CRYSTAL

Ashtray .... 4.00 To 7.50
Bowl, 4 1/2 In. 4.00
Bowl, 5 3/8 In. 7.50
Bowl, 7 1/2 In. .... 7.00 To 9.00

Bowl, 8 In. 9.50
Bowl, 9 In. .... 8.75 To 14.50
Bowl, 9 1/2 In. 15.00
Candleholder, Square, Pair 8.00
Candy Container, Cover 20.00
Coaster, 3 1/2 In. 7.00
Compote 15.00
Cookie Jar 50.00
Creamer .... 4.50 To 9.00
Cup 7.00
Cup & Saucer ..... 9.00 To 12.50
Decanter, Cover .... 10.00 To 12.75
Goblet, 4 Oz. 6.50
Jar, Mustard, Cover, Spoon 32.00
Pitcher, Juice ..... 12.00 To 19.00
Plate, 6 In. 3.00
Plate, 8 In. 6.00
Plate, 8 1/2 In. ..... 6.00 To 7.50
Plate, 10 1/4 In. .... 6.75 To 11.00
Relish, 4 Sections, Insert, 14 In. 17.00
Relish, 5 Sections, Insert, 14 In. 25.00
Salt & Pepper ..... 9.00 To 14.00
Salt & Pepper, Tray 18.00
Sherbet .... 3.50 To 7.00
Sugar 4.50
Sugar & Creamer .... 8.00 To 17.00
Tray, 2 Sections, 14 In. 11.00
Tray, 4 Sections, 14 In. 11.00
Tumbler .... 8.00 To 10.00
Water Set, 80 Oz.Tilted Pitcher, 9 Piece 60.00
Wine, 3 1/2 In. .... 2.25 To 6.25

PINK

Bowl, 5 3/8 In. 18.00
Bowl, 9 1/2 In. 23.00
Candy Container, 3-Footed 6.00
Compote 21.00
Cookie Jar 22.00
Pitcher, 42 Oz. 25.00
Pitcher, Ice Lip, 80 Oz. .... 25.00 To 30.00
Salt & Pepper .... 25.00 To 30.00
Sherbet 6.50
Sugar 5.00
Sugar & Creamer .... 10.00 To 15.00

Many Windows, see Roulette

Mayfair, see Rosemary

Mayfair Federal

The Mayfair patterns can easily be recognized; but if you are buying by mail, the names are sometimes confusing. Mayfair Federal is the pattern sometimes called Rosemary Arches. It was made in amber, crystal, or green by Federal Glass Company from 1934. The other pattern is called Mayfair Open Rose.

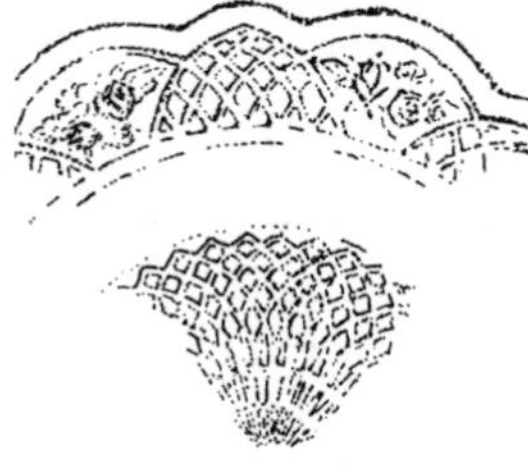

AMBER

Bowl, 6 In. 20.00
Creamer 8.00
Cup & Saucer ..... 6.00 To 12.00
Plate, 6 3/4 In. 5.00
Plate, 9 1/2 In. ..... 5.00 To 8.75
Plate, Grill, 9 1/2 In. .... 5.00 To 8.00
Saucer 1.50
Soup, Cream, 5 In. .... 8.50 To 10.00
Sugar 7.00
Sugar & Creamer 12.00
Tumbler, 4 1/2 In. 12.50

CRYSTAL

Creamer 5.00
Cup 4.00
Plate, Grill, 9 1/2 In. 5.50

GREEN

Bowl, 6 In. 25.00
Bowl, Vegetable, Oval, 10 In. 27.50
Sugar & Creamer 25.00

Mayfair Open Rose

Mayfair Open Rose was made by Hocking Glass Company from 1931 to 1937. It was made in light blue, crystal, green, pink, and yellow. The cookie jar and the whiskey glass have been reproduced.

BLUE

Bowl, 2 Handles, 11 In. 40.00
Bowl, 7 In. 18.00
Bowl, Vegetable, 10 In. 40.00
Butter, Cover .... 125.00 To 225.00
Pitcher, 6 In. 90.00
Pitcher, 8 In. 110.00
Pitcher, 8 1/2 In. ..... 100.00 To 135.00
Plate, 8 1/2 In. 22.00
Plate, 9 1/2 In. 39.00
Plate, Grill, 9 1/2 In. 25.00
Plate, Off-Center Indent, 6 1/2 In. 18.00
Vase, Sweet Pea .... 55.00 To 60.00

GREEN

Bowl, 11 3/4 In. 25.00
Bowl, 12 In. ..... 20.00 To 37.00
Sandwich Server, Center Handle 17.00
Vase, Sweet Pea 60.00

PINK

Bowl, 5 1/2 In. .... 12.00 To 15.00
Bowl, 7 In. 15.00
Bowl, 11 3/4 In. 27.00
Bowl, 12 In. ..... 36.00 To 48.00

Bowl, Vegetable, 10 In. 13.00
Bowl, Vegetable, Cover, 10 In. .... 50.00 To 60.00
Bowl, Vegetable, Oval, 9 1/2 In. 18.00
Butter, Cover 45.00
Cake Plate, Footed, 10 In. 15.00
Cake Plate, Handles, 12 In. 23.00
Candy Container, Cover .... 25.00 To 35.00
Celery, 9 In. 21.00
Cookie Jar, Cover .... 20.00 To 27.00
Creamer .... 10.00 To 14.00
Cup .... 10.00 To 12.00
Cup & Saucer 27.50
Decanter, Stopper 110.00
Pitcher, 6 In. .... 25.00 To 32.00
Pitcher, 8 In. .... 30.00 To 60.00
Pitcher, 8 1/2 In. 58.00
Plate, 5 3/4 In. 8.00
Plate, 6 1/2 In. 8.00
Plate, 8 1/2 In. 12.00
Plate, 9 1/2 In. 35.00
Plate, Off-Center Indent, 6 1/2 In. 18.00
Platter, Oval, 12 In. 14.00
Salt & Pepper, Flat 42.00
Sandwich Server, Center Handle 25.00
Saucer 20.00
Sherbet, 3 In. .... 9.50 To 12.00
Sugar 14.00
Tumbler, 3 1/2 In. .... 25.00 To 32.00
Tumbler, 4 1/4 In. .... 19.00 To 25.00
Tumbler, 5 1/4 In. .... 21.50 To 35.00
Tumbler, Footed, 3 1/4 In. .... 52.00 To 55.00
Tumbler, Footed, 6 1/2 In. .... 20.00 To 27.50
Vase, Sweet Pea 105.00
Whiskey 45.00
Wine 55.00

Meadow Flower, see No. 618

Meandering Vine, see Madrid

Melba, see Hammered Band

Miss America

Miss America, or Diamond Pattern, was made by Hocking Glass Company from 1933 to 1936. It was made in many colors including amber, crystal, green, ice blue, pink, red, and Ritz blue. In 1977 some reproduction butter dishes were made of amberina, crystal, green, ice blue, pink, or red. Saltshakers, pitchers, and tumblers are also being reproduced.

Miss America, see also English Hobnail

BLUE

Bowl, 5 In. 13.00
Creamer 6.50
Cup & Saucer 8.50
Plate, 5 3/4 In. 3.00
Salt & Pepper 26.00
Sugar 6.00

CRYSTAL

Bowl, 6 1/4 In. .... 5.00 To 6.50
Bowl, Vegetable, Oval, 10 In. 8.00
Cake Plate, Footed, 12 In. .... 14.00 To 18.00
Candy Jar, Cover, 11 3/4 In. 45.00
Celery, Oval, 10 1/2 In. .... 5.00 To 9.00
Compote, 5 In. .... 8.00 To 10.00
Creamer 5.25
Cup .... 3.25 To 6.00
Cup & Saucer .... 6.00 To 12.00
Goblet, 3 3/4 In. 10.00
Goblet, 4 3/4 In. 18.00
Goblet, 5 1/2 In. .... 12.00 To 15.00
Plate, 5 3/4 In. 2.00
Plate, 8 1/2 In. 5.00
Plate, 10 1/4 In. 9.00
Plate, Grill, 10 1/4 In. 7.00
Platter, Oval, 12 1/4 In. 8.00
Relish, 2 Sections, 8 3/4 In. 5.00
Relish, 4 Sections, 8 3/4 In. .... 6.00 To 9.00
Salt & Pepper .... 18.00 To 22.50
Saucer .... 1.25 To 2.00
Shaker 10.00
Sherbet .... 5.00 To 6.50
Sugar 4.80
Sugar & Creamer .... 11.00 To 13.00
Sugar, Metal Cover 15.00
Tumbler, 4 1/2 In. 12.00
Tumbler, 6 3/4 In. 20.00
Wine, 3 3/4 In. 13.00

GREEN

Cup 7.50
Plate, 5 3/4 In. .... 5.00 To 6.00
Salt & Pepper 175.00

PINK

Bowl, 6 In. 10.00
Bowl, 6 1/4 In. .... 8.80 To 13.50
Bowl, 8 3/4 In. 40.00
Bowl, Curved-In Top, 8 In. 47.50
Bowl, Vegetable, Oval, 10 In. 17.50
Butter, Cover 300.00
Cake Plate 22.00

If you display your collection at a library, museum, or commercial store, do not let the display include your street address or city name. It is best if you don't even include your name. A display is an open invitation to a thief.

Candy Container, Cover............78.00 To 98.00
Celery, Oval, 10 1/2 In.......13.00 To 15.00
Coaster............14.00 To 16.50
Compote..........10.50 To 15.00
Creamer..........10.00 To 13.00
Cup................12.00 To 15.00
Cup & Saucer....15.00 To 18.00

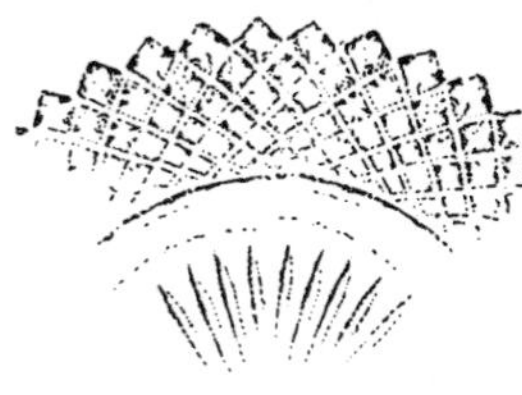

Goblet, 4 3/4 In.........45.00 To 50.00
Goblet, 5 1/2 In.........25.00 To 38.00
Jar, Jam, Cover, Spoon......65.00
Lamp, 9 1/2 In..............50.00
Pitcher, 8 In..................70.00
Pitcher, Ice Lip, 8 1/2 In.....................90.00
Plate, 5 3/4 In................5.00
Plate, 8 1/2 In...............14.00
Plate, 10 1/2 In.......15.00 To 17.50
Plate, Grill, 10 1/4 In........9.00 To 12.50
Platter, 12 1/4 In.......10.00 To 12.50
Relish, 4 Sections, 8 3/4 In..........9.00 To 14.00
Salt & Pepper....34.00 To 40.00
Saucer................3.00 To 4.00
Sherbet............8.00 To 12.50
Sugar..............10.00 To 12.00
Sugar & Creamer............24.50
Tumbler, 4 In...............38.00
Tumbler, 4 1/2 In.........19.00 To 27.50
Tumbler, 5 3/4 In..........48.00
Wine, 3 3/4 In..............45.00

Moderne Art, see Tea Room

Moderntone

Moderntone, or Wedding Band, was made by Hazel-Atlas Glass Company from 1935 to 1942. The cobalt blue and the simple pattern are popular today with Art Deco enthusiasts. The pattern was made of amethyst, cobalt blue, crystal, and pink glass. It was also made of a glass called platonite, which was covered with a variety of bright fired-on colors, including black, light or dark blue, light or dark green, red, orange, yellow, and white trimmed with a small colored rim.

AMETHYST

Plate, 8 In.....................5.00
Plate, 9 In.....................6.00
Plate, 10 1/2 In..............7.00
Salt & Pepper................32.00
Saltshaker, 5 In.............10.00 To 13.00
Soup, Cream......8.50 To 10.00
Sugar & Creamer............14.50
Tumbler, 12 Oz..............37.50

BLUE

Plate, 9 In.....................9.50
Salt & Pepper, Platonite....10.00

COBALT

Bowl, 5 In.........8.00 To 13.00
Bowl, 9 In....................35.00
Butter, Metal Top, Black Knob.................47.00
Creamer.............6.00 To 8.00
Cup.............................7.00
Cup & Saucer.....8.00 To 10.00
Custard........................10.00
Mustard, Cover..............15.00
Plate, 6 In..........2.50 To 5.00
Plate, 6 3/4 In......4.50 To 7.00
Plate, 7 3/4 In................5.00
Plate, 8 7/8 In................8.00
Plate, 10 1/2 In.............27.50
Platter, Oval, 11 In.............18.00 To 33.00
Salt & Pepper................25.00
Saucer..........................2.00
Saucer, With Sailboat........8.00
Sherbet...............6.00 To 8.00
Soup, Cream, 5 In..............11.00 To 12.00
Soup, Cream, Ruffled, 5 In..............14.00 To 22.00
Soup, Dish, 7 1/2 In........55.00
Sugar.................2.50 To 6.00
Sugar & Creamer.........11.00 To 15.00
Sugar, Metal Cover..........62.50

Tumbler, 9 Oz...............15.00
Whiskey..........15.00 To 17.00

CRYSTAL

Cup & Saucer.................8.00

GREEN

Bowl, 5 In. 3.00
Plate, 8 1/2 In. 1.50
Plate, 9 1/2 In. 2.00
Saucer 50
Sugar 2.50

PINK

Bowl, 5 In. 3.00
Creamer 2.50
Cup 1.50
Plate, 8 1/2 In. 1.50
Plate, 9 1/2 In. 2.00
Saucer 50
Soup, Cream, 5 In. 3.00

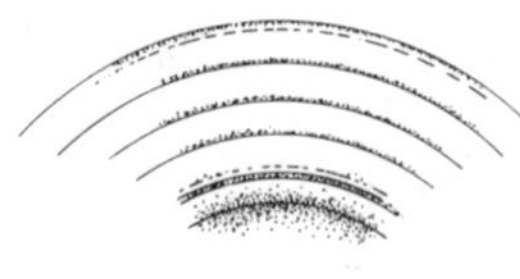

WHITE

Salt & Pepper ..... 8.00 To 10.00

YELLOW

Creamer 2.50
Cup 1.50
Plate, 8 1/2 In. 1.50
Plate, 9 1/2 In. 2.00
Saucer 50
Soup, Cream, 5 In. 3.00

Moderntone Little Hostess Party Set

The Moderntone Little Hostess Party Set was also made by Hazel–Atlas in the 1940s. This was a child's set of dishes made in platonite with fired–on colors. We have seen blue, gray, green, maroon, orange, pink, turquoise, and yellow, but other colors were probably made.

BLUE

Plate, 5 1/4 In. ...... 2.75 To 5.00
Saucer 1.75

GRAY

Cup 4.50
Cup & Saucer 8.00

GREEN

Cup 4.25
Plate 4.25
Saucer 2.50

MAROON

Cup & Saucer 8.00
Plate 3.50

ORANGE

Creamer .... 3.00 To 4.25
Cup .... 3.00 To 4.25
Plate 4.00
Sugar .... 3.50 To 4.25

PINK

Creamer .... 3.00 To 4.25
Plate 3.00
Sugar .... 3.50 To 4.25

TURQUOISE

Plate 4.00
Saucer 2.00

YELLOW

Cup .... 3.00 To 4.25
Plate .... 2.75 To 5.00
Saucer .... 1.50 To 2.50

Moondrops

The New Martinsville Glass Company, New Martinsville, West Virginia, made Moondrops from 1932 to the late 1940s. Collectors like the pieces with the fan–shaped knobs or stoppers. The pattern was made in amber, amethyst, black, cobalt, crystal, evergreen, ice blue, jade,

medium blue, light green, pink, Ritz Blue, rose, ruby, and smoke.

AMBER

Ashtray 9.00
Cordial 7.00
Cup & Saucer 19.00
Plate, 9 1/2 In. 8.00
Sugar & Creamer, Large 15.00
Sugar, 4 In. 5.00
Tumbler, 3 5/8 In. 5.00
Whiskey 6.00

AMETHYST

Cordial, 2 7/8 In. 10.00
Decanter, 10 1/2 In. 50.00
Sugar & Creamer, Miniature 24.00

COBALT

Butter, Cover 300.00
Tumbler, Footed, 3 1/4 In. 11.00
Whiskey, 2 3/4 In. 9.00
Wine, 4 In. 15.00

CRYSTAL

Sugar & Creamer, Miniature .... 13.00 To 25.00
Tray, 7 1/2 In. 10.00
Tumbler, Footed, 3 1/4 In. 8.00

DARK GREEN

Cordial, 2 7/8 In. 10.00
Sugar & Creamer, Miniature 25.00

LIGHT GREEN

Ashtray 9.00
Pitcher, 8 1/4 In. 175.00

Sugar & Creamer, Miniature, Tray 30.00
Whiskey, 2 3/4 In............ 6.00

PINK

Cup............................ 9.00
Cup & Saucer 12.00
Plate, 8 1/2 In................ 6.50
Relish, 3 Sections............ 20.00

RED

Ashtray........................ 25.00
Bowl, Ruffled, 3-Footed, 9 1/2 In..................... 18.00
Butter, Cover 275.00
Cocktail Shaker, Handle 40.00
Creamer, 2 3/4 In........... 13.00
Creamer, 3 3/4 In........... 12.00
Cup................... 7.50 To 9.00
Cup & Saucer .... 12.00 To 13.00
Decanter, 8 1/2 In.......... 55.00
Plate, 8 1/2 In................ 9.50
Plate, 9 1/2 In................ 8.00
Sherbet, 2 5/8 In............ 10.00
Sugar & Creamer......... 22.50 To 23.00

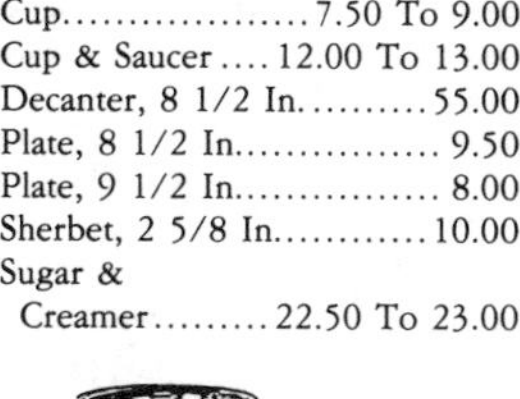

Sugar & Creamer, Miniature.................... 18.00
Sugar, Miniature......... 8.00 To 12.50
Tumbler, 3 5/8 In. 7.00
Tumbler, 4 3/8 In. 11.00
Tumbler, 4 7/8 In......... 12.00 To 15.00
Tumbler, 5 1/8 In. 10.00
Whiskey, 2 3/4 In............ 8.00
Wine, 4 In.................... 14.00
Wine, Metal Stem, 5 1/8 In.................... 11.00

Moonstone

The opalescent hobnails on this pattern gave it the name Moonstone. It was made by Anchor Hocking Glass Company, Lancaster, Ohio, from 1941 to 1946. A few pieces are seen in green.

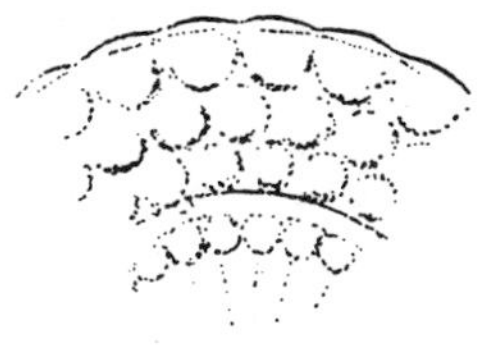

CRYSTAL

Bowl, 5 1/2 In. .... 5.00 To 7.50
Bowl, 7 3/4 In. .... 7.00 To 9.00
Bowl, 9 1/2 In......... 10.00 To 13.50
Bowl, Crimped, 5 1/2 In.... 6.00
Bowl, Crimped, 7 1/2 In.... 7.00
Bowl, Crimped, 9 1/2 In.................... 12.00
Bowl, Handle, 6 1/2 In. 5.50
Bowl, Ruffled, 5 1/2 In. 5.50
Candleholder, Pair .... 12.50 To 17.50
Candy Container, Cloverleaf Shape 8.50
Candy Container, Cover, 6 In.......................... 15.00
Candy Container, Heart Shape 8.50
Cigarette Box, Cover........ 18.50
Creamer .... 4.00 To 7.50
Cup & Saucer .... 7.00 To 8.00
Goblet, 9 Oz................ 12.00
Jar, Powder, Cover, 4 3/4 In......... 12.00 To 16.50
Plate, 6 1/4 In.............. 2.75
Plate, 8 In.................... 7.00
Plate, 10 In....... 15.00 To 22.50
Relish, 2 Sections, 7 3/4 In............ 6.00 To 8.50
Salt & Pepper 29.00

Saucer................ 2.00 To 2.50
Sherbet............... 3.00 To 5.50
Sugar................. 4.00 To 7.50
Sugar & Creamer.......... 5.25 To 12.00
Vase, 3 1/2 In............... 12.00
Vase, Bud, 5 1/2 In............ 7.50 To 8.00

Mt. Pleasant

Mt. Pleasant, sometimes called Double Shield, was made by I. F. Smith Company, Mt. Pleasant, Pennsylvania, from the mid-1920s to 1934. The pattern was made in black amethyst, a very deep purple that appears black unless held in front of a strong light, cobalt blue, green, and pink. Some pieces have gold trim.

BLACK

Bonbon, Curved Handles, 7 In............. 12.00 To 16.00
Bowl, 2 Handles, 8 1/2 In..................... 18.00
Cake Plate, Handles, 10 1/2 In................... 20.00
Candleholder, 2-Light, Pair .... 20.00 To 30.00
Creamer 10.00
Cup & Saucer ..... 9.00 To 10.00
Dish, Mayonnaise, 3-Footed, 5 1/2 In..................... 16.00
Plate, 2 Handles, 8 In. 12.00
Plate, 7 In.................... 10.00
Plate, 8 In................... 5.00
Plate, 8 1/2 In.............. 12.00
Plate, Grill, 9 In............. 6.00

Sherbet............ 8.50 To 11.00
Sugar.......................... 11.00
Sugar & Creamer......... 16.00 To 22.00
Tray, Center Handle, 9 1/2 In.................... 16.00

BLUE

Bowl, 2 Handles, 6 1/2 In.................... 19.00
Bowl, 3-Footed, 5 In. 17.00
Bowl, 3-Footed, 7 In. 17.00
Bowl, 4-Footed, Oval, 6 1/2 In.................... 15.00
Bowl, Center Handle, 6 In.............. 7.50 To 10.00
Bowl, Dish, Mayonnaise, 3-Footed, 5 1/2 In. 15.00
Bowl, Square, 8 In. 15.00
Candleholder, 2-Light, Pair.......................... 35.00
Creamer 12.00

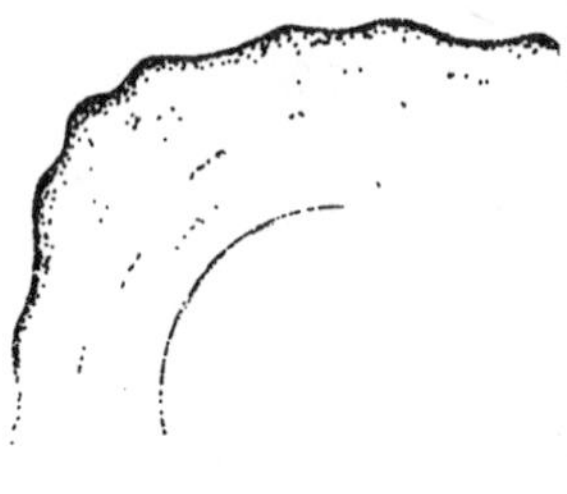

Cup............................ 8.00
Cup & Saucer............... 11.00
Plate, 2 Handles, 7 In. 9.75
Plate, 8 In.................. 11.00
Plate, Grill, 9 In............. 9.00
Plate, Leaf Shape, 8 In...... 10.00
Rose Bowl, Footed, 4 In.... 16.50
Sherbet....................... 12.00
Sugar & Creamer........... 16.00

GREEN

Bowl, 6 In.................. 15.00
Creamer 15.00
Cup & Saucer................ 9.50
Plate, 6 In.................... 3.00
Plate, 9 1/2 In.............. 15.00
Platter, Oval 15.00
Sandwich Server, 11 In. 12.00
Saucer......................... 2.50
Sherbet....................... 10.00
Sugar......................... 10.00

Mt.Vernon

Mt. Vernon was made in the late 1920s through the 1940s by the Cambridge Glass Company, Cambridge, Ohio. It was made in amber, blue, crystal, emerald green, heatherbloom, red, and violet.

CRYSTAL

Cup............................ 2.50
Cup & Saucer............... 10.00
Goblet, 6 1/4 In. 9.00
Plate, 6 In.................... 4.00
Plate, 8 In.................... 6.00
Plate, 15 1/2 In. 15.00
Plate, Tab Handle, 11 1/2 In.................. 11.50
Punch Bowl, Footed, 13 In........................ 10.00
Sherbet, Tall 12.00
Sugar.......................... 2.50
Tumbler, Footed, 3 Oz. 7.00
Tumbler, Footed, 7 Oz. 5.50

RED

Creamer 15.00
Plate, Square, 8 In.......... 12.00
Sherbet....................... 14.00

N

Navarre

Fostoria Glass Company, Fostoria, Ohio, made Navarre pattern glass from 1937 to 1980. It is an etched pattern. Some of the pieces were made on the Baroque glass blank, others on more modern shapes. It was made only in crystal.

CRYSTAL

Bell, 6 1/2 In.... 42.00 To 65.00
Bowl, Square, 4 In. 18.00
Cake Plate.................... 18.00
Candy Container, 3 Sections, Cover....................... 50.00

Champagne, 5 5/8 In....... 17.00
Cordial........................ 35.00
Creamer .... 15.00 To 18.50
Cup & Saucer............... 19.00
Goblet, 5 5/8 In. 25.00
Goblet, 6 In...... 18.00 To 24.00
Ice Bucket.................... 65.00
Plate, 14 In.................. 45.00
Relish, 2 Sections....... 20.00 To 25.00
Relish, 3 Sections........... 45.00
Sherbet....................... 18.00
Sugar, Individual 15.00
Tumbler, Footed, 5 3/8 In........ 15.00 To 22.00
Wine, 5 1/2 In........ 24.00 To 28.00

New Century

There is vast confusion about the patterns called New Century, Lydia Ray, Ovide, and related pieces. After studying all the

available books about Depression glass, the old advertisements, and checking with dealers who sell the glass, we have made these decisions. Most dealers and most people who advertise Depression glass call the pattern pictured here New Century. It has a series of ribs in the glass design. New Century was made by the Hazel–Atlas Glass Company, a firm with factories in Ohio, Pennsylvania, and West Virginia, from 1930 to 1935. It is found in amethyst, cobalt, crystal, green, and pink. In 1970 a book listed the pattern with ribs by Hazel–Atlas as Lydia Ray. In this same book, New Century was a very plain ware with no impressed or raised pattern. Sometimes it was made in black or white with fired–on colors and was called Ovide. Research shows that the ribbed pattern was advertised in the 1930s as New Century by Hazel–Atlas. The plain glassware was also called New Century. With added enamel designs, it was sometimes called Ovide, Floral Sterling, or Cloverleaf. In this book, we list no Lydia Ray or Floral Sterling. The plain glass we call Ovide.

New Century, see also Ovide

AMETHYST

Tumbler, 3 1/2 In. .... 4.75 To 6.00
Tumbler, 4 1/4 In. .... 4.00 To 6.50
Tumbler, 5 In. 8.50
Tumbler, 5 1/4 In. 7.00

COBALT

Pitcher, 8 In. .... 25.00 To 26.00
Tumbler, 3 1/2 In. .... 4.75 To 5.00
Tumbler, 4 1/4 In. 5.00
Tumbler, 5 In. 7.00

CRYSTAL

Butter, Cover .... 35.00 To 44.00
Creamer & Sugar 7.00
Cup 3.00
Goblet, 4 Oz. 10.00
Pitcher, 7 3/4 In. 21.00
Pitcher, Ice Lip, 7 3/4 In. 23.00
Saucer 1.00
Soup, Cream 6.00
Tumbler, 4 1/4 In. 8.00

GREEN

Butter, Cover 46.00
Creamer 6.00
Cup 4.00
Pitcher, 8 In. .... 25.00 To 27.00
Salt & Pepper .... 22.00 To 25.00
Saltshaker 12.00
Sherbet 6.00
Sugar 5.00
Sugar, Cover 12.00

PINK

Cup 15.00
Pitcher, Ice Lip, 8 In. 32.50
Tumbler, 4 1/4 In. 5.00
Tumbler, 5 1/4 In. 12.00

Newport

Newport, or Hairpin, was made by Hazel–Atlas Glass Company from 1936 to 1940. It is known in amethyst, cobalt blue, pink, platonite (white), and a variety of fired–on colors.

AMETHYST

Bowl, 4 1/4 In. .... 7.00 To 7.50
Bowl, 5 1/4 In. .... 12.00 To 18.50
Bowl, 8 1/4 In. .... 25.00 To 26.00
Creamer .... 6.50 To 9.50
Cup & Saucer .... 6.50 To 9.00
Plate, 6 In. .... 2.50 To 3.00
Plate, 8 1/2 In. .... 6.00 To 7.00
Plate, 11 1/2 In. .... 18.00 To 23.00
Platter, Oval, 11 3/4 In. 18.00
Salt & Pepper .... 25.00 To 45.00
Saucer .... 2.00 To 2.25
Sherbet .... 7.50 To 8.00
Soup, Cream .... 6.50 To 10.00
Sugar .... 6.00 To 9.50
Sugar & Creamer .... 14.00 To 15.00
Tumbler, 4 1/2 In. .... 16.50 To 19.00

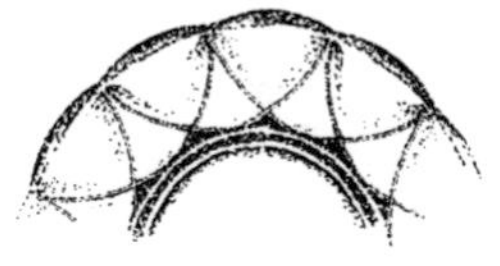

COBALT

Bowl, 4 1/4 In. 9.00
Bowl, 5 1/4 In. .... 22.00 To 25.00
Creamer .... 9.00 To 10.00
Cup 7.00
Cup & Saucer .... 9.00 To 12.00
Plate, 6 In. .... 3.50 To 4.00
Plate, 8 1/2 In. .... 7.00 To 7.50
Plate, 11 1/2 In. 22.00
Platter, Oval, 11 3/4 In. 28.00
Salt & Pepper .... 17.00 To 35.00
Saucer 2.50
Sherbet .... 6.00 To 9.50
Soup, Cream .... 8.00 To 12.00
Sugar & Creamer 20.00
Tumbler, 4 1/2 In. 25.00

WHITE

Salt & Pepper 22.00
Saltshaker 15.00

No. 601, see Avocado

No.610

Many patterns are listed both by the original pattern number and by a name. No. 610 is often called Pyramid or Rex. It was

made from 1926 to 1932 by the Indiana Glass Company. The pattern was made of crystal, green, pink, and yellow. In 1974 and 1975 reproductions were made in black.

CRYSTAL

Bowl, Oval, 9 1/2 In. 20.00

GREEN

Bowl, 9 1/2 In. 40.00

PINK

Sugar 17.50
Sugar & Creamer 35.00

YELLOW

Bowl, 9 1/2 In. 57.00
Sugar & Creamer,
 Tray .... 75.00 To 88.00
Tumbler, Footed, 8 Oz. 40.00

No.612

Indiana Glass Company, Dunkirk, Indiana, called this pattern No. 612, but collectors call it Horseshoe. It was made from 1930 to 1933 in green, pink, and yellow. Sugar and creamer sets were made in crystal. Plates came in two styles, one with the center pattern, one plain.

GREEN

Bowl, 6 1/2 In. 17.50
Bowl,
 9 1/2 In......... 20.00 To 24.00
Bowl, Oval, 10 1/2 In...... 13.00
Cup.................. 4.50 To 7.00
Cup & Saucer ..... 6.00 To 11.00
Pitcher,
 8 1/2 In...... 100.00 To 155.00
Plate, 8 3/8 In...... 4.00 To 5.00
Plate, 8 5/8 In............... 7.50
Plate, 9 3/8 In.... 6.00 To 15.00
Plate, 11 In........ 7.00 To 10.00
Platter, 10 3/4 In. 14.00

Relish,
 3 Sections .... 14.00 To 20.00
Saucer 4.00
Sherbet.......................... 9.00
Sugar .... 8.00 To 10.00
Sugar & Creamer 12.00
Tumbler, Footed, 9 Oz. 11.00

YELLOW

Bowl, 4 1/2 In. 16.00
Bowl, 6 1/2 In. 15.00
Bowl, 7 1/2 In. 10.00
Creamer 12.50
Cup.................. 6.00 To 7.50
Cup & Saucer 9.50
Plate, 6 In. .... 4.00 To 4.50
Plate, 8 3/8 In...... 6.00 To 7.00
Plate, 11 In.................. 11.00
Platter,
 10 3/4 In. ...... 14.00 To 19.00
Relish,
 3 Sections .... 18.00 To 25.00
Sherbet............ 9.00 To 11.50
Sugar .... 8.00 To 9.00
Tumbler, Footed, 9 Oz. 14.50

No.615

No. 615 is often called Lorain or sometimes Basket, Bridal Bouquet, Flower Basket, or Hanging Basket. It was made by the Indiana Glass Company from 1929 to 1932 of crystal, green, and yellow. Sometimes crystal pieces have blue, green, red, or yellow borders. Reproduction pieces were made of milk glass or olive green.

CRYSTAL

Cup & Saucer 11.50
Relish,
 4 Sections .... 10.00 To 15.00

If you go away on a driving trip, be sure to cover the window in your garage door so the missing car won't be noticed. New doors usually have no window at all for security reasons.

GREEN

Bowl, 6 In. 35.00
Bowl,
7 1/4 In. .... 25.00 To 45.00
Bowl, 8 In. 58.00
Bowl, 8 1/2 In. 55.00
Bowl, Oval, 9 3/4 In. 40.00
Creamer 9.00
Cup .... 8.00 To 10.00
Cup & Saucer .... 10.00 To 10.50
Plate, 7 1/2 In. 5.00
Plate, 7 3/4 In. 5.50
Plate,
8 3/8 In. .... 10.00 To 11.00
Plate,
10 1/4 In. .... 25.00 To 35.00
Platter, 11 1/2 In. 14.00
Saucer 3.25
Sherbet .... 10.00 To 17.50
Sugar .... 9.50 To 12.00
Sugar & Creamer 22.00
Tumbler,
4 3/4 In. .... 10.00 To 17.50

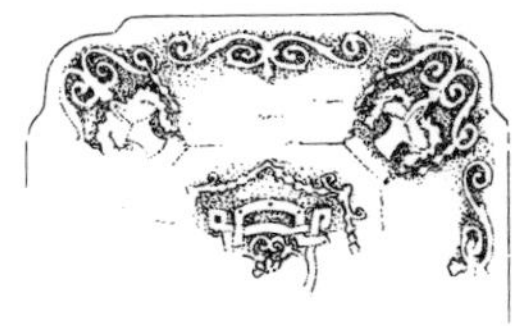

YELLOW

Bowl, 8 In. .... 115.00 To 130.00
Bowl, Oval,
9 3/4 In. .... 25.00 To 39.00
Bowl, Vegetable, Oval,
9 3/4 In. .... 25.00 To 38.50
Creamer .... 14.00 To 18.00
Cup & Saucer .... 13.50 To 15.00
Plate, 7 3/4 In. ... 7.00 To 10.00
Plate,
8 3/8 In. .... 15.00 To 22.00
Plate,
10 1/4 In. .... 38.00 To 43.00
Platter,
11 1/2 In. .... 27.00 To 32.00
Relish, 4 Sections,
8 In. .... 19.00 To 25.00
Sherbet .... 19.00 To 30.00
Sugar .... 13.00 To 16.00
Tumbler, 4 3/4 In. 15.00
Tumbler, Footed,
4 3/4 In. .... 15.00 To 20.00

No.616

No. 616 is called Vernon by some collectors. It was made by Indiana Glass Company from 1930 to 1932. The pattern was made in crystal, green, and yellow. Some crystal pieces have a platinum trim.

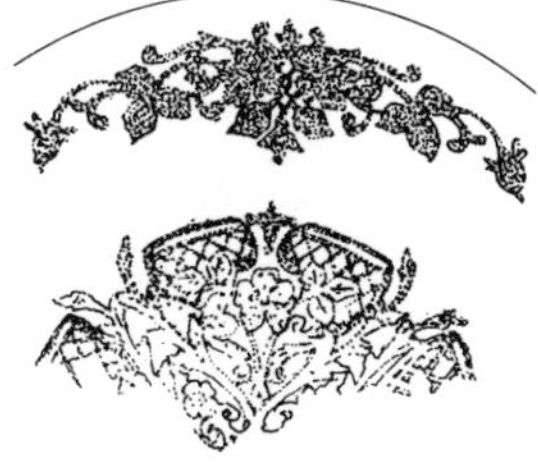

CRYSTAL

Creamer 8.00
Creamer, Platinum Rim 7.00
Cup 4.00
Cup & Saucer .... 6.25 To 9.50
Cup & Saucer,
Platinum Rim 5.00
Plate, 8 In. 3.75
Plate, 11 In. 7.50
Plate, 12 In. 5.00
Plate, Platinum Rim,
8 In. 3.50
Sugar 7.00

GREEN

Creamer 20.00
Cup 5.75
Cup & Saucer 15.00
Plate, 11 In. ...... 16.00 To 21.00

ROSE

Blue, Teapot 26.00

YELLOW

Creamer 8.00
Cup 9.50
Cup & Saucer 6.25
Plate, 8 In. .... 3.75 To 6.25
Saucer .... 3.00 To 3.75
Sugar 15.00
Tumbler, Footed, 5 In. 20.00

No.618

Another Indiana Glass Company pattern made from 1932 to 1937 was No. 618, or Pineapple & Floral. It is also called Meadow Flower, Lacy Daisy, or Wildflower. The pattern was made of amber, crystal, and fired-on green and red. Reproductions were made in olive green in the late 1960s.

AMBER

Bowl, 4 3/4 In. 12.00
Cup & Saucer 8.00
Plate, 6 In. 2.75
Plate, 8 3/8 In. 4.50
Plate, 9 3/8 In. ... 8.00 To 12.00
Soup, Cream 12.00
Sugar & Creamer 12.00

CRYSTAL

Ashtray .... 7.50 To 15.50
Bowl,
4 3/4 In. .... 30.00 To 35.00
Bowl, 6 In. .... 17.50 To 22.00
Bowl, 7 In. .... 3.50 To 7.00
Bowl, Flared, 12 In. 45.00
Bowl, Oval,
10 In. .... 15.00 To 18.00
Butter, Cover 145.00
Champagne 22.50
Claret 37.50

Creamer .... 4.50 To 5.00
Cup .... 5.50 To 8.00
Cup & Saucer ..... 7.00 To 10.00
Plate, 6 In. .... 2.00 To 2.25
Plate, 8 3/8 In. ..... 4.00 To 7.00
Plate, 9 In. 9.00
Plate, 9 3/4 In. 7.00
Plate,
11 1/2 In. .... 8.50 To 10.00

Plate, Indentation, 11 1/2 In. 10.00
Plate, Sugar, Diamond Shape 5.00
Platter, 11 In. .... 7.00 To 9.00
Relish, 3 Sections .... 10.00 To 16.00
Salt & Pepper 40.00
Saltshaker 20.00
Saucer .... 1.25 To 2.00
Sherbet .... 10.00 To 17.50
Soup, Cream 16.00
Sugar .... 3.00 To 6.00
Tumbler, 4 1/4 In. .... 18.00 To 25.00
Tumbler, 5 In. ... 31.00 To 45.00

No.620

No. 620, also known as Daisy, was made by Indiana Glass Company. In 1933 the pattern was made in crystal, and in 1940 in amber; in the 1960s and 1970s reproductions were made in dark green and milk glass.

AMBER

Bowl, 4 1/2 In. .... 5.50 To 6.00
Bowl, 6 In. .... 12.00 To 20.00
Bowl, 7 3/8 In. 18.50
Bowl, 9 3/8 In. .... 18.00 To 20.00
Bowl, Oval, 10 In. .... 11.00 To 12.50
Cake Plate, 11 1/2 In. .... 5.50 To 9.00
Creamer .... 6.00 To 7.00
Cup .... 3.50 To 3.75
Cup & Saucer .... 3.50 To 6.00
Plate, 6 In. .... 1.00 To 3.00
Plate, 7 3/8 In. ..... 4.00 To 6.00
Plate, 8 3/8 In. ..... 3.75 To 5.00
Plate, 9 3/8 In. ..... 4.00 To 6.00
Plate, 11 1/2 In. .... 7.00 To 10.00

Plate, Grill, 10 3/8 In. .... 8.50 To 10.00
Platter, 10 3/4 In. .... 7.00 To 10.00
Relish, 3 Sections, 8 3/8 In. .... 12.50 To 20.00
Saucer .... 1.75 To 2.00
Sherbet .... 4.00 To 7.25
Soup, Cream, 4 1/2 In. .... 4.50 To 7.50
Sugar .... 4.50 To 6.00
Sugar & Creamer .... 9.50 To 13.00
Tumbler, Footed, 9 Oz. .... 11.00 To 13.00
Tumbler, Footed, 12 Oz. .... 25.00 To 28.00
Vegetable, Oval 11.00

CRYSTAL

Bowl, 6 In. 9.00
Creamer 3.75
Cup .... 2.00 To 4.00
Cup & Saucer .... 3.50 To 5.00
Plate, 11 1/2 In. 4.50
Plate, Grill .... 3.00 To 5.00
Relish, 3 Sections ... 6.00 To 7.00
Sherbet 3.75
Soup, Cream, 4 1/2 In. .... 2.50 To 3.50
Tumbler, Footed, 9 Oz. 7.00

DARK GREEN

Bowl, 7 3/8 In. .... 3.50 To 5.00
Cake Plate, 11 1/2 In. 5.00
Cup & Saucer .... 3.50 To 4.00
Plate, 7 3/8 In. ..... 2.00 To 2.75
Plate, 8 3/8 In. ..... 2.50 To 3.00
Plate, 9 3/8 In. ..... 3.50 To 4.00
Plate, Grill 46.00
Saucer 1.50
Soup, Cream .... 2.50 To 4.00
Sugar .... 3.00 To 4.00

No. 622, see Pretzel

No. 624, see Christmas Candy

Normandie

A few Depression glass patterns were made in iridescent marigold color which has been collected as carnival glass. Iridescent Normandie appears in the carnival glass listings as Bouquet and Lattice; when the pattern is in the other known colors, it is called Normandie. Look for it in amber, crystal, iridescent, and pink. One author also lists green. It was made from 1933 to 1940.

AMBER

Bowl, 5 In. 4.00
Bowl, 6 1/2 In. 7.00
Bowl, Oval, 10 In. 12.50
Creamer 5.00
Cup .... 3.00 To 4.00
Cup & Saucer .... 4.00 To 7.00
Pitcher, 8 In. ..... 37.00 To 48.00
Plate, 8 In. 5.00
Plate, 9 1/4 In. ..... 5.25 To 6.00
Plate, 11 In. ...... 10.00 To 23.00
Platter, 11 3/4 In. 8.00
Salt & Pepper .... 30.00 To 32.00
Saltshaker .... 8.00 To 9.00
Saucer .... 1.00 To 2.00
Sherbet .... 3.00 To 5.00
Sugar & Creamer 9.00
Sugar, Cover ..... 60.00 To 70.00
Tumbler, 4 1/4 In. .... 8.00 To 11.00
Tumbler, 5 In. ... 12.00 To 19.00

CRYSTAL

Bowl, 5 In. 3.00
Bowl, 6 1/2 In. 4.50
Bowl, 8 1/2 In. 12.00
Bowl, Oval, 10 In. 12.00
Creamer 6.50
Cup & Saucer 6.50
Plate, 6 In. 2.00
Plate, 9 1/4 In. 9.50
Plate, 11 In. 12.00
Plate, Grill .... 4.50 To 7.25
Platter, 11 3/4 In. 12.00
Sherbet .... 4.00 To 6.50

Sugar.......................... 5.00
Tumbler, 4 In................20.00

IRIDESCENT

Bowl, 5 In...........2.25 To 3.50
Bowl, 6 1/2 In. ....4.00 To 5.25
Bowl, 8 1/2 In. ....7.00 To 8.00
Bowl, Oval,
10 In.............. 6.00 To 14.00
Cup & Saucer.......3.25 To 5.50
Plate, 6 In..................... 1.50
Plate, 11 In.......10.00 To 11.00
Plate, Grill ....2.25 To 7.50
Platter, 11 3/4 In. 8.00
Sherbet...............2.50 To 5.00
Sugar.................4.00 To 5.00
Sugar & Creamer............. 7.50

PINK

Bowl, 5 In..........4.75 To 5.00
Bowl, 8 1/2 In. 9.00
Cup & Saucer.......5.50 To 8.00
Pitcher, 8 In..................75.00
Plate, 8 In...........6.00 To 8.00
Sherbet...............3.00 To 7.50
Sugar & Creamer............14.50
Tumbler, 4 In................20.00

Oatmeal Lace, see Princess Feather

Octagon

Octagon, sometimes called Tiered Octagon or U.S. Octagon, was made by the U.S. Glass Company from 1927 to 1929. It was used by the Octagon Soap Company as a premium. The pieces were made in green and pink. Some pieces are found marked with the glass company trademark.

PINK

Dish, Mayonnaise............14.00
Plate, 6 In..................... 4.00
Plate, 8 In..................... 6.00

Old Cafe

Old Cafe is one of the few patterns with only one name. It was made by the Anchor Hocking Glass Company, Lancaster, Ohio, from 1936 to 1938. Pieces are found in crystal, pink, and red.

CRYSTAL

Bowl, 2 Handles,
5 In.................4.00 To 5.00
Bowl, 3 3/4 In. ....1.50 To 2.75
Bowl, 5 1/2 In. 4.00
Candy Container,
8 In.................3.50 To 4.50
Vase, 7 1/4 In............... 8.00

PINK

Candy Container,
8 In.................4.00 To 5.50
Cup............................ 6.00
Dish, Olive, 6 In. 4.00

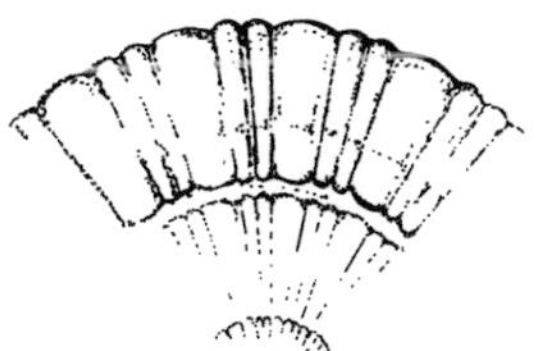

Plate, 10 In...................15.00
Tumbler, 3 In................. 5.00

RED

Candy Container,
8 In.............. 7.00 To 10.00
Cup............................. 5.50
Tumbler, 4 In................10.00

Old English

Old English, or Threading, was made by the Indiana Glass Company, Dunkirk, Indiana, in the late 1920s and early 1930s. It was first made in amber, crystal, emerald green, and light green. Pink was a later color.

CRYSTAL

Eggcup......................... 6.00

GREEN

Bowl, Footed, 9 In.........22.00
Pitcher........................60.00

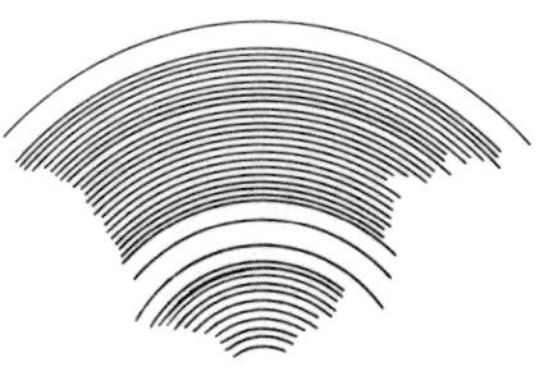

Old Florentine, see Florentine No. 1

Opalescent Hobnail, see Moonstone

Open Lace, see Lace Edge

Open Rose, see Mayfair Open Rose

Open Scallop, see Lace Edge

Optic Design, see Raindrops

Orange Blossom

Indiana Glass Company made Orange Blossom in 1957. The pattern is the same as Indiana Custard but the milk glass items are called Orange Blossom.

WHITE

Bowl, 4 7/8 In. 4.00
Bowl, 5 1/2 In. ....2.00 To 5.00
Creamer ....2.00 To 4.50
Cup & Saucer ....3.00 To 5.00
Plate, 6 In. 4.00
Plate, 9 3/4 In................ 3.50
Sugar........................... 4.50

Oregon Grape, see Woolworth

Oriental Poppy, see Florentine No. 2

Ovide

Hazel-Atlas made Ovide pattern from 1929 to 1935. It was made in green at first. By 1931–1932 it was black and by 1933–1935 platonite or opaque white glass was used with fired-on colors. A bright fired-on pattern of black, green, orange, yellow, and black circles and lines was one of the popular designs. Some other patterns were white with colored rims. There is great confusion between Ovide and New Century. Read the explanation under New Century.

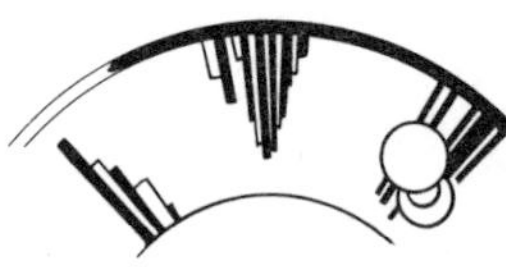

Ovide, see also New Century

BLACK

Creamer 6.00
Cup & Saucer ....5.50 To 6.00
Plate, 8 In. 4.50
Sherbet......................... 5.00
Sugar........................... 6.00

GREEN

Sugar & Creamer 5.00

WHITE

Cup & Saucer, Black Design 3.50
Plate, Black Design, 9 In.... 3.50
Sugar & Creamer, Footed, Fired-On Rust.............. 5.00
Tumbler, Black Design 6.50

Oxford, see Chinex Classic

Oyster & Pearl

Anchor Hocking Glass Company, Lancaster, Ohio, made Oyster & Pearl pattern from 1938 to 1940. It was made in crystal, pink, red, and white with fired-on colors. The outside of these fired-on pieces is white, the inside is either pink or green.

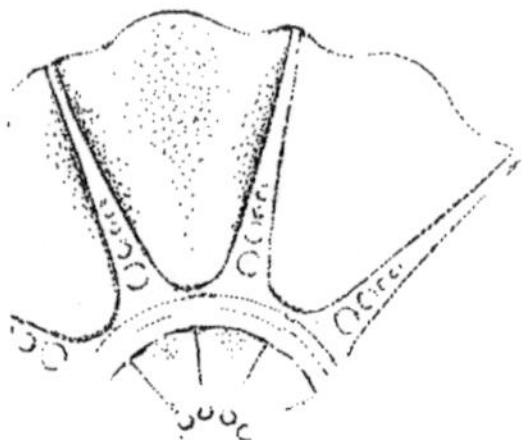

CRYSTAL

Bowl, 5 1/2 In. 4.00
Bowl, 10 1/2 In............12.00
Bowl, Heart Shape, 5 1/4 In...........2.50 To 6.00
Plate, 13 1/2 In. 10.00
Relish, 2 Sections, 10 1/4 In.........4.50 To 9.00

FIRED-ON GREEN

Candleholder, Pair...........12.50

FIRED-ON PINK

Bowl, 10 1/2 In............13.00
Candleholder, Pair...........11.00

PINK

Bowl, 10 1/2 In............17.00
Bowl, 2 Handles, 6 1/2 In...........6.00 To 8.00
Bowl, Heart Shape, 5 1/4 In...................... 6.00
Candleholder, Pair.............15.00 To 16.00
Plate, 13 1/2 In. 16.00
Relish, 2 Sections...5.00 To 6.00

RED

Bowl, 10 1/2 In............30.00
Bowl, 2 Handles, 6 1/2 In.....................15.00
Bowl, Handle, 5 1/2 In......... 7.75 To 12.00
Candleholder, Pair...........30.00
Plate, 13 1/2 In.......20.00 To 21.00

P

Paneled Aster, see Madrid

Paneled Cherry Blossom, see Cherry Blossom

Pansy & Doric, see Doric & Pansy

Parrot, see Sylvan

Patrician

Federal Glass Company, Columbus, Ohio, made Patrician, sometimes called Hinge or Spoke, from 1933 to 1937. Full dinner sets were made. It was made in amber, crystal, green, pink, and yellow.

AMBER

Bowl, 5 In. 5.75 To 8.00
Bowl, 6 In. 12.00 To 17.00
Bowl, 8 1/2 In. 25.00 To 27.00
Bowl, Oval, 10 In. 14.00 To 22.50
Butter, Cover 55.00 To 70.00
Cookie Jar, Cover 40.00 To 62.50
Creamer 5.00 To 7.00
Cup 4.50 To 8.50
Cup & Saucer 7.50 To 12.00
Dish, Jam 13.00 To 20.00
Pitcher, Molded Handle, 8 In. 65.00 To 72.00
Plate, 6 In. 5.00 To 7.00
Plate, 7 1/2 In. 8.00 To 10.00
Plate, 9 In. 4.50 To 7.50
Plate, 10 1/2 In. 3.00 To 7.00
Plate, Grill 5.00 To 9.50
Platter, 11 1/2 In. 11.00 To 20.00
Salt & Pepper 30.00 To 42.50
Saltshaker 15.00 To 18.50
Saucer 4.50 To 9.00
Sherbet 4.50 To 9.50
Soup, Cream 8.00 To 12.50
Sugar & Creamer, Cover 65.00
Sugar, Cover 30.00
Tumbler, 4 In. 20.00 To 25.00
Tumbler, 4 1/2 In. 15.00 To 20.00
Tumbler, 5 1/2 In. 18.00 To 28.00
Tumbler, Footed, 5 1/4 In. 28.00

CRYSTAL

Bowl, 5 In. 4.50 To 6.50
Bowl, 6 In. 11.00
Bowl, Oval, 10 In. 14.00
Creamer 4.75 To 6.50
Cup 3.75 To 4.00
Cup & Saucer 7.50
Plate, 9 In. 5.50
Plate, 10 1/2 In. 4.00
Plate, Grill 4.00 To 6.00
Platter, 11 1/2 In. 8.00
Salt & Pepper 34.50 To 35.00
Saucer 1.00 To 4.00
Sherbet 6.00
Sugar 4.00 To 7.50
Sugar & Creamer 11.00
Tumbler, 4 1/2 In. 16.00 To 21.50
Tumbler, Footed, 5 1/4 In. 32.50

GREEN

Bowl, 5 In. 6.00 To 7.50
Cookie Jar, Cover 200.00
Creamer 8.00
Cup 4.50 To 8.00
Cup & Saucer 9.00 To 12.50
Dish, Jam 19.50
Pitcher, Applied Handle, 8 1/4 In. 87.50
Plate, 6 In. 4.50
Plate, 7 1/2 In. 8.00
Plate, 9 In. 6.00 To 6.50
Plate, Grill 7.00 To 12.50
Platter, 11 1/2 In. 13.00 To 15.00
Salt & Pepper 39.00
Saucer 4.00 To 7.00
Sherbet 7.00 To 9.00
Soup, Cream 13.00
Sugar 6.00 To 9.00
Sugar & Creamer, Cover 48.00 To 55.00
Tumbler, 4 In. 19.00
Tumbler, 4 1/2 In. 17.00
Tumbler, Footed, 5 1/4 In. 36.00

PINK

Bowl, 5 In. 8.75
Bowl, 8 1/2 In. 12.00 To 16.00
Cup 7.00
Cup & Saucer 8.00 To 10.00
Dish, Jam 22.50
Plate, 10 1/2 In. 14.00
Salt & Pepper 55.00 To 65.00
Saltshaker 38.00
Saucer 1.50
Sherbet 7.00
Soup, Cream 13.00 To 15.00
Tumbler, 4 1/2 In. 17.50 To 19.50

Pear Optic

Pear Optic, sometimes called Thumbprint, was made in 1929 and 1930 by the Federal Glass Company. It was made only in green.

If you have to pack or store an oddly shaped antique, a footed bowl, or an unsteady figurine, try this trick. Get a damp polyurethane sponge, preferably the two-layer type with a stiffer bottom layer. Put the piece on the wet sponge. It will make the proper shaped indentation and when the sponge dries, the piece will be held safely in one position.

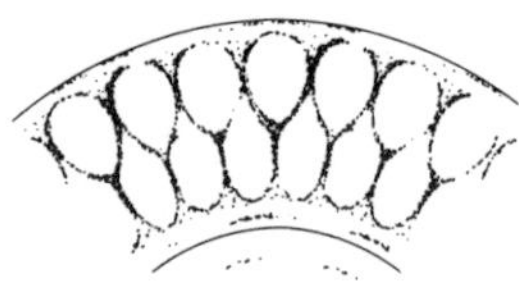

GREEN

Cup.................. 2.25 To 3.50
Cup & Saucer....... 3.50 To 5.00
Plate, 8 In.......... 2.00 To 3.75
Saucer................ 1.00 To 2.00
Sherbet.............. 3.50 To 4.50
Tumbler, 4 In....... 3.00 To 3.50
Tumbler, 5 In....... 4.00 To 6.00
Whiskey 3.00

Pebble Optic, see Raindrops

Pebbled Band, see Hammered Band

Penny Line

Paden City Glass Company, Paden City, West Virginia, made Penny Line in amber, Cheri-glo, crystal, green, royal blue, and ruby. It was No. 991 in the 1932 catalog.

GREEN

Goblet, 4 3/4 In. 5.25 To 5.50

RUBY

Cordial Set,
7 Piece.......... 62.00 To 65.00
Cup............................ 4.00
Cup & Saucer............... 10.00

Petalware

Macbeth-Evans made Petalware from 1930 to 1940. It was first made in crystal and pink. In 1932 the dinnerware was made in monax, in 1933 in cremax. The pattern remained popular and in 1936 cobalt blue and several other variations were made. Some pieces were hand-painted with pastel bands of ivory, green, and pink. Some pieces were decorated with a gold rim. Flower or fruit designs in bright colors were used on some. Bright bands of fired-on blue, green, red, and yellow were used to decorate some wares. All of these patterns have their own names. These include Aurora, Banded Petalware, Daisy Petals, Diamond Point, Petal, Shell, and Vivid Bands.

BLUE

Bowl, 5 3/4 In. 7.00
Creamer .... 8.50 To 12.75
Cup........................... 7.00
Cup & Saucer................ 8.00
Plate, 9 In.................... 8.00
Saucer......................... 2.00
Soup, Cream 14.00

COBALT

Cup & Saucer................ 8.00

CREMAX

Bowl, 5 3/4 In. .... 4.00 To 5.00
Bowl, 9 In................... 12.00
Cup.................. 2.75 To 4.00
Cup & Saucer....... 4.50 To 6.00
Cup & Saucer,
Gold Trim......... 4.00 To 6.00
Cup & Saucer,
Pastel Bands................ 8.00

Plate, 6 In.......... 1.50 To 2.00
Plate, 8 In.......... 2.50 To 5.00
Plate, 9 In.......... 3.25 To 6.00
Plate, Gold Trim, 6 In....... 2.00
Plate, Gold Trim, 8 In....... 4.00
Plate, Gold Trim, 9 In....... 5.00
Plate, Server, 11 In.......... 8.00
Plate, Server, Gold Trim,
11 In........................ 10.00
Platter, 13 In...... 7.00 To 14.00
Saucer............... 1.00 To 2.50
Sherbet............ 4.00 To 11.00
Soup, Cream .... 5.00 To 9.00
Soup, Cream, Gold Trim.... 9.00
Sugar................ 3.00 To 5.00
Sugar & Creamer... 7.50 To 8.25
Sugar, Gold Trim... 4.50 To 5.00

CRYSTAL

Ice Bucket.................... 14.00
Saucer.......................... 1.25
Soup, Cream 5.00
Tumbler, Gold Trim,
4 1/2 In...................... 5.00

MONAX

Bowl, 5 3/4 In. 6.00
Creamer .... 3.50 To 4.50
Cup & Saucer....... 4.00 To 9.00
Cup, Gold Trim 3.00
Lamp Shade................... 7.00
Plate, 6 In.......... 1.50 To 3.25
Plate, 8 In.......... 3.00 To 5.00
Plate, 9 In.................... 7.00
Plate, Gold Trim, 8 In....... 4.00
Plate, Gold Trim, 9 In....... 5.00
Plate, Server,
11 In............... 5.00 To 8.00
Plate, Server, Gold Trim,
11 In.......................... 9.00
Platter, 13 In...... 8.50 To 17.00
Saucer............... 1.00 To 2.25
Sherbet.............. 7.00 To 9.50
Soup, Cream .... 5.00 To 8.00
Sugar................ 3.50 To 5.00
Sugar & Creamer............ 9.00
Sugar & Creamer,
Gold Trim.................. 9.00

PINK

Bowl, 5 3/4 In. 5.00
Bowl, 9 In................... 12.00
Cake Plate........ 14.00 To 16.00
Creamer .... 5.00 To 8.00
Cup.................. 3.00 To 4.00

Cup & Saucer .... 6.75 To 7.00
Plate, 8 In. .... 2.50 To 4.00
Plate, 9 In. .... 3.25 To 6.50
Plate, Server, 11 In. 8.00
Platter, 13 In. 10.00
Soup, Cream .... 5.50 To 7.50
Sugar 3.00
Sugar & Creamer 8.00
Sugar, Cover ...... 8.00 To 15.00

YELLOW

Cup 4.00
Plate, 8 In. 4.00
Plate, 9 In. 8.00
Sugar & Creamer 10.00

Philbe

Philbe is a Fire–King dinnerware made by the Anchor Hocking Glass Company from 1937 to the 1940s. It was made in blue, crystal, green, and pink. The blue sometimes has platinum trim. Philbe is the dinnerware pattern; the matching kitchenware is called Fire–King Oven Glass.

Philbe, see also Fire–King

BLUE

Bowl, 5 1/2 In. 40.00
Cookie Jar 500.00
Cup 70.00
Plate, 8 In. 32.00
Tumbler, Footed, 3 1/2 In. 110.00
Tumbler, Footed, 6 1/2 In. 65.00

CRYSTAL

Bowl, 10 1/8 In. 20.00
Cup & Saucer 2.25
Plate, 8 In. 16.00

Plate, Grill, 10 1/2 In. 18.00
Plate, Server, 10 1/2 In. 2.25
Sugar & Creamer, Cover 9.00
Tumbler, 4 In. 25.00

Pie Crust, see Cremax

Pillar Flute

Pillar Flute was made by Imperial Glass Company, Bellaire, Ohio, in amber, blue, crystal, green, and a pink called Rose Marie. It was made about 1930.

BLUE

Bowl, 10 In. 18.00
Cup .... 5.50 To 8.00
Goblet, 7 1/2 In. 15.00
Plate, 8 In. 6.75
Relish, Oval 9.00

Pineapple & Floral, see No. 618

Pinwheel, see Sierra

Pioneer

Pioneer by Federal Glass Company, Columbus, Ohio, was first made in pink in the 1930s. In the 1940s the dishes were made

in crystal and the pattern continued to be made into the 1970s.

CRYSTAL

Ashtray 6.00
Bowl, 4 In. 10.00
Bowl, 5 3/8 In. 5.00
Bowl, 7 In. 4.00
Plate, 8 1/2 In. 5.00

PINK

Ice Bucket .... 32.00 To 40.00
Plate, 8 1/2 In. 3.00

Poinsettia, see Floral

Popeye & Olive

Line 994 was the original name for this Paden City Glass Company pattern. The popular name today is Popeye & Olive. It was made in cobalt blue, crystal, green, and red. The pattern was made in the 1930s and a 1932 ad shows the red as a new color.

BLUE

Bowl, Footed, 9 In. 18.00

GREEN

Plate, 6 In. 3.00

RED

Bowl, 8 In. 35.00
Bowl, Footed, 9 In. .... 18.00 To 20.00

Bowl, Ruffled, Footed, 7 In. 17.50
Bowl, Ruffled, Footed, 9 In. 25.00
Candleholder, Pair 20.00
Plate, 8 In. 10.00
Sherbet .... 10.00 To 15.00
Sugar 7.00
Sugar & Creamer 15.00
Tumbler, 9 Oz. 18.50
Tumbler, 12 Oz. 22.50

Poppy No. 1, see Florentine No. 1

Poppy No. 2, see Florentine No. 2

Pretty Polly Party Dishes, see Doric & Pansy

Pretzel

Pretzel, also called No. 622 or Ribbon Candy, was made by Indiana Glass Company, Dunkirk, Indiana, in the 1930s. Crystal and teal pieces were made. Some reproductions appeared in the 1970s.

CRYSTAL

Celery .... 4.50 To 6.00
Creamer .... 3.00 To 4.50
Cup .... 1.50 To 4.00
Cup & Saucer .... 3.00 To 5.00
Dish, Olive, Handle, 7 In. 2.25
Dish, Pickle, 8 1/2 In. 2.50
Plate, 6 In. .... 1.00 To 1.50
Plate, 9 3/8 In. ..... 2.75 To 4.00
Plate, 11 1/2 In. ... 7.00 To 8.75
Plate, Center Fruit Design, 6 In. 3.50
Plate, Center Fruit Design, 10 1/2 In. 6.00
Saucer .... 1.00 To 2.50

Sherbet 5.00
Soup, Dish .... 3.00 To 6.50
Sugar .... 2.50 To 5.00
Sugar & Creamer ... 7.00 To 7.50
Tumbler, 3 1/2 In. 4.50
Tumbler, 4 1/2 In. 16.00

Primo

Green and mandarin yellow are the two colors of Primo advertised in the 1932 catalog for U.S. Glass Company.

GREEN

Cake Plate 10.00
Cup .... 5.50 To 6.00
Saucer .... 1.25 To 1.50
Tumbler, Footed, 5 3/4 In. .... 10.00 To 11.50

YELLOW

Cup 6.50
Cup & Saucer 7.50
Plate, 7 1/2 In. 3.00

Plate, Grill 7.50
Saucer 1.00
Sugar & Creamer 13.00
Tumbler, 5 3/4 In. 10.00

Primus, see Madrid

Princess

Hocking Glass Company, Lancaster, Ohio, made the popular Princess pattern from 1931 to 1935. The first sets were made in green, then in topaz. The amber sometimes came out a rather yellow shade, so if you are assembling a set, be careful of the color variations. Pink was added last. There are blue pieces found in the West, but there is a debate about the age or origin of these pieces. Some pieces had a frosted finish, some are decorated with hand-painted flowers. Green is sometimes trimmed with gold, other colors are trimmed with platinum.

AMBER

Cup .... 5.00 To 7.00
Cup & Saucer 8.00
Pitcher, 8 In. ..... 50.00 To 55.00
Plate, 5 1/2 In. 4.00
Plate, 8 In. .... 6.00 To 7.00
Plate, Grill .... 4.50 To 6.00
Tumbler, 5 1/4 In. 18.00
Tumbler, Footed, 5 1/4 In. 15.00

CRYSTAL

Cup & Saucer 7.00
Plate, 9 In. 8.00
Sugar & Creamer 17.00
Tumbler, Footed, 5 1/4 In. 12.00

GREEN

Ashtray 30.00
Bowl, 4 1/2 In. .... 10.00 To 16.00
Bowl, 5 In. .... 16.00 To 19.50
Bowl, Hat Shape, 9 1/2 In. .... 17.50 To 27.50

Bowl, Octagon,
9 In. .... 21.00 To 25.00
Bowl, Oval,
10 In. .... 15.00 To 18.00
Butter, Cover .... 58.00 To 70.00
Cake Plate .... 13.00 To 27.50
Candy Container,
Cover .... 22.00 To 35.00
Coaster 22.00
Cookie Jar,
Cover .... 27.50 To 35.00
Creamer .... 9.50 To 15.00
Cup .... 5.00 To 8.00
Cup & Saucer ..... 9.00 To 12.50
Pitcher, 6 In. ..... 28.00 To 35.00
Pitcher, 8 In. ..... 28.00 To 40.00
Plate, 2 Handles,
11 1/2 In. ...... 15.00 To 16.00
Plate, 5 1/2 In. ..... 3.00 To 5.00
Plate, 8 In. .... 6.00 To 9.00
Plate, 9 In. .... 17.00 To 18.00
Plate, Grill, 9 1/2 In. 8.50
Plate, Grill, 11 1/2 In. 9.00
Platter, 12 In. .... 11.00 To 15.00
Salt & Pepper .... 28.00 To 45.00
Saltshaker .... 13.75 To 18.00
Saucer 5.00
Sherbet .... 11.00 To 14.00
Sugar & Creamer, Cover ... 35.00
Sugar, Cover 21.00
Tumbler,
4 In. .... 17.00 To 22.00
Tumbler,
4 1/2 In. .... 16.00 To 20.00
Tumbler, Footed,
5 1/4 In. .... 17.00 To 22.50
Vase, 8 In. 16.00

PINK

Bowl, 4 1/2 In. 14.00
Bowl, 5 In. .... 9.00 To 15.00
Bowl, Hat Shape,
9 1/2 In. 25.00
Bowl, Octagonal,
9 In. .... 14.00 To 28.00
Butter, Cover 75.00
Cookie Jar,
Cover .... 30.00 To 37.50
Cup .... 5.00 To 6.50
Cup & Saucer .... 6.50 To 8.50
Pitcher, 6 In. 25.00
Pitcher, 8 In. ..... 25.00 To 33.00
Plate, 5 1/2 In. 2.00
Plate, 9 In. .... 5.00 To 14.00
Platter, 12 In. 14.00
Sherbet 12.00

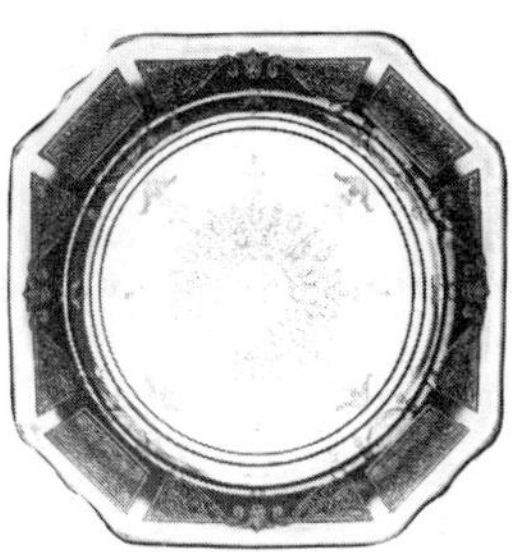

Tumbler, 3 In. ... 13.75 To 16.00
Tumbler, 4 In. ... 14.00 To 16.00
Tumbler, Footed,
5 1/4 In. .... 12.00 To 15.00
Tumbler, Footed,
6 1/2 In. 31.00

YELLOW

Bowl, 5 In. 18.00
Bowl, Oval, 10 In. 37.50
Creamer 8.00
Cup .... 4.00 To 10.00
Cup & Saucer 13.00
Plate, 5 1/2 In. ..... 3.00 To 4.00
Plate, 8 In. .... 5.75 To 7.00
Plate, 9 In. .... 9.00 To 14.00
Plate, Grill, Handle,
11 1/2 In. .... 6.00 To 15.00
Platter, 12 In. 50.00
Sugar, Cover 25.00
Tumbler, 3 In. 17.00
Tumbler, 4 In. ... 16.00 To 18.00
Tumbler,
5 1/4 In. .... 12.50 To 24.75
Tumbler, Footed,
5 1/4 In. .... 12.00 To 14.00

Princess Feather

Westmoreland Glass Company made Princess Feather pattern from 1939 through 1948. It was originally made in aqua, crystal, green, and pink. In the 1960s a reproduction appeared in an amber shade called Golden Sunset. The pattern is sometimes called Early American, Flower, Oatmeal Lace, Scroll & Star, or Westmoreland Sandwich.

AMBER

Creamer 12.00
Salt & Pepper 20.00

CRYSTAL

Bowl, 6 1/2 In. 11.00
Cordial, 4 1/2 In. 7.00
Creamer 6.00
Goblet, 4 3/8 In. 7.00
Goblet, 5 7/8 In. 12.50
Plate, 8 In. 8.00
Plate, 13 In. 28.50
Salt & Pepper .... 14.00 To 23.00
Saltshaker .... 10.00 To 12.50
Sherbet .... 4.50 To 6.75
Sugar 6.00

Prismatic Line, see Queen Mary

Provincial, see Bubble

Pyramid, see No. 610

Queen Mary

Queen Mary, sometimes called Prismatic Line or Vertical Ribbed, was made by Anchor Hocking Glass Company from 1936 to 1940. It was made in crystal, pink, and red.

CRYSTAL

Bowl, 6 In. .... 3.00 To 5.00
Bowl,
8 3/4 In. .... 6.50 To 10.00
Candy Container, Cover 19.00

If you live in an old house and the locks are old, check the new types. There have been many improvements and new locks give much better security.

Celery 5.00
Cigarette Holder 6.00
Compote 7.00
Creamer .... 2.00 To 4.00
Cup .... 3.00 To 3.50
Cup & Saucer 5.00
Plate, 6 In. .... 2.00 To 4.00
Plate, 8 1/2 In. .... 3.00 To 4.00
Plate, 9 3/4 In. .... 8.00 To 9.00
Plate, 12 In. 5.00
Relish, 3 Sections, 12 In. 7.00
Salt & Pepper .... 8.00 To 15.00
Sherbet 3.00
Sugar .... 2.00 To 4.00
Sugar & Creamer 6.00

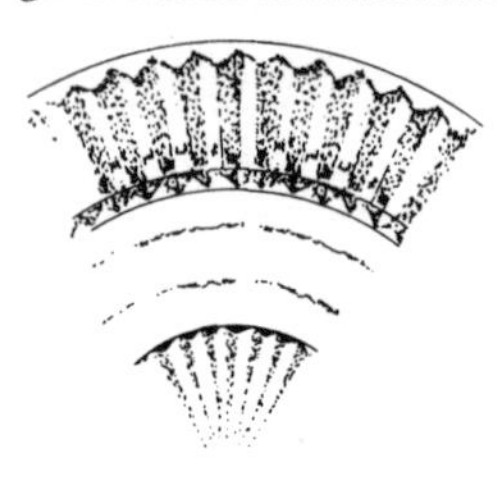

PINK

Bowl, 4 In. .... 2.00 To 3.00
Bowl, 6 In. .... 4.00 To 6.00
Bowl, Handle, 4 In. .... 3.75 To 4.00
Creamer .... 3.00 To 4.00
Cup .... 4.00 To 5.50
Cup & Saucer .... 6.50 To 9.00
Plate, 6 In. .... 1.25 To 3.00
Plate, 9 3/4 In. .... 18.50 To 25.00
Plate, Sandwich, 12 In. 12.00
Punch Cup 2.50
Sherbet .... 3.00 To 6.00
Sugar 4.00
Sugar & Creamer 14.00
Tumbler, 3 1/2 In. .... 6.00 To 9.00
Tumbler, 4 In. .... 6.50 To 9.00
Tumbler, Footed, 5 In. .... 20.00 To 25.00

R

Radiance

New Martinsville Glass Company, New Martinsville, West Virginia, made Radiance pattern from 1936 to 1939. It was made of amber, cobalt, crystal, emerald green, ice blue, and red.

AMBER

Celery 6.00
Creamer .... 7.00 To 10.00
Cup & Saucer 9.00
Pitcher, 10 In. 120.00
Punch Cup 4.00
Saucer 3.00
Sugar .... 9.00 To 10.00
Tumbler, 9 Oz. 8.00

CRYSTAL

Butter, Cover .... 100.00 To 125.00
Compote, 6 In. 7.00
Creamer 10.00
Cruet, Salt & Pepper, Red Tray 100.00
Punch Set, Star Cup, Ball Shape, Ladle, 10 Piece 135.00
Sugar 6.00
Sugar & Creamer .... 10.00 To 23.00

ICE BLUE

Candleholder, 2-Light 9.50
Cup & Saucer .... 13.00 To 15.00

Punch Cup 6.00
Sugar & Creamer 34.00

RED

Cordial 14.00
Creamer 15.00
Cruet, Crystal Top 95.00
Cup 8.50
Cup & Saucer 11.00
Decanter, Sterling Overlay 60.00
Dish, Pickle, 7 In. 35.00
Salt & Pepper 125.00
Sugar & Creamer 20.00
Tray 25.00

Raindrops

Watch out for confusion with Raindrops and another pattern called Thumbprint or Pear Optic. The pattern for Raindrops is on the inside of the pieces, the other pattern is on the outside. Federal Glass Company made crystal and green Raindrops dinnerware from 1929 to 1933.

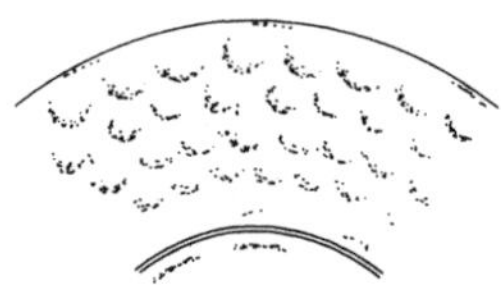

Raindrops, see also Colony

GREEN

Bowl, 4 1/2 In. 1.75
Bowl, 7 1/2 In. 13.00
Creamer 5.00
Cup 4.00
Cup & Saucer .... 4.75 To 8.00

Plate, 8 In. 4.00
Saucer 2.50
Sherbet .... 5.00 To 6.00
Tumbler,
2 1/8 In. .... 3.00 To 5.00
Tumbler, 3 In. ...... 3.50 To 4.50
Tumbler,
Whiskey .... 4.00 To 5.00

Raspberry Band, see Laurel

Rex, see No. 610

Ribbed, see Manhattan

Ribbon Candy, see Pretzel

Ribbon

Black, crystal, and green pieces were made in Ribbon pattern in the 1930s. It was made by the Hazel-Atlas Glass Company.

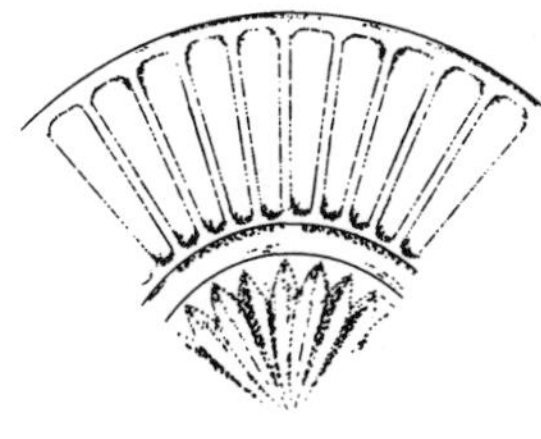

CRYSTAL

Bowl, 8 In. 13.50
Candy Container, Cover 23.00
Creamer 3.00
Plate, 6 In. 1.50
Plate, 8 In. 2.00
Salt & Pepper 15.00
Sherbet 4.00
Sugar .... 3.00 To 5.50

GREEN

Candy Container,
Cover .... 23.00 To 25.00
Creamer 6.00
Cup 3.00
Cup & Saucer 8.00
Plate, 6 1/4 In. ..... 1.25 To 2.00
Plate, 8 In. .... 2.00 To 4.50
Sherbet .... 3.25 To 4.50
Sugar .... 4.00 To 6.00
Tumbler, 6 In. 7.00

Ring

Hocking Glass Company made Ring from 1927 to 1932. The pattern is sometimes clear-colored glass and sometimes has colored rings added. The clear glass is crystal, green, or pink, which may or may not be decorated with rings of black, blue, orange, pink, platinum, red, or yellow.

CRYSTAL

Cocktail Shaker 5.00
Cocktail Shaker,
Multicolored Rings 9.00
Creamer, Platinum Rim 4.00
Cup & Saucer 4.50
Decanter, Stopper 20.00
Decanter, Stopper, Multicolored
Rings .... 17.00 To 25.00
Goblet, Platinum Rim,
7 1/4 In. 7.50
Ice Bucket .... 5.00 To 10.00
Pitcher, 8 In. .... 3.50 To 9.00
Pitcher, 8 1/2 In. 9.00
Plate, Off-Center Indent,
6 In. 2.00
Plate, Platinum Rim,
8 In. 2.00
Sandwich Server, Center Handle,
Platinum Rim 10.00

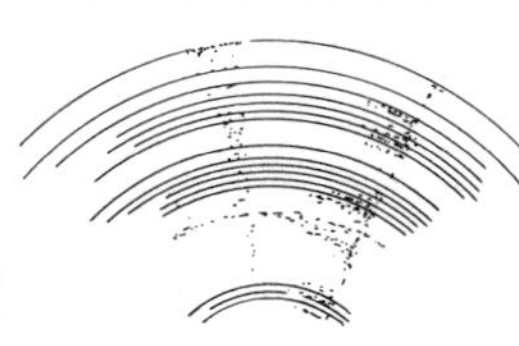

Sherbet, Footed,
4 3/4 In. .... 3.00 To 3.50
Sugar 2.50
Tumbler, 3 1/2 In. 2.50
Tumbler, 4 1/4 In. 3.00
Tumbler, Footed,
6 1/2 In. 3.00
Tumbler, Multicolored Rings,
3 1/2 In. 3.50
Vase, Multicolored Rings,
8 In. 10.00
Whiskey, Multicolored
Rings .... 3.50 To 4.50

GREEN

Creamer 4.50
Cup 3.00
Cup & Saucer 4.50
Pitcher,
8 1/2 In. .... 15.00 To 18.00
Plate, 6 1/4 In. ..... 2.00 To 2.50
Plate, 8 In. 3.50
Plate, Off-Center Ring,
6 1/2 In. 4.50
Plate, Platinum Rim,
6 1/4 In. 2.50
Plate, Platinum Rim,
8 In. 3.50
Salt & Pepper 50.00
Sandwich Server, Center
Handle .... 17.00 To 17.50
Sherbet, Low 7.00
Tumbler, 3 1/2 In. 3.75
Tumbler,
4 1/4 In. .... 4.50 To 7.50
Tumbler,
5 1/8 In. .... 4.00 To 5.75

Rock Crystal

Rock Crystal, sometimes called Early American Rock Crystal, was made in many solid colors by McKee Glass Company. Crystal was made in the 1920s. Amber, blue-green, cobalt blue, crystal, green, pink, red, and yellow pieces were made in the 1930s.

AMBER

Bowl, 4 In. 8.00
Cake Plate, 11 In. 25.00
Candleholder, 8 1/2 In. 20.00
Goblet, Cordial 40.00
Plate, 7 1/2 In. 6.00
Sandwich Server,
Clear Handle 22.00

COBALT BLUE

Candleholder, 2-Light 125.00

CRYSTAL

Bowl, 4 1/2 In. 8.00
Bowl, 5 In..................... 9.00
Bowl, Footed,
12 1/2 In.......20.00 To 30.00
Bowl, Oblong, 12 In........20.00
Candleholder, 2-Light,
Pair..........................25.00
Candleholder, 8 1/2 In.,
Pair..........................55.00
Champagne,
5 In.............. 9.00 To 15.00
Compote, 7 In. 22.00
Cordial, 1 Oz................25.00
Creamer, Footed.............25.00
Cruet, Stopper ... 40.00 To 75.00
Cup & Saucer .... 18.00 To 24.75
Eggcup........................ 9.00
Goblet,
3 1/2 Oz........10.50 To 18.00
Goblet, 8 Oz..... 12.00 To 18.50
Pitcher, 9 In.................45.00
Plate, 6 In..................... 6.25
Plate, 7 1/2 In................ 6.00
Plate, 8 1/2 In................ 7.00
Plate, 9 In....................12.00
Relish, 5 Sections,
12 In............20.00 To 22.50
Sherbet........................12.00
Tumbler, Concave,
9 Oz.........................20.00
Tumbler, Concave,
12 Oz...........10.00 To 15.00
Tumbler, Straight, 9 Oz.....20.00
Vase, Footed, 11 In. 60.00

GREEN

Plate, 8 1/2 In................ 6.00
Saltshaker, Bulbous..........65.00

PINK

Compote,
7 In.............32.00 To 35.00

RED

Bowl, Jelly, Footed,
5 In..........................75.00
Champagne, 6 Oz...........35.00
Cordial, 1 Oz................60.00
Goblet, 8 Oz.................35.00
Parfait.........................65.00
Plate, 7 1/2 In..............12.00
Plate, 8 1/2 In..............19.00
Plate, 9 In....................18.00
Sandwich Server,
Center Handle............ 120.00
Whiskey 45.00
Wine, 2 Oz.......35.00 To 47.50

Rope, see Colonial Fluted

Rose Cameo

Rose Cameo was made by the Belmont Tumbler Company, Bellaire, Ohio, in 1933. It has been found only in green.

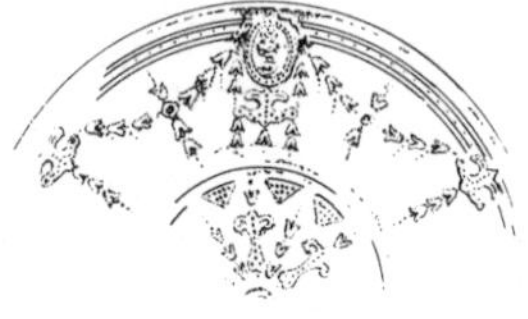

GREEN

Bowl, 4 1/2 In. ....3.00 To 6.50
Bowl, 5 In......... 9.00 To 10.00
Plate, 7 In.................... 5.00
Tumbler, Footed,
5 In.............. 7.00 To 10.00

Rose Lace, see Royal Lace

Rosemary

Rosemary, also called Cabbage Rose with Single Arch or Dutch Rose, was made by Federal Glass Company from 1935 to 1937. It was made in amber, green, and pink. Pieces with bases, like creamers or cups, are sometimes confused with Mayfair Federal. The lower half of the Rosemary pieces are plain, the lower half of Mayfair Federal has a band of arches.

Rosemary, see also Mayfair Federal

AMBER

Bowl, 5 In...........3.75 To 5.00
Bowl, 6 In........ 18.50 To 20.00
Bowl, Vegetable, Oval,
10 In.........................18.00
Creamer ....5.00 To 6.50
Cup & Saucer................. 6.00
Plate, 6 3/4 In......3.50 To 4.00
Plate, 9 In. ....3.75 To 6.00
Plate, Grill ....5.00 To 6.00
Platter, 12 In...... 6.00 To 18.00
Saucer.......................... 1.50
Soup, Cream ...... 6.00 To 11.00
Sugar.................5.00 To 9.00
Sugar & Creamer............18.00
Tumbler,
4 1/4 In......... 13.00 To 16.00

GREEN

Bowl, 5 In..................... 6.00
Bowl, 6 In....................25.00
Bowl, Vegetable, Oval,
10 In............22.50 To 27.50
Creamer 14.00
Cup...................6.00 To 8.00
Plate, 9 In....................11.00
Platter, Oval, 12 In..........12.00
Soup, Cream 14.00

PINK

Bowl, 5 In..................... 6.50
Bowl, Vegetable, Oval......10.00
Plate, 6 3/4 In................ 7.50
Plate, 9 In......... 9.00 To 12.50
Platter, Oval, 12 In..........17.50
Tumbler, 4 1/4 In. 21.00

Roulette

Anchor Hocking Glass Company made Roulette pattern from 1935 to 1939. It can be found in crystal, green, and pink. Collectors originally called the pattern Many Windows.

CRYSTAL

Tumbler, Footed, 5 1/2 In. 13.00

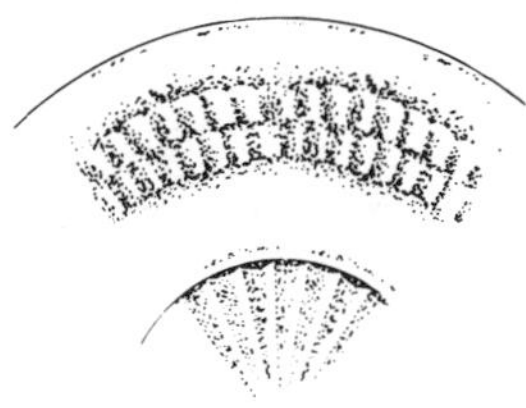

GREEN

Bowl, 9 In. .... 7.50 To 15.00
Creamer 15.00
Cup 2.00
Cup & Saucer .... 4.50 To 5.00
Pitcher, 8 In. 22.50
Plate, 6 In. .... 2.00 To 2.50
Plate, 8 1/2 In. .... 3.00 To 4.25
Plate, 12 In. .... 6.00 To 10.00
Saucer .... .75 To 2.00
Sherbet .... 3.00 To 7.50
Sugar, Footed 9.00
Tumbler, 4 1/8 In. .... 10.00 To 12.00
Tumbler, Footed, 5 1/2 In. .... 10.00 To 13.50
Whiskey 7.00

PINK

Cup & Saucer 18.00
Pitcher, 8 In. .... 18.00 To 28.00
Plate, Sherbet 6.00
Tumbler, 3 1/4 In. 6.50
Tumbler, 4 1/8 In. 12.50
Tumbler, 5 1/8 In. 7.50

Round Robin

Sometimes a pattern was advertised by the wholesaler, but the

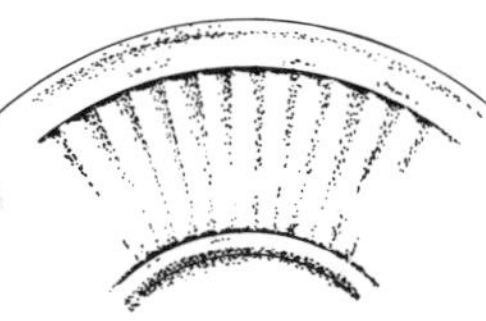

manufacturer is unknown today. One of these is Round Robin, sometimes called Accordion Pleats. It was pictured in the catalogs of the late 1920s and 1930s and offered in green, crystal, and iridescent marigold.

GREEN

Cup 3.00
Cup & Saucer 4.00
Plate, 8 In. 2.00
Tray 25.00

Roxana

Hazel-Atlas Glass Company made Roxana pattern in 1932. It was made in crystal, yellow, and white. Although there seems to be a full luncheon set, collectors cannot find a cup for the saucer.

CRYSTAL

Tumbler, 4 In. 8.00

YELLOW

Bowl, 5 In. 5.50
Plate, 6 In. .... 2.50 To 2.75
Sherbet .... 2.50 To 3.75

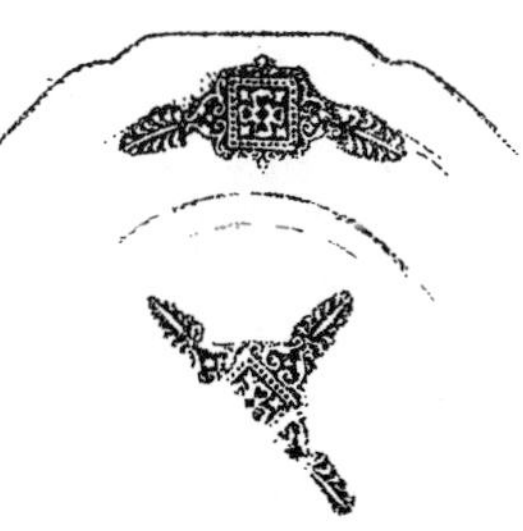

Royal Lace

Royal Lace was made from 1934 to 1941. The popular pattern by Hazel-Atlas Glass Company was made in amethyst, cobalt blue, crystal, green, and pink. It is sometimes called Gladiola or Rose Lace.

AMETHYST

Sherbet 6.00
Toddy Set 95.00

BLUE

Bowl, 5 In. 27.50
Bowl, 10 In. 37.00
Bowl, Footed, Rolled Edge, 10 In. 150.00
Bowl, Footed, Straight Edge, 10 In. 42.00
Butter, Cover 350.00
Cookie Jar, Cover 195.00
Creamer .... 24.00 To 35.00

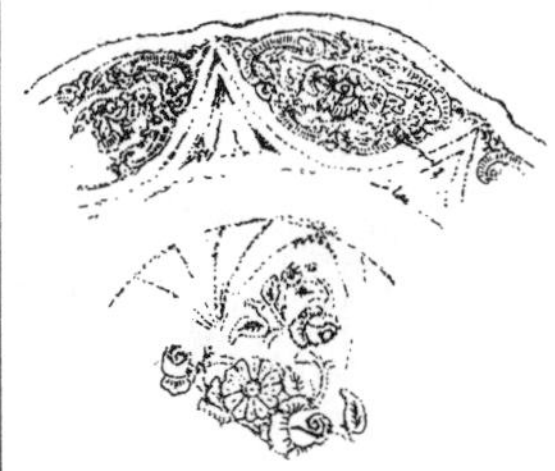

Cup .... 20.00 To 23.50
Cup & Saucer .... 25.00 To 30.00
Pitcher, 8 In. 115.00
Pitcher, Straight Side, 48 Oz. .... 68.00 To 80.00
Plate, 6 In. .... 7.50 To 8.25
Plate, 9 7/8 In. .... 25.00 To 30.00
Plate, Grill .... 21.00 To 22.50
Platter, Oval, 13 In. 45.00
Salt & Pepper .... 195.00 To 225.00
Saucer .... 5.50 To 7.50
Sherbet, Metal Holder 17.00
Soup, Cream .... 22.25 To 25.00
Sugar .... 16.00 To 25.00
Sugar, Cover .... 95.00 To 115.00
Toddy Set 125.00

Tumbler, 3 1/2 In. 27.00
Tumbler, 4 1/8 In.........20.00 To 27.00
Tumbler, 4 7/8 In. 50.00
Tumbler, 5 3/8 In. 37.50

CRYSTAL

Butter, Cover ....40.00 To 57.00
Candleholder, Ruffled, Pair 25.00
Cookie Jar, Cover............17.00 To 35.00
Creamer ....7.00 To 9.00
Cup...................3.00 To 6.50
Cup & Saucer ..... 9.50 To 10.00
Pitcher, 8 In.....25.00 To 30.00
Pitcher, 8 1/2 In.........40.00 To 43.00
Plate, 6 In. 4.00
Plate, 9 7/8 In......7.00 To 9.50
Platter, Oval, 13 In........... 9.00
Saltshaker......................17.50
Saucer.......................... 2.00
Sherbet......................... 5.00
Soup, Cream ...... 6.00 To 10.00
Sugar & Creamer, Cover ...29.00
Tumbler, 3 1/2 In.......... 7.00 To 11.00
Tumbler, 4 1/8 In...........7.00 To 9.00

GREEN

Bowl, 5 In....................25.00
Bowl, Oval, 11 In..........19.50
Cookie Jar, Cover............42.00 To 65.50
Creamer 17.50
Cup............................15.00
Plate, 6 In. 5.00
Plate, 8 1/2 In................ 8.00
Plate, Grill 15.00
Platter, Oval, 13 In............25.00 To 27.50
Salt & Pepper ....67.50 To 70.00
Saucer......................... 4.00
Sherbet............. 9.00 To 17.50
Soup, Cream .....20.00 To 22.00
Sugar, Cover 50.00
Tumbler, 4 1/8 In.........16.75 To 17.50
Tumbler, 4 7/8 In. 27.00

PINK

Bowl, 3-Footed, Straight Edge, 10 In.............13.00 To 20.00
Bowl, 5 In....................14.00
Bowl, Oval, 11 In.............14.00 To 15.00
Butter, Cover..........90.00 To 125.00
Candleholder, Rolled, Pair 32.50
Candleholder, Ruffled, Pair 40.00
Cookie Jar, Cover............32.00 To 37.00
Creamer .... 9.50 To 14.00
Cup................. 7.00 To 10.00
Cup & Saucer 11.00
Pitcher, 8 1/2 In. 62.00
Plate, 6 In. 3.00
Plate, 8 1/2 In................ 1.50
Plate, Grill 8.00
Platter, Oval, 13 In............12.00 To 16.00
Salt & Pepper ....40.00 To 51.50
Saltshaker.....................20.00
Sherbet...............8.00 To 9.50
Soup, Cream ...... 9.00 To 14.00
Sugar & Creamer, Cover ...45.00
Sugar, Cover 35.00
Tumbler, 3 1/2 In.........11.00 To 15.00
Tumbler, 4 1/8 In.......... 9.00 To 12.00
Tumbler, 5 3/8 In. 38.00

Royal Ruby

There is no reason to picture this pattern because it is the plain shape and bright red color that identifies it. Anchor Hocking Glass Company made it from 1939 to the 1960s and again in 1977. The same shapes were made in green and called by the pattern name Forest Green. Reproduction tumblers were made in 1977–1978.

Ashtray, Square, 4 1/2 In............2.50 To 5.00
Bowl, 4 1/4 In. ....3.00 To 4.50
Bowl, 8 1/2 In.........11.50 To 19.00
Card Holder 27.00
Creamer, Flat........5.50 To 6.00
Creamer, Footed....6.00 To 7.00
Cup...................3.00 To 3.50
Cup & Saucer ....4.00 To 7.00
Goblet, Ball Stem 8.00
Ice Bucket, Bail, Tongs.....40.00
Pitcher, Tilted, 22 Oz............20.00 To 22.00
Pitcher, Tilted, 3 Qt.........25.00
Pitcher, Upright, 3 Qt. 30.00
Plate, 6 1/2 In................ 4.00
Plate, 7 In. 4.00
Plate, 9 In. ....5.00 To 7.50
Plate, 13 3/4 In. 18.50

In snowy weather make tracks both in and out of your door. One set of tracks leaving the house is an invitation to an intruder. Or perhaps you could walk out of the house backward.

Punch Bowl ...... 23.00 To 35.00
Punch Cup .... 2.00 To 2.50
Punch Set, 14 Piece 47.50
Saucer .... 1.50 To 2.50
Sherbet .... 4.00 To 10.00
Soup, Dish 9.00
Sugar & Creamer .... 10.00 To 12.00
Tumbler, 3 1/2 Oz. 7.50
Tumbler, 5 Oz. ..... 4.00 To 6.00
Tumbler, 9 Oz. 5.00
Tumbler, 10 Oz. .... 3.50 To 5.00
Tumbler, 13 Oz. 6.00
Vase, Large 10.00
Vase, Small 5.00
Wine, 2 1/2 In. 7.25

Russian, see Holiday

S

S Pattern

Macbeth-Evans Glass Company made S Pattern, or Stippled Rose Band, from 1930 to 1935. It was made before 1932 in crystal, pink, topaz, and crystal with gold, blue, or platinum trim. The 1934–1935 listing mentions red, green, and monax. Other pieces were made in amber, ruby, Ritz Blue, and crystal with many colors of trim including amber, green, rose, platinum, red, or white.

AMBER

Bowl, 5 1/2 In. 4.00
Cup & Saucer 4.50
Plate, Grill .... 3.00 To 3.75
Sherbet 4.50
Sugar 4.50

CRYSTAL

Cake Plate, Footed, 11 In. 45.00
Creamer 3.50
Cup 2.00
Cup & Saucer .... 3.00 To 6.00
Plate, 8 In. .... 1.50 To 2.50
Saucer 1.00
Sugar & Creamer ... 4.00 To 6.00
Tumbler, 3 1/2 In. 3.00
Tumbler, 4 In. 3.00
Tumbler, 4 3/4 In. 4.00

TOPAZ

Bowl, 5 1/2 In. 6.50
Bowl, 8 1/2 In. 18.00
Creamer 5.50
Cup & Saucer 5.00
Plate, 8 In. 3.25
Plate, 9 1/4 In. 7.50
Sherbet 6.00

Sail Boat, see White Ship

Sailing Ship, see White Ship

Sandwich Anchor Hocking

Many patterns were called Sandwich. Each company seemed to have one design with that name.

The Anchor Hocking Glass Company Sandwich pattern was made from 1939 to 1964. Pink and royal ruby were used in 1939–1940; crystal, forest green, and opaque white were used in the 1950s and 1960s; amber was used in the 1960s. A reproduction line was introduced in 1977 by another company in amber, blue, crystal, and red.

AMBER

Bowl, 6 1/2 In. 6.50
Cookie Jar, Cover .... 20.00 To 30.00
Cup & Saucer .... 3.00 To 6.50
Plate, 7 In. 2.50
Plate, 9 In. .... 3.00 To 5.00
Sherbet 10.00

CRYSTAL

Bowl, 4 7/8 In. 4.00
Bowl, 5 1/4 In. 6.00
Bowl, 6 1/2 In. .... 3.25 To 5.50
Bowl, Oval, 8 1/4 In. 3.00
Bowl, Scalloped, 4 7/8 In. 4.00
Bowl, Scalloped, 8 In. .... 5.00 To 6.00
Butter, Cover .... 14.00 To 28.00
Cookie Jar, Cover .... 20.00 To 30.00
Creamer .... 1.50 To 4.00
Cup .... 1.25 To 4.00
Cup & Saucer .... 2.00 To 6.00
Custard Cup .... 2.00 To 3.00
Custard Cup, Scalloped .... 6.00 To 7.00
Dresser Set, 9 Piece 30.00
Pitcher, 1/2 Gal. .... 39.50 To 56.00
Plate, 7 In. 5.00
Plate, 8 In. .... 2.00 To 4.00
Plate, 9 In. .... 7.50 To 12.00
Plate, Gold Trim, 7 In. 4.00
Punch Bowl 12.00
Punch Cup .... 1.25 To 2.00
Punch Cup, Gold Trim 1.50
Punch Set, 14 Piece .... 20.00 To 40.00
Saucer .... 1.00 To 1.50
Sherbet .... 3.00 To 5.00
Sugar, Cover 12.00
Tumbler, 5 Oz. ..... 3.75 To 4.50

Tumbler, 9 Oz. 5.00
Tumbler, Footed, 9 Oz. 9.50

FOREST GREEN

Bowl, 4 3/8 In. 1.50
Bowl, 6 1/2 In. 21.00
Bowl, 8 In....................35.00
Bowl, Scalloped, 6 1/2 In.....................22.00
Cookie Jar, Cover 14.00
Creamer ....10.00 To 14.00
Cup................11.00 To 18.50
Cup & Saucer ....15.00 To 18.00
Custard Cup.................. 3.50
Pitcher, 6 In......70.00 To 80.00
Plate, 9 In. ....39.00 To 50.00
Saucer.......................... 6.00
Sherbet........................10.00
Sugar............... 9.00 To 12.00
Sugar & Creamer............28.00
Tumbler, 5 Oz. 1.50
Tumbler, 9 Oz. 2.50

RUBY RED

Bowl, 5 1/4 In.........10.00 To 13.00
Bowl, 6 1/2 In. 10.00
Bowl, Scalloped, 8 In. 25.00

WHITE

Punch Cup 1.50
Punch Set, 14 Piece.........35.00

Sandwich Indiana

Another Sandwich pattern was made by the Indiana Glass Company, Dunkirk, Indiana, from the 1920s through the 1980s. Only the colors changed through the years. Amber was made from the late 1920s to the 1970s, crystal in the late 1920s to the 1980s, light green in the 1930s, pink in the late 1920s through the 1930s, red from 1933 to the 1970s, and teal blue in the 1950s. The scroll design varies with the size of the plate. In 1969 reproduction dinner sets were made in amber, blue, crystal, green, and red. Other items have been reproduced in amber and light green since 1982.

AMBER

Bowl, 4 1/4 In. ....3.00 To 4.00
Candleholder, 3 1/2 In., Pair..........................15.00
Decanter Set, Stopper, Tray, 10 Piece.....................50.00
Goblet, 9 Oz...... 8.00 To 12.00
Goblet, Wine, 4 Oz............. 8.00 To 12.00

CRYSTAL

Ashtray Set, 4 Piece........... 8.00 To 15.00
Ashtray, Club ....1.00 To 3.50
Bowl, 4 1/4 In. ....1.75 To 3.00
Butter.........................45.00
Creamer ....4.00 To 5.00
Cruet, Stopper, Individual..................32.50
Cup & Saucer ....2.50 To 6.00
Decanter, Stopper 55.00
Goblet, 9 Oz...... 9.00 To 12.00
Plate, 6 In. 2.00
Plate, 8 In. 1.75
Plate, 10 1/2 In. 8.00
Plate, 13 In.................... 5.50
Plate, Sandwich, 13 In. 12.00
Sandwich Server, Center Handle ....12.00 To 13.00
Saucer.......................... 1.50
Sherbet..............2.50 To 5.00
Sugar................3.50 To 4.00
Sugar & Creamer, Tray, Rectangular................15.00
Tumbler, Footed, 12 Oz....12.00

GREEN

Bowl, Mayonnaise, Footed.......................18.00
Plate, 8 In. 4.00

PINK

Decanter, Stopper 90.00

Sawtooth, see English Hobnail

Saxon, see Coronation

Scroll & Star, see Princess Feather

Shamrock, see Cloverleaf

Sharon

Sharon or Cabbage Rose was made by the Federal Glass Company from 1935 to 1939. The pattern was made in amber, crystal, green, and pink. A cheese dish was reproduced in 1976 in amber, blue, dark green, light green, and pink. Other items have been reproduced in various colors.

AMBER

Bowl, 8 1/2 In. ....3.00 To 3.50
Bowl, 10 1/2 In.......10.00 To 16.00
Bowl, Jam, 7 1/2 In.........20.00 To 23.00
Bowl, Oval, 9 1/2 In..........8.00 To 9.50
Butter, Cover ....35.00 To 38.00
Cake Plate...................20.00
Candy Container, Cover...........27.00 To 35.00

Cheese Dish, Cover 100.00
Creamer .... 4.00 To 6.00
Cup................... 5.00 To 7.00
Cup & Saucer ..... 6.00 To 15.00
Pitcher,
 Ice Lip.......... 75.00 To 95.00
Plate, 6 In.................... 1.75
Plate, 7 1/2 In.... 6.00 To 10.00
Plate, 9 1/2 In.... 7.00 To 13.00
Platter,
 12 1/2 In........ 7.50 To 11.00
Salt & Pepper .... 19.00 To 35.00
Saltshaker..................... 18.00
Saucer................ 3.00 To 8.50
Sherbet.............. 7.00 To 8.50
Soup, Cream ..... 15.00 To 17.00
Soup, Dish .... 20.00 To 32.50
Sugar................ 4.75 To 5.00
Sugar &
 Creamer......... 12.50 To 22.00
Tumbler,
 4 1/8 In......... 19.00 To 21.00
Tumbler, Footed,
 6 1/2 In.................... 65.00

GREEN

Bowl, 5 In........... 8.50 To 9.75
Bowl, 8 1/2 In. 18.00
Bowl,
 10 1/2 In....... 18.00 To 24.75
Bowl, Oval,
 9 1/2 In.......... 9.00 To 13.00
Butter, Cover 67.00
Candy Container,
 Cover...................... 125.00
Cup............................ 9.00
Cup & Saucer ..... 7.50 To 14.00
Dish, Jam..................... 30.00
Plate, 6 In. .... 4.00 To 5.50
Plate,
 7 1/2 In......... 11.00 To 12.50
Plate, 9 1/2 In.... 7.25 To 12.50
Platter,
 12 1/2 In........ 7.00 To 16.00
Salt & Pepper .... 39.00 To 55.00
Saltshaker..................... 22.00
Sherbet....................... 25.00
Soup, Cream ..... 25.00 To 27.50

PINK

Bowl, 5 In........... 5.00 To 7.00
Bowl, 6 In........ 12.00 To 18.00
Bowl,
 8 1/2 In......... 12.00 To 15.00

Bowl,
 10 1/2 In....... 15.00 To 20.00
Bowl, Oval,
 9 1/2 In......... 13.00 To 15.00
Butter, Cover .... 27.00 To 37.00
Cake Plate........ 17.00 To 25.00
Candy Container,
 Cover........... 25.00 To 35.00
Creamer .... 6.00 To 9.75
Cup................ 6.50 To 10.00
Cup & Saucer ..... 7.25 To 13.50
Pitcher,
 Ice Lip.......... 95.00 To 120.00
Plate, 6 In. .... 2.50 To 3.00
Plate, 7 1/2 In.............. 13.75
Plate, 9 1/2 In.... 9.00 To 12.00
Platter,
 12 1/2 In....... 10.00 To 14.00
Salt & Pepper .... 13.00 To 28.00
Saltshaker..................... 16.00
Saucer................ 3.00 To 4.50
Sherbet............ 7.50 To 13.00
Soup, Cream ..... 18.00 To 27.00
Soup, Dish .... 20.00 To 25.00
Sugar & Creamer, Cover ... 32.00
Sugar, Cover 29.00
Tumbler, Footed,
 6 1/2 In......... 29.00 To 35.00
Tumbler, Thick,
 4 1/8 In.................... 22.00
Tumbler, Thick,
 5 1/4 In.................... 32.00
Tumbler, Thin,
 4 1/8 In......... 19.00 To 23.00
Tumbler, Thin,
 5 1/4 In......... 28.00 To 29.00

Sheffield, see Chinex Classic

Shell, see Petalware

Shirley Temple

Shirley Temple is not really a pattern, but the dishes with the white enamel decoration picturing Shirley have become popular with collectors. The most famous were made as giveaways with cereal from 1934 to 1942. Companies, including Hazel-Atlas Glass Company and U.S. Glass, made the glassware. Sugars and creamers, bowls, plates, and mugs were made. The milk pitcher and mug have been reproduced since 1982 and the bowl has been reproduced since 1986. Other items with the Shirley Temple decal include Fostoria Mayfair green sugar bowl and tea cup, white mug, and a 8 7/8-inch Moderntone cobalt plate. In 1972 Libbey glass made 6 different sized tumblers.

BLUE

Bowl, Cereal ..... 42.50 To 45.00
Creamer .... 22.00 To 35.00
Mug............... 12.00 To 20.00
Plate......................... 275.00
Sugar.......................... 45.00

Sierra

Sierra, or Pinwheel, was made by Jeannette Glass Company from 1931 to 1933. It is found in green and pink.

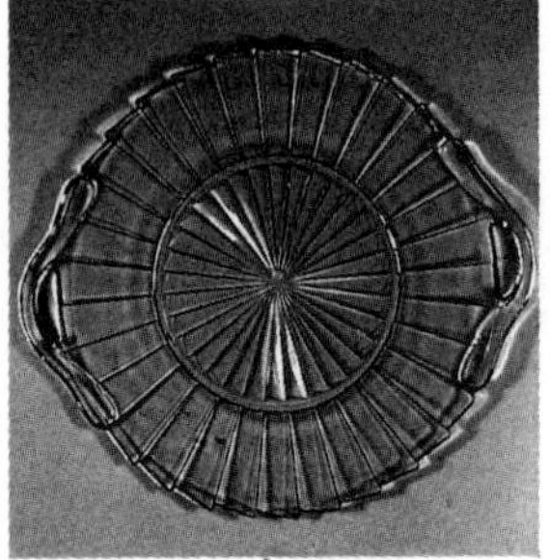

GREEN

Bowl, 5 1/2 In. .....5.50 To 7.50
Bowl, 8 1/2 In.........13.00 To 28.00
Butter, Cover ....39.50 To 57.50
Creamer 10.00
Cup & Saucer 11.00
Pitcher, 6 1/2 In.........65.00 To 75.00
Plate, 9 In. ....11.00 To 13.50
Plate, Cup & Saucer.........14.00
Plate, Salt & Pepper.........37.50
Plate, Tray, 2 Handles, 10 1/4 In. 12.50
Plate, Tumbler, Footed, 4 1/2 In.....................47.50
Salt & Pepper....15.00 To 25.00
Saucer................3.00 To 4.00
Sugar, Cover .....18.50 To 25.00
Tumbler, Footed, 4 1/2 In.........40.00 To 42.00

PINK

Bowl, 5 1/2 In. .....5.00 To 7.00
Bowl, 8 1/2 In......... 7.00 To 10.50
Bowl, Oval, 9 1/4 In. 22.00
Butter, Cover ....22.00 To 42.50
Creamer 7.00
Cup...................5.00 To 8.00
Cup & Saucer..... 8.00 To 11.50
Pitcher, 6 1/2 In.........42.50 To 55.00
Plate, 9 In. .... 8.00 To 10.00
Platter........................25.00

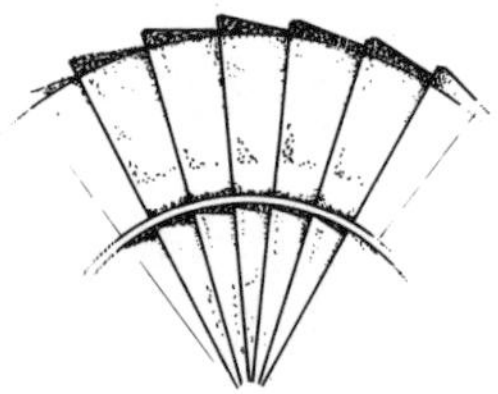

Platter, 11 In.................24.00
Salt & Pepper.... 18.00 To 33.00
Saltshaker.....................12.50
Saucer.......................... 3.50
Sugar, Cover 18.00
Tray, 2 Handles, 10 1/4 In. .... 8.00 To 15.00
Tumbler, Footed, 4 1/2 In.....................22.00

Smocking, see Windsor

Snowflake, see Doric

Spiral

It is easy to confuse Spiral and Twisted Optic patterns. Ask to be shown examples of each, because even a picture will not be much help. In general, the rule is that Twisted Optic spirals to the right, or counterclockwise; Spiral goes to the left, or clockwise. There are a few pieces that are exceptions. The spiral pattern was made from 1928 to 1930 in green and pink by Hocking Glass Company.

GREEN

Bowl, 4 3/4 In. 4.75
Bowl, 8 In..................... 8.00
Cup............................ 5.00
Cup & Saucer.......4.50 To 5.50

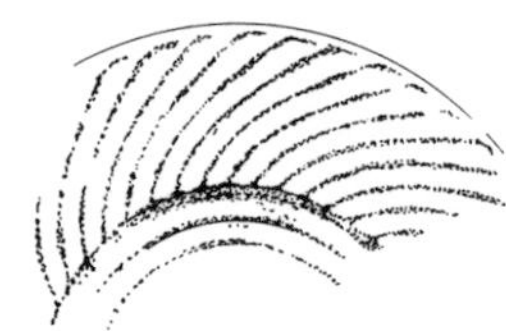

Ice Bucket........12.00 To 17.00
Jar, Jam, Cover 17.50
Pitcher, 7 5/8 In. 23.00
Plate, 6 In. 1.00
Plate, 8 In. ....2.00 To 3.00
Salt & Pepper................18.00
Sherbet..............2.50 To 5.00
Sugar & Creamer, Footed.......................17.50
Sugar, Footed ....8.00 To 9.00
Tumbler, 5 In. 5.00

PINK

Ice Bucket....................35.00
Sherbet..............2.75 To 5.00
Sugar, Footed 8.00

Spiral Flutes

Duncan and Miller Glass Company, Washington, Pennsylvania, made Spiral Flutes pattern. It was made of amber, crystal, and green glass in 1924, pink in 1926. A few pieces are reported with gold trim and in blue or vaseline-colored glass.

AMBER

Bowl, 2 In..................... 6.00
Bowl, 6 3/4 In. 6.00
Bowl, 8 1/2 In.........12.00 To 15.00
Compote, 6 5/8 In. 15.00
Creamer 7.50
Cup............................ 7.50
Cup & Saucer 10.00
Cup & Saucer, Demitasse...19.00
Plate, 6 In. ....3.00 To 3.50
Plate, 8 3/8 In......4.00 To 5.50
Sugar................6.00 To 8.00
Vase, 10 1/2 In. 22.00

GREEN

Bowl, 6 3/4 In. 6.00
Bowl, 7 1/2 In. 19.50
Bowl, 8 1/2 In. 17.50
Cruet, Stopper 225.00
Finger Bowl.................. 7.50
Plate, 8 3/8 In......6.50 To 8.50
Saucer......................... 2.00
Sherbet, 3 3/4 In............ 6.00
Sherbet, 4 3/4 In............ 9.00

Install large windows in your house—burglars avoid shattering them because of noise. Put up glass shelves, fill them with inexpensive, colorful bottles. A burglar would have to break everything, with accompanying noise, to get in.

Sugar 8.50
Tray, 2 Handles 25.00
Vase, 8 1/2 In. 14.00
Vase, 10 1/2 In. 30.00

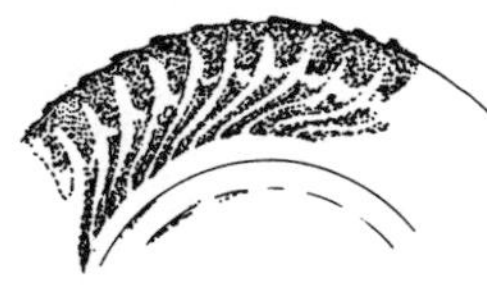

PINK

Plate, 7 1/2 In. 7.50
Sherbet, 4 3/4 In. 9.00

Spiral Optic, see Spiral

Spoke, see Patrician

Sportsman Series

Hazel-Atlas Glass Company made an unusual Depression glass pattern in the 1940s. It was made of cobalt blue, amethyst, or crystal with fired-on decoration. Although the name of the series was Sportsman, designs included golf, sailboats, hunting, angelfish, and a few strange choices like windmills. We list Windmill and White Ships separately, although they are sometimes considered part of this pattern.

BLUE & WHITE

Cocktail Shaker, Fish .... 20.00 To 22.00
Ice Bucket, Fish... 3.25 To 15.00
Tumbler, 3 3/4 In., Fish 7.50
Tumbler, 3 3/4 In., Hunter On Horse 7.50
Tumbler, 3 Oz., Horse's Head 8.00
Tumbler, 5 Oz., Fish 8.00
Tumbler, Juice, Golf .... 7.50 To 15.00
Tumbler, Skier, Roly Poly... 6.50

Square

Fire-King dinnerware by Anchor Hocking Glass Company, Lancaster, Ohio, was made in 5 patterns: Alice, Jane-Ray, Square, Swirl Fire-King, and Turquoise Blue. Square, named for its shape, was made in the 1940s-1960s and came in a variety of colors.

BLUE

Bowl, 4 3/4 In. 3.00
Cup 2.50
Plate 8 3/8 In. 2.75
Saucer .... .50

CRYSTAL

Bowl, 4 3/4 In. 3.50
Bowl, 7 3/8 In. 5.00
Cup 2.00
Saucer .... .50

JADITE

Bowl, 7 3/8 In. 5.00
Cup 2.00
Plate, 9 1/4 In. 3.00
Saucer .... .50

Starlight

Starlight was made by the Hazel-Atlas Company of Wheeling, West Virginia, in the 1930s. Full table settings were made of cobalt blue, crystal, pink, and white. The pattern is pressed, not etched.

COBALT BLUE

Bowl, 11 1/2 In. 40.00
Bowl, Handle, 8 1/2 In. ... 35.00

CRYSTAL

Bowl, 5 1/2 In. .....2.00 To 2.50
Bowl, 11 1/2 In. 10.50
Creamer .... 2.50 To 3.00
Cup 3.75
Cup & Saucer 5.50

Plate, 8 1/2 In......2.50 To 3.50
Plate, 9 In...........3.00 To 4.50
Salt & Pepper....12.00 To 22.00
Saltshaker.....................10.00
Saucer..........................1.25
Sherbet.........................7.50
Sugar & Creamer.............6.50

WHITE

Cup & Saucer.......2.00 To 3.50

Stippled, see Craquel

Stippled Rose Band, see S Pattern

Strawberry

Strawberry and Cherry–Berry are similar patterns. The U.S. Glass Company made this pattern in the early 1930s with strawberry decoration. It was made in crystal, green, pink, and iridescent marigold.

Strawberry, see also Cherry–Berry

CRYSTAL

Bowl, 4 In.....................5.00
Creamer, 4 5/8 In...........13.00
Sugar, Small...................7.00

GREEN

Bowl, 4 In.........8.50 To 10.00
Bowl, 7 1/2 In. 12.00
Butter,
Cover.........115.00 To 120.00
Pitcher,
7 3/4 In......105.00 To 115.00
Sherbet..............5.00 To 8.75
Sugar, Large..................12.00
Tumbler, 3 5/8 In. 19.00

PINK

Bowl, 4 In.....................9.00
Bowl,
7 1/2 In.........7.00 To 18.00
Compote,
5 3/4 In........16.00 To 18.00
Dish, Pickle..................35.00
Pitcher,
7 3/4 In........98.00 To 125.00
Plate, 6 In.....................5.00
Sherbet.........................6.00
Sugar, Small..................10.00
Tumbler,
3 5/8 In........20.00 To 22.50

Sunburst

Crystal dinner sets were made in Sunburst pattern from 1938 to 1941 by Jeannette Glass Company of Jeannette, Pennsylvania.

CRYSTAL

Candleholder,
2–Light............8.00 To 9.00
Cup............................3.50
Plate, 6 In.....................2.00
Plate, 8 1/2 In................3.00
Relish, Oval, 2 Sections......6.00
Sugar...........................5.00

Sunflower

Sunflower was made by Jeannette Glass Company, Jeannette, Pennsylvania, in the late 1920s and early 1930s. It is found in delphite, pink, and two shades of green.

GREEN

Ashtray...............5.50 To 7.50
Cake Plate.........7.00 To 10.00
Creamer..........10.00 To 12.50
Cup................7.50 To 10.00
Cup & Saucer................13.50
Plate, 9 In.........8.50 To 14.00
Sugar...............9.50 To 12.50
Sugar &
Creamer.........25.00 To 26.00
Tumbler, Footed,
4 3/4 In.........7.00 To 18.00

PINK

Ashtray...............5.00 To 6.00
Cake Plate...........7.00 To 9.00
Cup.............................8.00
Cup & Saucer....10.00 To 11.00
Plate, 9 In.....................8.50
Sugar...........................9.00
Sugar & Creamer............25.00
Tumbler, Footed,
4 3/4 In.........11.00 To 15.50

Swankyswigs

In October 1933, Kraft Cheese Company began to market cheese spreads in decorated, reusable glass tumblers. The tumbler was made in a 5–ounce size. It had a smooth beverage lip and a permanent color decoration. The designs were tested and changed as public demand indicated. Hazel–Atlas Glass Company made the glasses, which were decorated by hand by about 280 girls, working in shifts around the clock. In 1937 a silk screen process was developed and the Tulip design was made by this new, faster method. The glasses were made thinner and lighter in weight. The decorated Swankyswigs were discontinued from 1941 to 1946, the war years. They were made again in 1947 and were continued through 1958. Then plain glasses were used for most of the cheese, although a few specially decorated Swankyswigs have been made since that time.

Antique, Black ...... 1.25 To 3.00
Antique, Blue .... 1.25 To 3.00
Antique, Brown ..... 1.25 To 3.00
Antique, Green ..... 1.25 To 3.00
Band No.1, Red & Black 2.50
Band No.2, Black & Red .... 2.00 To 4.00
Band No.3, Blue & White 3.00
Bustlin' Betsy, Blue .... 1.25 To 1.75
Bustlin' Betsy, Brown 1.75
Bustlin' Betsy, Green .... 1.50 To 2.50
Bustlin' Betsy, Orange .... 1.50 To 2.00
Bustlin' Betsy, Red .... 1.25 To 1.75
Bustlin' Betsy, Yellow .... 1.25 To 1.50
Centennial, Texas, Blue 25.00
Checkerboard, Blue 15.00
Circle & Dot, Black .... 2.50 To 5.00
Circle & Dot, Blue .... 3.00 To 4.00
Circle & Dot, Green .... 2.50 To 3.50
Circle & Dot, Red .... 2.50 To 3.50
Kiddie Cup, Black .... 1.25 To 1.50
Kiddie Cup, Blue ... 1.25 To 2.00
Kiddie Cup, Green .... 1.25 To 2.00
Kiddie Cup, Orange .... 1.75 To 2.00
Kiddie Cup, Red 1.75
Posy Cornflower No.1, Light Blue 2.00
Posy Cornflower No.2, Dark Blue 2.00
Posy Cornflower No.2, Red 2.00
Posy Cornflower No.2, Yellow 2.00
Posy Forget-Me-Not, Black 2.00
Posy Forget-Me-Not, Blue .... 2.50 To 3.00
Posy Forget-Me-Not, Dark Blue .... 1.25 To 3.00
Posy Forget-Me-Not, Red .... 1.50 To 3.00
Posy Forget-Me-Not, Yellow .... 1.25 To 3.00
Posy Jonquil, Yellow .... 2.00 To 2.50
Posy Tulip, Red 1.75
Posy Violet, Green 2.50
Sailboat No.1, Blue .... 8.50 To 10.00
Sailboat No.2, Blue .... 8.00 To 12.00
Sailboat No.2, Green .... 8.00 To 12.00
Star, Black 2.50
Star, Blue .... 2.50 To 3.00
Star, Green .... 2.50 To 3.00
Star, Red 2.50
Tulip No.1, Blue 6.00
Tulip No.1, Green .... 2.75 To 3.00
Tulip No.1, Red .... 2.00 To 3.00
Tulip No.2, Green 2.00
Tulip No.3, Blue ... 2.00 To 2.25
Tulip No.3, Red .... 2.00 To 3.00
Tulip No.3, Yellow .... 2.00 To 2.50
Tulip, Red 2.50
Tulip, Yellow 1.50

Sweet Pear, see Avocado

Swirl

Swirl, sometimes called Double Swirl or Petal Swirl, was made by Jeannette Glass Company during 1937 and 1938. It was made of amber, delphite, ice blue, pink, and a green-blue color called ultramarine.

DELPHITE

Bowl, 5 1/4 In. 4.75
Bowl, 9 In. 10.00

PINK

Bowl, 5 1/4 In. .... 3.00 To 4.50
Bowl, 9 In. 8.00
Butter, Cover 90.00
Candy Container, Cover 39.00
Creamer 7.00
Cup & Saucer 5.50
Salt & Pepper 35.00
Saucer 1.50
Sugar & Creamer 12.00

ULTRAMARINE

Bowl, 5 1/4 In. .... 5.00 To 8.00
Bowl, 9 In. .... 11.00 To 15.00
Bowl, Closed Handle, Footed, 10 In. .... 14.00 To 18.00
Candlestick, 2-Light, Pair .... 15.00 To 25.00
Candy Container, 3-Footed .... 8.00 To 8.50
Coaster .... 5.00 To 5.25
Creamer .... 6.00 To 9.00
Cup .... 5.00 To 8.00
Cup & Saucer ..... 7.50 To 10.00
Plate, 6 1/2 In. ..... 2.00 To 6.00
Plate, 7 1/4 In. ..... 5.00 To 6.00
Plate, 8 In. 8.00
Plate, 9 1/4 In. .... 6.50 To 10.00
Plate, 9 1/2 In. ..... 8.00 To 9.00
Plate, Sandwich, 12 1/2 In. .... 9.50 To 12.00
Salt & Pepper .... 18.00 To 24.00
Saltshaker 9.00
Saucer .... 1.00 To 3.00
Sherbet .... 5.50 To 11.00
Sugar .... 7.00 To 8.00
Sugar & Creamer .... 11.00 To 15.00
Tumbler, 4 In. 14.00
Tumbler, Footed, 9 Oz. 18.00

Vase, Footed, 6 1/2 In. 15.00
Vase, Footed,
8 1/2 In. .... 9.00 To 18.00

Swirl Fire-King

Swirl Fire-King is named for its wide swirled border. It was made in blue, jadite, pink, white with gold trim, and ivory with trim from 1955 to the 1960s. Other related sections in this book are Alice, Fire-King, Jane-Ray, Square, and Turquoise Blue.

BLUE

Creamer 2.50
Plate, 7 In. 2.25
Plate, 9 In. 2.50

IVORY

Bowl, 5 In. 1.50
Creamer, Red Trim 3.00

JADITE

Bowl Set, 4 Piece 15.00
Bowl, 8 1/2 In. 5.50

PINK

Creamer 2.50
Cup & Saucer 2.50
Plate, 7 1/2 In. 2.25

WHITE

Cup & Saucer 2.00
Plate, 10 In. 2.00
Soup, Dish 2.00

Swirled Big Rib, see Spiral

Swirled Sharp Rib, see Diana

Sylvan

Sylvan is often called Parrot or Three Parrot because of the center pattern on the plates. It was

made by Federal Glass Company in 1931 and 1932 in amber, blue, crystal, and green.

AMBER

Cup & Saucer 28.00
Plate, 9 In. 26.00
Plate, Grill .... 12.00 To 14.00
Platter, 11 1/4 In. 35.00
Sherbet .... 9.50 To 10.00
Tumbler, 5 1/2 In. 125.00

CRYSTAL

Plate, 5 3/4 In. 13.00

GREEN

Bowl, 8 In. .... 30.00 To 45.00
Bowl, Oval,
10 In. .... 30.00 To 33.00
Creamer .... 17.00 To 18.00
Cup .... 18.00 To 21.00
Cup & Saucer 35.00
Plate, 7 1/2 In. 13.75
Plate, 9 In. .... 21.00 To 27.00
Plate, Grill 18.50
Platter,
11 1/4 In. ...... 20.00 To 27.00
Salt &
Pepper .... 210.00 To 215.00
Sherbet 12.50
Sugar 20.00
Sugar & Creamer 25.00
Sugar, Cover .... 60.00 To 100.00

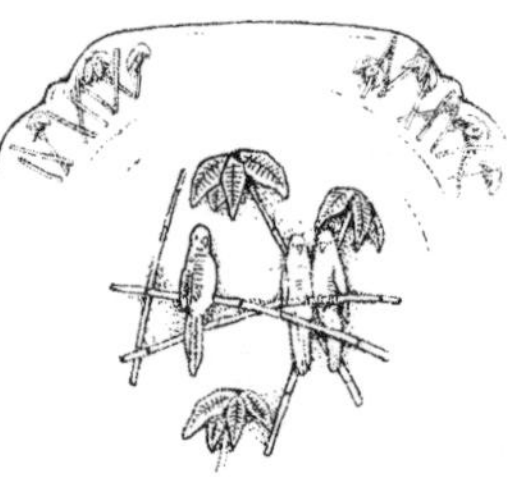

Tumbler, 4 1/2 In. 95.00
Tumbler,
5 1/2 In. .... 75.00 To 90.00
Tumbler, Footed,
5 3/4 In. .... 95.00 To 100.00

T

Tea Room

The very Art Deco design of Tea Room has made it popular with a group of collectors; it is even called Moderne Art by some. The Indiana Glass Company, Dunkirk, Indiana, made it from 1926 to 1931. Dinner sets were made of amber, crystal, green, and pink glass.

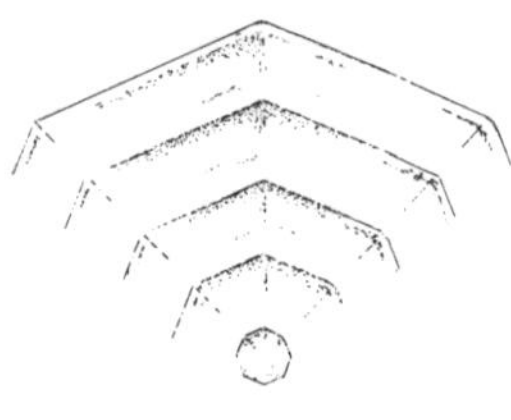

CRYSTAL

Bowl, Ruffled, 9 In. 18.00
Dish, Sundae, Footed 21.00
Mustard, Cover 40.00
Relish, 2 Sections 9.00
Salt & Pepper 38.00
Sherbet, Low, Footed 18.00

GREEN

Bowl, Vegetable, Oval,
9 In. .... 38.00 To 45.00
Candleholder, Pair 50.00
Celery, 8 1/2 In. 22.00
Creamer 13.50
Creamer, Footed,
4 1/2 In. 12.50
Cup 25.00
Cup & Saucer 48.00
Dish, Sundae,
Footed .... 60.00 To 85.00
Goblet, 9 Oz. .... 50.00 To 65.00

Ice Bucket........42.50 To 65.00
Parfait........................55.00
Pitcher, 64 Oz. 180.00
Plate, 6 1/2 In..............12.00
Plate,
8 1/4 In.........30.00 To 35.00
Relish,
2 Sections.......13.00 To 15.00
Salt & Pepper................65.00
Saucer.........................16.00
Sherbet, Flared...............20.00
Sherbet, Low, Footed 16.00
Sherbet, Tall, Footed........35.00
Sugar & Creamer, Tray,
3 1/2 In.....................52.00
Sugar, 4 In. ......10.00 To 12.00
Sugar, Footed,
4 1/2 In.........12.50 To 15.00
Tumbler, Footed,
12 Oz...........30.00 To 37.00
Vase, Ruffled,
11 In...........85.00 To 100.00

PINK

Banana Boat, Flat,
7 1/2 In.................. 110.00
Bowl, Vegetable, Oval,
9 1/2 In.........35.00 To 45.00
Candleholder.................14.00
Creamer, Footed,
4 1/2 In.....................10.00
Cup & Saucer................40.00
Dish, Sundae, Footed 18.00
Goblet, 9 Oz.................60.00
Ice Bucket........42.00 To 55.00
Lamp, 9 In....................37.50
Mustard, Cover 110.00
Pitcher, 64 Oz. 75.00
Plate, 2 Handles,
10 1/2 In..................60.00
Plate, 8 In...................25.00
Saltshaker.....................13.00
Sugar &
Creamer.........20.00 To 24.00
Sugar & Creamer, Tray,
3 1/2 In.........25.00 To 37.50
Sugar, Footed, 4 1/2 In. 9.00
Tray, Center Handle...... 105.00
Tray, For Sugar & Creamer,
Oval 45.00
Tumbler, Flat,
8 1/2 Oz................. 100.00
Tumbler, Footed,
9 Oz............15.00 To 20.00
Vase, Ruffled, 6 1/2 In.....45.00
Vase, Straight, 11 In. 60.00

Tear Drop

Tear Drop, a pattern available in full dinnerware sets, was made by Duncan and Miller Glass Company, Washington, Pennsylvania, from 1934 to 1955. It was made only in crystal.

CRYSTAL

Ashtray, 3 In. ....3.50 To 4.50
Bonbon, 4 Handles,
6 In.............. 7.00 To 13.00
Bowl, 2 Handles, 5 In. 6.50
Bowl, 5 In.................... 5.00
Bowl, Flared, 11 1/2 In....25.00
Butter, Silver-Plated Cover,
1/4 Lb.......................18.00
Candleholder, 4 In., Pair...18.00
Candy Container, Heart Shape,
7 1/2 In.........10.50 To 16.00
Celery, 3 Sections, 12 In. 18.00
Champagne, 5 In. 8.50
Cocktail, Oyster,
2 3/4 In.......... 8.00 To 12.00
Cruet, Stopper 12.00
Cup............................ 7.00
Cup & Saucer, Tea 6.00
Dish, Mayonnaise, 2 Sections,
3 Piece 20.00
Dish, Nut,
2 Sections........ 6.00 To 12.00
Dish, Olive, 2 Sections,
6 In.............. 6.50 To 10.00
Dish, Pickle, 6 In............10.00
Goblet, 5 5/8 In. 9.00
Goblet, 7 In......11.00 To 13.00
Mustard, Cover 12.00
Pitcher, 5 In..................38.00
Pitcher, Amber Handle,
8 1/2 In.....................95.00
Plate, 2 Handles, 11 In.....22.00
Plate, 4 Handles, 7 In. 7.00
Plate, 7 1/2 In............... 4.75
Plate, Cheese & Cracker,
11 In.........................30.00
Relish, 2 Sections, Handle,
7 In..........................10.00
Relish, 2 Sections, Heart Shape,
7 1/2 In.......... 9.50 To 14.00
Relish, 3 Sections,
9 In............15.00 To 18.00
Relish, 3 Sections,
12 In............15.00 To 20.00
Relish, 5 Sections, 12 In....25.00
Sherbet,
3 1/2 In.......... 6.00 To 12.00
Sugar & Creamer, 3 Oz...... 9.00
Sugar & Creamer, 8 Oz.....15.00
Tumbler,
3 1/4 In.......... 8.00 To 10.00
Tumbler, 4 1/2 In. 7.50
Tumbler, 5 1/4 In. 14.00
Tumbler, Juice,
3 1/2 In.....................10.00
Tumbler, Juice, Footed,
4 In........................... 8.00
Vase, Fan, Footed, 9 In.....60.00
Wine,
4 3/4 In.........18.00 To 25.00

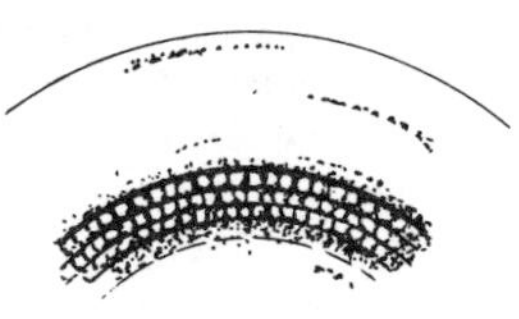

Thistle

Thistle pattern was made by Macbeth–Evans Glass Company from 1929 to 1930. The pattern pictured large thistles on green, crystal, pink, and yellow dishes.

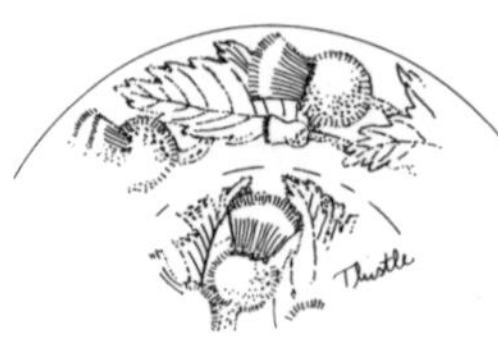

CRYSTAL

Bowl, 5 1/2 In. 6.00
Plate, 8 In. 14.75

GREEN

Bowl, 10 1/4 In. 100.00
Cake Plate, 13 In. 50.00
Cup & Saucer .... 15.00 To 27.00
Plate, 8 In. .... 6.00 To 8.00
Plate, Grill, 10 1/4 In. 10.00

PINK

Bowl, 5 1/2 In. 10.00
Plate, 8 In. .... 2.50 To 6.00

Threading, see Old English

Three Parrot, see Sylvan

Thumbprint, see Pear Optic

Tiered Octagon, see Octagon

Tradition

Imperial Glass Company of Bellaire, Ohio, made Tradition pattern glass in the 1930s. It was made in amber, amethyst, blue, crystal, green, pink, and red.

AMBER

Goblet, 5 1/2 In. 9.50
Sherbet 8.00
Tumbler, 12 Oz. 7.50

AMETHYST

Tumbler, Juice, Footed 7.50

BLUE

Bowl, 4 1/2 In. 9.50
Goblet,
5 1/2 In. .... 8.50 To 15.00

Pitcher, Water 95.00
Plate, 10 1/2 In. 9.50
Sherbet 9.50
Tumbler,
12 Oz. .... 10.00 To 15.00

BROWN

Sherbet 5.00

CRYSTAL

Goblet, 5 1/2 In. 9.50
Relish, 2 Sections 15.00
Sherbet 5.00

GREEN

Bowl, 4 1/2 In. 9.50
Butter, Cover 45.00
Goblet,
5 1/2 In. .... 9.00 To 14.00
Jar, Jam, Cover 45.00
Sherbet .... 9.50 To 12.00
Tray, Muffin 48.00
Tumbler, 4 1/4 In. 14.00
Tumbler, Juice, Footed 14.00
Wine 9.00

PINK

Salt & Pepper 65.00
Sherbet 15.00
Wine 20.00

Protect your home and antiques from theft. Use a timer on your lights at all times, even when you are at home. This will set a pattern of certain lights going on and off each day. When you are away, the house will appear to have normal activity. If possible, when you are away, park a car near the front of the house. The car will block your driveway so a burglar cannot load up through your garage. Have someone keep your trash cans filled. This will help to make the house look occupied. Keep the grass mowed. Stop your mail and paper deliveries.

RED

Goblet, 5 1/2 In. 10.00
Tumbler, 12 Oz. 12.50

Trojan

The Fostoria Glass Company made Trojan. The etched glass dishes were made in rose from 1929 to 1935, topaz from 1929 to 1938, and gold tint from 1938 to 1944. Crystal bases were used on some pieces from 1931 to 1944.

GREEN

Candy Container, Cover, 1/2 Lb. 95.00
Goblet, 8 1/4 In. 21.00

PINK

Champagne, 6 In. 38.00
Creamer 27.50
Goblet, 8 1/4 In. .... 32.00 To 40.00
Plate, 6 In. 6.00
Sherbet, 6 In. 18.00
Soup, Cream 24.00
Sugar 27.50
Vase, 8 In. 175.00

YELLOW

Bonbon 29.50
Bowl, 5 In. .... 17.50 To 17.50
Bowl, 6 In. 25.00
Bowl, 6 1/2 In. 21.00
Bowl, 12 In. 35.00
Bowl, 2 Handles, 9 In. 45.00
Bowl, Lemon, 2 Handles ... 19.00
Candleholder, 3 1/4 In., Pair 45.00
Candy Container, Cover, 1/2 Lb. 150.00
Celery, 11 1/2 In. .... 30.00 To 32.50
Chop Plate, 13 1/2 In. 55.00
Compote, 6 In. 35.00
Creamer .... 14.00 To 24.00
Cup 10.00
Cup & Saucer .... 12.00 To 20.00
Cup & Saucer, Demitasse ... 49.50
Decanter 475.00

Dish, Sweetmeat 25.00
Finger Bowl ...... 22.00 To 29.50
Goblet, Cordial, 4 In. .... 40.00 To 55.00
Goblet, Water, 8 1/4 In. ... 18.00
Goblet, Wine, 5 1/2 In. 30.00
Ice Bucket .... 65.00 To 67.50
Mayonnaise Set, 3 Piece 95.00
Parfait .... 21.00 To 35.00
Pitcher, Water 225.00
Plate, 6 In. .... 3.00 To 6.00
Plate, 7 In. 4.50
Plate, 7 1/2 In. ...... 4.50 To 7.50
Plate, 8 3/4 In. ...... 6.00 To 9.50
Plate, 9 1/2 In. .... 9.00 To 17.50
Plate, 10 1/2 In. 27.00
Plate, 13 3/4 In. 45.00
Relish, 2 Sections 35.00
Relish, 3 Sections 24.00
Salt & Pepper 75.00
Sauce 67.50

Sherbet, 4 1/4 In. .... 10.00 To 14.00
Sherbet, 6 In. .... 13.50 To 18.00
Soup, Cream 17.50
Sugar .... 14.00 To 24.00
Sugar & Creamer 15.00
Sugar & Creamer, Footed 32.00
Tray, Center Handle, 11 In. 32.00
Tray, Plate, 10 1/4 In. 35.00
Tumbler, Footed, 5 1/4 In. 16.00
Tumbler, Footed, 6 In. 22.00

Turquoise Blue

Turquoise Blue, one of the patterns made by Anchor Hocking Glass Company, is a plain pattern named for its color. It was made in the 1950s. Related sections in this book are Alice, Fire-King, Jadite, Jane-Ray, Square, and Swirl Fire-King.

Bowl, 4 1/2 In. 2.25
Bowl, 5 In. 4.00
Bowl, 8 1/4 In. 5.75
Bowl, Mixing, 1 Qt. 4.00
Creamer .... 3.00 To 3.50
Cup & Saucer .... 1.50 To 2.00
Mug .... 10.00 To 15.00
Plate, 7 In. 2.50
Plate, 6 7/8 In. 2.75
Plate, 9 1/8 In. 2.25
Relish, 3 Sections 6.50
Sugar 3.50
Sugar & Creamer 5.25

Twisted Optic

Twisted Optic is the pattern sometimes confused with Spiral. Be sure to look at the information about that pattern. Imperial Glass Company made Twisted Optic from 1927 to 1930 in amber, blue, canary yellow, green, and pink.

AMBER

Candleholder, 3 In., Pair .... 9.00 To 10.00
Plate, 6 In. .... 1.00 To 4.00
Plate, Oval, 9 In. 3.50

BLUE

Creamer 4.25

GREEN

Candleholder, 3 In., Pair .... 10.00 To 12.00

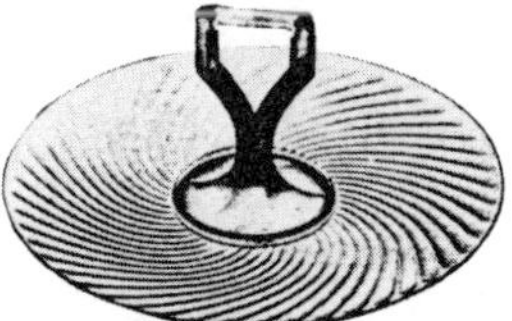

Candy Container, Cover 15.00
Creamer 4.25
Plate, 8 In. .... 2.00 To 3.50
Sugar 4.25

PINK

Candy Container, Cover 28.00
Cup .... 2.50 To 4.00
Plate, 8 In. .... 2.00 To 3.50
Sherbet .... 4.00 To 4.75
Sugar .... 4.00 To 4.50

YELLOW

Candy Container, Cover 35.00
Plate, 8 In. .... 3.00 To 3.50
Sherbet 6.00

U.S. Octagon, see Octagon

Vernon, see No. 616

Versailles

Versailles by Fostoria Glass Company was made in many colors during the years of production, 1928 to 1944. Azure, green, and rose were made from 1928 to 1944, topaz from 1929 to 1938, gold tint from 1938 to 1944. Crystal bases were used with colored glass from 1931 to 1944.

AMBER

Bowl, 5 In. 18.00

AZURE

Ashtray 55.00
Bowl, 5 In. 29.50
Bowl, 12 In. 45.00
Candleholder, 3 In., Pair 55.00
Candleholder, 5 In. 37.50
Celery, 11 1/2 In. 70.00
Champagne, 6 In. .... 37.50 To 65.00
Chop Plate, 13 1/2 In. 85.00
Compote, 7 In. 65.00
Creamer 32.50
Cup & Saucer 35.00
Cup & Saucer, Demitasse 75.00
Finger Bowl .... 30.00 To 32.50
Goblet, 5 1/4 In. 29.50
Goblet, 8 1/4 In. 45.00
Ice Bucket, Tongs 125.00
Oyster Cocktail 38.00
Parfait, 5 1/4 In. 65.00
Plate, 6 In. 8.50
Plate, 7 1/2 In. .... 8.00 To 12.50
Plate, 8 3/4 In. 15.00
Plate, 10 1/4 In. 65.00
Saucer 9.50
Sherbet 25.00
Sugar 32.50
Tumbler, Footed, 5 1/4 In. 29.50
Tumbler, Footed, 6 In. .... 27.50 To 37.50
Vase, Fan, 8 1/2 In. 225.00
Wine, 5 1/2 In. 50.00

BLUE

Cup & Saucer 27.50
Tumbler, Footed, 6 In. 24.00

GREEN

Ashtray 45.00
Bonbon .... 20.00 To 35.00
Bowl, 5 In. 22.50
Bowl, 12 In. 45.00
Bowl, Baker, 9 In. 65.00
Cake Plate 35.00
Candleholder, 2 In., Pair .... 37.50 To 40.00
Candy Container, 3 Sections, Cover 60.00
Cheese & Cracker Set, 11 In. 85.00
Claret, 6 In. 45.00
Cordial, 4 In. 60.00
Cup & Saucer 20.00
Cup & Saucer, Demitasse 45.00
Finger Bowl 29.50
Goblet, 5 1/4 In. 35.00
Goblet, 8 1/4 In. 28.00
Parfait 40.00
Pitcher, Water 350.00
Plate, 6 In. 4.50
Plate, 7 1/2 In. .... 6.00 To 6.50
Plate, 8 3/4 In. 9.50
Plate, 9 1/2 In. 22.50
Platter, 12 In. 65.00
Salt & Pepper 120.00
Sauce 175.00
Sherbet, 4 1/4 In. 18.00
Soup, Cream 39.50
Soup, Dish 39.50
Sugar & Creamer, Cover 175.00
Sugar & Creamer, Demitasse 95.00
Sugar Pail 150.00
Tumbler, Footed, 5 1/4 In. 20.00
Tumbler, Footed, 6 In. 27.50
Vase, 8 In. 175.00
Vase, Fan, 8 1/2 In. 175.00

PINK

Ashtray 45.00
Bowl, 5 In. .... 15.00 To 22.50
Bowl, Baker, 9 In. 65.00
Bowl, Grapefruit 125.00
Bowl, Lemon 22.00
Candleholder, 3 In., Pair 32.00
Candy Container, Cover 125.00
Cheese & Cracker, 11 In. 85.00
Claret, 6 In. 45.00
Creamer 25.00
Cup & Saucer .... 16.00 To 20.00
Cup & Saucer, Demitasse 45.00
Finger Bowl 29.50
Goblet, 5 1/4 In. .... 24.50 To 35.00
Parfait .... 32.00 To 40.00
Pitcher 350.00

Plate, 6 In. 4.50
Plate, 7 1/2 In...... 6.00 To 6.50
Plate, 8 3/4 In................ 9.50
Plate, 9 1/2 In............... 10.00
Plate, 10 1/4 In. 49.50
Platter, 12 In................ 65.00
Salt & Pepper 126.00
Sauce....................... 175.00
Saucer.......................... 3.00
Sherbet, 4 1/4 In............ 18.00
Soup, Cream 39.50
Soup, Dish 39.50
Sugar & Creamer,
Cover...................... 175.00
Sugar Pail 150.00
Sugar, Cover 95.00
Tumbler, Footed,
5 1/4 In..................... 20.00
Tumbler, Footed,
6 In............. 15.00 To 25.00
Vase, 8 In. 175.00
Vase, Fan, 8 1/2 In. 175.00

TOPAZ

Bowl, 5 In.................... 18.00
Bowl, 12 In. 35.00
Bowl, Grapefruit............ 65.00
Bowl, Lemon..... 12.50 To 19.50
Celery,
11 1/2 In....... 39.50 To 48.00
Claret, 6 In................... 45.00
Compote, 6 In. 45.00
Cordial, 4 In. 60.00
Creamer .... 23.00 To 27.50
Cup........................... 12.00
Cup & Saucer 25.00
Finger Bowl.................. 20.00
Goblet, 5 1/4 In. 28.00
Goblet,
8 1/4 In......... 18.00 To 25.00
Ice Bucket.................... 95.00
Mayonnaise, 3 Piece 110.00
Plate, 2 Handles, 10 In..... 32.00
Plate, 6 In. 5.00
Plate, 7 1/2 In................ 7.50
Plate, 8 3/4 In...... 9.00 To 9.50
Platter, Oval, 12 In.......... 35.00
Salt & Pepper 120.00
Sherbet....................... 15.00
Sherbet, 4 1/4 In........... 18.00
Soup, Cream ..... 16.00 To 18.00
Sugar......................... 27.50
Sugar & Creamer 25.00
Tumbler, Footed,
6 In............. 20.00 To 27.50
Wine, 5 1/2 In. 45.00

YELLOW

Bowl, Lemon................ 19.50
Finger Bowl.................. 24.00

Vertical Ribbed, see Queen Mary

Vesper

Vesper was made by the Fostoria Glass Company of Ohio and West Virginia, from 1926 to 1934. Dinner sets were made in amber, crystal, green, and blue.

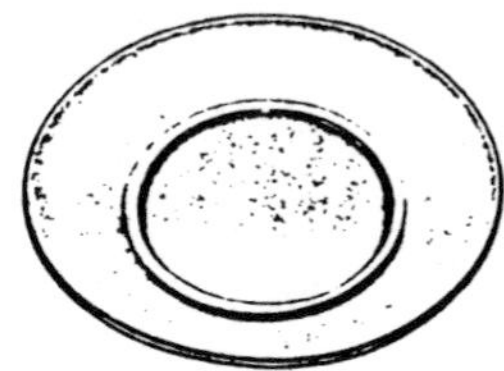

AMBER

Cup & Saucer 12.00
Goblet, 7 1/2 In. 25.00
Ice Bucket, Bail............. 75.00
Pitcher, 8 1/2 In. 8.00
Plate, 8 1/2 In................ 6.00
Sherbet....................... 18.00

BLUE

Berry Bowl, 5 1/2 In....... 15.00
Vase, 8 In. 125.00

GREEN

Bowl, 5 1/2 In. 9.75
Cup........................... 12.00
Ice Bucket.................... 40.00
Plate, 6 In. 5.00
Platter, 12 In................. 35.00
Soup, Cream 8.00

Victory

The Diamond Glass-Ware Company, Indiana, Pennsylvania, made Victory pattern from 1929 to 1932. It is known in amber, black, cobalt blue, green, and pink. A few pieces have gold trim.

AMBER

Bowl, 6 1/2 In. 8.00
Bowl, 12 In. 22.00
Candleholder, Pair........... 18.00
Compote, 6 In. 15.00
Creamer .... 4.00 To 12.00
Cup & Saucer ..... 4.50 To 10.00
Plate, 6 In. .... 2.00 To 2.50
Plate, 8 In. 4.00

Plate, 9 In. 12.50
Sandwich Server, Center
Handle .... 15.00 To 16.00
Saucer.......................... 1.75
Sugar............................ 8.00
Sugar & Creamer 16.00

BLACK

Sugar & Creamer 48.00

COBALT

Cup........................... 10.00

GREEN

Bowl, 6 1/2 In. 8.00
Cup............................ 6.00
Cup & Saucer .... 4.50 To 6.00
Plate, 8 In. .... 2.00 To 7.00
Plate, 9 In. 11.00
Sandwich Server, Center
Handle .... 15.00 To 23.00

Saucer 4.00
Sugar & Creamer 10.00

PINK

Bowl, 6 1/2 In. 7.50
Compote, Gold Edge, 6 In. 15.00
Creamer .... 7.00 To 15.00
Cup & Saucer .... 6.00 To 7.00
Plate, 7 In. .... 3.00 To 5.00
Plate, 9 In. 12.50
Sandwich Server, Center Handle .... 18.50 To 24.00
Saucer 2.00

Vitrock

Vitrock is both a kitchenware and a dinnerware pattern. It has a raised flowered rim and so is often called Floral Rim or Flower Rim by collectors. It was made by Hocking Glass Company from 1934 to 1937. It was made of white with fired-on colors, solid red, green, and decal-decorated centers.

WHITE

Bowl, 4 In. .... 3.00 To 3.25
Bowl, 7 1/2 In. .... 3.00 To 4.00
Creamer .... 2.50 To 5.00
Cup .... 2.00 To 3.00
Cup & Saucer .... 3.00 To 3.75
Plate, 7 1/4 In. 2.00
Plate, 10 In. 3.50
Platter, 12 In. 13.00
Salt & Pepper 8.00
Soup, Cream 8.00
Sugar .... 2.50 To 5.00
Sugar & Creamer .... 5.00 To 6.00

Vivid Bands, see Petalware

W

Waffle, see Waterford

Waterford

Waterford, or Waffle, pattern was made by Anchor Hocking Glass Company from 1938 to 1944. It was made in crystal, pink, yellow, and white. In the 1950s some forest green pieces were made.

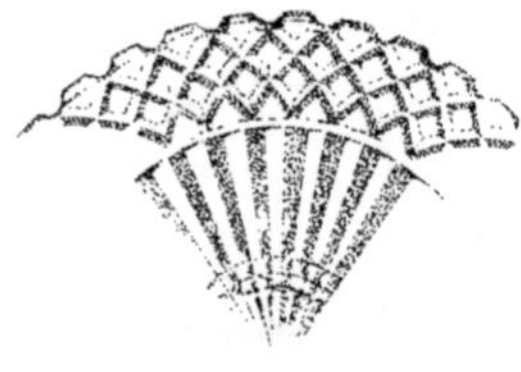

CRYSTAL

Ashtray .... 2.50 To 3.50
Bowl, 4 3/4 In. .... 3.00 To 4.00
Bowl, 5 1/2 In. .... 6.00 To 7.50
Bowl, 8 1/4 In. .... 4.50 To 7.00
Butter, Cover .... 12.00 To 15.00
Cake Plate .... 4.50 To 6.00
Cake Plate, 10 1/4 In. 3.50
Coaster, 4 In. 3.00
Creamer .... 2.00 To 4.50
Cup & Saucer .... 4.00 To 6.50
Goblet, 5 1/4 In. 8.00
Pitcher, 42 Oz. .... 12.00 To 17.50
Pitcher, 80 Oz. .... 18.00 To 21.50
Plate, 6 In. .... 1.25 To 1.75
Plate, 7 1/8 In. .... 1.00 To 3.00
Plate, 9 5/8 In. .... 3.50 To 5.50
Plate, 13 3/4 In. .... 7.50 To 10.00
Relish, 5 Sections .... 10.00 To 15.00
Salt & Pepper .... 4.00 To 6.00
Saltshaker 2.75
Sherbet .... 2.00 To 3.50
Sugar & Creamer, Cover .... 6.50 To 7.50
Sugar, Cover .... 5.00 To 7.00
Tumbler, Footed, 4 7/8 In. .... 5.50 To 8.50

GREEN

Coaster 10.00

PINK

Ashtray 27.50
Bowl, 4 3/4 In. .... 6.00 To 8.50
Bowl, 8 1/4 In. 10.00
Cake Plate, 10 1/4 In. 6.50
Cup 5.00
Cup & Saucer 10.50
Plate, 7 1/8 In. .... 3.00 To 4.50
Plate, 9 5/8 In. .... 8.50 To 12.50
Sandwich Server, 13 3/4 In. .... 18.00 To 20.00
Saucer .... 2.50 To 4.00
Sherbet .... 6.50 To 7.00
Sugar & Creamer 22.00
Tumbler, Footed, 4 7/8 In. .... 10.00 To 12.00

Wedding Band, see Moderntone

Westmoreland Sandwich, see Princess Feather

White Sail, see White Ship

White Ship

White Ship, also called Sailing Ship, Sail Boat or White Sail, is really part of the Sportsman series made by Hazel-Atlas in 1938. The ships are enamel decorations on cobalt blue glass.

BLUE

Cocktail Shaker .... 14.00 To 25.00
Ice Bowl .... 15.00 To 25.00
Pitcher, Ice Lip, 36 Oz. 45.00
Pitcher, Large 45.00
Plate, 5 7/8 In. 16.00
Plate, 6 In. 16.00
Plate, 8 In. 19.00
Plate, 9 In. 15.00

Roly Poly 6.00
Tumbler, 3 3/4 In. .... 5.50 To 8.00
Tumbler, 4 5/8 In. .... 7.00 To 8.00
Tumbler, Old Fashioned, 3 3/8 In. 4.75
Tumbler, Roly Poly .... 6.00 To 7.50
Tumbler, Water, Straight, 3 3/4 In. 8.00
Tumbler, Whiskey 80.00

Wildflower, see No. 618

Wildrose, see Dogwood

Wildrose With Apple Blossom, see Flower Garden with Butterflies

Windmill

Windmill, or Dutch, is also a part of the Sportsman series made by Hazel-Atlas in 1938. Of course it pictures a landscape with a windmill.

BLUE

Bowl, Mixing 12.00
Cocktail Shaker 30.00
Tumbler, Juice, 3 3/4 In. ... 8.50
Tumbler, Roly Poly 6.50

Windsor

Windsor pattern, also called Diamond, Smocking, or Windsor Diamond, was made by Jeannette Glass Company, Jeannette, Pennsylvania, from 1936 to 1946. The pattern is most easily found in crystal, green, and pink, although pieces were made of amberina, blue, delphite, and red.

CRYSTAL

Ashtray 25.00
Bowl, Pointed Edge, 8 In. 10.50
Butter, Cover .... 13.00 To 20.00
Cake Plate, 10 3/4 In. 4.00
Candleholder, Pair .... 10.00 To 12.00
Chop Plate, 13 5/8 In. 8.00
Compote 6.00
Creamer .... 1.50 To 3.50
Cup .... 1.50 To 2.25
Cup & Saucer .... 3.50 To 4.50
Pitcher, 4 1/2 In. .... 7.00 To 10.00
Pitcher, 5 In. ...... 8.00 To 12.00
Plate, 9 In. 5.00
Powder Jar 5.50
Relish, 2 Sections ... 4.50 To 5.00
Salt & Pepper 15.00
Sugar .... 2.00 To 5.00
Tumbler, 3 1/4 In. 3.50
Tumbler, 5 In. ...... 5.50 To 6.00

GREEN

Bowl, 4 3/4 In. 5.50
Bowl, Boat Shape 18.00
Bowl, Oval, 9 1/2 In. 14.50
Butter, Cover 57.00
Chop Plate 16.75
Coaster .... 6.00 To 12.50
Creamer 9.50
Cup .... 7.00 To 7.50
Cup & Saucer 11.50
Pitcher, 6 3/4 In. .... 38.00 To 50.00
Plate, 6 In. 5.00
Plate, 9 In. .... 8.50 To 11.00
Salt & Pepper .... 28.00 To 38.00
Saltshaker 18.00
Saucer 2.50
Sherbet .... 5.00 To 11.50
Soup, Cream 15.50
Sugar, Cover 20.00
Tumbler, 3 1/4 In. 25.00
Tumbler, 4 In. 16.00
Tumbler, 5 In. 20.00

PINK

Ashtray .... 22.00 To 31.25
Bowl, 4 3/4 In. .... 4.25 To 4.50
Bowl, 5 In. .... 8.50 To 10.00
Bowl, 8 1/2 In. .... 9.00 To 10.00
Bowl, 9 In. 14.00
Bowl, 10 1/2 In. 60.00
Bowl, 2 Handles, 8 In. .... 8.50 To 12.00
Bowl, Boat Shape 22.50
Bowl, Footed, 7 1/8 In. .... 12.00 To 15.75
Bowl, Oval, 9 1/2 In. 6.00
Butter, Cover .... 25.00 To 38.00
Candleholder, Pair .... 60.00 To 75.00

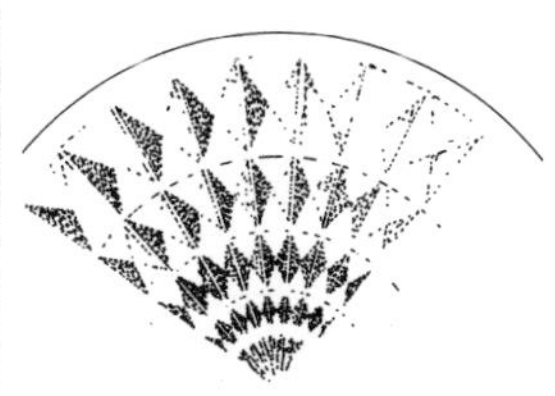

Chop Plate .... 13.00 To 17.50
Coaster 5.00
Compote 55.00
Creamer 6.50
Cup .... 5.00 To 6.00
Cup & Saucer ..... 7.00 To 10.25
Pitcher,
 6 3/4 In. .... 13.00 To 17.00
Plate, 6 In. .... 1.75 To 3.50
Plate, 7 In. .... 14.00 To 18.00
Plate, 9 In. .... 9.00 To 12.00
Plate, Sandwich Server,
 10 1/4 In. .... 6.00 To 7.50
Platter,
 11 1/2 In. .... 9.00 To 9.50
Salt & Pepper 23.00
Saucer .... 2.50 To 3.50
Sherbet .... 5.50 To 7.50
Sugar & Creamer,
 Cover .... 13.75 To 25.00
Sugar, Cover ..... 12.00 To 15.00
Tray, 4 In. 4.25
Tray, 8 1/2 X 9 3/4 In. ... 35.00
Tumbler,
 3 1/4 In. .... 6.00 To 9.00
Tumbler, 4 In. ...... 8.00 To 8.50
Tumbler, 5 In. ... 11.00 To 14.50
Water Set, 7 Piece 54.00

Windsor Diamond, see Windsor

Winged Medallion, see Madrid

Woolworth

Woolworth was made by Westmoreland Glass Company, Grapeville, Pennsylvania, in the early 1930s. The design, showing bunches of grapes, was also called Oregon Grape, but it is not the same as the pattern just called Grape. It was made of crystal, blue, green, and pink glass.

Woolworth, see also Grape

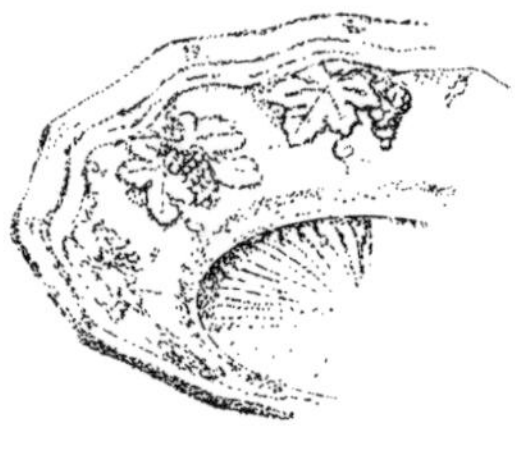

GREEN

Basket, 5 1/2 In. 18.00
Pitcher, 80 Oz. 25.00
Tumbler, 5 1/2 In. 11.00

X

X Design

X Design, or Criss Cross, was another Hazel-Atlas pattern made from 1928 to 1932. The name indicates that the pattern has rows of x's in grids. It was made in crystal, green, pink, and white opaque glass. Only a breakfast set was made.

CRYSTAL

Bowl, 6 1/2 In. 8.00
Bowl, 8 1/2 In. 4.00
Bowl,
 9 1/2 In. .... 9.00 To 10.00
Bowl, 10 1/2 In. 14.00
Butter, Cover,
 1 Lb. .... 12.00 To 15.00
Reamer .... 5.00 To 9.00
Relish, 4 X 8 In. 7.00

GREEN

Bowl, 7 1/2 In. 15.00
Butter, Cover,
 1/4 Lb. .... 33.00 To 35.00
Butter, Cover, 1 Lb. 32.00
Dish, Refrigerator, Cover,
 4 X 8 In. .... 14.00 To 28.00
Reamer .... 12.00 To 15.00

PINK

Butter, Cover, 1/4 Lb. 22.00
Butter, Cover, 1 Lb. 32.50
Dish, Refrigerator, Cover,
 4 X 4 In. 15.00
Reamer, Lemon 200.00
Reamer, Orange 185.00
Relish, 8 X 8 In. 17.00

DEPRESSION GLASS

Reproductions

PATTERN	OBJECT	COLORS	DATES
Adam	Butter dish	Green, pink	1981
American	Two-piece candle night light, 10-inch oval bowl, 10-inch 3-footed bowl, 6¼-inch 3-footed bowl, sugar and creamer, covered, candy container and cover, 10-inch divided relish, 12½-inch cake plate, 14-ounce footed tumbler		1987
Avocado	Cream and sugar, cup and saucer, handled dish, nappy, pickle, pitcher	Blue, burnt honey, frosted pink, pink, red amethyst, yellow	1974
Avocado	Pitcher	Green	1979
Avocado	Tumbler	Blue, frosted pink, green, pink, red amethyst, yellow	1974
Avocado	Berry, olive, 5½-inch plate, relish, sundae	Various colors	
Bubble	Ashtray, bowl, ivy ball, punch cup, vase	Red	1977–1978
Cameo	Child's dishes	Green, pink, yellow	
Cameo	Shaker	Green	1982
Candlewick	Bowl, candelabra, cup & saucer, cream & sugar, 2-handled jelly, plate, basket	Alexandrite, blue, pink	1987
Cape Cod	Cruet		1986
Cape Cod	Dinner set		1978
Caprice	Butter, cream & sugar, footed juice, footed water glass, relish, square dish	Cobalt, light blue	1985
Cherry Blossom	Almost all items have been reproduced in various colors since 1972		
Diana	Bowl	Pink	1986
Early American Sandwich	Ashtray, berry set, bowl, bridge set, napkin holder, platter, pitcher, snack set, 3-part relish, tidbit, tumbler, vase, basket, boxes, candleholder, egg plate	Amber, light green	1982

PATTERN	OBJECT	COLORS	DATES
English Hobnail	18 pieces	Red	1980
English Hobnail	26 pieces	Pink	1983
English Hobnail	Pedestal salt dip		1986
Hazel Atlas Quilt	Kitchen shaker	Pink	1987
Heritage	5-inch bowl	Amber, crystal	1987
Iris	Candy dish (bottom only), vase	Multicolored	1976
Madrid (called Recollection)	Various items	Blue, crystal, pink	1982
Madrid	Dinner set	Amber	1976–1979
Mayfair	Cookie jar	Pink, green	1982
Mayfair	Salt & pepper	Cobalt blue	1988
Mayfair	Shot glass	Blue, green, pink	1977
Miss America	Butter dish	Amberina, crystal, green, ice blue, pink	1977
Miss America	Pitcher, tumbler	Crystal, green	1982
Miss America	Salt & pepper	Crystal, green, pink	1977
Miss America	Shaker	Crystal, green, pink	
Miss America	Various items	Cobalt blue	1987
Petalware	Dinner set	Blue, crystal, peach/pink, smoke	1988
Pyramid	Berry bowl, relish, tray, tumbler	Black	1974
Royal Ruby	Tumbler: 7-ounce, 9-ounce, 12-ounce, 16-ounce	Red	1977–1978
Sandwich Anchor Hocking	Covered cookie jar	Crystal	1977
Sandwich Indiana	Basket, bridge set, candleholder, goblets, napkin holder, nappy, punch set, snack set, tidbit, vase, wine set	Amber	1982
Sandwich Indiana	Basket, candleholder, snack set, wine set	Light green	1982
Sandwich Indiana	Dinner set	Amber, crystal, dark blue, red	1969
Sandwich Indiana	Various items	Amber, blue, crystal, green, red	
Sharon	Butter dish	Amber, blue, dark green, light green, pink	1976
Sharon	Covered candy dish	Green, pink	1984
Sharon	Cheese dish	Green, pink	1977
Sharon	Salt & pepper shakers	Green, pink, and other colors	1980
Sharon	Covered sugar & creamer	Pink, green	1982
Shirley Temple	Milk pitcher, mug	Cobalt blue	1982
Shirley Temple	6½-inch bowl		1986
Westmoreland Sandwich	1- and 2-piece reamers, "Gillespie" measuring cup	Various colors	1986

DEPRESSION GLASS

Factories

NAME	LOCATION	DATES
Akro Agate	Clarksburg, West Virginia	1914–1951
Bartlett-Collins	Sapulpa, Oklahoma	1914-present
Belmont Tumbler Company	Bellaire, Ohio	c.1920–1952
Cambridge Glass Company	Cambridge, Ohio	1901–1958
Central Glass Works	Wheeling, West Virginia	1860s–1939
Consolidated Lamp & Glass Company	Coraopolis, Pennsylvania	1894–1933; 1936–1967
Co-Operative Flint Glass Company	Beaver Falls, Pennsylvania	1879–1934
Dell Glass Company	Millville, New Jersey	1930s
Diamond Glass-Ware Company	Indiana, Pennsylvania	1891–1931
Dunbar Flint Glass Corporation/Dunbar Glass Corporation	Dunbar, West Virginia	1913–1953
Duncan & Miller Glass Company	Washington, Pennsylvania	1893–1955
Federal Glass Company	Columbus, Ohio	1900–1971
Fenton Art Glass Company	Williamstown, West Virginia	1906–present
Fostoria Glass Company	Fostoria, Ohio; Moundsville, West Virginia	1887–1986
Hazel Atlas Glass Company	Washington, Pennsylvania; Zanesville, Ohio; Clarksburg, West Virginia; Wheeling, West Virginia	1902–1956
A. H. Heisey & Company	Newark, Ohio	1893–1956
Hocking Glass Company/Anchor Hocking Glass Corporation	Lancaster, Ohio	1905–present (Anchor Hocking from 1937)
Imperial Glass Company	Bellaire, Ohio	1904–1982

NAME	LOCATION	DATES
Indiana Glass Company	Dunkirk, Indiana	1907–present
Jeannette Glass Company	Jeannette, Pennsylvania	c.1900–present
Jenkins Glass Company	Kokomo Indiana; Arcadia, Indiana	1901–1932
Lancaster Glass Company	Lancaster, Ohio	1908–1937
Libbey Glass Company	Toledo, Ohio	1892–present
Liberty Works	Egg Harbor, New Jersey	1903–1932
Louie Glass Company	Weston, West Virginia	1926–present
Macbeth-Evans Glass Company	(several factories); Toledo, Ohio; Charleroi, Pennsylvania; Corning, New York	1899–1936 (acquired by Corning)
McKee Glass Company	Jeannette, Pennsylvania	1853–1961
Morgantown Glass Works	Morgantown, West Virginia	Late 1800s–1972
New Martinsville Glass Manufacturing Company	New Martinsville, West Virginia	1901–1944
Paden City Glass Manufacturing Company	Paden City, West Virginia	1916–1951
Seneca Glass Company	Fostoria, Ohio; Morgantown, West Virginia	1891–present
Silex (division of Macbeth-Evans)	Corning, New York	mid-1930s
L. E. Smith Glass Company	Mt. Pleasant, Pennsylvania	1907–present
Standard Glass Manufacturing Company (Subsidiary of Hocking/Anchor Hocking)		1924–present
United States Glass Company	Pennsylvania (several factories); Tiffin, Ohio; Gas City, Indiana	1891–1966
Westmoreland Glass Company	Grapeville, Pennsylvania	1890–1985

DEPRESSION GLASS
Pattern List

Note: (R) = pattern has been reproduced
* = Prices & paragraph in body of book

PATTERN NAME	CROSS-REFERENCES	MANUFACTURER AND DATES	COLORS AND DESCRIPTION
ABC Stork		Belmont	Crystal, green; child's plate
Accordian Pleats	See Round Robin		
*Adam (R)	Chain Daisy; Fan & Feather	Jeannette, 1932–1934	Crystal, green, pink, yellow
Aero Optic		Cambridge, 1929	Crystal, emerald, Peach-blo, Willow Blue
Afghan & Scottie Dog		Hazel Atlas, 1938	Blue with white decorations
*Akro Agate		Akro Agate, 1932–1951	Marbleized colored glass
*Alice	See also Fire-King Oven Ware; Jadite; Jane-Ray; Square; Swirl Fire-King; Turquoise Blue	Anchor Hocking 1940s	Jadite, opaque white; blue, pink borders
*Alpine Caprice	See also Caprice	Cambridge, 1936	Blue, crystal, pink; satin finished
*American (R)	Fostoria	Fostoria, 1915–1986	Amber, crystal, green, milk glass
American Beauty	See English Hobnail		
*American Pioneer		Liberty Works, 1931–1934	Amber, crystal, green, pink
*American Sweetheart	Lily Medallion	Macbeth-Evans, 1930–1936	Blue, cremax, monax, pink, red; gold, green, pink, platinum, red, smokey black trim
Angel Fish	See Sportsman Series		
*Anniversary		Jeannette, 1947	Amethyst, crystal, milk glass, pink; 1970–1972—crystal, iridescent amber
Apple Blossom	See Dogwood		
Apple Blossom Border	See Blossoms & Band		
April		Macbeth-Evans	Pale pink
Aramis		Dunbar, 1936	Luster colors
Arcadia Lace		Jenkins, c.1930	
Arctic		Hocking, 1932	Red & white decorations
Art Moderne		Morgantown, 1929	Rose, green; black stem & foot
Artura		Indiana, c.1930	Crystal, green, pink
Athos		Dunbar, 1936	Colored stripes
*Aunt Polly		U.S. Glass, late 1920s	Blue, green, iridescent, pink
Aurora	See Petalware		

PATTERN NAME	CROSS-REFERENCES	MANUFACTURER AND DATES	COLORS AND DESCRIPTION
Autumn		McKee, 1934	French ivory, jade green
*Avocado (R)	No. 601; Sweet Pear	Indiana Glass, 1923–1933	Crystal, green, pink; reproductions in amber, amethyst, blue, frosted pink, green, pink, red yellow
B Pattern	See Dogwood		
Ballerina	See Cameo		
Bamboo Optic	See also Octagon Bamboo Optic	Liberty, 1929	Green, pink
Bananas		Indiana, c.1930	Green, pink
Banded Cherry	See Cherry Blossom		
Banded Fine Rib	See Coronation		
Banded Petalware	See Petalware		
Banded Rainbow	See Ring		
Banded Ribbon	See New Century		
Banded Rings	See Ring		
Barbra		Dunbar, 1928	Pink
*Baroque		Fostoria, 1936–1966	Blue, crystal, green, yellow
Basket	See No. 615		
*Beaded Block	Frosted Block	Imperial, 1927–1930s	Amber, crystal, green, ice blue, pink, red, vaseline; iridescent (frosted) colors
Bee Hive	See also Queen Anne	U.S. Glass, 1926	Crystal; amber, green, pink trim
Belmont Ship Plate		Belmont	Amber, crystal, green, iridescent
Berwick	See Boopie		
Beverages with Sailboats	See White Ship		
Bibi		Anchor Hocking, 1940s	Forest Green, red
Big Rib	See Manhattan		
Blackberry Cluster	See Loganberry		
Blaise		Imperial, c.1930	Amber, crystal, green, Rose Marie
Blanche		Standard, c.1930	Crystal
Block	See Block Optic		
*Block Optic	Block	Hocking, 1929–1933	Crystal, green, pink, yellow; black stem
Block with Rose	Rose Trellis	Imperial	Crystal, green, pink
Block with Snowflake	Snowflake on Block		Green, pink; plates only
Block with Windmill	See Windmill & Checkerboard		
Blossoms & Band	Apple Blossom Border	Jenkins, 1927	Crystal, green, iridescent marigold, pink
*Boopie	Berwick	Anchor Hocking, late 1940s-1950s	Crystal, Forest Green, Royal Ruby; glasses
Bordette	See also Chinex Classic; Cremax	Macbeth-Evans, 1930–1940	Chinex, cremax
Bouquet & Lattice	See Normandie		

PATTERN NAME	CROSS-REFERENCES	MANUFACTURER AND DATES	COLORS AND DESCRIPTION
*Bowknot		Late 1920s	Crystal, green
Bridal Bouquet	See No. 615		
Bridget		Jeannette, 1925	Green, topaz; bridge set
*Bubble (R)	Bullseye; Provincial	Anchor Hocking, 1934–1965	Crystal, dark green, pale blue, pink; 1960s—milk white, ruby red, yellow; 1980s—green, jadite, pink, royal ruby
Bullseye	See Bubble		
*Burple		Anchor Hocking, 1940s	Crystal, Forest Green, Ruby Red; dessert sets, bowls
Butterflies & Roses	See Flower Garden with Butterflies		
Buttons & Bows	See Holiday		
*By Cracky		Smith, late 1920s	Amber, canary, crystal, green
Cabbage Rose	See Sharon		
Cabbage Rose with Single Arch	See Rosemary		
Camellia		Jeannette, 1947–1951	Crystal
*Cameo (R)	Ballerina; Dancing Girl	Hocking, 1930–1934	Crystal with platinum, green, pink, yellow; 1981—pink, green salt and pepper shakers; green, pink, yellow children's dishes
*Candlewick (R)		Imperial, 1937–1982	Black, blue, brown, crystal, green, lavender, pink, red, yellow; crystal with gold; fired-on gold, red, blue, green beading
*Cape Cod (R)		Imperial, 1932	Amber, azalea, cobalt blue, crystal, green, light blue, milk glass, ruby; 1978—dinner set; 1986—cruet
*Caprice (R)	See also Alpine Caprice	Cambridge, 1936–1953	Amber, amethyst, cobalt blue, crystal, emerald green, light green, milk glass, moonlight blue, pink
Carolyn	See Yvonne		
*Caribbean	Wave	Duncan & Miller, 1936–1955	Amber, crystal, blue, red
Catalonian		Consolidated, 1927–1936	Amethyst, emerald green, Honey, jade, Spanish Rose
Centaur	Sphinx	Lancaster, 1930s	Green, yellow
*Century		Fostoria, 1926–1986	Crystal
Chain Daisy	See Adam		
*Chantilly		Jeannette, 1960s	Crystal, pink
Charade			Amethyst, dark blue, pink
Chariot		Hocking, 1932	Red & white decorations
Cherry	See Cherry Blossom		

PATTERN NAME	CROSS-REFERENCES	MANUFACTURER AND DATES	COLORS AND DESCRIPTION
*Cherry-Berry	See also Strawberry	U.S. Glass, early 1930s	Amber, crystal, green, pink
*Cherry Blossom (R)	Banded Cherry; Cherry; Paneled Cherry Blossom	Jeannette, 1930–1939	Crystal, delphite, green, jadite, pink; reproductions—blue, delphite, green, pink
Chesterfield		Imperial, c.1930	Amber, green, Rose Marie; iced tea set
Chico		Louie, 1936	Black, green, pink, royal blue, ruby, topaz; crystal handles; beverage set
*Chinex Classic	See also Cremax; Bordette; Oxford; Pie-Crust; Sheffield	Macbeth-Evans, c.1938–1942	Ivory; decal decorated; colored edges
Chintz		Fostoria, 1940–1972	Crystal
*Chintz		Heisey, 1931–1938	Crystal, green, orchid, pink, yellow
*Christmas Candy	Christmas Candy Ribbon; No. 624	Indiana, 1937	Crystal, emerald green, Seafoam Green, teal blue; luncheon sets
Christmas Candy Ribbon	See Christmas Candy		
*Circle	Circular Ribs	Hocking, 1930s	Crystal, green, pink
Circular Ribs	See Circle		
Classic	See Chinex Classic		
*Cleo		Cambridge, 1930	Amber, blue, crystal, green, pink, yellow
Clico		McKee, 1930	Crystal with black, green feet, jade green transparent green, rose pink
*Cloverleaf	Shamrock	Hazel Atlas, 1930–1936	Black, crystal, green, pink, topaz
*Colonial	Knife & Fork	Hocking 1934–1938	Crystal, green, opaque white, pink
*Colonial Block		Hazel Atlas	1930s—crystal, green, pink; 1950s—white
*Colonial Fluted	Rope	Federal, 1928–1933	Crystal, green
*Colony	Elongated Honeycomb; Hexagon Triple Band	Hazel Atlas, 1930s	Crystal, green, pink
Colony		Fostoria	
Columbia		Federal, 1938–1942	Crystal, pink
Columbus		Anchor Hocking	Amber; plate only
Comet	Scroll	U.S. Glass, mid-1920s	Crystal, green, pink
Corded Optic		Federal, 1928	Crystal, green
*Coronation	Banded Fine Rib; Saxon; see also Lace Edge	Anchor Hocking, 1936–1940	Crystal, dark green, pink, ruby red
Cracked Ice		Indiana, 1930s	Green, pink
Crackled	See Craquel		

PATTERN NAME	CROSS-REFERENCES	MANUFACTURER AND DATES	COLORS AND DESCRIPTION
*Craquel	Crackled; Stippled; Tree of Life	U.S. Glass, 1924	Crystal with green trim, blue, yellow
*Cremax	See also Bordette; Chinex Classic; Ivex; Oxford; Pie-Crust; Sheffield	Macbeth-Evans, 1930s–1940s	Cream-colored opaque; decal decorated; colored edges
Criss Cross	See X Design		
Crossbar		Federal, mid-1930s	Crystal, Golden Glow, Green, Rose Glow
Crystal Leaf		Macbeth-Evans, 1928	Crystal, green, pink
Cube	See Cubist		
Cubist	Cube	Jeannette, 1929–1933	Amber, blue, canary yellow, crystal, green, pink, ultramarine, white; reproductions—amber, avocado, opaque white
*Cupid		Paden City, 1930s	Black, green, light blue, pink, yellow
Daisy	See No. 620		
Daisy J		Jeannette, 1926	Amber, green
Daisy Petals	See Petalware		
Daisy Spray & Lattice		Federal, 1928	Crystal, green
Dance of the Nudes		Consolidated, 1920s	Crystal, pink
Dancing Girl	See Cameo		
D'Artagnan		Dunbar, 1936	Lusters
Dear		Jeannette, 1930s	
Debbra		Hocking, 1931–1933	Green, rose, topaz
*Decagon		Cambridge, 1930s	Amber, cobalt blue, green, Moonlight Blue, pink, red
*Della Robbia		Westmoreland, 1920s–1930s	Amber, crystal, green, pink
Dewdrop		Jeannette, 1954–1955	Crystal
Diamond	See Windsor		
Diamond Arch	Diamond Lattice	Federal, 1938–1940	Crystal, green, pink
Diamond Dart		Macbeth-Evans, 1928	Crystal, emerald green
Diamond Lattice	See Diamond Arch		
Diamond Panel	See Diamond Point Columns		
Diamond Pattern	See Miss America		
Diamond Point	See Petalware		
Diamond Point Columns	Diamond Panel	Hazel Atlas, late 1920s–1930s	Crystal, green, iridescent, pink
*Diamond Quilted	Flat Diamond	Imperial, 1920s–1930s	Amber, black, blue, crystal, green, pink, red
Diamond Squat		Federal, 1928	Water set
*Diana (R)	Swirled Sharp Rib	Federal, 1937–1941	Amber, crystal, green, pink; 1987—pink bowl

PATTERN NAME	CROSS-REFERENCES	MANUFACTURER AND DATES	COLORS AND DESCRIPTION
Diner		U.S. Glass, 1927	Amber, green, pink
Dixie		Macbeth-Evans, 1931	Green, pink; water set
*Dogwood	Apple Blossom; B Pattern; Magnolia; Wildrose	Macbeth-Evans, 1929–1934	Cremax, crystal, green, monax, pink, red, yellow
Doreen		Westmoreland, 1924	Amber, blue, crystal, green, rose
*Doric	Snowflake	Jeannette, 1935–1938	Delphite, green, pink, white, yellow
*Doric & Pansy	Doric with Pansy; Pansy & Doric; see also Pretty Polly Party Dishes	Jeannette, 1937–1938	Crystal, pink, ultramarine
Doric with Pansy	See Doric & Pansy		
Do-Si-Do		Smith, 1930s	Black, black with crystal
Double Shield	See Mt. Pleasant		
Double Swirl	See Swirl		
Drape & Tassel	See Princess		
Dutch	See Windmill		
Dutch Rose	See Rosemary		
Early American	See Princess Feather		
Early American Hobnail	See also Hobnail	Imperial, 1930s	Amber, black, blue, crystal, green, pink, red
Early American Lace		Duncan & Miller, 1932	Amber, crystal, green, rose, ruby
Early American Rock Crystal	See Rock Crystal		
Early American Sandwich (R)		Duncan & Miller, 1925–1949	Amber, chartreuse, crystal, green, pink, ruby
Early American Scroll		Heisey, 1932	
Early American Thumbprint		Heisey, 1932	Crystal, golden yellow, green, rose
Egg Harbor		Liberty, 1929	Green, rose
Elongated Honeycomb	See Colony		
*English Hobnail (R)	American Beauty; Sawtooth; see also Miss America	Westmoreland, 1920–1970s	Amber, blue, cobalt, crystal, green, pink, red, turquoise; 1960s—dark amber; 1980s—pink, red
Everglades		Cambridge, 1933–1934	Amber, Carmen, crystal, Eleanor Blue, Forest Green
*Fairfax		Fostoria, 1927–1944	Amber, black, blue, green, orchid, pink, ruby, topaz
Fan & Feather	See Adam		
Fanfare		Macbeth-Evans	Pale pink
Feather Scroll	See Scroll Fluted		
Fieldcrest		Jenkins	Crystal, green, iridescent amber
Fine Rib	See Homespun (Jeannette)		

PATTERN NAME	CROSS-REFERENCES	MANUFACTURER AND DATES	COLORS AND DESCRIPTION
Fire-King Dinnerware	See Alice; Jane-Ray; Jadite; Square; Swirl Fire-King; Turquoise Blue		
*Fire-King Oven Glass	See also Philbe	Anchor Hocking, 1942–1960s	Crystal, pale blue
*Fire-King Oven Ware	See also Alice; Jadite; Jane-Ray; Philbe; Square; Swirl Fire-King; Turquoise Blue	Anchor Hocking, 1950s	Opaque; blue, ivory with gold or colored trim, jadite, pink, white
*Flanders		U.S. Glass, 1914–1935	Crystal, pink or yellow with crystal trim
Flat Diamond	See Diamond Quilted		
Flora		Imperial, c.1925	Amber, green, Rose Marie
Floradora	Floral Bouquet	Imported, 1929	Amber, amethyst, green
*Floragold	Louisa	Jeannette, 1950s	Crystal, ice blue, iridescent, red-yellow, shell pink
*Floral	Poinsettia	Jeannette, 1931–1935	Amber, crystal, delphite, green, jadite, pink, red, yellow
*Floral & Diamond Band		U.S. Glass, 1920s	Black, crystal, green, pink
Floral Bouquet	See Floradora		
Floral Rim	See Vitrock		
Floral Sterling		Hazel Atlas, early 1930s	
*Florentine No. 1	Old Florentine; Poppy No. 1	Hazel Atlas, 1932–1935	Cobalt, crystal, green, pink, yellow; hexagonal plates
*Florentine No. 2	Oriental Poppy; Poppy No. 2	Hazel Atlas, 1932–1935	Amber, cobalt, crystal, green, ice blue, pink
Flower	See Princess Feather		
Flower & Leaf Band	See Indiana Custard		
Flower Band		McKee, 1934	French Ivory, Jade Green, Poudre Blue
Flower Basket	See No. 615		
Flower Garden	See Flower Garden with Butterflies		
*Flower Garden with Butterflies	Butterflies & Roses; Flower Garden; Wildrose with Apple Blossom	U.S. Glass, late 1920s	Amber, black, blue, crystal, green, pink, yellow
Flower Rim	See Vitrock		
Forest		Co-Operative Flint, 1928	Blue, green, pink
*Forest Green		Anchor Hocking, 1950–1957	Green
*Fortune		Anchor Hocking, 1937–1938	Crystal, pink
Fostoria	See American		
Fountain Swirl		Imperial, 1928–1930	Crystal, green, pink
Franklin		Fenton, 1934	Amber, crystal, ruby; beverage glasses

PATTERN NAME	CROSS-REFERENCES	MANUFACTURER AND DATES	COLORS AND DESCRIPTION
Frosted Block	See Beaded Block		
Frosted Ribbon		Anchor Hocking, 1940	Red
*Fruits		Hazel Atlas, 1931–1933	Crystal, green, iridescent, pink
Full Sail		Duncan & Miller, 1925	Amber, green
Garland		Indiana	Crystal—1935; decorated milk glass—1950s
Georgian		Hocking, 1935	Crystal, green; beverage sets
*Georgian	Lovebirds	Federal, 1931–1935	Crystal, green
Georgian		Duncan & Miller, 1928	Amber, crystal, green, rose
*Georgian Fenton		Fenton, c.1930	Amber, black, cobalt blue, crystal, green, pink, ruby, topaz
Gladiola	See Royal Lace		
*Gloria		Cambridge, c.1930	Amber, crystal, emerald green, green, heatherbloom, pink, yellow
Gothic Arches	Romanesque	L. E. Smith, 1920s	Amber, crystal, green, yellow
Grand Slam		Federal, 1930	Crystal; bridge set
Grape	See also Woolworth	Standard, 1930s	Green, rose, topaz
Groucho		Louie, 1936	Black, green, pink, royal blue, ruby, topaz; crystal handles; beverage set
Hairpin	See Newport		
*Hammered Band	Melba; Pebbled Band	L. E. Smith, early 1930s	Amethyst, black, green, pink
Hanging Basket	See No. 615		
*Harp		Jeanette, 1954–1957	Crystal, crystal with gold trim, light blue, pink
Harpo		Louis, 1936	Black, green, pink, royal blue, ruby, topaz; crystal handles; beverage set
Hazel Atlas Quilt (R)		Hazel Atlas, 1937–1940	Amethyst, cobalt blue, green, pink
Hazen		Imperial, c.1930	
*Heritage (R)		Federal, late 1930s–1960s	Crystal, blue, light green, pink; 1987—amber, crystal; bowls
Hex Optic	See Hexagon Optic		
*Hexagon Optic	Hex Optic; Honeycomb	Jeannette, 1928–1932	Green, pink; c.1960—blue-green, iridized
Hexagon Triple Band	See Colony		
High Point		Anchor Hocking	Ruby; water set
Hinge	See Patrician		
Hob		Jenkins, 1927–1931	Crystal, green
*Hobnail	See also Early American Hobnail; Moonstone	Hocking, 1934–1936	Crystal, pink; red rims; black base

PATTERN NAME	CROSS-REFERENCES	MANUFACTURER AND DATES	COLORS AND DESCRIPTION
Hobstars Intaglio		Imperial, c.1930	Crystal, green, pink
*Holiday	Buttons & Bows; Russian	Jeannette, 1947–1949	Crystal, iridescent, pink, shell pink opaque
*Homespun	Fine Rib	Jeannette, 1939–1940	Crystal, light blue, pink
Homespun		Hazel Atlas	Cobalt blue, crystal
Homestead		Smith, 1930s	Amber, black, green, pink
Honeycomb	See Hexagon Optic		
Horizontal Fine Rib	See Manhattan		
Horizontal Ribbed	See Manhattan		
Horizontal Rounded Big Rib	See Manhattan		
Horizontal Sharp Big Rib	See Manhattan		
Horseshoe	See No. 612		
Huck Finn		Jenkins, c.1930	
Huckabee		Imperial, c.1930	
Huges		Morgantown, 1932	Black, crystal, green, Ritz Blue, ruby; beverage set
Ida		Imperial, c.1930	Blue, crystal, green, ruby
Imperial Hunt		Cambridge, 1932	
Imperial Optic Rib	Optic Rib	Imperial, 1927	Amberina, blue, crystal, green, iridescent
Imperial Plain Octagon	Molly	Imperial, 1927	Crystal, green, pink
Indian		Federal, c.1930	Green
*Indiana Custard	Flower & Leaf Band; see also Orange Blossom	Indiana, 1930s–1950s	Custard, ivory; bands of pastel colors
*Iris (R)	Iris & Herringbone	Jeannette, 1928–1932, 1950s, 1970s	Crystal, iridescent, pink; later wares—blue-green, red-yellow
Iris & Herringbone	See Iris		
Ivex	See also Chinex Classic; Cremax	Macbeth-Evans, 1930–1940	Chinex, cremax
Jack Frost		Federal, 1928	Crackled; water, iced tea & lemonade sets
*Jadite	See also Alice; Fire-King Oven Ware; Jadite; Jane-Ray; Philbe; Square; Swirl Fire-King; Turquoise Blue	Jeannette, 1936–1938	Jadite
Jamestown	See Tradition		
Jane		Lancaster, c.1930	Green, pink, topaz
*Jane-Ray	See also Alice; Fire-King Oven Ware; Jadite; Philbe; Square; Swirl Fire-King; Turquoise Blue	Anchor Hocking, 1945–1963	Jadite
Jenkins' Basket		Jenkins	Crystal, green, iridescent amber

PATTERN NAME	CROSS-REFERENCES	MANUFACTURER AND DATES	COLORS AND DESCRIPTION
John		Federal, mid-1930s	Crystal, Golden Glow, green, Rose Glow
*Jubilee		Lancaster, early 1930s	Pink, yellow
*June (R)		Fostoria, 1928–1952	Azure blue, crystal, gold-tinted, green, rose, topaz; reproductions—blue, crystal, pink, yellow
Kimberly		Duncan & Miller, 1931	Amber, crystal, green, rose
King Arthur		Indiana, c.1930	Green, pink
Knife & Fork	See Colonial		
Krinkle		Morgantown, 1924	
*Lace Edge	Loop; Open Lace; Open Scallop; see also Coronation; Queen Mary	Hocking, 1935–1938	Crystal, pink
Lacy Daisy	See No. 618		
Lake Como		Hocking, 1934–1937	Opaque white with blue decoration
Langston		Morgantown, 1932	Black, crystal, green, Ritz Blue, ruby
Lariette		U.S. Glass, 1931	
*Laurel	Raspberry Band; see also Scottie Dog	McKee, 1930s	Ivory, jade, powder blue, white opal; child's set—colored rim
Leaf		Macbeth-Evans, early 1930s	Crystal, green, pink
Lenox		McKee, 1930s	Crystal, green, Ritz Blue, Rose Pink
Lido		Federal, mid-1930s	Crystal, Golden Glow, green, Rose Glow
Lily Medallion	See American Sweetheart		
Lily Pons		Indiana, c.1930	Green
Lincoln Drape	See Princess		
*Lincoln Inn		Fenton, 1928	Amber, amethyst, black, cobalt, crystal, green, jadite, light blue, pink, red
Lindburgh	Scalloped Panels	Imperial, c.1930	Crystal, green, ross pink
Line 92	See Twitch		
Line 191	Party Line; Tiered Block, Tiered Semi-Optic	Paden City, 1928	Amber, blue, Cheri-Glo, crystal, green, mulberry
Line 300	See Peacock & Wild Rose		
Line 412	See Peacock Reverse		
Line 550	See Sheraton		
Line 994	See Popeye & Olive		
Little Bo Peep		Anchor Hocking, 1940	Green & orange on ivory; child's line
Little Hostess	See Moderntone Little Hostess		

PATTERN NAME	CROSS-REFERENCES	MANUFACTURER AND DATES	COLORS AND DESCRIPTION
Little Jewel	See also New Jewel	Imperial, late 1920s–1930	Crystal, green, pink, white
Little Orphan Annie	See Orphan Annie		
Loganberry	Blackberry Cluster	Indiana, c.1930	Green, pink
Lombardi		Jeannette, 1938	Light blue; bowl only
Loop	See Lace Edge		
Lorain	See No. 615		
Lorna		Cambridge, 1930	Amber, crystal, emerald, Gold Krystol, Peach-Blo
Lotus		Westmoreland, 1920s–1930s	Amber, blue, crystal, green, rose
Louisa	See Floragold		
Lovebirds	See Georgian		
Lydia Ray	See New Century		
*MacHOB		Macbeth-Evans, 1928	Crystal, monax, pink
*Madrid (R)	Meandering Vine; Paneled Aster; Primus; Winged Medallion	Federal, 1932–1939	Amber, blue, crystal, green, pink; 1976—amber; 1980s—blue, crystal, pink
Magnolia	See Dogwood		
*Manhattan	Horizontal Fine Rib; Horizontal Ribbed; Horizontal Rounded Big Rib; Horizontal Sharp Big Rib, Ribbed	Anchor Hocking, 1938–1941	Crystal, green, pink, red
Manor		Fostoria, 1931–1944	Crystal, green, topaz
Many Windows	See Roulette		
Mapleleaf		Westmoreland, 1923	Plate only
Marguerite		Westmoreland, 1924	Amber, blue, crystal, green, rose
Marilyn		Morgantown, 1929	Green, pink
Martha Washington		Cambridge, 1932	Amber, crystal, forest green, Gold Crystol, royal blue, ruby
Mary		Federal, mid-1930s	Crystal, Golden Glow, green, Rose Glow
Mayfair	See Mayfair Open Rose		
*Mayfair Federal	See also Rosemary Arches	Federal, 1934	Amber, crystal, green
*Mayfair Open Rose (R)	Mayfair; Open Rose	Hocking, 1931–1937	Crystal, green, ice blue, pink, yellow
Meadow Flower	See No. 618		
Meandering Vine	See Madrid		
Melba	See Hammered Band		
Melon		Morgantown, 1932	Black, blue, green, ruby, opal with colors; beverage set

PATTERN NAME	CROSS-REFERENCES	MANUFACTURER AND DATES	COLORS AND DESCRIPTION
Memphis		Central, 1923	Amethyst, black, blue, canary, green
Millay		Morgantown, 1932	Black, blue, crystal, green, ruby; beverage set
*Miss America (R)	Diamond Pattern; see also English Hobnail	Hocking, 1933–1936	Amber, crystal, green, ice blue, pink, red, Ritz Blue; 1977—amberina, crystal, green, ice blue, pink, red
Moderne Art	See Tea Room		
*Moderntone	Wedding Band	Hazel Atlas, 1935–1942	Amethyst, cobalt blue, crystal, pink, platonite with fired-on colors
*Moderntone Little Hostess	Little Hostess	Hazel Atlas, 1940s	Fired-on colors
Molly	See Imperial Plain Octagon		
Monarch		Anchor Hocking	Ruby
Monticello		Imperial	Crystal
Moondrops		New Martinsville, 1932–1940s	Amber, amethyst, black, cobalt blue, crystal, Evergreen, ice blue, jade, light green, medium blue, pink, Ritz Blue, ruby, smoke
*Moonstone	Opalescent Hobnail; see also Hobnail	Anchor Hocking, 1941–1946	Crystal with opalescent hobnails, green
*Mt. Pleasant	Double Shield	L. E. Smith, mid 1920s–1934	Black amethyst, cobalt blue, green, pink; gold trim
*Mt. Vernon		Cambridge, 1920s–1940s	Amber, blue, crystal, emerald green, Heatherbloom, red, violet
Mt. Vernon		Imperial, c.1930	Crystal
Mutt'N Jeff		Federal, 1928	Crystal, green; water set
Naomi		Seneca, mid-1930s	Blue, crystal
Nautilus		Cambridge, 1933–1934	Amber, crystal, royal blue
*Navarre		Fostoria, 1937–1980	Crystal
*New Century	Banded Ribbon; Lydia Ray; see also Ovide	Hazel Atlas, 1930–1935	Amethyst, cobalt blue, crystal, green, pink
New Jewel	See also Little Jewel	Imperial, 1931	Crystal, green, pink, white
*Newport (R)	Hairpin	Hazel Atlas, 1936–1940	Amethyst, cobalt blue, fired-on monax, pink, platonite
No. 601	See Avocado		
*No. 610 (R)	Pyramid; Rex	Indiana, 1926–1932	Crystal, green, pink, yellow: 1974–1975—black
*No. 612	Horseshoe	Indiana, 1930–1933	Green, pink, yellow; crystal sugar and creamer
*No. 615	Basket; Bridal Bouquet; Flower Basket; Hanging Basket; Lorain	Indiana, 1929–1932	Crystal, crystal with colored borders, green, yellow; reproduction—milk glass, olive green
*No. 616	Vernon	Indiana, 1930–1932	Crystal, crystal with platinum trim, green, yellow

PATTERN NAME	CROSS-REFERENCES	MANUFACTURER AND DATES	COLORS AND DESCRIPTION
*No. 618	Lacy Daisy; Meadow Flower; Pineapple & Floral; Wildflower	Indiana, 1932–1937	Amber, crystal, fired-on green and red; 1960s—olive green
*No. 620	Daisy	Indiana	1933—crystal; 1940—amber; 1960s–1970s—dark green, milk glass
No. 622	See Pretzel		
No. 624	See Christmas Candy		
Nora Bird		Paden City, 1929	Amber, blue, Cheri-Glo, green
*Normandie	Bouquet & Lattice	Federal, 1933–1940	Amber, crystal, green, iridescent, pink
Oatmeal Lace	See Princess Feather		
Ocean Wave	Ripple	Jenkins, c.1930	
*Octagon	Tiered Octagon; U.S. Octagon	U.S. Glass, 1927–1929	Green, pink
Octagon Bamboo Optic	See also Bamboo Optic	Liberty, 1929	Green, pink
Octagon Edge		McKee	Green, pink
*Old Cafe		Anchor Hocking, 1936–1938	Crystal, pink, red
Old Central Spiral		Central, 1925	
*Old English	Threading	Indiana, late 1920s-early 1930s	Amber, crystal, emerald green, light green, pink
Old Florentine	See Florentine No. 1		
Opalescent Hobnail	See Moonstone		
Open Lace	See Lace Edge		
Open Rose	See Mayfair Open Rose		
Open Scallop	See Lace Edge		
Optic Design	See Raindrops		
Optic Rib	See Imperial Optic Rib		
*Orange Blossom	See also Indiana Custard	Indiana, 1957	Milk glass
Orchid		Paden City, early 1930s	Cobalt blue, green, pink, yellow
Oregon Grape	See Woolworth		
Oriental Poppy	See Florentine No. 2		
Orphan Annie		Westmoreland, 1925	Amber, blue, crystal, green; breakfast set
*Ovide	See also New Century	Hazel Atlas, 1929–1935	Black, green, platonite, white, trimmed with fired-on colors
Oxford	See also Chinex Classic; Cremax	Macbeth-Evans, 1930–1940	Chinex, cremax
*Oyster & Pearl		Anchor Hocking, 1938–1940	Crystal, pink, red, white; fired-on green, pink
Palm Optic		Morgantown, 1929	Green, pink
Panel	See Sheraton		

PATTERN NAME	CROSS-REFERENCES	MANUFACTURER AND DATES	COLORS AND DESCRIPTION
Paneled Aster	See Madrid		
Paneled Cherry Blossom	See Cherry Blossom		
Panelled Ring-Ding		Hocking, 1932	Black, green, orange, red, yellow, painted bands
Pansy & Doric	See Doric & Pansy		
Pantryline		Hocking, 1920s–1930s	
Parrot	See Sylvan		
Party Line	See Line 191		
*Patrician	Hinge; Spoke	Federal, 1933–1937	Amber, crystal, green, pink, yellow
Patrick		Lancaster, c.1930	Rose, topaz
Peacock & Rose	See Peacock & Wild Rose		
Peacock & Wild Rose	Line 300; Peacock & Rose	Paden City, 1930s	Black, cobalt blue, green, pink, red
Peacock Optic		Morgantown, 1929–1930	Green, pink
Peacock Reverse	Line 412	Paden City, 1930s	Cobalt blue, red, yellow
*Pear Optic	Thumbprint; see also Raindrops	Federal, 1929–1930	Green
Pebble Optic	See Raindrops		
Pebbled Band	See Hammered Band		
*Penny Line		Paden City, 1932	Amber, Cheri-Glo, crystal, green, royal blue, ruby
Petal	See Petalware		
Petal Swirl	See Swirl		
*Petalware	Aurora; Banded Petalware; Daisy Petals; Diamond Point, Petal; Shell; Vivid Bands	Macbeth-Evans, 1930–1940	Cremax, crystal, monax, pink; gold trim; hand-painted fruit designs; fired-on blue, green, red, yellow
*Philbe	Fire-King Dinnerware; see also Fire-King Oven Glass	Anchor Hocking, 1937–1940s	Blue, blue with platinum trim, crystal, green, pink
Pie-Crust	See also Chinex Classic; Cremax	Macbeth-Evans, 1930–1940	Chinex, cremax
*Pillar Flute		Imperial, c.1930	Amber, blue, crystal, green, pink
Pillar Optic		Hocking, 1935	Green
Pineapple & Floral	See No. 618		
Pineapple Optic		Morgantown, 1929	Green, rose
Pinwheel	See Sierra		
*Pioneer		Federal, 1930s–1970s	Crystal, pink
Plymouth		Fenton, 1933	Amber, green, ruby
Poinsettia	See Floral		
Polar Bear		Hocking, 1932	Red & white decorations
Polo		Hazel Atlas, 1938	Blue with white decorations

PATTERN NAME	CROSS-REFERENCES	MANUFACTURER AND DATES	COLORS AND DESCRIPTION
*Popeye & Olive	Line 994	Paden City, early 1930s	Cobalt blue, crystal, green, red
Poppy No. 1	See Florentine No. 1		
Poppy No. 2	See Florentine No. 2		
Pretty Polly Party Dishes	See also Doric & Pansy	Jeannette, 1937–1938	Children's dishes
*Pretzel (R)	No. 622; Ribbon Candy	Indiana, 1930s	Crystal; teal
*Primo		U.S. Glass, 1932	Green, yellow
Primrose Lane		Morgantown, 1929	Green, pink
Primus	See Madrid		
*Princess	Drape & Tassell; Lincoln Drape; Tassell	Hocking, 1931–1935	Amber, blue, green, pink, topaz; frosted finish; gold, platinum trim, painted flowers
*Princess Feather (R)	Early American; Flower; Oatmeal Lace; Scroll & Star; Westmoreland Sandwich	Westmoreland, 1939–1948	Aqua, crystal, green, pink; 1960s—amber
Prisma		Anchor Hocking	
Prismatic Line	See Queen Mary		
Provincial	See Bubble		
Punties		Duncan & Miller, 1931	Amber, crystal, green, rose
Puritan		Duncan & Miller, 1929	
Pyramid	See No. 610		
Pyramid Optic		Hocking	Crystal, green
Queen Anne	See also Bee Hive	Anchor Hocking; late 1930s	Crystal, pink; beverage set
*Queen Mary	Prismatic Line; Vertical Ribbed; see also Lace Edge	Anchor Hocking, 1936–1940	Crystal, pink, red
*Radiance		New Martinsville, 1936–1939	Amber, cobalt blue, crystal, green, ice blue, red
*Raindrops	Optic Design; Pebble Optic; see also Pear Optic	Federal, 1929–1933	Crystal, green
Raspberry Band	See Laurel		
Rex	See No. 610		
Ribbed	See Manhattan		
*Ribbon		Hazel Atlas, 1930s	Black, crystal, green
Ribbon Candy	See Pretzel		
Ried		Federal, Fry, 1930	Crystal with blue, green trim
*Ring	Banded Rainbow; Banded Rings	Hocking, 1927–1932	Crystal, green, pink; rings of black, blue, orange, pink, platinum, red, yellow
Ring-Ding		Hocking, 1932	Painted bands of green, orange, red, yellow

PATTERN NAME	CROSS-REFERENCES	MANUFACTURER AND DATES	COLORS AND DESCRIPTION
Ringed Target		Macbeth-Evans, 1931	Crystal, green, pink; iced tea set
Ripple	See Ocean Wave		
Rock Crystal	Early American Rock Crystal	McKee, 1920s–1930s	Amber, blue-green, cobalt blue, crystal, green, pink, red, yellow
Romanesque	See Gothic Arches		
Rope	See Colonial Fluted		
Rose		Standard, c.1930	Topaz
Rose & Thorn	See Thorn		
*Rose Cameo		Belmont Tumbler, 1933	Green
Rose Lace	See Royal Lace		
Rose Trellis	See Block with Rose		
*Rosemary	Cabbage Rose with Single Arch; Dutch Rose; see also Mayfair Federal	Federal, 1935–1937	Amber, green, pink
*Roulette	Many Windows	Anchor Hocking, 1935–1939	Crystal, green, pink
*Round Robin	Accordian Pleats	Late 1920s–1930s	Crystal, green, iridescent marigold
*Roxana		Hazel Atlas, 1932	Crystal, white, yellow
*Royal Lace	Gladioli; Rose Lace	Hazel Atlas, 1934–1941	Amethyst, cobalt blue, crystal, green, pink
*Royal Ruby (R)		Anchor Hocking, 1939–1960s, 1977	Red
Russian	See Holiday		
*S Pattern	Stippled Rose Band	Macbeth-Evans, 1930–1935	Amber, crystal, green, monax, pink, red, ritz blue, topaz; trimmed in amber, blue, gold, green, pink, platinum, red, rose, white
Sail Boat	See White Ship		
Sailing Ship	See White Ship		
*Sandwich Anchor Hocking (R)		Anchor Hocking, 1939–1964	Amber, crystal, forest green, pink, red, opaque white
*Sandwich Indiana (R)		Indiana, 1920s–1980s	Amber, crystal, light green, pink, red, teal blue
Saturn		Heisey, 1937	Crystal, pale green
Sawtooth	See English Hobnail		
Saxon	See Coronation		
Scallop Edge		McKee	Green, pink
Scalloped Panels	See Lindburgh		
Scottie Dog	See also Laurel	McKee, 1930s	Children's set
Scrabble		Macbeth-Evans, 1931	Crystal, green, pink; iced tea set and tumblers
Scramble		Westmoreland, 1924	Amber, blue, crystal, green, rose
Scroll	See Comet		
Scroll & Star	See Princess Feather		

PATTERN NAME	CROSS-REFERENCES	MANUFACTURER AND DATES	COLORS AND DESCRIPTION
Scroll Fluted	Feather Scroll	Imperial, c.1930	Crystal, green, pink
Seafood Buffet		McKee, 1936	
Sea-Side		Jenkins	Crystal, green, iridescent amber
Semper		Louie, 1931	Green, pink, topaz; refreshment set
Shaffer		Imperial, c.1930	Amber, blue, crystal, green
Shamrock	See Cloverleaf		
*Sharon (R)	Cabbage Rose	Federal, 1935–1939	Amber, crystal, green, pink
Sheffield	See also Chinex Classic; Cremax	Macbeth-Evans, 1930–1940	Chinex, cremax
Shell	See Petalware		
Sheraton	Line 550; Panel	Barlett Collins, 1930s	
*Shirley Temple (R)		Hazel Atlas; U.S. Glass; and others; 1934–1942	Cobalt blue & white
*Sierra	Pinwheel	Jeannette, 1931–1933	Green, pink
Simplicity		Morgantown	Green, pink
Smocking	See Windsor		
Snowflake	See Doric		
Snowflake on Block	See Block with Snowflake		
Soda Fountain		Indiana, c.1930	Green, pink
Soda Shop		Smith, mid-1920s	
Sommerset		Morgantown, 1932	Black, blue, crystal, green, ruby; beverage set
Spanish Fan	Spanish Lace		Crystal, green
Spanish Lace	See Spanish Fan		
Sphinx	See Centaur		
*Spiral	Spiral Optic; Swirled Big Rib; see also Twisted Optic	Hocking, 1928–1930	Green, pink
*Spiral Flutes		Duncan & Miller, 1924—early 1930s	Amber, crystal, crystal with gold trim, green, light blue, pink, vaseline
Spiral Optic	See Spiral		
Spoke	See Patrician		
*Sportsman Series	See also White Ship; Windmill	Hazel Atlas, 1940s	Amethyst, cobalt blue, crystal with fired-on decorations
Spring Flowers		Imperial, 1920s	Plate only
Spun		Imperial, 1935	Aqua, crystal, fired-on orange, pastel colors, red
*Square	See also Alice; Fire-King Oven Ware; Jadite; Jane-Ray; Swirl Fire-King; Turquoise Blue	Anchor Hocking, 1940s–1960s	
Square		Morgantown, 1928	

PATTERN NAME	CROSS-REFERENCES	MANUFACTURER AND DATES	COLORS AND DESCRIPTION
Squat Optic		Federal, 1928	Water set
Squirt		Macbeth-Evans, 1931	Crystal, emerald green; water sets
*Starlight		Hazel Atlas, 1930s	Cobalt blue, crystal, pink, white
Stippled	See Craquel		
Stippled Rose Band	See S Pattern		
*Strawberry	See also Cherry-Berry	U.S. Glass, 1930s	Crystal, green, iridescent marigold, pink
Strawflower		Imperial, c.1930	Amber, crystal, green, Rose Marie
Stripe		Hocking, 1932	Red and white bands
*Sunburst		Jeannette, 1938–1941	Crystal
*Sunflower		Jeannette, late 1920s—early 1930s	Delphite, emerald green, light green, pink
*Swankyswigs		Hazel Atlas, 1933–1940; 1947–1958	5-oz. decorated tumblers
Sweet Pear	See Avocado		
*Swirl	Double Swirl; Petal Swirl	Jeannette, 1937–1938	Amber, delphite, ice blue, pink, ultramarine
*Swirl Fire-King	See also Fire-King Oven Ware; Alice; Jadite; Jane-Ray; Square; Turquoise Blue	Anchor Hocking, 1955–1960s	Blue, ivory with trim, jadite, pink, white with gold trim
Swirled Big Rib	See Spiral		
Swirled Sharp Rib	See Diana		
*Sylvan	Parrot; Three Parrot	Federal, 1931–1932	Amber, blue, crystal, green
Tall Boy		Federal, 1928	Green; iced tea sets
Tassell	See Princess		
*Tea Room	Moderne Art	Indiana, 1926–1931	Amber, crystal, green, pink
*Tear Drop		Duncan & Miller, 1934–1955	Crystal
Terrace		Duncan & Miller, 1935	Amber, blue, crystal, ruby
*Thistle		Macbeth-Evans, 1929–1930	Crystal, green, pink, yellow
Thorn	Rose & Thorn	U.S. Glass, 1930s	Black, crystal, green, pink
Threading	See Old English		
Three Bands		Hocking, 1930s	Opaque white with three enameled bands
Three Parrot	See Sylvan		
Thumbprint	See Pear Optic		
Tiered Block	See Line 191		
Tiered Octagon	See Octagon		
Tiered Semi-Optic	See Line 191		
Tom & Jerry		Hazel Atlas, 1930s	Opaque white, enameled decorations

PATTERN NAME	CROSS-REFERENCES	MANUFACTURER AND DATES	COLORS AND DESCRIPTION
Tom & Jerry		McKee, 1940s	Black, ivory, white with black, gold, green, red decorations
Tradition	Jamestown	Imperial, 1930s	Amber, amethyst, blue, crystal, green, pink red
Tree of Life	See Craquel		
*Trojan		Fostoria, 1929–1944	Gold tint, green, rose, topaz
Trudy		Standard, c.1930	Green, pink
Truman		Liberty, 1930	Green, pink
Trump Bridge		Federal, 1928	Colored enamel decorations; luncheon set
Tudor Ring		Federal, 1928	Crystal, green; water set
*Tulip		Dell, 1930s	Amber, amethyst, blue, crystal, green
*Turquoise Blue	See also Fire-King Oven Ware; Alice; Jadite; Jane-Ray; Square; Swirl Fire-King	Anchor Hocking, 1950s	Turquoise
Twentieth Century		Hazel Atlas, 1928–1931	Crystal, green, pink
Twin Dolphin		Jenkins	Crystal, green, iridescent amber
*Twisted Optic	See also Spiral	Imperial, 1927–1930	Amber, blue, canary yellow, green, pink
Twitch	Line 92	Bartlett-Collins, early 1930s	Green
U.S. Octagon	See Octagon		
Vernon	See No. 616		
*Versailles		Fostoria, 1928–1944	Azure, crystal bases with colored glass, gold tinted, green, rose, topaz
Verticle Ribbed	See Queen Mary		
*Vesper		Fostoria, 1926–1934	Amber, crystal, green, blue
*Victory		Diamond Glass, 1929–1932	Amber, black, cobalt blue, green, pink; gold trim
Victory Model		Silex, 1938–1942	Amber, cobalt, green, pink; coffee pot
Viking		Imperial, 1929	Green, rose
*Vitrock	Floral Rim; Flower Rim	Hocking, 1934–1937	Green, red, white with fired-on colors; decal decorations
Vivid Bands	See Petalware		
Waffle	See Waterford		
Wagner		Westmoreland, 1924	Amber, blue, green, rose
Wakefield		Westmoreland, 1933–1960s	Crystal
Washington Bi-Centennial		1932	Topaz; tumbler

PATTERN NAME	CROSS-REFERENCES	MANUFACTURER AND DATES	COLORS AND DESCRIPTION
*Waterford	Waffle	Anchor Hocking, 1938–1944	Crystal, pink, white, yellow; 1950s—forest green
Wave	See Caribbean		
Weatherford		Cambridge, 1926	Amber-Glo, emerald, Peach-Blo
Wedding Band	See Moderntone		
Westmoreland Sandwich	See Princess Feather		
Wheat		Federal, early 1930s	Crystal, green, pink
Whirly-Twirly		Anchor Hocking, 1940s	Forest green, red
White Sail	See White Ship		
*White Ship	Beverages with Sailboats; Sail Boat; Sailing Ship; White Sail	Hazel Atlas, 1938	Blue with white decorations
Wiggle		McKee, 1925	Amethyst, amber, blue, canary, green
Wildflower	See No. 618		
Wildrose	See Dogwood		
Wildrose with Apple Blossom	See Flower Garden with Butterflies		
*Windmill	Dutch; see also Sportsman Series	Hazel Atlas, 1938	Blue with white decorations
Windmill & Checkerboard	Block with Windmill		Crystal, green
*Windsor	Diamond; Smocking; Windsor Diamond	Jeannette, 1936–1946	Amberina, blue, crystal, delphite, green, pink, red
Windsor Diamond	See Windsor		
Winged Medallion	See Madrid		
Woodbury		Imperial, c.1930	Amber, crystal, green, Rose Marie
*Woolworth	Oregon Grape; see also Grape	Westmoreland, early 1930s	Blue, crystal, green, pink
Wotta Line		Paden City, 1933	Amber, amethyst, Cheri-Glo, crystal, ebony, green, royal blue, ruby, topaz
*X Design	Criss Cross	Hazel Atlas, 1928–1932	Crystal, green, pink, white; breakfast set
Yankee		Macbeth-Evans, 1931	Crystal, green, pink; water set
Yoo-Hoo		Jenkins, c.1930	
Yo-Yo		Jenkins, c.1930	
Yvonne	Carolyn	Lancaster, mid-1930s	Green, yellow
Zeppo		Louie, 1936	Black, green, pink, royal blue, ruby, topaz; crystal handles; beverage set

We welcome any additions or corrections to this chart. Please write to us c/o Crown Publishers, Inc., 225 Park Avenue South, New York, NY 10003.

AMERICAN DINNERWARE

AMERICAN DINNERWARE

Introduction

Many patterns of ceramic dinnerware were made in America from the 1930s through the 1950s. Some collectors refer to it as "Depression dinnerware," but the name used by the manufacturers was "American dinnerware," and that is the name used by most collectors and dealers.

Pottery, porcelain, semiporcelain, ironstone, and other ceramic wares are included in the category of dinnerware. Most were made in potteries located in southern Ohio and in West Virginia near the Ohio River. Each factory made many patterns for sale to gift shops and department stores. The potteries also made special patterns for use as premiums and free giveaways or to sell for low prices as store promotions.

American dinnerware patterns fall into six categories. The first patterns to be rediscovered by collectors and the first to be reproduced have been the solid-colored pottery lines such as Fiesta or Harlequin. Some of this type of dinnerware was also made in California potteries before 1950.

Many manufacturers preferred hand-painted decorations on their dinnerware. Included in this group are the pieces made by Southern Potteries under the name Blue Ridge and the pottery by Stangl of New Jersey picturing fruit, flowers, or birds.

An unusual type of dinnerware made by Harker and others was Cameoware: a solid-colored plate embellished with a white decoration that appears to be cut into the colored glaze.

Particular patterns can be found by using either the Depression Glass or American Dinnerware main listings, both of which are arranged alphabetically. Depression Glass begins on page 7 and American Dinnerware on page 123. There is no index of pattern names in this book as it would only duplicate the main listings. However, we have compiled lists of known Depression glass and American Dinnerware patterns along with information on manufacturers, dates, alternate names, and descriptions. These can be found at the end of each section.

Realistically shaped pieces resembling corn were produced by several makers. The most important was Corn King by the Shawnee Pottery Company. Green and yellow dishes were made in full sets. Other sets of dishes in three-dimensional shapes include the Red Riding Hood line, many cookie jars, and salt and pepper shakers.

Some of the dishes were made in very modern shapes with solid-colored decorations. The innovative shapes and subtle earth-tone colorings made them favorites in the 1940s and 1950s, for example, wares designed by Russel Wright and made by several firms, and the Lu-Ray pattern by Taylor, Smith, and Taylor.

Most of the dinnerware was decorated with decal designs: colored, printed patterns applied to the dishes. The most famous of these designs, Autumn Leaf, was made for and sold by the Jewel Tea Company. Mexican-inspired designs such as Mexicana by Homer Laughlin were popular during the late 1930s. The Hall China Company made many decal-decorated wares, including Poppy, Red Poppy, and Crocus. Black silhouette designs against light-colored dishes were popular in the 1930s, for example, Silhouette by the Crooksville China Company and Taverne by the Hall China Company.

Because the dishes were made by so many manufacturers, there is a problem with variations in vocabulary. Most sugar bowls made for these dinnerware sets had covers. Today many have lost the original cover and are sold as open sugars. We do not include the word "open" in the description, but we do indicate if there is a cover.

The terms "kitchenware" and "dinnerware" are used in the original sense. A dinnerware set includes all the pieces that might have been used on a dinner table, including dishes, bowls, platters, tumblers, cups, pitchers, etc. A kitchenware set has bowls and storage dishes of the type used in a kitchen and does not include dinner plates or cups.

Colors often were given romantic names; and, whenever necessary, we have used more ordinary language. So although we may describe a set as "surf green" or "Persian Cream," we will list it as green or ivory. Some colors, like camellia (rose), cadet (light blue), Indian red (orange), or Dresden (deep blue), are explained in the paragraph descriptions. A list of known patterns and makers is included at the end of the book.

It is important to remember that the descriptions of dinnerware may include many strange names. Some are the factory names, some names refer to the pattern (decorations applied to the piece), and many of the names were used by the factory to describe the shape: for example, Taverne is a pattern, Laurel is the shape of the dish used to make that pattern, and Taylor, Smith, and Taylor is the name of the company that made the dinnerware. Sometimes a name refers to both a pattern and a shape.

Pieces of American dinnerware are constantly being discovered in attics, basements, garage sales, flea markets, and antiques shops. The publications that offer them through the mail use descriptions that often include both the pattern and the shape name. Learn to recognize the shapes that were used by each maker. Authors of some of the other books about dinnerwares have arbitrarily named the pieces. Sometimes these names, although referring to the same piece, are different in different books. We have tried to cross-reference these names so you can locate them in any of the other books.

Although hundreds of patterns are included in this book, many patterns were not seen at sales this year and were not included. Prices listed in this book are actual prices asked by dealers at shows, shops, and through national advertising. It is not the price you would pay at a garage sale or church bazaar. Prices are not estimates. If a high and low are given, we have recorded several sales. There is a regional variation in the prices, especially for the solid-colored wares. In general, these pieces are high priced in the East and West, lower in the center of the country.

There have been a few reissues of dinnerwares. Harlequin was put back into production in 1979; the Woolworth Company was sole distributor. Complete dinner sets were made in the original colors, except that the salmon is a deeper color than the original. The sugar bowls were made with closed handles. A Fiesta look-alike was made by Franciscan since 1978 under the name Kaleidoscope. Fiesta was reissued by Homer Laughlin China Company in 1986. The original molds and marks were used. The new Fiesta has a china body that shrinks a little more than the semi-vitreous clay body used before. This means that most pieces are slightly smaller than the old ones. Dinner plates and soup-cereal bowls, however, were made slightly larger to accommodate modern tastes. New molds were made for these pieces. The dinner plates are 10½ inches. The new dishes are made in cobalt blue (darker than the original), black, white, apricot, and rose. A few of the pieces have been slightly redesigned since 1986 and there are variations in handles and bases.

If you plan to collect dinnerwares, be sure to do further research into your patterns in the books listed in the Bibliography that follows.

AMERICAN DINNERWARE
Bibliography

Bougie, Stanley J. and David A. Newkirk. *Red Wing Dinnerware.* Privately printed, 1980 (Rte. 3, Box 141, Monticello, MN 55362).

Catalina Art Pottery Price List and General Sales Instructions, 1942 (catalog reprint). Privately printed, 1982 (Delleen Enge, 912 N. Signal, Ojai, CA 93023).

Chipman, Jack and Judy Stangler. *Bauer Pottery 1982 Price Guide.* Privately printed, 1982 (16 East Holly Street, Pasadena, CA 91003).

Cunningham, Jo. *Autumn Leaf Story Price Guide, 1979/1980.* Privately printed, 1979 (Box 4929, Springfield, MO 65808).

Cunningham, Jo. *Collector's Encyclopedia of American Dinnerware.* Paducah, Kentucky: Collector Books, 1982.

Cunningham, Jo. *Hall China Price Update.* Privately printed, 1982 (Box 4929, Springfield, MO 65808).

Derwich, Jenny and Mary Latos. *Dictionary Guide to United States Pottery & Porcelain (19th and 20th Century).* Privately printed, 1984 (P.O. Box 674, Franklin, MI 48025).

Dole, Pat. *Purinton Pottery.* Privately printed, 1984 (P.O. Box 4782, Birmingham, AL 35206).

Duke, Harvey. *Superior Quality Hall China: A Guide for Collectors.* Privately printed, 1977 (Box HB, 12135 N. State Road, Otisville, MI 48463).

Enge, Delleen. *Franciscan Ware.* Paducah, Kentucky: Collector Books, 1981.

Eva Zeisel: Designer for Industry. Chicago: University of Chicago Press, 1984.

Farmer, Linda D. *Farmer's Wife's Fiesta Inventory & Price Guide.* Privately printed, 1984 (P.O. Box 10371, Pittsburgh, PA 15234).

Fridley, A. W. *Catalina Pottery: The Early Years 1927–1937.* Privately printed, 1977 (P.O. Box 7723, Long Beach, CA 90807).

From Kiln to Kitchen: American Ceramic Design in Tableware. Springfield, Illinois: Illinois State Museum, 1980.

Hayes, Barbara and Jean Bauer. *California Pottery Rainbow.* Privately printed, 1975 (1629 W. Washington Boulevard, Venice, CA 90291).

Homer Laughlin China Company: A Fiesta of American Dinnerware. Newell, West Virginia: Homer Laughlin China Co., 1985.

Huxford, Sharon and Bob. *Collectors Encyclopedia of Fiesta,* 6th Edition. Paducah, Kentucky: Collector Books, 1987.

Huxford, Sharon and Bob. *Collectors Encyclopedia of Roseville Pottery.* Paducah, Kentucky: Collector Books, 1976.

Keillor, Winnie. *Dishes What Else? Blue Ridge of Course!* Privately printed, 1983 (5731 Gorivan Road, Frankfort, MI 49635).

Kerr, Ann. *Russel Wright and His Dinnerware.* Privately printed, 1981 (P.O. Box 437, Sidney, OH 45365).

Kerr, Ann. *Russel Wright Dinnerware: Designs for the American Table.* Paducah, Kentucky: Collector Books, 1985.

Kerr, Ann. *Steubenville Sage.* Privately printed, 1979 (P.O. Box 437, Sidney, OH 45365).

Klein, Benjamin. *Collector's Illustrated Price Guide to Russel Wright Dinnerware.* Smithtown, New York: Exposition Press, Inc., 1981.

Kovel, Ralph and Terry. *Kovels' Antiques & Collectibles Price List,* 20th Edition. New York: Crown Publishers, 1987.

Kovel, Ralph and Terry. *Kovels' Guide to Selling Your Antiques & Collectibles.* New York: Crown Publishers, 1987.

Kovel, Ralph and Terry. *Kovels' Know Your Collectibles.* New York: Crown Publishers, 1981.

Kovel, Ralph and Terry. *Kovels' New Dictionary of Marks Pottery & Porcelain 1850 to the Present.* New York: Crown Publishers, 1986.

Lehner, Lois. *Complete Book of American Kitchen and Dinner Wares.* New York: Wallace-Homestead Book Co., 1980.

Nelson, Maxine Feek. *Versatile Vernon Kilns.* Privately printed, 1978 (P.O. Box 1686 Huntington Beach, CA 92647).

Nelson, Maxine. *Versatile Vernon Kilns Book II.* Paducah, Kentucky: Collector Books, 1983.

Newbound, Betty. *Gunshot Guide to Values of American Made China & Pottery.* Privately printed, 1981 (4567 Chadsworth, Union Lake, MI 48085).

Newbound, Betty. *Gunshot Guide to Values of American Made China & Pottery.* Privately printed, 1984 (4567 Chadsworth, Union Lake, MI 48085).

Newbound, Bill and Betty. *Southern Potteries Inc. Blue Ridge Dinnerware,* Revised 2nd Edition. Paducah, Kentucky: Collector Books, 1984.

Newkirk, David A. *Guide to Red Wing Prices.* Privately printed, 1982 (Rte. 3, Box 146, Monticello, MN 55362).

Pottery 1880–1960. Encino, California: Orlando Gallery, 1973.

Rehl, Norma. *Abingdon Pottery.* Privately printed, 1981 (P.O. Box 556, Milford, NJ 08848).

Rehl, Norma. *Collectors Handbook of Stangl Pottery.* Privately printed, 1979 (P.O. Box 556, Milford, NJ 08848).

Rehl, Norma. *Stangl Pottery Part II.* Privately printed, 1982 (P.O. Box 556, Milford, NJ 08848).

Riederer, LaHoma and Charles Bettinger. *Fiesta III, A Collector's Guide to Fiesta Dinnerware.* Privately printed, 1980 (P.O. Box 2733, Monroe, LA 71201).

Roberts, Brenda. *Collectors Encyclopedia of Hull Pottery.* Paducah, Kentucky: Collector Books, 1980.

Schneider, Robert. *Coors Rosebud Pottery.* Privately printed, 1984 (Box 10382S Pike Place Station, Seattle, WA 98101).

Simon, Dolores. *Red Wing Pottery with Rumrill.* Paducah, Kentucky: Collector Books, 1980.

Simon, Dolores. *Shawnee Pottery.* Paducah, Kentucky: Collector Books, 1977.

Supnick, Mark E. *Collecting Shawnee Pottery.* Privately printed, 1983 (8524 N.W. 2nd Street, Coral Springs, FL 33065).

Teftt, Gary and Bonnie. *Red Wing Potters & Their Wares.* Privately printed, 1981 (W174 N9422 Devonwood Road, Menomonee Falls, WI 53051).

Whitmyer, Margaret & Kenn. *Collector's Guide to Hall China.* Paducah, Kentucky: Collector Books, 1985.

AMERICAN DINNERWARE

Clubs and Publications

CLUBS

Abingdon Pottery Collectors Club, *Abingdon Pottery Collectors Newsletter,* Route 6, Box 59, Galesburg, IL 61401.

Blue & White Pottery Club, *Blue & White Pottery Club* (newsletter), 224 12th Street NW, Center Point, IA 52405.

Corn Items Collectors Association, *Corn Items Collectors Newsletter,* c/o Mr. Val Ferrin, 11825 South Harding, Chicago, IL 60655.

Novelty Salt & Pepper Shakers Club, *Novelty Salt & Pepper Shakers Club Newsletter,* R.D. 2, Box 2131, Stroudsburg, PA 18360.

Red Wing Collectors Society, *Red Wing Collectors Newsletter,* Route 3, Box 146, Monticello, MN 55362.

Willow Society, *Willow Transfer Quarterly* (newsletter), 39 Medhurst Road, Toronto, Ontario, M4B 1B2, Canada.

PUBLICATIONS

American Clay Exchange (newsletter), 800 Murray Drive, El Cajon, CA 92020.

American Willow Report (newsletter), 1733 Chase Street, Cincinnati, OH 45223.

Antique Trader Weekly (newspaper), P.O. Box 1050, Dubuque, IA 52001.

Depression Glass Daze (newsletter), Box 57, Otisville, MI 48463.

Hall China Connection (newsletter), P.O. Box 401, Pollock Pines, CA 95726.

Hot Tea (newsletter), Handle on the Teapot Enthusiast Association, 882 South Mollison Avenue, El Cajon, CA 92020.

Kovels on Antiques and Collectibles (newsletter), P.O. Box 22200, Beachwood, OH 44122.

Matching Services: China, Silver, Crystal (leaflet), Ralph and Terry Kovel (P.O. Box 22900, Beachwood, OH 44122).

National Blue Ridge Newsletter, c/o Norma Lilly, Highland Drive, Route 5, Box 62, Blountville, TN 37617.

The New Glaze (newsletter), P.O. Box 4782, Birmingham, AL 35206.

Vernon Views (newsletter) (Vernon Kilns pottery), P.O. Box 945, Scottsdale, AZ 85252.

Floragold

Beaded Block

Doric & Pansy

No. 620

Doric

Sharon

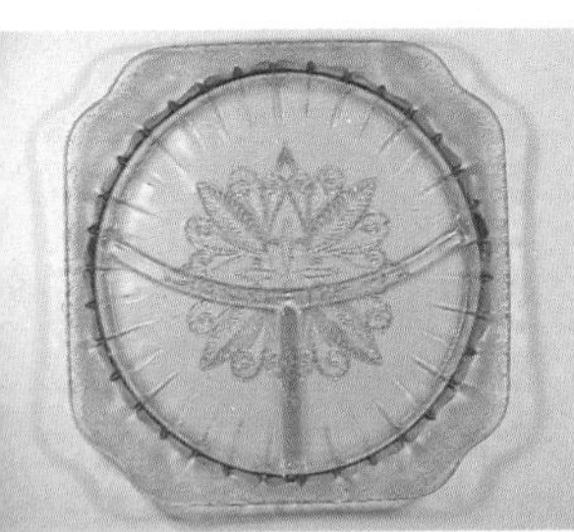

Adam

Swirl

Cubist

Iris

SWANKYSWIGS
Antique Posy Cornflower No. 1 Posy Forget-Me-Not Bustlin' Betsy

Alice

Ring

Bubble

Mayfair Federal

Cameo

Block Optic

Sandwich Indiana

Forest Green

Chinex Classic

Manhattan

Corn King

Center: Iroquois
Left & Right: American Modern

Harlequin

Cat-tail

Rustic Plaid

Crocus

Rose Bud

Cameo Shellware

California Provincial

Gingham

Refrigerator Ware

Riviera

Fiesta

Flora

Blueberry

Blue Willow

Ballerina

Country Garden

Amberstone

Fiesta is a popular dinnerware pattern found in solid colors. In 1967 Amberstone was made by the Homer Laughlin China Company, Newell, West Virginia, using the Fiesta shapes. The pieces were glazed a rich brown. Some pieces had black machine-stamped underglaze patterns. The pieces were used for supermarket promotions and were called Genuine Sheffield dinnerware. Full sets of dishes were made.

Bowl, 5 1/2 In. 2.50
Creamer 3.50
Cup & Saucer .... 3.50 To 4.50
Plate, 6 3/8 In................ 2.00
Plate, 7 1/4 In................ 3.00
Plate, 10 In.................... 3.00
Salt & Pepper .... 7.00 To 9.00
Saucer.......................... 1.00

American Modern

Russel Wright was a designer who made dinnerware in modern shapes for many companies. American Modern was made by the Steubenville Pottery Company, Steubenville, Ohio, from

Russel Wright
MFG. BY
STEUBENVILLE

1939 to 1959. The original dishes were made in Seafoam (blue-green), white, Coral, Chartreuse, Granite Gray, and Bean Brown (a shaded brown). The brown was replaced with Black Chutney (dark brown), during World War II. Cantaloupe, Glacier Blue, and Cedar Green were added in the 1950s. Matching linens and glassware were made.

BEAN BROWN

Baker, Small.................. 16.00
Bowl, Vegetable, Cover,
  12 In......................... 35.00
Bowl, Vegetable, Open,
  10 In......................... 15.00
Celery......................... 22.00
Creamer 8.00
Cup & Saucer 12.50
Pitcher, Water 55.00
Plate, 6 1/4 In............... 4.25
Plate, 10 In.......... 5.00 To 7.50
Plate, Chop.................. 25.00
Platter......................... 20.00
Salt & Pepper 12.00
Sugar, Cover 10.00

BLACK CHUTNEY

Bowl, Soup, Lug Handle ... 16.00
Bowl, Vegetable, Open..... 15.00
Casserole, Cover 37.00
Celery......................... 22.00
Creamer 8.00
Cup............................. 6.00
Cup & Saucer 12.50
Pitcher, Water 55.00
Plate, 6 1/4 In...... 3.00 To 4.25
Plate, 10 In.................... 7.50
Plate, Chop.................. 25.00
Platter......................... 20.00
Salt & Pepper 12.00
Sugar, Cover 10.00

CANTALOUPE

Cup & Saucer 12.50
Plate, 6 1/4 In............... 4.25
Plate, 10 In.................... 7.50

CEDAR GREEN

Bowl, Fruit, Lug Handle 7.00
Casserole, Cover 30.00
Celery......................... 18.00
Creamer 8.00
Cup & Saucer ..... 7.00 To 10.00
Gravy Boat....... 10.00 To 12.00
Mug............................ 28.00
Pitcher, Water 30.00
Plate, 6 1/4 In............... 4.25
Plate, 10 In.......... 5.00 To 7.50
Plate, Chop.................. 20.00
Salt & Pepper 10.00
Sugar........................... 7.00

CHARTREUSE

Bowl, Fruit, Lug Handle 7.00
Bowl, Soup, Lug Handle 6.00
Bowl, Vegetable, 10 In. 9.00
Casserole, Cover 25.00
Celery......................... 15.00
Creamer 6.00
Dish, Pickle 6.00
Pitcher, Water ... 18.00 To 25.00
Plate, 6 1/4 In............... 1.75
Plate, 8 1/4 In............... 4.00
Plate, 10 In.......... 4.00 To 5.00
Platter............. 9.00 To 12.00
Sugar........................... 8.00

CORAL

Ashtray............ 8.00 To 10.00
Baker.......................... 15.00
Bowl, 5 In..................... 7.00
Bowl, Fruit,
  Lug Handle...... 7.00 To 10.00
Bowl, Salad.................. 30.00

Bowl, Vegetable,
2 Sections 35.00
Bowl, Vegetable, Cover 25.00
Bowl, Vegetable, Open,
10 In. 12.00
Butter, Cover 95.00
Casserole,
Cover .... 27.00 To 35.00
Celery .... 12.00 To 22.00
Coffeepot, 5 In. X 8 In. 40.00
Creamer 8.00
Cup .... 6.50 To 7.00
Cup & Saucer 15.00
Dish, Pickle 9.00
Gravy Boat .... 8.00 To 10.00
Pepper Shaker 4.00
Pitcher, Cover 65.00
Pitcher, Water 55.00
Plate, 6 1/4 In. ..... 1.75 To 3.00
Plate, 8 1/4 In. 4.00
Plate, 10 In. .... 4.00 To 8.00

Plate, Chop, Square,
13 In. 20.00
Platter .... 15.00 To 20.00
Saltshaker 4.00
Setting For 4, 16 Piece 60.00
Soup, Dish .... 7.00 To 10.00
Stack Set 85.00
Sugar, Cover ...... 8.00 To 10.00
Teapot 30.00

GLACIER BLUE

Ashtray 8.00
Baker 18.00
Cup & Saucer 12.50
Plate, 6 1/4 In. 4.25

GRANITE GRAY

Ashtray .... 10.00 To 12.00
Bowl, 10 In. 10.00
Bowl, Fruit,
Lug Handle .... 5.00 To 7.00

Bowl, Salad, 11 In. 32.00
Bowl, Vegetable, Cover 35.00
Bowl, Vegetable, Open,
10 In. 12.00
Casserole, Cover 30.00
Casserole,
Stick Handle .... 30.00 To 35.00
Celery .... 15.00 To 17.00
Creamer 10.00
Cup .... 5.00 To 6.00
Cup & Saucer .... 5.00 To 9.00
Dish, Pickle 10.00
Gravy Boat .... 13.00 To 15.00
Pitcher, Water ... 30.00 To 50.00
Plate, 6 1/4 In. ..... 2.00 To 3.00
Plate, 8 In. 7.00
Plate, 10 In. .... 4.50 To 8.50
Platter, Rectangular 20.00
Salt & Pepper ..... 6.00 To 10.00
Saltshaker .... 4.00 To 5.00
Saucer 2.00
Setting For 4, 16 Piece 60.00
Sugar, Cover ...... 7.00 To 10.00

SEAFOAM BLUE

Ashtray 8.00
Baker, 7 1/2 In. 22.00
Bowl, Fruit, Lug Handle 7.50
Bowl, Salad 30.00
Bowl, Soup, Dish, 6 In. 6.00
Bowl, Vegetable,
Cover .... 20.00 To 25.00
Bowl, Vegetable,
Oval .... 12.00 To 18.00
Casserole, Cover 27.00
Celery 15.00
Creamer .... 8.00 To 9.00
Cup & Saucer ..... 7.00 To 15.00
Gravy Boat 15.00
Pitcher, Water ... 35.00 To 50.00
Plate, 6 1/4 In. ..... 2.00 To 3.50
Plate, 10 In. .... 4.00 To 8.00
Plate, Chop 20.00
Platter,
13 1/2 In. ...... 13.00 To 22.00
Salt & Pepper ..... 8.00 To 12.00
Saltshaker 6.50
Sugar 10.00
Teapot .... 35.00 To 40.00

Apple Franciscan

Franciscan Pottery made Apple pattern dishes from 1940. The pattern is still being made, although the company is now part of Wedgwood Inc.

Bowl, 5 1/4 In. .... 3.25 To 4.00
Bowl, 6 In. .... 4.00 To 7.50
Bowl, 6 1/2 In. 19.00
Bowl, 7 1/2 In. 15.00
Bowl, 8 1/2 In. 14.00
Bowl, 9 In. 22.00
Bowl, Footed, 7 In. 8.00
Butter, 1/4 Lb. 10.00
Butter, Cover, 1/4 Lb. 22.00
Casserole, Cover 15.00
Casserole, Handle 30.00
Celery, Oval 22.00
Cookie Jar, Cover 85.00
Creamer .... 10.00 To 14.00
Cup 5.00
Cup & Saucer ..... 6.50 To 15.00
Cup & Saucer, Cover 25.00
Cup & Saucer, Demitasse ... 18.00
Eggcup 10.00
Gravy Boat,
Attached Plate 25.00
Mug .... 14.00 To 17.50
Pitcher, 8 1/2 In. 6.00
Pitcher,
Ice Lip .... 30.00 To 65.00
Plate, 6 1/4 In. 3.50
Plate, 8 In. .... 4.00 To 6.00

Plate, 10 In. ....5.50 To 9.00
Plate, 10 1/2 In. 8.00
Plate, Chop, Round, 12 In. 22.00
Plate, Chop, Round, 14 In. 35.00
Platter, 12 In. ....25.00 To 30.00
Platter, 14 In. 28.00
Relish, 3 Sections...........15.00
Salt & Pepper 10.00
Saucer...............1.50 To 3.00
Shaker, 6 In. 10.00
Sherbet, Footed 12.00
Soup, Dish .... 7.00 To 10.00
Sugar, Cover .....15.00 To 18.00
Tumbler, 5 1/4 In. 14.00

Apple Watt

The Watt Pottery Company was incorporated in Crooksville, Ohio in 1922. They made a variety of hand decorated potteries. The most popular is Apple pattern. It was made from the 1930s as dinnerware sets and also in kitchenwares. The company burned to the ground in 1965.

Bean Pot..........35.00 To 70.00
Bowl, 8 In. 15.00
Bowl, 12 In. 55.00
Bowl, No.5...................15.00
Bowl, No.6...................12.50
Bowl, Spaghetti ....40.00 To 50.00
Canister, Coffee, Cover 70.00
Canister, Flour, Cover 70.00
Canister, Sugar...............42.00
Casserole, Cover, No.601 ....45.00

Pie Plate 43.00
Pitcher, No. 5 ....35.00
Pitcher, No. 6 ....25.00
Pitcher, No.15 ....35.00
Salt & Pepper 10.00
Saltshaker 65.00

Arcadia

Arcadia pattern was made by Vernon Kilns of Los Angeles, California, about 1947.

Cup, Demitasse 8.00
Plate, 7 1/2 In. 5.00
Soup, Dish, 7 In. 8.00
Teapot 20.00

Autumn Leaf

One of the most popular American dinnerware patterns, Autumn Leaf, was made for the Jewel Tea Company, a grocery chain, beginning in 1936. Hall China Company of East Liverpool, Ohio, Crooksville China Company of Crooksville, Ohio, Harker Potteries of Chester, West Virginia, and Paden City Pottery of Paden City, West Virginia, made dishes with this design. The Autumn Leaf pattern always has the same shades of dark yellow and rust leaves. The shape of the dish varied with the manufacturer. Several special terms are used to describe these shapes, such as the word "bud-ray," which describes a bowl lid with a knob surrounded by raised rays. Collectors can find Autumn Leaf pattern tinware, plastic tablecloths, glassware, clocks, even painted

furniture. There are several books about Autumn Leaf and a collectors club listed at the back of this book.

Baker, French, 3 Sections...15.00
Baker, Oval 75.00
Bouillon 18.00
Bowl, 5 1/2 In. ....3.00 To 3.50
Bowl, 6 1/4 In. ....7.50 To 9.00
Bowl, 9 In. .... 8.00 To 12.00
Bowl, Salad, 8 In. 5.00
Bowl, Vegetable, 2 Sections ......50.00 To 100.00
Bowl, Vegetable, Cover, Oval 26.00
Bowl, Vegetable, Oval, 10 1/2 In. .... 8.50 To 12.00
Butter, 1/4 Lb. 125.00
Cake Carrier 25.00
Cake Plate ....10.00 To 16.00
Candy Container, Footed..................... 245.00
Canister, 6 In. 12.50
Casserole, Oval 56.00
Clock, Electric.............. 345.00
Coffee Server, Cover........25.00
Cookie Jar, Big Ear.........85.00 To 100.00
Cookie Jar, Peanut 85.00
Cookie Jar, Tootsie..........75.00
Creamer 6.00
Cup...................4.00 To 6.00

A vase that is drilled for a lamp, even if the hole for the wiring is original, is worth 30 to 50 percent of the same vase without a hole.

Cups are best stored by hanging them on cup hooks. Stacking cups inside each other can cause chipping.

Cup & Saucer .... 4.50 To 7.00
Custard, Individual 4.00
Dish, Souffle, 10 Oz. 15.50
Flour Sifter, Metal 100.00
Gravy Boat .... 9.50 To 15.00
Gravy Boat, Underplate 21.00
Jar, Grease, Cover 9.50
Jar, Jam, Cover, Underplate 37.00
Mixing Bowl Set, Sunshine, 6, 7, & 8 In. 20.00
Mixing Bowl, 6, 7, 7 1/2 & 9 In., 3 Piece 32.00
Mixing Bowl, Radiance, No.3, 6 In. 10.00
Mixing Bowl, Radiance, No.5, 9 In. 14.00
Mug .... 50.00 To 55.00
Mustard, Cover 24.00
Percolator, Electric 215.00
Pie Plate, 9 1/2 In. 9.00
Pitcher, Ball 16.00
Pitcher, Ice Lip 17.50
Pitcher, Milk 12.50
Plate, 6 In. .... 1.50 To 2.25
Plate, 7 1/4 In. 4.00
Plate, 8 1/4 In. 6.00
Plate, 9 In. .... 3.50 To 5.00
Plate, 10 In. .... 9.50 To 12.00
Platter, 11 1/4 In. 8.00
Platter, 13 1/2 In. ...... 13.00 To 17.00
Salt & Pepper 5.00
Saucer 1.50
Soup, Cream ..... 11.00 To 22.00
Soup, Dish .... 6.50 To 8.00
Sugar 6.00
Sugar, Cover, Rayed 9.50
Teapot, Aladdin, Infusor 38.00
Tidbit, 3-Tier 55.00
Tumbler, 3 3/4 In. 20.00
Tumbler, Frosted, 5 1/2 In. .... 13.00 To 25.00
Warmer, Oval 100.00
Warmer, Round 85.00

B

Ballerina

Solid-colored pottery was popular in the 1950s. The Universal Potteries of Cambridge, Ohio, made Ballerina from 1947 to 1956. Ballerina was very modern in shape and had solid-colored glazes. A later line was decorated with abstract designs. The original solid-colored Ballerina dinnerware was offered in Dove Gray, Jade Green, Jonquil Yellow, and Periwinkle Blue. In 1949 Chartreuse and Forest Green were added. By 1955 Burgundy, Charcoal, and Pink were added, while some other colors had been discontinued. There was also a line called Ballerina Mist which was a pale blue-green with decal decorations.

BLUE

Bowl, 2 Handles, 6 1/2 In. 5.00

BURGUNDY

Butter, 1/4 Lb. 9.00
Cup 2.75
Cup & Saucer 3.00
Gravy Boat 5.00
Pitcher, 12 In. 7.00
Saucer 1.00
Soup, Dish, Lug Handle 3.00

CHARTREUSE

Plate, 9 In. 3.50
Saucer 1.00

DOVE GRAY

Cup 2.75
Cup & Saucer 3.00
Pitcher 3.50
Plate, 9 In. 2.50
Plate, Handle, 10 In. 4.00
Salt & Pepper 4.50
Saucer 1.25
Shaker 4.50
Soup, Dish 3.50
Sugar, Cover 4.00

FOREST GREEN

Bowl, 9 In. .... 5.00 To 7.00
Creamer 2.50
Cup & Saucer 3.00
Gravy Boat .... 4.50 To 6.00
Pitcher, 6 In. 1.75
Plate, 6 In. 1.75
Plate, 7 1/2 In. 3.00
Plate, 10 In. 4.00
Platter, 2 Handles, 11 3/4 In. 8.00
Salt & Pepper .... 4.50 To 6.00
Saucer 1.00
Sugar, Cover 4.50

JADE GREEN

Bowl, Vegetable, 9 In. 4.00

Plate, 9 In. 2.50
Tidbit, 2 Tiers 5.00

JONQUIL YELLOW

Gravy Boat 6.00
Saucer 1.00

Banded

Banded is a kitchenware pattern made by the Hall China Company of East Liverpool, Ohio, beginning in 1937. Ridges forming a band are molded into the pieces. Banded is the name of both a solid-color line and the shape for some decal-decorated pieces. The solid pieces are usually found in Chinese Red.

CHINESE RED

Jug, 6 1/4 In. 15.00
Jug, Sunshine, Cover, Silver Trim, 4 1/8 In. 37.00

Betty

Betty is a Blue Ridge pattern made on the Candlewick shape. It features a red flower, a yellow flower, and green leaves.

Creamer 3.50
Cup & Saucer 4.00
Plate, 9 In. 3.50
Platter, 15 In. 10.00

Blue Ridge
Hand Painted
Underglaze
Southern Potteries, Inc.
MADE IN U. S. A.

Bittersweet

Blue Ridge, Hall, Universal, and Stangl potteries made patterns named Bittersweet. Listed here is the Universal Bittersweet pattern made from 1942 to 1949. It has bright orange and yellow decal decorations.

Casserole, Cover 15.00
Cup & Saucer 4.00
Plate, 9 In. 4.00
Salt & Pepper 5.00

Blossom Time

Blossom Time by Red Wing Pottery was made in 1947. It is a dinnerware with modern shapes, red flowers, and green leaves. Yellow and green accessory pieces were made.

Bowl, 5 In. 3.00
Bowl, 8 1/2 In. 6.00
Cup & Saucer 6.00
Plate, 6 1/2 In. 2.00
Plate, 10 1/2 In. 5.00

Blue Bouquet

Standard Coffee of New Orleans, Louisiana, gave Blue Bouquet pattern dinnerware and kitchenware as a premium from the early 1950s to the early 1960s. Although it was made by the Hall China Company, East Liverpool, Ohio, it is most easily found in the South. The pattern is very plain with a thin blue border interrupted by roses.

Baker, French 7.00
Bowl, 9 In. 22.00
Coffeepot, Large 25.00
Pie Plate 50.00
Plate, 9 In. 15.00
Sugar, Lid, Boston 12.00

Blue Garden

Blue Garden is a line of Hall kitchenware made in 1939. The body is cobalt blue, the design is a floral decal pattern.

Batter Jug 100.00
Bowls, Nested, 8, 9, 10 In. 40.00

Creamer 20.00
Salt & Pepper 25.00
Teapot, New York 100.00

Blue Parade, see Rose Parade

Blue Willow

Willow pattern pictures a bridge, three figures, birds, trees, and a Chinese landscape. The pattern was first used in England by Thomas Turner in 1780 at the Caughley Pottery Works. It was inspired by an earlier Chinese pattern. The pattern has been copied by makers in almost every country. Many pieces of Blue Willow were made by Homer Laughlin, Sebring, and other American makers; but we list dishes here from these and foreign firms.

Bowl, 5 In., Homer Laughlin 2.75
Bowl, 5 In., Royal 1.50
Bowl, 6 In., Homer Laughlin 4.00
Carafe, Japan 47.50
Casserole, Cover, Royal..... 28.00
Coffee Warmer, Japan 60.00
Creamer, 1 3/4 In.......... 10.00
Creamer, Child's, 2 In. 12.00
Creamer, Japan, 3 1/4 In.... 9.00
Creamer, Royal 2.75
Creamer, U.S.A. 3.50
Cup & Saucer, Child's, 2 1/4 In. 4.75
Cup & Saucer, Japan 7.50
Cup & Saucer, U.S.A. 4.50
Cup, Stack, Homer Laughlin 2.50
Eggcup, Homer Laughlin 9.00
Gravy Boat, Royal........... 10.00
Plate, 6 In., Royal 1.50
Plate, 6 In., U.S.A. 2.00
Plate, 6 1/4 In., Homer Laughlin .... 1.75 To 2.75
Plate, 9 In., Homer Laughlin 4.50
Plate, 9 In., Royal 2.25
Plate, 10 In., Homer Laughlin 8.00
Plate, 10 In., Meakin 12.00
Plate, 12 In., Royal 12.00
Plate, Child's, 3 3/4 In. 4.75
Plate, Child's, 4 1/2 In. 5.00
Plate, Royal, 12 In. 9.00
Platter, 11 1/2 In., Homer Laughlin 12.00
Platter, 12 1/2 In., Japan 16.50
Platter, Child's, Oval, 6 In. 18.00
Soup, Dish 6.00
Soup, Dish, Child's, 4 3/4 In. 24.75
Soup, Dish, U.S.A. 4.00
Sugar, Cover, Royal 4.00
Teapot, Sugar & Creamer 75.00

Blueberry

Stangl Pottery of Trenton, New Jersey, made Blueberry (pattern No. 3770) before 1942. The heavy red pottery dishes were glazed with a yellow border and a sgraffito decoration of blueberries in the center.

Bowl, 5 1/2 In. 4.00
Creamer, 2 3/4 In. 4.00
Cup 3.00
Dish, Pickle 10.00
Plate, 6 In. 5.00

Plate, 9 In. 6.00
Teapot 15.00

Bob White

Bob White was made by Red Wing Potteries from 1956 to 1967. It was one of the most popular dinnerware patterns made by the factory. The pattern, a modern hand-painted design, shows a stylized bird and background.

Bowl, 5 1/2 In. 5.00
Bowl, 9 In.................... 14.00
Bowl, Nut, Large............ 20.00
Bowl, Vegetable, 2 Sections,
 14 In............. 15.00 To 20.00
Casserole,
 Cover............ 28.00 To 35.00
Cup............................ 4.00
Cup & Saucer ..... 6.00 To 10.00
Dish, Hors D'Oeuvre Holder,
 Bird Shape...... 24.00 To 32.00
Pitcher, 12 In. 23.00
Pitcher, Tall.................. 32.00
Plate, 6 1/2 In...... 1.50 To 3.00
Plate, 10 1/2 In. ... 6.00 To 8.00
Platter, Oval,
 20 In............ 15.00 To 22.50
Salt & Pepper, Tall.......... 18.00
Saucer.......................... 2.75

Brittany

Brittany is a pattern made by Red Wing in 1941. It pictures a yellow rose and a yellow band on the rim of the plates.

Bowl, 5 1/2 In. 3.00
Bowl, 9 1/2 In. 10.00
Plate, 6 In. 4.00
Plate, 7 In. 5.00
Plate, 10 In.................... 6.00
Platter, 14 In.................. 8.00
Shaker.......................... 4.50

Brown-Eyed Susan

Brown-Eyed Susan was first made by Vernon Kilns, Vernon, California, in the 1940s.

Butter Chip................... 10.00
Butter, Cover, 1/4 Lb. 10.00
Coaster.......................... 8.00
Creamer 3.00
Cup & Saucer 9.00
Cup & Saucer, Demitasse... 12.00
Eggcup.......................... 9.00
Gravy Boat 9.00

Plate, 10 1/2 In. 7.00
Platter, Round, 12 In. 10.00
Salt & Pepper 7.50
Syrup........................... 30.00
Teapot 25.00
Tumbler, 14 Oz.............. 11.00

Cactus

Cactus is a Mexican-inspired pattern first made by Hall China in 1937. It was made in kitchenware, not dinnerware, pieces.

Coffeepot, Viking............ 25.00
Platter, 12 In................. 15.00
Saltshaker..................... 12.00
Teapot, French............... 45.00

Calico

Calico is one of the plaid designs made by Vernon Kilns of Vernon, California. The design was pink and blue with a blue border. Other related plaids are Coronation Organdy (gray and rose), Gingham (green and yellow), Homespun (cinnamon, yellow, and green), Organdie (brown and yellow), Tam O'Shanter (green, lime, and cinnamon), and Tweed (gray and blue).

Plate, 9 In. 6.00
Saucer 1.50
Sugar & Creamer 10.00

Calico Fruit

Dinnerware and kitchenware were made in Calico Fruit pattern in the 1940s. It was made by Universal Potteries, Cambridge, Ohio; matching tinware and glass pieces were also made by other firms. The design of the fruit is a vivid red and blue on a plain white dish. Unfortunately, the decals often fade.

Cookie Jar 16.50
Plate, 10 In. 7.00
Plate, 9 In. 5.00

Caliente

Every pottery company, it seemed, made a solid-colored dinnerware in the 1940s. Paden City Pottery Company, Paden City, West Virginia, made Caliente, a semi-porcelain, in blue, green, tangerine, and yellow. There is also matching ovenproof cooking ware.

BLUE

Cup & Saucer 4.25
Salt & Pepper 10.00

GREEN

Bowl, 5 In. 3.00
Bowl, 6 1/4 In. 4.00
Cup & Saucer 8.00
Plate, 6 In. 2.50
Teapot 30.00

TANGERINE

Bowl, 5 In. 3.00
Bowl, 6 1/4 In. 4.00
Cup & Saucer .... 4.25 To 9.50
Plate, 6 In. 2.25
Plate, 9 In. 4.00
Saucer 3.00

YELLOW

Bowl, 5 In. 3.00
Mixing Bowl, 8 In. 5.00
Plate, 9 In. 4.00
Saucer 1.50

California Provincial

California Provincial dinnerware pictures a rooster in the center. The rooster is maroon, green, and yellow. The border is green and coffee brown. It was made by Metlox in 1965.

Bowl, Vegetable 25.00
Canister, Flour 25.00
Cup & Saucer 8.00
Gravy Boat 25.00
Pitcher, Milk 25.00
Plate, Dinner 10.00
Platter, 13 In. 25.00

Cameo Rose Hall

Cameo Rose made by Hall China Company has gray and white

decal decorations and a gold trim. It was not made by the cameo process used for cameo shellware and other designs.

Bowl, 5 1/4 In. 2.50
Bowl, Oval, 10 1/2 In....... 8.50
Bowl, Vegetable, Cover 35.00
Creamer ....4.00 To 4.50
Cup & Saucer 5.00
Gravy Boat...................10.00
Plate, 6 1/2 In............... 2.00
Platter, 11 1/4 In. 9.50
Platter, 13 In................10.00
Saltshaker...................... 6.50
Sugar.........................10.00

Cameo Rose Harker

The names of the various cameo ware shapes and designs are confusing. One pattern is Cameo Rose, made by Harker China Company, Chester, West Virginia, from about 1940. The design is of solid white roses against a blue, pink, gray, or yellow background.

Cameo Rose Harker, see also Cameo Shellware; White Rose

BLUE

Beanpot.......................50.00
Creamer 6.50
Cup............................ 4.00
Cup & Saucer..... 5.00 To 12.00
Plate, Square, 8 3/4 In. 5.50

Plate, Square, 9 1/2 In. 6.50
Soup, Dish 4.00
Tea Tile 9.00

Cameo Shellware

Another cameo pattern, Cameo Shellware, has the same design as Cameo Rose, but the dishes are fluted.

BLUE

Bonbon 25.00
Bowl, Footed, Oval 15.00
Compote, 6 In. 8.00
Plate, 9 In..................... 4.50
Powder Jar 8.00
Relish 25.00
Snack Set, 8 Piece...........20.00
Sugar, Cover 6.00

Don't store dishes for long periods of time in old newspaper wrappings. The ink can make indelible stains on china.

Some tea and coffee stains on dishes can be removed by rubbing them with damp baking soda.

YELLOW

Pitcher, Cover 7.00

Carnival

Carnival is a pottery decorated with abstract star-like patterns, made by Stangl Pottery, Trenton, New Jersey, from 1954 to 1957.

Bowl, 9 In. 6.50
Bowl, 10 In. 8.00
Butter, Corn Shape, 1/4 Lb. 10.00
Creamer 6.50
Eggcup 10.00
Plate, 6 In. 2.00
Plate, 14 1/2 In. 14.00

Casualstone

Casualstone is another in the family of Fiesta dinnerware. Homer Laughlin Company, Newell, West Virginia, made the dishes for supermarket promotions under the trade name Coventry in 1970. Antique Gold Fiesta Ironstone dishes were decorated with a gold-stamped design on some pieces. Small, deep dishes were left in solid colors.

Bowl, 5 1/2 In. 3.00
Cup & Saucer 4.00
Plate, 6 In. 2.00
Plate, 9 In. 5.00
Saucer .... .50

Cat-Tail

Cat-Tail pattern dishes must have been found in most homes in America in the 1940s. Sears, Roebuck and Company featured the pattern from 1934 to 1956. It was made by the Universal Potteries of Cambridge, Ohio. The red and black cat-tail design was used for dinnerware and matching tinware, kitchenware, glassware, furniture, and table linens.

Bean Pot, Amethyst 2.50
Berry Bowl 5.50
Bottle, Water, Cover 32.00
Bowl, 5 1/4 In. 6.00
Bowl, 8 3/4 In. .... 9.00 To 15.00
Bowl, 9 1/4 In. 20.00
Bowl, Salad 22.50
Bowl, Vegetable, Oval, 10 In. 16.50
Bowl, Vegetable, Round.... 14.50
Butter 38.00
Cake Plate, Circus Handle 18.00
Cake Safe 17.00

Canister Set, Red Top, Tin, Set of 4 .... 40.00
Casserole, Cover, Handle, 8 1/2 In. 16.50
Cup 4.50
Cup & Saucer .... 5.00 To 9.50
Custard Cup 3.75
Gravy 11.00
Jug, Stopper 18.50
Jug, Tilt, Stopper, 1 Qt. 15.00
Pepper Shaker 5.00
Pie Plate, 10 In. 15.00
Pie Server 15.00
Pitcher, Milk, 6 In. 15.00
Plate, 6 In. 2.50
Plate, 9 1/4 In. 6.00
Plate, Dinner 6.25
Plate, Dinner, 10 In. 10.00
Platter, Oval, 11 1/2 In. 7.50
Platter, Oval, 13 In. 22.50
Platter, Oval, 13 1/2 In. 9.00
Platter, Oval, 14 1/2 In. ...... 10.00 To 12.00
Scale, Kitchen 18.00
Soup, Dish 10.00
Sugar & Creamer 12.00
Sugar, Cover 10.00
Teapot, Cover 18.00
Waste Can, Tin, Oval, 12 In. 20.00
Water Set, 7 Piece 75.00

Century

Century pattern was made by the Homer Laughlin China Company. The ivory dinnerware had floral decals.

Bonbon, 3-Footed 12.00
Bowl, 8 In. 30.00

Candy Container, Cover, 7 In. 45.00
Compote, Round 13.50
Mustard, Cover 45.00
Pickle, 8 In. 12.00
Pitcher, Milk 40.00

Plate, 10 In. 18.00
Relish, 3 Sections 19.00
Sandwich Server, Center Handle 35.00
Sugar & Creamer .... 14.00 To 22.50
Vase, Bud, 6 In. 12.00

Chinese Red

Chinese Red is a color used by Hall China Company, East Liverpool, Ohio. This bright red was used on many shapes of dishes. A few are listed here that are not included in the more recognizable sets.

Chinese Red, see also Banded; Saf-handle

Bean Pot 30.00
Bowl, Batter, Saf-Handle ... 55.00
Casserole, Cover, 3 Qt. 20.00
Cookie Jar 47.00
Creamer, Sani-Grid 8.50
Cup & Saucer 9.00
Jug, Sani-Grid, 5 1/4 In. 11.00
Jug, Sani-Grid, 7 1/2 In. 16.00
Pepper Shaker 6.50
Saltshaker 6.50
Sugar & Creamer 12.00
Sugar, Sani-Grid 8.50
Teapot, Sani-Grid, 6-Cup 22.00

Cock O' The Morn

Cock O' the Morn was made by Southern Potteries, Erwin, Tennessee. The hand-painted pattern shows a rooster crowing at the sun, just rising over a distant barn. Another similar pattern by Southern Potteries is called Rooster.

Cup & Saucer 5.00
Plate, 6 In. 3.00
Plate, 9 In. 4.50
Platter, 14 In. 9.00

Colonial

Colonial, also called Medallion, was the first kitchenware line made by Hall China Company, East Liverpool, Ohio. It was first made in 1932. The first pieces were made in ivory or ivory with lettuce-colored exteriors. Later pieces were made in Chinese Red, Delphinium (blue), Golden Glo, or with decal decorations. Some are still being made. The Stangl Colonial pattern is also listed here.

BLUE

Bowl, 6 In., Stangl .... 3.00 To 3.75
Cup & Saucer, Stangl .... 3.00 To 5.00
Gravy Boat, Stangl .... 9.00 To 14.00
Jug, No.3, 5 In., Hall 10.00
Plate, 7 In., Stangl .... 2.00 To 3.00
Plate, 9 In., Stangl .... 3.00 To 3.75
Sugar & Creamer, Cover, Stangl 12.00

GREEN

Bowl, 6 In., Stangl .... 3.00 To 3.75
Cup & Saucer, Stangl .... 3.00 To 5.00
Plate, 7 In., Stangl .... 2.00 To 3.00
Plate, 9 In., Stangl 3.75

LETTUCE

Baker, French, Hall 18.00
Jug, No.3, 5 In., Hall 17.00
Salt & Pepper, Hall 38.00
Sugar & Creamer, Hall 9.00

PERSIAN YELLOW

Bowl, 6 In., Stangl .... 3.00 To 3.75
Plate, 7 In., Stangl .... 2.00 To 3.00
Plate, 9 In., Stangl .... 3.00 To 3.75

RED

Bowl, 6 In., Stangl 3.75
Cup, Stangl 3.50
Plate, 9 In., Stangl .... 3.00 To 3.75

Colonial Homestead

Colonial Homestead was one of many patterns made by Royal China Company of Sebring, Ohio. The dinnerware was made in the 1940s and 1950s.

GREEN

Bowl, 5 In. 1.25
Bowl, 9 In. 5.00
Bowl, 10 In. 6.00
Creamer 2.25
Cup & Saucer 2.00
Gravy Boat 5.00
Pitcher, Handle, 10 1/4 In. 4.00
Plate, 6 1/2 In. 1.25
Plate, 9 In. 2.00
Plate, 10 In. 2.00
Plate, 2 Handles, 10 1/2 In. 4.00

Plate, Chop, 12 In. 6.00
Salt & Pepper 6.00
Soup, Cream 3.00
Soup, Dish 3.00
Teapot 20.00

Conchita

Mexican-inspired designs became the rage for dinnerwares in the late 1930s. Conchita was one of several made by Homer Laughlin Company, Newell, West Virginia. The dinnerware was a decal-decorated ware made on the Century shape line. The decoration pictured three pots of cactus in one corner, and on large flat pieces, like plates, a group of hanging gourds and peppers. There is a thin red border trim. Conchita decals were also used on kitchenwares made on the Kitchen Kraft shapes.

HOMER LAUGHLIN

Bowl, 5 In. 6.00
Cup & Saucer 8.00
Plate, 5 In. 3.00
Plate, 9 In. 4.50

Conchita Kitchen Kraft

Conchita pattern decals of three pots of cactus were used to decorate the Oven-serve and Kitchen Kraft oven-to-table kitchenwares made by Homer Laughlin Company, Newell, West Virginia, in the 1930s.

Bowl, Mixing, 9 In. 22.00
Bowl, Mixing, 10 In. 24.00
Plate, 10 1/2 In. 18.00

GENUINE
OVEN SERVE
WARE
U·S·A

Coors, see Rosebud

Corn King

Dishes shaped like ears of corn? This novel idea became a popular reality when Corn King pattern was sold by Shawnee Pottery Company, Zanesville, Ohio, before 1954. The green and yellow dishes, three-dimensional representations of ears of corn, ranged from dinner plates to small salt and pepper shakers. Corn King has darker yellow corn kernels and lighter green leaves than a later pattern called Corn Queen.

Shawnee
U. S. A.

Bowl, No.5 .... 16.50
Casserole, 3 Piece 40.00
Casserole, Cover 38.00
Cookie Jar 35.00
Creamer 12.00
Mug 22.00
Pitcher, 1 1/2 Qt. 35.00
Plate, 10 In. 25.00
Salt & Pepper 15.00

Salt & Pepper, Large........16.00
Sugar & Creamer, Cover...35.00

Corn Queen

Corn King was redesigned slightly by Shawnee Pottery Company, Zanesville, Ohio, and continued to be marketed from 1954 to 1961. The kernels of the new line were lighter yellow and the foliage was a deeper green. It was called Corn Queen.

Cookie Jar....................22.00
Creamer......................10.00
Pitcher, Milk.................20.00
Plate, 10 In...................18.00
Tray, Relish...................7.00

Shawnee
U.S.A.

Coronado

Franciscan dinnerware was made in Los Angeles, California. Coronado was a popular plain-colored art ware made by Franciscan from 1935 to 1942. Fifty different shapes and fifteen different colors were made. Another pattern called Coronado was made by Vernon Kilns. The Franciscan pieces are listed in this book.

CORAL

Ashtray, Shell.................6.50
Bowl, 7 1/2 In..............7.00
Casserole, Cover............10.00
Creamer......................6.00
Cup..................2.75 To 4.00
Cup & Saucer.................6.00
Plate, 6 In...................3.00
Plate, 6 3/8 In...............2.25
Plate, 7 1/2 In......3.25 To 5.00
Plate, 8 In....................4.50
Plate, 9 1/4 In...............6.00

Plate, 12 In..................13.00
Saucer..........................2.00
Sugar, Cover..................9.00

GRAY

Bowl, 7 1/2 In. 8.50

IVORY

Sugar, Cover..................6.00

MAROON

Cup.............................2.75
Cup & Saucer.................3.50
Saucer..........................1.25
Teapot, Glazed..............25.00

REDWOOD

Bowl, 6 In..........2.00 To 3.00
Pitcher.........................3.00
Saucer..........................1.00
Sherbet, 5 In.................4.00

TURQUOISE

Bowl, 6 In.....................3.00
Butter, Cover................10.00
Cup & Saucer................5.00
Cup & Saucer, Demitasse....7.00
Olive Dish, 9 1/2 In.........5.00
Pitcher, 6 3/8 In. 2.00
Plate, 6 3/8 In...............2.25
Plate, 8 In.....................4.50
Plate, 12 In..................10.00
Plate, 14 In..................12.00
Platter, 13 In................12.00
Saucer..........................1.25
Sherbet, 5 In.................4.00
Soup, Cream, Underplate...10.50
Sugar & Creamer, Cover...10.00
Teapot........................30.00

WHITE

Bowl, Oval, 13 In..........20.00
Cup & Saucer.................6.00
Plate, 10 1/4 In.............6.00

YELLOW

Ashtray, Shell, Individual....6.50
Bowl, 6 In..........2.00 To 3.00
Cup.............................3.00
Olive Dish, 9 1/2 In.........5.00
Pitcher, 6 3/8 In. 3.00
Plate, 6 1/2 In...............2.00
Plate, 9 1/2 In...............4.00
Platter, 13 3/4 In. 5.00
Saucer..........................1.00
Sherbet, 5 In.................4.00
Soup, Dish....................4.00
Sugar, Cover..................4.75

Country Garden

Three raised flowers are pictured on the Country Garden dinnerware. The pattern was made by Stangl Pottery of Trenton, New Jersey, from 1956 to 1974.

Casserole, Cover............18.00
Cup & Saucer, 5 1/2 In. 7.50
Pickle Dish, 10 In..........12.00
Pitcher, 4 1/2 In. 12.00
Plate, Chop, 14 1/2 In. 15.00
Salt & Pepper, 2 Cruets, Tray.........................28.00
Sauce Boat...................10.00
Teapot, Cover...............25.00

Crab Apple

One of the most popular Blue Ridge dinnerware patterns made by Southern Potteries of Erwin, Tennessee, under the name Blue Ridge was Crab Apple. This brightly colored hand-painted dinnerware was decorated with red apples and green leaves. A thin red spatter border was used. Matching glassware was made. The pattern was in production after 1930 and was discontinued when the factory went out of business in 1957.

Bowl, Round, 9 In. 7.00
Creamer 4.00
Cup & Saucer 6.00
Plate, 8 1/2 In................ 4.00
Plate, 9 1/2 In................ 5.00
Platter, Oval,
13 In............ 10.00 To 13.00
Platter, Oval, 15 In.......... 12.00
Salt & Pepper,
Blossom Top 24.00

Crocus

Crocus was a popular name for dinnerware patterns. Prices listed

are for the Crocus pattern by Hall China Company of East Liverpool, Ohio, in the 1930s. The decal-decorated dinnerware was sometimes called Holland. The design was a border of oddly shaped crocuses in black, lavender, red, green, and pink. Most pieces have platinum trim. Other firms, including Stangl Pottery and Blue Ridge, had very different-looking dinnerwares called Crocus.

Bowl, 9 In.................... 18.00
Casserole, Sunshine.......... 22.00
Coffeepot, Drip-O-Lator ... 45.00
Cup.................. 5.00 To 6.00

Cup & Saucer 8.00
Jar, Pretzel 55.00
Leftover, Rectangular 20.00
Mixing Bowl,
6 In.............. 9.00 To 12.00
Mixing Bowl, 9 In........... 15.00
Pepper Shaker, Handle 10.00
Platter, 13 In..... 16.00 To 18.00
Range Set 30.00
Salt & Pepper 24.00
Saltshaker, Handle, 2 In. 9.00
Teapot, Colonial 35.00
Teapot, Metal Drip.......... 32.00

Cumberland

Large hand-painted blue and white flowers with green leaves and reddish flowerlets are centered on the plates of Cumberland pattern. The pattern was made by Southern Potteries, Erwin, Tennessee, about 1948.

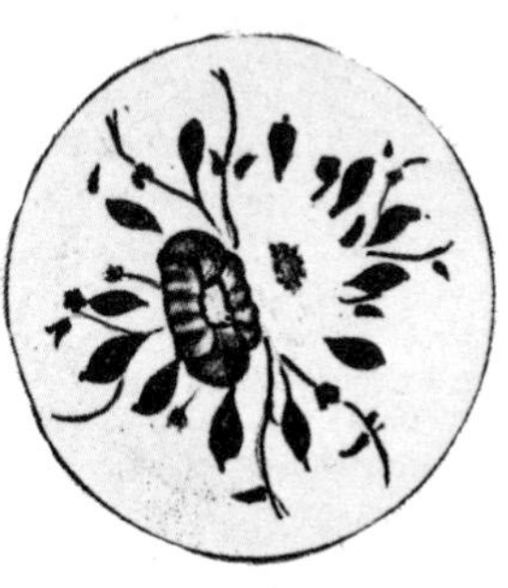

Blue Ridge
Hand Painted
Underglaze
Southern Potteries, Inc.
MADE IN U. S. A.

Bowl, 5 1/2 In. 4.00
Cup & Saucer 5.00
Plate, 9 In. 4.00

Curiosity Shop, see Old Curiosity Shop

Currier & Ives

Currier & Ives was made by the Royal China Company of Sebring, Ohio, from the 1940s. It is a blue and white pattern that was popular as a store premium. The pattern is still being made.

Ashtray...............3.25 To 4.50
Bowl, 3 3/4 In. ....1.50 To 3.50
Bowl, 5 1/2 In. 1.50
Bowl, 6 In.................... 3.50
Bowl, Vegetable, Round, 10 In......................... 7.50
Butter.........................16.50
Butter, Cover 10.00
Casserole..........20.00 To 35.00
Creamer 3.00
Cup & Saucer ....2.50 To 4.50

Custard, 4 Piece 3.00
Gravy Boat, Saucer..........10.00
Mixing Bowl, 6 1/4 In. 3.00
Mixing Bowl, 8 1/2 In. 4.00
Mug........................... 2.00
Plate, 6 In..........1.50 To 2.50
Plate, 7 In..................... 3.00
Plate, 10 In..........2.00 To 4.50
Plate, Handle, 10 1/2 In.... 6.00
Platter, 13 In.................12.00
Salt & Pepper 10.00
Soup, Dish ....3.75 To 6.50
Sugar & Creamer, Cover...............7.50 To 9.50
Sugar, Cover 4.25
Teapot ....28.00 To 35.00
Tumbler, 4 3/4 In. 4.25
Tumbler, 5 1/2 In. 4.50

D

Daffodil

Daffodil is a pattern made by Southern Potteries, Erwin, Tennessee, under the trademark Blue Ridge. It pictures a large single yellow and orange daffodil realistically painted on each plate. The dinnerware shape has a piecrust edge.

Blue Ridge
Hand Painted
Underglaze
Southern Potteries, Inc.
MADE IN U. S. A.

Bowl, 5 1/2 In. 4.00
Bowl, Salad.................... 5.50
Cup & Saucer 5.00
Plate, 9 In..................... 4.00

Daisy

Daisy, or Hawaiian 12-point Daisy, is a Fiesta Casual pattern. Two designs, Daisy and Yellow Carnation, were made by the Homer Laughlin Company of Newell, West Virginia. They were first made in 1962 and discontinued in 1968. Daisy pattern, on the familiar Fiesta shape, has a turquoise rim and turquoise and brown daisies in the center.

Bowl, 5 1/2 In. 3.00
Cup & Saucer 3.00
Plate, 8 In..................... 4.00
Plate, 10 In.................... 4.50

Delicious

Delicious pattern pictures two Delicious apples with green and yellow leaves. It has a beaded edge. The hand-painted Blue Ridge pattern was made by Southern Potteries of Erwin, Tennessee, before 1957, when the firm went out of business.

Blue Ridge
Hand Painted
Underglaze
Southern Potteries, Inc.
MADE IN U. S. A.

Plate, 6 In. 1.50
Plate, 9 In. 7.00
Sugar & Creamer 12.00

Desert Rose

Desert Rose by Franciscan is one of the popular patterns with today's collectors. It was introduced in 1941. The name is for a shape, not for the decoration on the plate.

Bowl, 5 1/4 In. .... 3.50 To 9.00
Bowl, 5 3/4 In. 7.50
Bowl, 8 In. 20.00
Bowl, 8 1/2 In. 10.00
Bowl, 9 In. 22.00
Butter, Cover, 1/4 Lb. 11.00
Casserole, Cover, Handle ... 45.00
Celery, 11 In. 22.00
Creamer .... 9.00 To 14.00
Cup .... 4.50 To 8.00
Cup & Saucer ..... 6.00 To 10.00
Gravy Boat, Attached Underplate ...... 25.00 To 28.00
Pitcher, Quart 32.00
Plate, 5 1/2 In. 3.50
Plate, 6 1/4 In. 4.00
Plate, 7 In. 4.00
Plate, 8 In. 7.50
Plate, 9 1/2 In. 7.50
Plate, 10 1/2 In. ... 6.00 To 9.50
Platter, Oval, 12 In. 20.00
Platter, Oval, 14 In. 25.00
Platter, Round ... 18.00 To 25.00
Soup, Dish 14.00
Sugar, Cover ..... 11.00 To 15.00
Teapot, Cover 45.00
Tumbler, 5 1/2 In. 13.00

Dogwood

Dogwood pattern was made by Homer Laughlin China Company of Newell, West Virginia. It is a decal-decorated line of dinnerware. The edges are gold, the pattern realistic pink and white sprays of dogwood. It was made in the 1960s. Another pattern named Dogwood was made by Stangl Pottery Company, Zanesville, Ohio, in 1965. It is a heavy pottery dinnerware. Other factories also used the Dogwood name for dinnerware patterns.

Bowl, 5 1/2 In. 2.50
Plate, 9 In. 3.00
Saucer 1.00

Dolores

Dolores is a Vernon Kilns pattern made in the 1940s. It has a floral border.

Bowl, 5 1/2 In. 4.00
Bowl, Vegetable, Oval, 10 In. 9.00
Bowl, Vegetable, Round, 9 In. 9.00
Creamer 6.00
Cup 6.00
Cup & Saucer 5.00
Plate, 7 1/2 In. 4.00
Plate, 9 1/2 In. 5.00
Plate, 10 1/2 In. ... 5.00 To 6.00
Plate, Bread & Butter 3.00
Plate, Chop, 12 In. 8.00
Platter, 14 In. 12.00
Salt & Pepper 9.00
Sugar 7.00
Sugar & Creamer .... 10.00 To 12.00

E

El Patio

El Patio is one of many solid-color dinnerware patterns made by Franciscan from 1936–1956. It comes in twenty colors.

BLUE

Cup & Saucer 7.00

GREEN

Plate, 9 In. 6.50
Tumbler, Spring Handle..... 6.50

FRANCISCAN WARE
MADE IN CALIFORNIA U.S.A.

MAROON

Cup............................ 4.00

ORANGE

Gravy Boat, Saucer.......... 18.00
Plate, 9 In. 6.50

PINK

Plate, 9 In. 6.50
Tumbler, Spring Handle..... 6.50

TURQUOISE

Plate, Chop, 14 In. 12.00
Salt & Pepper 7.00
Syrup, Small.................. 6.00

YELLOW

Cup & Saucer 7.00
Tumbler, Spring Handle..... 6.50

F

Fantasia

Fantasia is an abstract leaf pattern made by Blue Ridge on the Skyline shape. It is brown, blue, and yellow.

Bowl, Vegetable, Round, Open, 9 In. 7.00
Cup............................ 3.50
Cup & Saucer 5.00

Blue Ridge
Hand Painted
Underglaze
Southern Potteries, Inc.
MADE IN U.S.A.

Plate, 6 In. 2.00
Plate, 7 3/4 In. 2.50
Plate, 10 In. 5.00
Salt & Pepper, Handle....... 8.00
Sugar & Creamer 5.00

Fiesta

Fiesta ware was introduced in 1936 by the Homer Laughlin China Company, Newell, West Virginia. The line was redesigned in 1969 and withdrawn in 1973. The design was characterized by a band of concentric circles, beginning at the rim. Cups had full-circle handles until 1969, when partial-circle handles were made. The original Fiesta colors were bright green, dark blue, Fiesta red, and yellow. Later old ivory, turquoise, gray, rose, forest green, light green, and chartreuse were added. From 1970 to 1972 the redesigned Fiesta Ironstone was made only in mango red, antique gold, and turf green (medium green). Most Fiesta ware was marked with the incised word Fiesta. Some pieces were hand-stamped before glazing. The Fiesta shape was also made with decal decorations, but these are not considered Fiesta by collectors; instead they are collected by the pattern names. There is also a Fiesta Kitchen Kraft line, a group of kitchenware pieces made in the early 1940s in blue, green, red, or yellow. These were bake-and-serve wares. Glassware and linens were made to match the Fiesta colors. Homer Laughlin reissued Fiesta in 1986 using the original marks and molds.

Fiesta, see also Amberstone; Casualstone; Daisy; Fiesta Ironstone; Fiesta Kitchen Kraft; Yellow Carnation

BLUE

Bowl, 4 3/4 In. 8.00
Bowl, No.2, 6 In. 26.00
Bowl, No.4, 8 In. 30.00
Bowl, No.5, 9 In. 50.00
Bowl, No.6, 10 In. 45.00
Carafe, 3 Pt. 90.00
Casserole, Cover, Individual 19.00
Cup & Saucer 17.00
Cup & Saucer, After Dinner.... 16.00 To 26.00
Eggcup............ 9.00 To 20.00
Plate, 9 In. 7.00
Plate, 10 1/2 In. 10.00
Plate, Grill, 10 1/2 In. 9.00
Plate, Grill, 11 1/2 In. 18.00
Saltshaker 4.50
Saucer, After Dinner 4.00
Soup, Cream 16.00
Sugar, Cover 10.00
Teapot, 6-Cup 45.00
Tray, Figure 8 .... 28.00
Vase, 8 In. 165.00
Vase, 12 In. 250.00

CHARTREUSE

Bowl, 4 3/4 In. .... 8.00 To 14.00
Bowl, 8 1/2 In. 25.00
Coffeepot, Cover 80.00
Creamer .... 8.50 To 11.00
Cup & Saucer .... 18.50 To 22.00

Gravy Boat....27.00
Jug, 2 Pt....40.00
Mug....11.00 To 15.00
Plate, 6 In....4.75 To 6.00
Plate, 7 In....4.00 To 7.50
Plate, 9 In.... 7.00 To 10.00
Plate, 10 In....14.00 To 18.00
Plate, Deep, 8 In....20.00 To 22.00
Platter, Oval, 12 1/2 In....20.00
Salt & Pepper....16.00
Saucer....2.00 To 5.00
Soup, Cream....20.00 To 24.00
Sugar....8.50
Sugar & Creamer, Cover....26.50
Sugar, Cover, Small....12.00

DARK BLUE

Ashtray....22.00
Bowl, 4 3/4 In....12.00
Bowl, 5 1/2 In....13.50
Bowl, 6 In....18.00
Bowl, 8 1/2 In....22.00
Creamer....7.50
Cup....8.00
Cup & Saucer....16.50 To 18.00
Gravy Boat....22.00
Mug....28.00
Plate, 6 In....3.50
Plate, 7 In....4.50
Plate, 9 In....5.00 To 7.50
Plate, 10 In....12.75
Plate, Chop, 12 1/4 In....14.00
Plate, Chop, 14 1/2 In....17.00
Plate, Deep, 8 In....18.00
Plate, Grill, 10 1/2 In....14.00 To 18.00
Plate, Grill, 11 5/8 In....25.00 To 28.00
Platter, Oval, 12 1/2 In....18.00
Relish, 5 Inserts....20.00
Salt & Pepper....12.00
Saucer....2.00
Soup, Cream....18.00
Tumbler, 5 Oz....18.00
Tumbler, 10 Oz....21.50 To 25.00
Vase, Bud, 6 3/8 In....40.00

FOREST GREEN

Bowl, 4 3/4 In....14.00 To 16.00
Bowl, 5 1/2 In....16.00
Bowl, 6 In....17.00
Bowl, 8 1/2 In....19.00
Casserole....65.00
Casserole, Cover....75.00
Coffeepot....85.00
Creamer....9.50 To 12.50
Cup & Saucer....23.00
Gravy Boat....25.00 To 27.00
Jug, 2 Pt....45.00
Mug....35.00
Plate, 6 In....4.75
Plate, 7 In....5.00
Plate, 9 In....8.50 To 10.00
Plate, 10 In....18.00
Plate, Deep, 8 In....20.00 To 22.50
Plate, Grill, 10 1/2 In....14.00
Platter, Oval, 12 In....24.50
Salt & Pepper....16.50
Saucer....2.00 To 4.50
Sugar....9.00
Sugar, Cover....23.00

GRAY

Bowl, 4 3/4 In....16.50
Bowl, 6 In....25.00
Bowl, 8 1/2 In....18.00 To 28.50
Casserole, Cover....90.00
Creamer....11.00
Cup....15.00
Cup & Saucer....21.00 To 23.00
Mug....30.00 To 35.00
Plate, 6 In....5.00
Plate, 7 In....5.00 To 7.50
Plate, 9 In....10.00
Plate, 10 In....18.00
Plate, Deep, 8 In....22.50
Platter, 12 In....22.00
Shaker....6.00
Soup, Cream....15.00 To 29.00
Sugar, Cover....20.00 To 25.00

LIGHT GREEN

Bowl, 4 3/4 In....8.00 To 12.00
Bowl, 5 1/2 In....13.00
Bowl, 6 In....12.00 To 18.00
Bowl, 8 1/2 In....22.00
Bowl, 9 1/4 In....18.00 To 27.00
Bowl, No.2, 6 In....20.00
Bowl, No.4, 8 In....35.00
Bowl, No.5, 9 In....39.00
Bowl, No.7, 11 1/2 In....97.00
Bowl, Salad, Footed....115.00 To 120.00
Cake Plate....20.00
Candleholder, Bulb....15.00
Candleholder, Tripod, Pair....115.00 To 120.00
Carafe, 3 Pt....46.00 To 70.00
Coffee Set, After Dinner, 6 Cups & Saucers....185.00
Coffeepot, Cover....32.00 To 60.00
Compote, 10 1/4 In....18.00
Compote, 12 In....40.00
Creamer....7.00
Cup....18.00
Cup & Saucer....14.00 To 23.00
Cup & Saucer, After Dinner....28.00
Eggcup....9.00
Gravy Boat....12.00 To 23.00
Mustard, Cover....45.00
Pitcher, Ice, 2 Qt....32.00
Plate, 6 In....2.00 To 3.50
Plate, 7 In....1.50 To 4.75
Plate, 9 In....4.50 To 7.00
Plate, 10 In....9.00 To 12.00
Plate, Chop, 12 In....13.00 To 14.00
Plate, Chop, 14 In....15.00 To 17.00
Plate, Deep, 8 In....12.00 To 18.00
Platter, Oval, 12 In....11.00 To 18.00
Relish, 5 Blue & Yellow Inserts....100.00
Relish, 5 Inserts....15.00
Salt & Pepper....8.00 To 10.00
Soup, Cream....18.00
Soup, Onion, Cover....45.00 To 95.00
Sugar, Cover....10.00 To 16.00
Syrup, Cover....65.00 To 100.00
Tray, Utility....18.00

Tumbler, 5 Oz. .... 11.50 To 18.00
Tumbler, 10 Oz. .... 20.00 To 25.00
Vase, 8 In. 170.00
Vase, 8, 10 & 12 In., 3 Piece 900.00
Vase, 12 In.... 265.00 To 285.00
Vase, Bud, 6 3/8 In. 22.00

MEDIUM GREEN

Bowl, 5 1/2 In. 21.00
Bowl, 6 In. 18.00
Bowl, 7 5/8 In. 45.00
Cup .... 15.00 To 22.00
Cup & Saucer .... 13.50 To 23.00
Gravy Boat 5.00
Mug 35.00
Plate, 6 In. .... 1.75 To 4.00
Plate, Chop, 13 In. 48.00
Platter, Oval, 12 1/2 In. ... 13.00
Relish, 5 Inserts 58.00
Teapot 25.00
Tumbler, 5 Oz. 12.50

OLD IVORY

Ashtray 21.00
Bowl, 4 3/4 In. .... 5.50 To 12.00
Bowl, 5 1/2 In. .... 8.50 To 13.50
Bowl, 6 In. .... 18.00 To 18.50
Bowl, 8 1/2 In. 22.00
Bowl, No.6, 10 In. 75.00
Candleholder, Bulb, Pair .... 34.00 To 42.00
Candleholder, Tripod, Pair 115.00
Compote, 10 1/2 In. 18.00
Compote, 12 In. 40.00
Creamer .... 6.50 To 7.50
Cup 5.00
Cup & Saucer .... 14.50 To 18.00
Cup & Saucer, After Dinner.... 20.00 To 24.00
Eggcup 25.00
Gravy Boat .... 12.00 To 23.00
Jar, Jam, Cover 85.00
Jug, 2 Pt. .... 21.00 To 25.00
Mug .... 28.00 To 37.00
Mustard, Cover 60.00
Pitcher, Disk, 2 Qt. .... 30.00 To 38.00
Plate, 6 In. .... 2.00 To 3.50
Plate, 7 In. .... 4.00 To 5.00
Plate, 8 In. 11.50
Plate, 9 In. .... 5.00 To 7.50
Plate, 10 In. .... 7.50 To 12.75
Plate, Chop, 13 In. .... 10.00 To 14.00
Plate, Chop, 15 In. 25.00
Plate, Deep, 8 In. 18.00
Plate, Grill, 11 5/8 In. 20.00
Platter, Oval, 12 1/2 In. ... 18.00
Salt & Pepper ..... 8.00 To 10.00
Saucer .... 1.00 To 3.50
Soup, Cream ..... 13.00 To 20.00
Soup, Onion, Cover 150.00
Sugar 7.00
Sugar & Creamer, Cover ... 18.00
Sugar, Cover 16.00
Syrup 75.00
Teapot 5.00
Tray, Utility 18.50
Tumbler, 5 Oz. .... 11.50 To 18.00
Tumbler, 10 Oz. .... 20.00 To 25.00
Vase, 8 In. 195.00
Vase, Bud, 6 3/8 In. 28.00

RED

Ashtray .... 25.00 To 35.00
Bowl, 4 3/4 In. .... 12.00 To 14.00
Bowl, 5 1/2 In. .... 13.00 To 25.00
Bowl, 6 In. .... 18.00 To 26.00
Bowl, 7 5/8 In. 42.00
Bowl, 8 1/2 In. .... 20.00 To 27.00
Bowl, No.1, 5 In. 30.00
Bowl, No.4, 8 In. 35.00
Candleholder, Bulb, Pair .... 45.00 To 50.00
Carafe, 3 Pt. .... 95.00 To 105.00
Casserole, Cover 85.00
Coffeepot .... 85.00 To 95.00
Coffeepot, After Dinner .... 125.00 To 145.00
Compote, 10 1/4 In. 22.00
Compote, 12 In. .... 45.00 To 85.00
Compote, Sweets .... 33.00 To 37.00
Creamer, Stick Handle .... 12.00 To 14.00
Cup .... 15.00 To 20.00
Cup & Saucer .... 21.00 To 22.50
Cup & Saucer, After Dinner .... 29.00 To 39.00
Eggcup .... 15.00 To 32.00
Gravy Boat 26.00
Jar, Jam, Cover .... 110.00 To 135.00
Jug, 2 Pt. .... 39.00 To 55.00
Mug .... 31.00 To 35.00
Mustard .... 70.00 To 85.00
Pitcher, Disk, 2 Qt. 47.00
Pitcher, Disk, Juice, 30 Oz. .... 80.00 To 110.00
Pitcher, Ice, 2 Qt. .... 65.00 To 75.00
Plate, 6 In. .... 4.00 To 4.50
Plate, 7 In. .... 6.00 To 7.50
Plate, 9 In. .... 10.00 To 13.50
Plate, 10 In. ...... 14.00 To 18.00
Plate, Chop, 13 In. 18.00
Plate, Chop, 15 In. .... 20.00 To 22.00
Plate, Deep, 8 In. .... 20.00 To 24.00
Plate, Grill, 10 1/2 In. ...... 20.00 To 22.00
Plate, Grill, 11 5/8 In. 20.00
Platter, Oval, 12 In. .... 20.00 To 25.00
Salt & Pepper .... 13.00 To 16.75
Saucer .... 2.00 To 3.00
Soup, Cream 20.00
Soup, Onion, Cover 175.00
Sugar, Cover 22.00
Syrup .... 100.00 To 110.00
Teapot, 6–Cup ... 59.00 To 62.00
Teapot, 8–Cup 75.00
Tumbler, 5 Oz. .... 10.00 To 20.00
Tumbler, 8 Oz. 35.00
Tumbler, 10 Oz. .... 27.00 To 35.00
Vase, 10 In. 100.00
Vase, Bud, 6 3/8 In. 40.00

Always wash antique china in a sink lined with a rubber mat or towels. This helps prevent chipping. Wash one piece at a time. Rinse and let it air dry. If you suspect a piece has been repaired, do not wash it. Clean with a soft brush dampened in a solution of ammonia and water.

ROSE

Bowl, 4 3/4 In. 15.00
Bowl, 8 In........27.00 To 30.00
Casserole,
Cover...........85.00 To 100.00
Creamer ....10.00 To 14.00
Cup.............................15.00
Cup & Saucer 22.00
Gravy Boat.......27.00 To 29.00
Mug...............32.00 To 35.00
Pitcher, Disk, 2 Qt..........80.00
Plate, 6 In...........4.75 To 6.00
Plate, 7 In...........5.00 To 7.50
Plate, 9 In......... 8.00 To 10.00
Plate, 10 In.......14.00 To 16.00
Plate, Chop, 13 In...........17.50
Plate, Chop, 15 In...........25.00
Plate, Deep, 8 In. 20.00
Plate, Grill, 10 1/2 In. 19.00
Platter, Oval, 12 In..........26.00
Saucer................2.50 To 3.50
Soup, Dish, 8 In.............22.50
Sugar..........................10.00
Sugar & Creamer............30.00
Sugar, Cover 25.00
Teapot, 6-Cup...50.00 To 85.00
Tumbler, 5 Oz................14.00

TURQUOISE

Ashtray........................20.00
Bowl,
4 3/4 In.......... 5.00 To 12.00
Bowl,
5 1/2 In.......... 8.50 To 13.50
Bowl, 6 In....................18.50
Bowl,
8 1/2 In.........14.50 To 22.00
Bowl, 9 1/2 In. 25.00
Bowl,
11 3/4 In....100.00 To 120.00
Bowl, No.5, 9 In. 40.00
Bowl, No.6, 10 In...........55.00
Candleholder, Tripod 60.00
Carafe, 3 Pt. ....70.00 To 100.00
Casserole,
Cover............48.00 To 55.00
Coffeepot.........60.00 To 75.00
Compote, 12 In..............75.00
Compote,
Sweets...........18.00 To 23.00
Creamer ....6.50 To 8.00
Creamer, Stick Handle......13.50
Cup & Saucer....12.00 To 18.00
Cup & Saucer,
After Dinner................25.00
Eggcup........................23.00
Gravy Boat.......12.00 To 19.00
Jug, 2 Pt......................30.00
Mug...............25.00 To 28.00
Pitcher, Disk, 2 Qt..........27.00
Pitcher, Ice, 2 Qt............40.00
Plate, 6 In. ....2.50 To 3.50
Plate, 7 In. ....3.00 To 5.00
Plate, 9 In. ....4.00 To 7.50
Plate, 10 In........ 7.50 To 12.75
Plate, Chop,
13 In............13.00 To 17.00
Plate, Deep, 8 In. 18.00
Plate, Grill,
10 1/2 In.......10.00 To 18.00
Platter, Oval,
12 In............11.00 To 18.00
Relish,
5 Multicolored Inserts.....75.00
Salt & Pepper..... 8.00 To 12.50
Saltshaker............4.00 To 6.00
Saucer................1.50 To 2.50
Shaker......................... 5.00
Soup, Cream 18.00
Sugar.................5.50 To 7.00
Sugar, Cover 16.00
Syrup.............65.00 To 85.00
Teapot ....45.00 To 48.00
Tumbler,
5 Oz. ....11.00 To 12.50
Tumbler,
10 Oz...........22.00 To 24.00
Vase, Bud, 6 3/8 In. 32.00

YELLOW

Ashtray........................21.00
Bowl Set, Nested,
7 Piece 360.00
Bowl,
4 3/4 In.......... 3.00 To 11.00
Bowl,
5 1/2 In.......... 5.50 To 10.00
Bowl, 6 In........12.00 To 18.00
Bowl,
7 5/8 In.........38.00 To 40.00
Bowl, No.2,
6 In.............19.00 To 25.00
Bowl, No.3, 7 In. 22.00
Bowl, No.4, 8 In. 29.50
Bowl, No.5, 9 In. 45.00
Bowl, No.6, 10 In...........45.00
Bowl, Salad,
9 1/2 In.........38.00 To 46.00
Cake Plate 20.00
Candleholder, Bulb,
Pair ....28.00 To 32.00
Carafe, 3 Pt. 70.00
Casserole,
Cover............48.00 To 52.00
Casserole, French 95.00
Compote,
12 In.............42.00 To 65.00
Creamer ....6.00 To 7.00
Creamer, Stick Handle......13.00
Cup & Saucer....12.00 To 17.00
Cup & Saucer,
After Dinner................20.00
Eggcup........................25.00
Gravy Boat.......16.00 To 20.00
Jar, Jam, Cover 50.00
Juice Set, Pitcher,
6 Tumblers 85.00
Mug...............25.00 To 28.00
Mustard, Cover 60.00
Pitcher, Disk, Juice,
30 Oz.........................16.00
Plate, 6 In. ....2.50 To 3.50
Plate, 7 In. ....3.00 To 5.00

Plate, 9 In. ....4.00 To 6.50
Plate, 10 In. .... 7.50 To 12.75
Plate, Chop, 13 In. ....12.00 To 15.00
Plate, Chop, 15 In. 17.00
Plate, Deep, 8 In. ....12.00 To 17.00
Plate, Grill, 10 1/2 In. .... 9.00 To 14.00
Plate, Grill, 11 3/4 In. ......24.00 To 28.00
Platter, Oval, 12 In. ....11.00 To 18.00
Relish, 5 Inserts.........45.00 To 55.00
Salt & Pepper ....7.00 To 9.00
Saucer................1.50 To 4.00
Soup, Onion, Cover.........65.00
Sugar & Creamer, Individual 28.00
Sugar, Cover 12.00
Sugar, Creamer & Tray 90.00
Syrup........................ 105.00
Teapot, 6–Cup 48.00
Teapot, 8–Cup 58.00
Tumbler, 5 Oz. ....10.00 To 18.00
Tumbler, 10 Oz. ....22.00 To 25.00
Vase, 10 In. 80.00

Fiesta Casual, see Daisy; Yellow Carnation

Fiesta Ironstone

Fiesta Ironstone by Homer Laughlin Company, Newell, West Virgina, was made from 1970 to 1972. It was made in antique gold, turf green, and mango red.

ANTIQUE GOLD

Cup............................ 5.00

TURF GREEN

Ashtray........................15.00
Bowl, 5 1/2 In. 8.00
Saucer................1.50 To 4.00

Fiesta Kitchen Kraft

Fiesta Kitchen Kraft was a bake-and-serve line made in the early 1940s by Homer Laughlin Company, Newell, West Virginia. It was made in red, yellow, green, and blue.

BLUE

Jug, Cover, Original Stickers.......... 110.00

GREEN

Bowl, 10 In. 110.00
Cake Plate........21.00 To 30.00
Cake Server 40.00

YELLOW

Cake Plate....................21.00
Green & Red, Refrigerator Jars, Stacking 65.00

Pie Plate......................19.00
Platter.........................38.00

Flora

Flora is a 1941 Stangl pattern with a yellow band and pink, blue, and yellow flowers.

Cup & Saucer................ 3.75
Plate, 6 In..................... 1.50
Plate, 9 In..................... 4.50
Plate, 10 In. 6.00

Flower Ring

Flower Ring is another of the many Blue Ridge patterns made on the Colonial shape. A red, a yellow, and a blue flower are pictured near the border. Green leaves and a green rim finish the decoration.

Don't put china with gold designs in the dishwasher. The gold will wash off.

Bowl, 5 In. 2.00 To 3.00
Bowl, 9 In. 10.00
Cup. 5.00
Plate, 10 1/2 In. 8.00
Saucer 1.50 To 2.00
Soup, Lug Handle 5.00
Sugar & Creamer, Cover ... 10.00
Tidbit, 2 Tiers 20.00

Flowerpot

Hall China Company, East Liverpool, Ohio, made Flowerpot pattern kitchenware. The decal shows a flowerpot with a plant growing up a trellis. The bowls are made from the banded shapes.

Mixing Bowl 20.00 To 25.00
Syrup, Cover 20.00 To 25.00

Frontenac

Frontenac is a modern-looking pattern made by Red Wing Potteries on the Futura shape about 1960. It has an abstract border design of yellow and turquoise.

Bowl, 5 In. 5.00
Butter, Cover 15.00
Creamer 7.00
Plate, 6 1/2 In. 3.00
Plate, 8 1/2 In. 5.00

Plate, 10 1/2 In. 7.00
Saucer 2.00
Trivet, 6 3/4 In. 45.00

Fruit

Stangl Pottery, Trenton, New Jersey, made Fruit pattern from 1942 to 1974. The dishes had center designs that were different fruits. Some pictured apples, some pears, grapes, or other fruit. This pattern, No. 3697, was sometimes called Festive Fruit. It was marked Terra Rose.

Bowl, 10 In. 10.00 To 12.00
Coaster 3.00
Cup & Saucer 4.50 To 9.00

Pitcher, 1 Quart 15.00
Plate, 9 In. 5.00
Plate, 11 In. 6.00
Plate, 12 1/2 In. 12.00
Sauce Boat 7.50
Soup, Dish 5.50

Fruit & Flowers

Fruit & Flowers pattern, No. 4030, was made by Stangl Pottery, Trenton, New Jersey, from 1957 to 1974. The design shows a mixed grouping of flowers, leaves, grapes, and fanciful shapes. Pieces have a colored border.

Cup & Saucer 4.50
Plate, 6 1/4 In. 2.00
Plate, 10 In. 4.00

G

Gay Plaid

Gay Plaid, or Plaid, was made by Blair Ceramics from 1946 to the 1950s. The brown, green, and yellow bold plaid was the most successful pattern made by the Ozark, Missouri, firm. Many of the pieces are rectangular.

Bowl, 4 3/4 In. 4.50
Bowl, 8 In. 9.00
Creamer 3.25
Cup. 5.00
Cup & Saucer 7.00
Plate, 6 1/4 In. 2.75
Plate, 7 In. 4.00
Plate, 10 In. 6.00
Salt & Pepper 12.00

Sugar 5.50
Sugar, Cover 8.00
Tray, 5 X 10 In. 6.00

Gingham

Vernon Kilns, Vernon, California, made six different plaid patterns. Each plaid was given a special name. Gingham is the pattern with a dark green border and green and yellow plaid. Other related plaids are Calico (pink and blue), Coronation Organdy (gray and rose), Home–spun (cinnamon, yellow, and green), Organdie (brown and yellow), Tan O'Shanter (green, lime, and cinnamon), and Tweed (gray and blue).

Bowl, 5 1/2 In. 3.00
Bowl, Chowder 4.50
Butter Chip, Individual 5.00
Carafe 16.00
Casserole,
Cover .... 24.00 To 28.00
Creamer 4.00
Cup 5.00
Cup, Demitasse 8.00
Eggcup .... 8.00 To 9.00
Gravy Boat 9.00
Plate, 6 In. 2.25
Plate, 7 1/2 In. 3.00
Plate, 9 3/4 In. ..... 4.00 To 5.00
Plate, 10 In. 6.00
Platter, 14 In. 10.00
Soup, Lug Handle 4.00
Sugar, Cover 6.00
Syrup, Cover 30.00

Golden Harvest

Golden Harvest was made by Stangl Pottery from 1953 to

1973. The pattern pictured yellow flowers on a gray background.

Bowl, 12 1/4 In. 13.50
Coffee Warmer, Round 8.75
Cup 3.00
Cup & Saucer 5.50
Plate, 6 In. 1.50
Plate, 8 In. 3.50
Plate, 10 In. 4.00
Salt & Pepper 8.00
Teapot, Cover 10.00

H

Hacienda

Another Mexican–inspired pattern, Hacienda was made by Homer Laughlin China Company, Newell, West Virginia, in 1938. The dinnerware was made on Century shape. A decal showed a

bench, cactus, and a portion of the side of a Mexican home. Most pieces have red trim at the handles and at the edge of the plate well.

Bowl, 5 In. 4.50
Creamer 4.00
Creamer & Sugar 12.00
Cup & Saucer 9.00
Plate, 6 In. 2.50
Plate, 9 In. 4.00

Saucer 2.00
Soup, Flat, 8 In. 7.00

Hall Teapots

Teapots of all sizes and shapes were made by the Hall China Company of East Liverpool, Ohio, starting in the 1920s. Each pot had a special design name such as Airflow or Boston. Each shape could be made in one of several colors, often with names like Cadet (light blue), Camellia (rose), Dresden (deep blue), Delphinium (purple blue), and Indian Red (orange). Coffeepots were also made.

Airflow, Canary &
Gold .... 19.00 To 40.00
Airflow, Cobalt &
Gold .... 28.00 To 40.00
Aladdin, Black &
White .... 20.00 To 25.00

Aladdin, Canary & Gold............22.50 To 25.00
Aladdin, Cobalt, Infuser....40.00
Aladdin, Emerald & Gold...........20.00
Albany, Mahogany & Gold............22.00 To 30.00
Albert, Celadon.............17.00
Automobile, Chinese Red.............. 145.00
Automobile, Maroon...... 265.00
Basket, Chinese Red...... 100.00
Basket, Emerald & Silver...87.00
Boston, Addison.............35.00
Boston, Daffodil, 6–Cup....20.00
Boston, Emerald.............20.00
Boston, Maroon & Gold............15.00 To 16.00
Boston, Pink & Gold.......20.00
Boston, Poppy & Gold.....50.00
Boston, Stock Brown........10.00
Boston, Stock Brown & Gold....... 7.50
Cleveland, Emerald & Gold............28.00 To 45.00
Cleveland, Warm Yellow & Gold............35.00 To 45.00
Disraeli, Emerald...........25.00
Disraeli, Pink.... 16.00 To 25.00
Doughnut, Poppy........155.00 To 195.00
Football, Chinese Red..... 325.00
French, Black & Gold............13.00 To 20.00
French, Cobalt & Gold............20.00 To 25.00
French, Stock Brown & Gold............19.00 To 30.00
French, Turquoise & Gold............18.00 To 45.00
Globe, Camellia.............75.00
Hollywood, Emerald & Gold...........30.00
Hollywood, Ivory...........15.00
Hollywood, Lettuce.........25.00
Hollywood, Maroon & Gold...........20.00
Hook Cover, Blue & Gold...............22.50
Los Angeles, Canary & Gold............30.00
Los Angeles, Stock Green & Gold.......40.00
Los Angeles, Warm Yellow & Gold.....26.00
McCormick, Canary, Infuser......................35.00

McCormick, Forest...........20.00 To 22.00
McCormick, Maroon........13.00
McCormick, Turquoise, Infuser.......................20.00
Melody, Chinese Red.......60.00
Melody, Poppy..........80.00 To 125.00
Moderne, Canary...........10.00
Nautilus, Turquoise & Gold.........70.00
New York, Canary & Gold............35.00
New York, Emerald & Gold............16.00 To 32.00
New York, Forest & Gold.............19.00
New York, Ivory & Gold... 9.50
New York, Stock Brown & Gold......19.00
New York, Turquoise & Gold.........20.00
Parade, Canary & Gold............10.00 To 20.00
Parade, Daffodil & Gold...20.00
Parade, Emerald & Gold...35.00
Parade, Rose.....26.00 To 32.00
Philadelphia, Emerald & Gold...........30.00
Philadelphia, Pink & Gold...............16.00
Philadelphia, Turquoise & Gold............30.00 To 40.00
Rhythm, Canary & Gold....60.00
Sani–Grid, Chinese Red....25.00
Streamline, Canary & Silver...........45.00
Streamline, Chinese Red....30.00 To 45.00
Streamline, Delphinium 200.00 To 225.00
Streamline, Poppy..........85.00
Streamline, Warm Yellow & Gold.....55.00
Surfside, Emerald........42.00 To 55.00
Twinspout, Turquoise.......48.00
Windshield, Camellia........45.00
Windshield, Maroon & Gold............16.00 To 24.00
World's Fair, Cobalt & Gold........... 375.00

Harlequin

Harlequin, a solid–color dinnerware made by Homer Laughlin Company of Newell, West Virginia, was less expensive than Fiesta. It was made from 1938 to 1964 and sold unmarked in Woolworth stores. The rings molded into the plate were at the edge of the plate well and the rim was plain. Dishes were made in blue, yellow, turquoise, gray, rose, forest green, dark blue, light green, chartreuse, maroon, mauve blue, spruce green, ivory, and tangerine (red).

BLUE

Bowl, 5 1/2 In.............. 4.00
Cup & Saucer, After Dinner................22.00
Dish, Nut...................... 5.00
Plate, 7 In..................... 8.50
Plate, Deep, 8 In...........10.00

CHARTREUSE

Bowl, 7 In........12.00 To 14.00
Cup & Saucer.......3.50 To 6.50
Gravy Boat.......11.00 To 18.00
Plate, 6 In..................... 2.00
Plate, 7 In..................... 2.50
Sugar, Cover.................15.00
Teapot........................28.00

FOREST GREEN

Bowl, 5 1/4 In.............. 8.50
Creamer............6.00 To 9.00
Cup & Saucer.......5.00 To 9.00
Gravy Boat..................... 8.00
Jug, 22 Oz....................18.00
Saltshaker...................... 8.50
Sugar, Cover.................16.00

GRAY

Bowl, 5 1/2 In. 6.50
Bowl, 6 1/2 In. 10.00
Bowl, 7 In. 17.00
Creamer .... 5.00 To 11.00
Creamer, Novelty 23.00
Cup 6.75
Cup & Saucer .... 7.50 To 8.50
Eggcup 8.00
Gravy Boat 12.00
Plate, 6 In. .... 2.75 To 4.00
Plate, 7 In. 3.25
Plate, 9 In. .... 5.00 To 12.00
Plate, 10 In. 10.00
Plate, Deep, 8 In. 7.50
Platter, 13 In. 10.00
Saucer 1.00
Soup, Cream 18.00
Sugar 7.00
Sugar, Cover 18.00

LIGHT GREEN

Butter, Cover 30.00
Creamer, Novelty 10.00
Cup & Saucer 8.00
Plate, 7 In. 5.00
Teapot 35.00
Tumbler, Car Decal 30.00

MAROON

Bowl,
5 1/2 In. .... 3.00 To 10.00
Butter, Cover 55.00
Creamer 11.00
Cup & Saucer ..... 5.00 To 11.00
Dish, Nut .... 4.00 To 8.00
Jug, 22 Oz. 15.00
Plate, 9 In. .... 4.00 To 7.00
Platter 9.00
Saltshaker .... 6.50 To 8.00
Sugar, Cover 16.00
Teapot 40.00
Tumbler .... 22.00 To 28.00

MAUVE BLUE

Bowl, 5 1/2 In. 6.00
Bowl, 6 1/2 In.,
Set of 7 .... 50.00
Candleholder, Pair 85.00
Creamer 9.00
Creamer, Individual 15.00
Creamer, Novelty 13.00
Cup & Saucer 5.50
Cup & Saucer,
After Dinner 25.00
Cup, After Dinner 18.00
Dish, Nut 6.00
Eggcup, Individual 17.00
Plate, 7 In. .... 3.00 To 3.50
Plate, 8 In. 2.50
Plate, 10 In. 10.00
Plate, Deep, 8 In. 10.00
Platter, 11 In. 8.00
Platter, 13 In. 12.50
Salt & Pepper 10.00
Soup, Cream 12.00
Sugar & Creamer, Cover ... 18.00
Tumbler .... 22.00 To 25.00

MEDIUM GREEN

Bowl, 5 1/4 In. 7.75
Bowl, 6 1/2 In. 30.00
Cup & Saucer 9.00
Plate, 9 In. 9.00

ROSE

Ashtray, Basketweave 30.00
Bowl, 5 1/2 In. 4.00
Bowl, 6 1/2 In. 5.50
Bowl, 7 In. 12.00
Bowl, 9 In. 9.00
Casserole 65.00
Creamer 7.00
Creamer, Novelty 16.00
Cup .... 2.50 To 5.00
Cup & Saucer 8.00
Cup & Saucer,
After Dinner .... 18.00 To 30.00
Cup, After Dinner 15.00
Eggcup 13.00
Gravy Boat .... 11.00 To 13.00
Jug, 22 Oz. 20.00
Pitcher, Water 40.00
Plate, 6 1/4 In. 2.00
Plate, 7 1/2 In. 3.00
Plate, 9 In. .... 3.00 To 7.00
Plate, 10 In. 10.00
Plate, Deep,
8 In. .... 7.50 To 10.00
Platter, 11 In. 11.00
Salt & Pepper 13.00
Saucer 1.00
Soup, Cream 11.00
Sugar, Cover 16.00

SPRUCE GREEN

Jug, 22 Oz. 29.00
Pepper Shaker 7.00
Syrup, Red Cover 95.00
Tumbler 22.00

TANGERINE

Ashtray 20.00
Bowl, 5 1/2 In. .... 3.00 To 6.50
Bowl, 6 1/2 In.,
Set of 7 .... 50.00
Candleholder, Pair 85.00
Creamer 9.00
Cup & Saucer 32.00
Dish, Nut .... 4.00 To 6.00
Eggcup .... 8.00 To 13.00
Gravy Boat 26.00
Jug, 22 Oz. .... 17.00 To 22.00
Pitcher, Water 30.00
Plate, 7 In. .... 4.00 To 4.50
Platter, 11 In. 11.00
Platter, 13 In. 22.00
Relish, 4 Inserts 26.00
Salt & Pepper 8.50
Soup, Cream 18.00
Sugar & Creamer, Cover ... 18.00
Sugar, Cover ...... 6.00 To 12.00
Syrup .... 125.00 To 150.00
Teapot 50.00
Tumbler 20.00

TURQUOISE

Ashtray,
Basketweave .... 20.00 To 22.00
Bowl, 5 1/2 In. .... 3.50 To 4.00
Bowl, 6 1/2 In. .... 4.50 To 5.50
Bowl, 7 In. .... 7.00 To 8.00
Bowl, 9 In. .... 8.50 To 14.00

Bowl, Baker, Oval, 9 In. ... 10.00
Butter, Cover ... 55.00
Creamer, Individual ... 14.50
Creamer, Novelty ... 14.00
Cup ... 2.50 To 4.00
Cup & Saucer ... 4.50
Cup & Saucer, After Dinner ... 22.00 To 27.00
Cup, After Dinner ... 15.00 To 18.00
Eggcup ... 8.00
Eggcup, Individual ... 13.00
Gravy Boat ... 7.50
Jar, Jam ... 65.00
Jug, 22 Oz. ... 15.00 To 18.00
Plate, 7 In. ... 2.50 To 2.75
Plate, 9 In. ... 3.25 To 4.00
Plate, 10 In. ... 4.00 To 10.00
Plate, Deep, 8 In. ... 7.50 To 10.00
Platter, 11 In. ... 6.00 To 9.00
Platter, 13 In. ... 9.00
Salt & Pepper ... 6.00
Soup, Cream ... 6.50
Sugar ... 5.00
Sugar & Creamer ... 10.00
Teapot ... 30.00 To 40.00
Tumbler ... 20.00

YELLOW

Bowl, 5 1/2 In. ... 4.00
Bowl, 7 In. ... 7.00 To 8.00
Bowl, 8 3/4 In. ... 6.00 To 7.00
Casserole, Cover ... 38.00
Creamer ... 3.50 To 6.00
Creamer, Individual ... 14.50
Cup ... 3.00 To 5.00
Cup & Saucer, After Dinner ... 18.00 To 22.50
Dish, Nut ... 4.00
Gravy Boat ... 6.00 To 9.00
Jug, 22 Oz. ... 14.00 To 18.00
Mixing Bowl, 10 In. ... 65.00
Plate, 6 In. ... 2.00
Plate, 7 In. ... 1.50 To 3.00
Plate, 9 In. ... 4.00
Plate, 10 In. ... 9.50
Plate, Deep, 8 In. ... 8.00
Platter, 11 In. ... 6.00 To 7.00
Platter, 13 In. ... 10.00
Salt & Pepper ... 10.00
Soup, Cream ... 6.50 To 12.00
Sugar & Creamer, Cover ... 16.00
Sugar, Cover ... 5.00 To 10.00
Teapot ... 25.00 To 40.00
Tumbler ... 18.00 To 22.00

Hawaiian Daisy, see Daisy

Hawaiian Flowers

Hawaiian Flowers was a well-known Vernon Kilns, Vernon, California, tableware designed by Don Blanding. It was first made in 1939.

Bowl, 9 In. ... 8.00
Coffeepot ... 50.00
Cup & Saucer ... 8.00
Plate, 7 1/2 In. ... 5.00
Plate, 9 1/2 In. ... 6.00
Plate, 10 1/2 In. ... 7.00
Plate, 6 1/2 In. ... 4.00

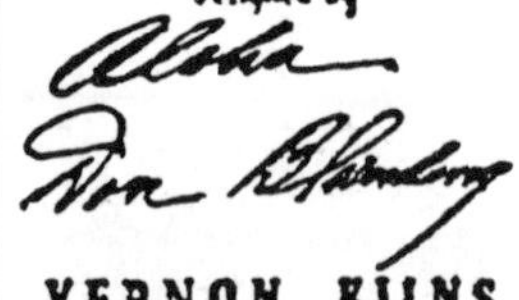

Hawaiian Fruit

Hawaiian Fruit is a colorful Blue Ridge pattern by Southern Potteries. The hand-painted design pictures a pineapple and two other fruits in blue, yellow, and brown. The border repeats the three colors. This pattern was

Blue Ridge
Hand Painted
Underglaze
Southern Potteries, Inc.
MADE IN U. S. A.

made on two different plate shapes.

Bowl, 5 In. ... 3.00
Plate, 7 In. ... 4.00
Plate, 10 In. ... 7.00
Platter, 16 In. ... 12.00
Saucer ... 2.00
Sugar & Creamer, Cover ... 12.00

Heather Rose

Heather Rose is a decal-decorated Hall Pottery pattern. Both dinnerware and utility ware pieces were made with this decoration. It pictures a realistic-looking pale pinkish purple rose on a stem with many leaves.

Bowl, 5 1/4 In. ... 2.00
Creamer ... 4.50

Cup & Saucer ... 4.00
Pitcher ... 11.00
Plate, 6 1/4 In. ... 2.00
Plate, 10 In. ... 4.50
Platter, 13 1/2 In. ... 10.00
Sugar, Cover ... 7.00

Hilda

A large red flower and an assortment of blue and yellow flowers surround the rim of the Hilda plate. The pattern, made on the

Candlewick shape, was made by Southern Potteries, Erwin, Tennessee.

Bowl, Cereal, 6 In. 3.50
Plate, 6 In. 1.00
Plate, 9 1/2 In. 3.00

Blue Ridge
Hand Painted
Underglaze
Southern Potteries, Inc.
MADE IN U. S. A.

Holland, see Crocus

Homespun

Homespun, a yellow, green, and reddish brown plaid pattern, was made by Vernon Kilns, Vernon, California. Other related plaids are Calico (pink and blue), Coronation Organdy (gray and rose), Gingham (green and yellow), Organdie (brown and yellow), Tam O'Shanter (green, lime, and cinnamon), and Tweed (gray and blue).

Bowl, Vegetable, 9 In. 9.00
Butter, Cover 35.00
Casserole, Cover 35.00
Coaster .... 4.00 To 8.00
Creamer 4.00
Cup & Saucer .... 6.00 To 7.50
Cup, Demitasse ..... 7.00 To 9.00
Mug 12.00
Pitcher 38.00
Plate, 6 In. .... 2.00 To 3.00
Plate, 7 1/2 In. 3.50
Plate, 9 1/2 In. 5.00
Plate, 10 1/2 In. 7.00
Soup, Dish, 8 1/2 In. 4.50

Sugar, Cover 6.00
Teapot 24.00
Tumbler, 14 Oz. 12.00

Homestead

Homestead, or Homestead in Winter, was a popular pattern by the Crooksville China Company of Crooksville, Ohio. It pictured a realistic winter scene in shades of brown and blue.

Bowl, Divided,
Stick Handle 12.50
Butter, Cover 17.50

Gravy Boat 15.00
Sugar & Creamer 17.50

I

Iris

Iris pattern was made by the Red Wing Pottery about 1947. The plates were white, the accessory pieces were mulberry. The iris pattern was in natural colors.

Cup & Saucer 6.00
Plate, 7 In. .... 2.00 To 3.00
Soup, Dish 5.00
Tray, Supper 5.00

Iroquois

Russel Wright was an important industrial designer. His dinnerwares were made by at least four companies. Iroquois Casual China was a Russel Wright modern design made by Iroquois China Company, Syracuse, New York. The dinnerware was less expensive than American Modern, heavier and less breakable. It was advertised as cook-and-serve. The first pieces were marked China by Iroquois with the signature of Russel Wright. In the 1950s the ware was redesigned and the mark was changed to Iroquois Casual China by Russel

Wright. The dishes were made in a number of colors, designed to be mixed and matched. Sets were often sold with pieces in several colors. The original Iroquois was glazed Ice Blue, Forest Green, Avocado Yellow, Lemon Yellow, Nutmeg Brown, or Sugar White. In 1951 more colors were added, including Lettuce Green, Charcoal, Ripe Apricot, Pink Sherbet, Parsley Green, Canteloupe, Oyster Gray, Aqua, Brick Red, or Grayed-Blue. In 1959 some Iroquois pieces were decorated with patterns and sold under other names. Glass tumblers were made in matching colors.

IROQUOIS
CASUAL
CHINA
by
Russel
Wright

AVOCADO YELLOW

Bowl, 5 In. 5.00
Bowl, 5 1/2 In. .....4.00 To 5.00
Cup............................ 5.00
Cup & Saucer 7.50
Plate, 6 1/2 In................ 2.00
Plate, 7 1/2 In................ 4.00
Plate, 9 1/2 In................ 5.00
Plate, 10 In..........5.00 To 7.50
Platter, 14 In................ 16.00
Platter, Oval, 12 3/4 In. ... 10.00
Platter, Oval, 14 1/2 In. ... 15.00
Saucer.......................... 3.00
Sugar & Creamer........... 15.00

CHARCOAL

Bowl, Vegetable,
8 1/2 In.................... 13.00
Cup & Saucer 8.00
Plate, 6 1/2 In................ 2.00

ICE BLUE

Bowl, 5 1/2 In. 5.00
Bowl, Divided, 10 In. 19.00
Bowl, Vegetable,
8 1/2 In.................... 16.00
Butter......................... 45.00
Carafe......................... 45.00
Cup............................ 6.00
Plate, 6 1/2 In................ 3.50
Plate, 9 1/2 In................ 4.00
Saucer.......................... 2.50

LEMON YELLOW

Bowl, 5 1/2 In. 3.25
Butter, 1/2 Lb. 50.00
Cup............................ 6.00
Pitcher 25.00
Plate, 7 1/2 In................ 4.00
Plate, 10 In.................... 5.00

LETTUCE GREEN

Bowl, 5 1/2 In. 3.25
Butter......................... 45.00
Cup & Saucer 7.00
Pitcher, 5 1/4 In. 25.00

OYSTER GRAY

Bowl, Vegetable, 10 In. 16.00
Casserole, Cover, 8 In. 22.00
Casserole, Divided, Cover,
10 In........................ 24.00
Sugar & Creamer, Stacking,
4 In.............14.00 To 18.00

PARSLEY GREEN

Bowl, 8 1/2 In. 12.00
Bowl, 10 In. .....18.00 To 20.00
Casserole, 2 Qt., 8 In. 15.00
Creamer 7.00
Cup, 7 Oz. 6.00
Plate, 6 1/2 In................ 2.00
Plate, 7 1/2 In................ 4.00
Platter, 12 3/4 In. 10.00
Salt & Pepper, Stacking..... 10.00
Saucer.......................... 2.00
Soup, Dish 4.00
Sugar & Creamer........... 14.00

PINK SHERBET

Butter, Cover, 1/2 Lb. 45.00
Carafe......................... 55.00
Cup & Saucer 7.00
Mug........................... 25.00
Plate, 6 1/4 In................ 2.50
Plate, 7 1/2 In................ 4.00
Plate, 9 In. 4.50
Plate, 10 In.................... 5.00
Salt & Pepper, Stacking..... 16.00
Sugar & Creamer,
Stacking 18.00

RIPE APRICOT

Bowl, 5 1/2 In. .....4.00 To 4.50
Bowl, 5 In...................... 5.00
Butter, Cover, Apricot...... 40.00
Casserole, 4 Qt., 8 In. 28.00
Dish, Soup 6.00
Plate, 6 1/2 In......2.50 To 3.00
Plate, 7 1/2 In................ 4.00
Plate, 9 1/2 In......4.00 To 4.50
Salt & Pepper, Stacking..... 12.00
Saucer.......................... 3.00
Sugar & Creamer, Stacking,
4 In.............15.00 To 18.00

SUGAR WHITE

Bowl, Cereal, 5 In............ 5.00
Plate, 6 1/2 In................ 3.50
Plate, 9 1/2 In................ 5.50
Saucer.......................... 2.50
Sugar & Creamer,
Stacking 20.00

Ivy

Ivy is a hand-painted pattern made by Franciscan Pottery from 1948.

Cup........................... 10.00
Cup & Saucer .... 10.00 To 14.00
Cup & Saucer, 14 Oz. 15.00
Jug, Cover.................... 45.00
Pitcher, 1 Qt. 40.00
Pitcher, 6 1/4 In. 4.50
Plate, 10 In.................... 9.00
Plate, Dinner.................. 4.00
Plate, Salad.................... 4.00
Platter, 11 1/2 In. 20.00
Platter, 12 3/4 In. 23.00
Platter, Round,
14 1/4 In.................. 28.00
Relish, 3 Sections........... 20.00

Saucer 2.00
Soup, Dish 6.00
Soup, Flat...................... 8.00
Sugar, Open.................... 4.00
Tumbler 10.00

K

Kitchen Kraft

Kitchen Kraft oven-to-table pieces were made by Homer Laughlin China Company, Newell, West Virginia, from the early 1930s. The pieces were made in plain, solid colors or with decals. If decorated with decals, they are listed in this book under the decal's name. If solid colors, they are listed here.

BLUE

Cake Plate,
11 In............ 32.00 To 35.00
Casserole, Cover,
Individual 80.00
Spoon .... 40.00 To 45.00

GREEN

Cake Plate,
11 In............ 32.00 To 35.00
Cake Server ...... 42.00 To 45.00
Fork 45.00
Mixing Bowl, 6 In........... 37.00
Pie Plate,
9 In............. 30.00 To 35.00
Platter, Metal Holder 75.00

RED

Cake Plate,
11 In............ 29.00 To 33.00
Casserole, Cover,
Individual 85.00
Fork 40.00
Salt & Pepper .... 48.00 To 50.00
Spoon 45.00
Stack Set, Cover 85.00

YELLOW

Casserole, Cover,
Individual 55.00
Fork 45.00
Platter, Metal Holder 40.00
Spoon 42.00
Sugar & Creamer,
Individual 65.00

L

Lipton

Lipton is the name of a line of teapots, sugars, and creamers marked with the words Lipton Tea on the bottom. These pieces were made by Hall China Company. The teapot is the French shape, the sugar and creamer are Boston shape.

CADET

Sugar & Creamer 15.00
Teapot 15.00

HI-BLACK

Creamer 5.00
Sugar.......................... 7.00

MAROON

Teapot 14.00

YELLOW

Creamer 9.00
Sugar.......................... 8.50
Sugar, Cover 9.00

Lu-Ray

The characteristic slightly speckled glaze of the solid-colored Lu-Ray makes it easy to identify. Taylor, Smith, and Taylor, Chester, West Virginia, made this pattern after 1938. Pastel colors include Windsor Blue, Persian Cream, Sharon Pink, Surf Green, and Chatham Gray.

BLUE

Bowl, 5 1/2 In. .... 2.50 To 3.50
Bowl, 9 In......... 7.50 To 12.00
Bowl, 10 In. 14.00
Bowl, Vegetable, Oval,
9 In. 5.00
Creamer, Oval 6.00
Cup............................ 2.75
Cup & Saucer .... 5.00 To 8.50
Cup & Saucer,
After Dinner................ 10.00
Eggcup......................... 9.00
Plate, 6 In. .... 1.00 To 1.50
Plate, 7 1/2 In............... 3.00
Plate, 9 In. .... 4.00 To 6.75
Plate, 10 In................... 5.00
Platter,
11 1/2 In.......... 7.00 To 9.75
Platter,
13 1/2 In........ 8.00 To 11.75
Saltshaker...................... 6.00
Saucer................ 1.50 To 2.00
Soup, Cream ..... 10.00 To 16.00
Soup, Dish .... 6.00 To 8.00
Sugar.......................... 10.00
Sugar & Creamer 12.00
Sugar, Cover,
After Dinner................ 15.00

CREAM

Bowl, 5 1/4 In. 5.50
Cup & Saucer 8.50
Plate, 6 1/4 In............... 2.75
Plate, 9 1/4 In............... 6.75
Plate, 14 1/2 In. 12.00

Don't put dishes or glassware with gold borders in the microwave oven.

Platter, 13 1/2 In. 11.75
Soup, Cream, 6 In. 10.00

GRAY

Bowl, 6 In. 7.00
Cup 7.00
Saucer 3.00
Soup, Dish 8.00

GREEN

Bowl, 5 1/2 In. .... 3.00 To 5.50
Bowl, 9 In. .... 5.00 To 6.00
Bowl, Vegetable, Oval 5.00
Creamer 3.50
Cup & Saucer .... 5.00 To 8.50
Cup & Saucer, After Dinner 10.00
Cup, After Dinner 6.50
Eggcup .... 9.00 To 12.50
Gravy, Twin 12.00
Plate, 6 In. .... 1.50 To 2.25
Plate, 7 1/2 In. 3.00
Plate, 9 In. .... 6.75 To 6.75
Plate, 10 In. 8.00
Plate, 13 In. 9.00
Plate, Grill .... 10.00 To 14.00
Platter, 11 3/4 In. 7.00
Platter, 13 1/2 In. .... 7.00 To 11.75
Salt & Pepper 7.00
Saucer .... 1.00 To 1.50
Soup, Cream 10.00
Soup, Dish .... 5.00 To 7.50
Sugar, Cover .... 4.50 To 8.50

PINK

Bowl, 5 1/2 In. .... 1.50 To 4.50
Bowl, 9 In. .... 6.00 To 12.00
Bowl, Vegetable .... 5.00 To 8.00
Creamer 3.50
Cup .... 7.00 To 8.00
Cup & Saucer .... 5.50 To 8.50
Cup & Saucer, After Dinner .... 10.00 To 11.00
Eggcup 12.50
Gravy Boat .... 12.50 To 14.00
Plate, 6 In. .... 1.50 To 2.75
Plate, 9 In. .... 5.50 To 6.75
Plate, 10 In. 10.00
Plate, 15 In. 20.00
Salt & Pepper 8.00
Soup, Dish .... 6.00 To 7.50
Teapot 10.00

YELLOW

Bowl, 5 1/2 In. .... 1.50 To 3.00
Bowl, 9 In. 5.00
Bowl, Oval, 10 In. .... 7.00 To 12.00
Chop Plate, 14 In. .... 10.00 To 15.00
Creamer 5.00
Cup 2.75
Cup & Saucer 4.00
Cup & Saucer, After Dinner 10.00
Dish, Pickle 6.00
Eggcup .... 9.00 To 10.00
Gravy Boat .... 12.50 To 14.00
Plate, 6 In. .... 1.00 To 2.25
Plate, 7 1/2 In. 3.00
Plate, 9 In. .... 2.50 To 4.00
Plate, 10 In. 5.00
Plate, 13 In. 9.00
Platter, 11 3/4 In. 7.00
Relish, 4 Sections 55.00
Salt & Pepper 8.00
Saucer 1.50
Soup, Dish .... 5.00 To 7.50
Sugar, Cover 8.00
Teapot 35.00

M

Magnolia

A wide, bright, cranberry-red band borders Magnolia pattern by Stangl Pottery, Trenton, New Jersey. The pattern, No. 3870, was made from 1952 to 1962. Another version of Magnolia by Red Wing does not have the banded edge. It was made in 1947. Both are listed here.

CRANBERRY

Creamer, Stangl 6.00
Plate, 10 In., Stangl 8.00
Teapot, Stangl 23.00

LIME

Coffee Server, Red Wing 3.00
Gravy Boat, Tray, Red Wing 6.00
Pitcher, Tall, Red Wing 8.00
Sugar & Creamer, Cover, Red Wing 6.00
Vegetable, Divided, Red Wing 8.00

YELLOW

Candleholder, Pair, Red Wing.................24.00

Mardi Gras

Southern Potteries, Erwin, Tennessee, made Mardi Gras, a hand-painted dinnerware. A large blue daisy and a large pink-petaled flower are surrounded by leaves and buds. The design is placed so that only parts of the flowers are seen on the plate.

Bowl, 5 In..........2.00 To 3.00
Bowl, 6 In.................... 4.00
Cup........................... 6.00
Cup & Saucer................. 4.00

Blue Ridge
Hand Painted
Underglaze
Southern Potteries, Inc.
MADE IN U. S. A.

Pie Plate.....................20.00
Plate, 6 In.................... 2.00
Plate, 9 1/2 In............... 5.00
Platter, 11 1/4 In. 6.00

Max-i-cana

The Mexican-inspired dinnerwares can be confusing. Max-i-cana is a Homer Laughlin China Company pattern. The decal design shows a Mexican napping amid pottery jars and cactus. It was made on a Yellowstone shape with octagonal plates. Do not confuse it with Mexicana.

Bowl, 6 In.................... 5.00
Eggcup.......................12.00
Plate, 9 In.................... 4.50
Platter, 11 1/2 In.......10.00 To 12.00

HOMER LAUGHLIN

Mayflower

Mayflower is a pattern by Southern Potteries.

Bowl, Oval, 9 In............10.00
Bowl, Round, 9 In. 10.00
Platter, 13 1/2 In. 12.00

Blue Ridge
Hand Painted
Underglaze
Southern Potteries, Inc.
MADE IN U. S. A.

Mexi-Gren

W. S. George made Mexi-gren pattern in the 1930s when the Mexican designs became popular. The dishes had a green rim and a decal design in the center picturing an arch, pots, and a blanket.

Cup, Bolero.................. 4.00
Cup, Lido..................... 4.00
Plate, Bolero, 9 1/4 In...... 5.00
Saucer, Ranchero............ 1.50

Mexicana

The first of the Mexican-inspired patterns that became popular as a dinnerware in the 1930s was Mexicana. This decal-decorated set was first offered in 1938. The design shows a collection of orange and yellow pots with a few cacti. The edge of the dish well is rimmed with red or occasionally yellow, green, or blue. Almost all of the pieces are Century line, a popular Homer Laughlin dinnerware shape.

HOMER LAUGHLIN

Bread Plate.................. 2.00
Cup........................... 4.00
Eggcup.......................12.00
Eggcup, Dark Green........45.00
Plate, 9 1/2 In............... 5.00
Platter, 13 In................12.00
Saucer........................ 1.50
Tumbler, Blue............... 7.00
Tumbler, Green ....6.00 To 7.00
Tumbler, Orange............ 6.00
Tumbler, Yellow ...6.00 To 7.00

Mod Tulip

Two red and yellow striped tulips with green leaves are the decorations on the Blue Ridge pattern called Mod Tulip. It is on the Colonial shape.

Blue Ridge
Hand Painted
Underglaze
Southern Potteries, Inc.
MADE IN U. S. A.

Bowl, 5 1/4 In. 1.50
Bowl, 6 In. .... 2.25 To 2.75
Creamer 2.00
Cup & Saucer 3.00
Gravy, Underplate 3.00
Pitcher, Square, 6 3/4 In. ... 2.00
Plate, 6 1/8 In. ..... 1.25 To 1.50
Plate, Square, 6 3/4 In. 2.00
Salt & Pepper 4.50
Soup, Dish 3.00

Modern California

Modern California was made in the 1930s by Vernon Kilns, Vernon, California. Colors include azure blue, orchid, pistachio, straw, sand, and gray.

AZURE

Bowl, 5 1/2 In. 2.00
Bowl, 9 In. 7.00
Cup & Saucer, Demitasse 6.00
Pitcher, 9 1/2 In. 3.50

Salt & Pepper 4.00
Saucer 1.25
Soup, Dish 4.00

GRAY

Chop Plate, 12 In. 7.00
Cup 2.75
Saucer 1.25

ORCHID

Bowl, Round, 9 In. 7.00
Cup & Saucer,
Demitasse .... 6.00 To 15.00
Plate, 9 1/2 In. 4.00

PISTACHIO

Bowl, Soup, Dish 4.00
Creamer 3.50
Cup 2.75
Gravy Boat 18.00
Plate, 9 1/2 In. 4.00
Plate, 10 1/2 In. 6.00
Platter, 13 In. 8.00
Salt & Pepper 4.00
Saucer 3.50

STRAW

Bowl, Oval, 9 1/2 In. 9.00
Plate, 7 1/4 In. 3.00
Plate, 10 In. 6.00
Platter 8.00
Sugar, Cover 4.75
Teapot 17.00

Morning Glory

From 1942 to 1949 the Hall China Company, East Liverpool, Ohio, made a dinnerware called Morning Glory. The outside of the pieces was Cadet Blue, the inside had a Morning Glory decal decoration.

Casserole, Lip 5.00
Pepper Shaker 6.00
Salt & Pepper 20.00

Moss Rose

Moss Rose was made by Southern Potteries, Erwin, Tennessee, under the trade name Blue Ridge, from 1920 to 1957. It was a hand-painted pattern. Another pattern called Moss Rose was made by the Universal Potteries, Cambridge, Ohio, from 1953 to 1955. It had decal decorations.

Canister Set, Child's,
3 Piece 95.00
Chocolate Set, Child's,
3 Piece 45.00
Plate, Child's, 4 1/2 In. 3.00
Sugar, Child's, Cover,
3 1/4 In. 12.00

Blue Ridge
Hand Painted
Underglaze
Southern Potteries, Inc.
MADE IN U. S. A.

Mt. Vernon

Mt. Vernon is a pattern made by the Hall China Company for Sears, Roebuck and Company in the 1940s. It has pink and green flowers in the design.

Coffeepot, Drip 75.00
Creamer 5.00
Cup & Saucer 6.00
Gravy & Underplate 18.00
Pitcher, 10 In. 10.00
Plate, 6 In. 2.50
Plate, 10 In. 7.50
Platter, 11 1/2 In. 10.00
Platter, 13 In. 9.00
Soup, Dish .... 7.00 To 8.50
Sugar, Cover .... 8.00 To 8.50

Mums

Mums pattern was made by Taylor, Smith, and Taylor of West Virginia and Ohio.

PINK

Bowl, 6 In. 9.00
Bowl, Open Drip 7.00
Gravy 12.00
Pepper, Handle 10.00
Sugar, Cover, Colonial 12.00

N

Native California

Vernon Kilns of Vernon, California, made a pastel-colored dinnerware called Native California from 1942 to 1947. The dishes had a leaf border on the plates. Colors used were aqua, blue, green, pink, and yellow.

AQUA

Plate, 10 1/4 In. 10.00
Soup, Dish 10.00

BLUE

Bowl, 5 3/4 In. 3.50
Bowl, Vegetable, Oval 9.00
Cup & Saucer 10.00
Nappy, 5 1/2 In. 2.50
Plate, 6 In. 2.50
Plate, 10 1/2 In. 8.50
Soup, Cream 6.00

GREEN

Bowl, 5 3/4 In. 3.50
Cup & Saucer ..... 4.00 To 10.00
Nappy, 5 1/2 In. 2.50

NATIVE CALIFORNIA VERNON KILNS AUTHENTIC CALIFORNIA POTTERY MADE IN U.S.A.

Plate, 6 In. 2.50
Plate, 10 1/2 In. ... 3.00 To 8.50
Platter, 13 1/2 In. 13.00
Soup, Cream 6.00

PINK

Bowl, 5 3/4 In. 3.50
Bowl, 9 In. .... 5.00 To 9.00
Bowl, Vegetable, Oval 10.00
Chop Plate 14.00
Cup & Saucer 10.00
Nappy, 5 1/2 In. 2.50
Plate, 6 In. 2.50
Plate, 10 1/2 In. .... 8.50 To 10.00
Soup, Cream 6.00
Soup, Dish 10.00

YELLOW

Bowl, 5 3/4 In. 3.50
Bowl, 9 In. .... 5.00 To 9.00
Cup & Saucer ..... 4.00 To 10.00
Nappy, 5 1/2 In. 2.50
Plate, 6 In. 2.50
Plate, 10 1/2 In. .... 8.50 To 10.00
Soup, Cream 6.00

Nautilus

Nautilus is a Homer Laughlin pattern. The decorations were put on Century-shaped dishes.

Bowl, Vegetable, Cover 15.00
Creamer 2.50
Cup & Saucer 3.00
Gravy Boat 6.00
Soup, Dish 3.00
Sugar, Cover 4.00

Norma

Norma pattern by Stangl is a heavy pottery dinnerware. It has

a pear branch in the center and rings of color on the rim. The plates are marked Della-Ware.

Cup & Saucer 7.00
Plate, 6 In. 3.00
Plate, 10 In. 6.00

Normandy

Red Wing Pottery made a number of dishes using the Provincial shape. These 1940s dishes were hand decorated. One of the popular patterns was Normandy. At first it was a plain white plate with blue and maroon bands. Later it pictured an apple in either Dubonnet or Forest Green.

Bowl, 5 1/4 In. 2.50
Cup 4.00
Pitcher, 8 In. 3.50
Plate, 9 In. 4.00
Salt & Pepper 5.00

O

Old Curiosity Shop

The Old Curiosity Shop is one of many patterns made by Royal China Company of Sebring, Ohio, in the 1940s. It pictures a view of the shop and an elaborate border.

Bowl, 5 1/2 In. .... 1.25 To 1.50
Bowl, 5 3/4 In. 2.50
Bowl, 10 In. .... 2.50 To 7.00
Butter, 1/4 Lb. 9.00
Butter, Cover 8.00

Creamer .... 2.25 To 3.00
Cup & Saucer .... 2.00 To 2.50
Gravy Boat .... 4.00 To 6.00
Plate, 6 In. 3.00
Plate, 10 In. .... 2.00 To 3.00
Plate, Handle,
10 1/2 In. .... 4.50 To 5.00
Salt & Pepper 6.00
Sugar, Cover .... 3.50 To 4.00
Tidbit, 3-Tier 11.00

Orange Poppy, see Poppy

Orchard Song

Orchard Song was made by Stangl Pottery, Trenton, New Jersey, from 1962 to 1974.

Celery, 15 In. 18.00
Gravy, Tray 18.00
Platter, Round, 12 In. 15.00
Sandwich Server, Center Handle,
10 In. 15.00
Sugar, Cover 5.00

Organdie

Organdie is one of six different plaid patterns, made by Vernon Kilns, Vernon, California. It is an overall brown pattern with a yellow and brown plaid border. Other related plaids are Calico (pink and blue), Coronation Organdy (gray and rose), Gingham (green and yellow), Homespun (cinnamon, yellow, and green), Tam O'Shanter (green, lime, and cinnamon), and Tweed (gray and blue).

Bowl, 5 1/2 In. .... 1.50 To 3.00
Bowl, 9 In. .... 5.00 To 9.00
Bowl, Vegetable, 9 In. 9.00
Bowl, Vegetable, Divided ... 7.00

Butter Chip.................. 10.00
Butter, Cover, 1/4 Lb. 12.50
Carafe......................... 17.00
Casserole, Cover............ 20.00
Chop Plate, 12 In............ 6.00
Creamer 8.00
Cup & Saucer .... 3.00 To 6.00
Eggcup......................... 3.00
Gravy Boat................... 12.00
Pitcher, 48 Oz. 12.50
Plate, 6 In. .... 1.50 To 2.25
Plate, 7 1/2 In...... 2.00 To 3.00
Plate, 9 In. 3.00
Plate, 10 In................... 6.00
Platter, Oval, 12 In.......... 4.00
Salt & Pepper..... 6.00 To 12.00
Saucer......................... 2.00
Soup, Cream 2.50
Soup, Dish 4.50
Sugar & Creamer,
Cover............... 7.00 To 9.00
Syrup............. 20.00 To 25.00
Teapot .... 16.00 To 24.00
Teapot, Cover, 1-Cup 10.00
Tidbit, 2 Tiers 12.00
Tumbler, 5 1/2 In. 10.00
Vase, Underplate, 3 In...... 15.00

Organdy

Organdy by Homer Laughlin is very different from the Organdie pattern by Vernon Kilns. Homer Laughlin made a plain, pastel-bordered, semi-porcelain set with very clean, modern shapes. Colors included green, yellow, blue, and pink. Each set had green handles.

PINK

Cup & Saucer 3.00
Plate, 6 In. 1.50
Plate, 8 In. 2.50
Sugar & Creamer,
Individual 10.00
Syrup.......................... 9.00
Toast, Cover 18.00

Painted Daisy

Red, blue, yellow, and green were the colors used to hand paint the flowers on the Painted Daisy pattern by Blue Ridge. It is on the Colonial shape.

Bowl, 5 In. 3.00
Bowl, 6 In. 4.50
Cup & Saucer 6.50

Blue Ridge
Hand Painted
Underglaze
Southern Potteries, Inc.
MADE IN U.S.A.

Plate, 6 In. 2.00
Soup, Dish 5.00

Patio

Patio is a Paden City Mexican-decal-decorated dinnerware. It was made on the Shell-Crest Shape. The Paden City, West Virginia, pottery made dinnerwares from 1907 to the 1950s. The Patio decal shows a doorway and a group of pots in blue, purple, and yellow. One orange blossom on a long stem is pictured in a pot. The handled

For emergency repairs to chipped pottery, try coloring the spot with a wax crayon or oil paint. It will look a little better.

pieces often have red trim on the edge.

Bowl, 11 In. 18.00
Plate, 6 1/4 In................ 5.00
Plate, 12 In...................15.00

Pepe

Pepe is a dinnerware made by Red Wing. It is hand painted and

was advertised in 1963 as color-fast, oven-proof, and detergent-safe. The design is very simple and modern in shades of bittersweet, green, and dark bluish purple.

Bean Pot......................22.00
Coffeepot, Tall...............22.00
Plate, 10 In..................10.00
Teapot 18.00

Poppy

Poppy, sometimes called Orange Poppy by collectors, was made by the Hall China Company, East Liverpool, Ohio, from 1933 through the 1950s. The decals picture realistic groups of orange poppies with a few leaves. Another Hall pattern called Red Poppy has bright red stylized flowers with black leaves and trim.

Baker, French................18.00
Bean Pot, New England ....57.00 To 60.00
Bowl, 5 1/2 In. ....3.00 To 4.00
Bowl, 9 1/8 In. 15.00
Butter, Yellow Base.........12.00
Casserole, Oval, 8 1/2 In.....................40.00
Coffeepot, Golden Key ....30.00 To 45.00
Cup..................3.00 To 5.50
Cup & Saucer 7.00

Custard..............3.50 To 5.00
Jar, Pretzel ....35.00 To 65.00
Jug, No.5, 6 1/2 In.........10.00 To 20.00
Mixing Bowl, 7 1/2 In. 8.50
Pepper Shaker, Handle ....11.00 To 12.50
Plate, 7 In................... 2.00
Plate, 7 3/4 In............... 4.50
Plate, 9 1/4 In......6.50 To 7.50
Platter, Oval, 11 1/4 In. ...10.00
Platter, Oval, 13 In............12.00 To 19.00
Salt & Pepper 14.00
Salt & Pepper, Oven, Handle, Pair 18.00
Saucer.......................... 2.00
Sugar & Creamer, Cover...........12.00 To 15.00
Teapot, Streamline......... 100.00

Poppy & Wheat

Poppy & Wheat is a design that seems to have been made in the 1930s. It was made by Hall China Company, East Liverpool, Ohio. The design shows a realistic spray of orange flowers and wheat heads. It is sometimes called Wheat.

Bowl, 5 1/2 In. 14.00
Bowl, 9 1/2 In. 20.00
Casserole......................10.00

Creamer 20.00
Mixing Bowl, 5 1/8 In. 12.00
Mixing Bowl, 7 3/8 In. 15.00
Mixing Bowl, 8 3/4 In. 20.00
Mixing Bowl, 9 1/2 In. 30.00
Pepper 15.00
Pitcher 30.00
Saltshaker, Handle...........20.00
Shaker, Flour, Handle 20.00

Poppy Trail

Metlox Poppy Trail Manufacturing Company of California made many dinnerwares marked with the words Metlox or Poppy Trail. Solid-colored wares and hand-decorated pieces were made. Listed here are solid pieces marked Metlox Poppy Trail.

IVORY

Butter, Cover 18.00
Coffeepot 35.00
Creamer 8.00
Pepper Shaker, Handle 6.00
Plate, 6 In. 3.50
Plate, 8 In. 7.00
Plate, 9 1/4 In. 8.00
Plate, 10 1/4 In. 9.50
Platter, Oval, 13 In. 15.00
Soup, Dish, 7 In. 8.50
Sugar, Cover 10.00

ORANGE

Bowl, 4 1/2 In. 2.00
Bowl, 5 1/4 In. 2.25
Carafe, Wooden Handle 9.00
Plate, 6 In. 1.50
Plate, 10 In. 3.00

TURQUOISE

Bowl, 4 1/2 In. 2.00
Bowl, 5 1/4 In. 2.25
Creamer 3.00
Cup 2.25
Plate, 6 In. 1.50
Plate, 10 In. 3.00
Plate, Chop, 12 1/2 In. 6.00
Sugar 3.00
Sugar & Creamer 6.00

YELLOW

Plate, 10 In. 3.00
Teapot 12.00

Prelude

Prelude is a pattern with a stylized flower design. It was made by Stangl Pottery, Trenton, New Jersey, from 1949 to 1957.

Cup & Saucer 5.00
Plate, 6 1/4 In. 2.25
Plate, 8 In. 4.00
Plate, 10 In. 5.00

Priscilla

Priscilla was made by Homer Laughlin China Company, Newell, West Virginia. It is a decal-decorated ware with pale pink roses and sprigs of flowers.

Bowl, 5 In. .... 2.00 To 2.50
Bowl, Vegetable, Oval, 9 In. 6.00
Cake Plate, 10 3/4 In. .... 5.00 To 7.00

Creamer 3.00
Cup & Saucer 4.00
Gravy Boat .... 4.50 To 7.00
Mixing Bowl, 10 1/2 In. 12.00
Plate, 6 In. 1.75
Plate, 8 In. .... 3.00 To 3.50
Plate, 9 In. 4.00
Platter, 13 1/2 In. 10.00
Soup, Dish, 8 1/2 In. 4.00
Sugar, Cover 4.75
Teapot 25.00

Provincial

Provincial is a bordered plate with a floral center made by Stangl Pottery, Trenton, New Jersey, from 1957 to 1967.

Bowl, 5 1/4 In. 4.00
Cup & Saucer 6.50
Plate, 9 In. 5.00
Soup, Lug Handle 5.00

Quilted Fruit

Southern Potteries of Erwin, Tennessee, made Quilted Fruit in the 1950s. The hand-painted decorations resembled pieces of fruit made from printed calicoes. Stitching outlines the leaves and the fruit.

Cup & Saucer 6.00
Plate, 6 In. 1.50
Plate, 9 In. 4.00
Sugar & Creamer, Cover ... 18.00

Blue Ridge
Hand Painted
Underglaze
Southern Potteries, Inc.
MADE IN U. S. A.

Random Harvest

Random Harvest is a Red Wing dinnerware pattern that is color-fast and oven-proof. It was made in the 1960s. The design is hand painted in brown,

copper, green, turquoise, and coral on a flecked dish.

Bowl, 5 In. 2.50
Bowl, Vegetable, 2 Sections,
10 In. 9.00
Plate, 8 1/2 In. 3.50
Plate, 10 1/2 In. 7.00
Salt & Pepper 10.00

Red Poppy

Bright red flowers and black leaves were used on this popular Hall pattern called Red Poppy.

The pattern, made in East Liverpool, Ohio, from 1930 through 1950 was a premium item for Grand Union Tea Company. Matching metal pieces were made, such as wastebaskets and bread boxes; glass tumblers are known.

Bowl, 5 1/2 In. .... 2.50 To 3.00
Coffeepot .... 18.00 To 22.50
Cup 4.00
Jug, No.5 .... 13.00 To 15.00
Mixing Bowl, No.5, 9 In. ... 8.00
Pepper Shaker, Handle 8.00
Plate, 7 In. 3.00
Salt & Pepper, Handle 18.50
Saltshaker, Teardrop 6.00
Teapot 25.00
Teapot, New York 45.00
Tumbler, Frosted,
10 Oz. 15.00

Red Riding Hood

One of the easiest patterns of American dinnerware to recognize is Red Riding Hood. Three-dimensional figures of the little girl with the red hood have been adapted into saltshakers, teapots, and other pieces. The pattern was made by the Hull Pottery Company, Crooksville, Ohio, from 1943–1957.

Bank, Standing 225.00
Butter .... 110.00 To 150.00
Canister, Sugar 90.00
Cookie Jar .... 40.00 To 135.00
Creamer .... 35.00 To 80.00
Grease Jar, Wolf Figural,
Cover 300.00
Lamp 550.00
Matchbox ...... 325.00 To 350.00
Mustard, Spoon 110.00
Pitcher,
8 In. .... 135.00 To 150.00
Pitcher, Milk 85.00

Salt & Pepper, 3 In. 15.00
Salt & Pepper, 5 In. 29.00
Salt & Pepper, Gold Trim 50.00
Saltshaker, Tall 20.00
Spice Set, 6 Piece 1600.00
Sugar .... 35.00 To 40.00
Sugar & Creamer .... 52.00 To 70.00
Teapot .... 80.00 To 118.00
Tray, Wolf, Metal, 7 1/2 X 5 1/2 In. 30.00
Wall Pocket ... 120.00 To 150.00

Hull Ware
Little Red Riding Hood
Patent Applied For
U.S.A.

Refrigerator Ware

Refrigerator sets were made by the Hall China Company, East Liverpool, Ohio, from the late 1930s. For Westinghouse the company made Patrician in 1938, Emperor in 1939, Aristocrat in 1940–1941 and Prince in 1952. They also made King and Queen ovenware to match the Refrigerator Ware. Sears, Roebuck, Montgomery Ward, Hotpoint and General Electric also used Hall Refrigerator Ware. The company also made some pieces sold with the Hall name. They were Bingo in the late 1930s, Plaza in the 1930s to the 1960s, and Norris.

G.E., Leftover, Prince, Addison, Rectangular 12.00
G.E., Leftover, Prince, Addison, Round 7.00
G.E., Leftover, Prince, Daffodil, Rectangular 12.00
G.E., Leftover, Prince, Daffodil, Round 7.00
Westinghouse, Leftover, Aristocrat, Garden 7.50
Westinghouse, Leftover, Aristocrat, Sunset 7.50
Westinghouse, Leftover, Emperor, Canary 7.50
Westinghouse, Leftover, Prince, Blue, Rectangular 12.00

Made Exclusively for
WESTINGHOUSE By
The Hall China Co.
MADE IN U.S.A.

Westinghouse, Leftover, Prince, Blue, Round 6.50
Westinghouse, Water Server, Emperor, Delphinium 55.00

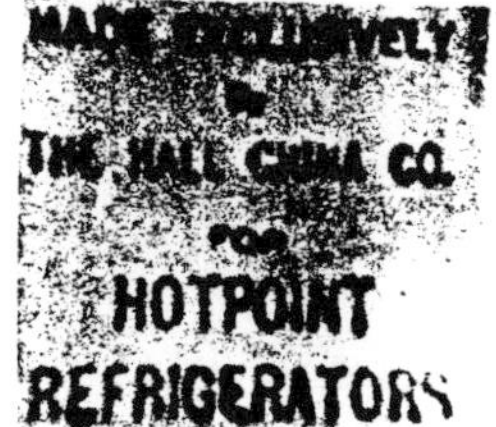

Rhythm

Rhythm is a solid-color dinnerware made by Homer Laughlin from about 1951 to 1958. It is a pattern with simple, modern shapes. The dishes were made in many of the Harlequin colors including chartreuse, forest green, gray, maroon, and yellow.

CHARTREUSE

Bowl, 5 1/2 In. 4.00
Bowl, 9 In. 7.00
Creamer 4.00
Gravy Boat 5.50
Plate, 9 In. 3.50
Platter, 11 1/2 In. 6.00
Salt & Pepper 5.00
Soup, Dish, 8 1/4 In. 6.00

FOREST GREEN

Bowl, 5 1/2 In. 2.50
Bowl, 9 In. 7.00
Gravy Boat 5.00
Plate, 9 In. 3.50
Soup, Dish, 8 1/4 In. 6.00

GRAY

Soup, Dish, 8 1/4 In. 5.00

YELLOW

Bowl, 9 In. 7.00
Soup, Dish, 8 1/4 In. 2.00

Rhythm Rose

Rhythm Rose was made by Homer Laughlin China Company, Newell, West Virginia, from the mid-1940s to the mid-1950s. The pattern featured a center rose decal.

Bowl, Round, 8 In. 7.50
Cake Plate, 10 1/2 In. .... 5.00 To 6.00

HOMER LAUGHLIN

Casserole, Cover.............15.00
Coffeepot.....................19.00
Creamer........................4.00
Gravy Boat.....................8.00
Pie Plate.......................8.00
Pitcher, Milk.................14.00
Plate, 6 In........................75
Plate, 7 In.....................1.50
Plate, 10 In..........3.00 To 4.00
Platter, 12 In..................8.50
Soup, Dish.....................4.50
Sugar, Cover..................5.00

Ring

Ring, sometimes called Beehive, was made by J. A. Bauer Company, Los Angeles, California, from 1932 to 1962. It was made in many colors. Bright shades include black, burnt orange, green, ivory, maroon, orange, and yellow. Pastel shades were chartreuse, gray, green, light yellow, olive, pale blue, pink, turquoise, and white.

BURNT ORANGE

Plate, 10 1/2 In.............7.00

GREEN

Bowl, 5 5/8 In..............5.00

IVORY

Plate, 10 1/2 In.............7.00

MAROON

Coffee Server, Cover........40.00

ORANGE

Carafe, Copper Lid,
Wooden Handle...........17.00

PINK

Casserole, Cover,
Copper Handle.............12.00

TURQUOISE

Bowl, 9 1/2 In.............12.00
Plate, 10 1/2 In.............7.00

YELLOW

Plate, 6 1/4 In................2.75
Plate, 10 1/2 In.............7.00
Salt & Pepper.................8.00

BAUER POTTERY
LOS ANGELES

Riviera

Riviera was solid-color ware made by Homer Laughlin China Company, Newell, West Virginia, from 1938 to 1950. It was unmarked and sold exclusively by the Murphy Company. Plates and cup handles were squared. Colors were ivory, light green, mauve blue, red, yellow, and, rarely, dark blue.

IVORY

Cup.............................4.50
Jug, Cover....................45.00
Plate, 9 In.....................5.00
Soup, Cream.....13.50 To 18.00

LIGHT GREEN

Bowl, 5 1/2 In..............4.50
Cup.............................5.00
Cup & Saucer................8.50

Plate, 9 In.....................5.50
Platter, 11 1/2 In............9.50
Saltshaker......................3.00
Tumbler,
Handle..........35.00 To 38.00

MAUVE BLUE

Casserole, Cover,
10 1/2 In.....................35.00
Creamer........................4.50
Cup.............................5.00
Platter, 11 1/2 In..........10.00
Platter, 13 1/2 In..........14.00
Saucer..........................1.50

RED

Butter, 1/2 Lb...............42.50
Creamer........................6.00
Plate, 9 In....................12.00
Platter, 11 1/2 In..........14.00
Saltshaker......................3.50
Syrup..........................65.00
Teapot.........................20.00

YELLOW

Bowl, 5 In.....................4.50
Bowl, 5 1/2 In...............4.00
Butter, 1/2 Lb...............45.00
Creamer........................5.50
Cup.............................4.00
Pitcher, Juice.................55.00
Platter, 11 In.................10.00
Salt & Pepper.................6.00
Saltshaker......................3.50
Soup, Flat......................9.50

Glue broken china with any invisible mending cement that is waterproof.

Sugar, Cover........7.00 To 8.00
Tumbler, Juice................ 4.00

Rooster

Roosters of many sorts were used as decorations on Southern Pot-

teries pieces. The Rooster crowing from the fence top with a sun and a barn in the distance is a pattern called Cock o' the Morn. Most other patterns picturing the bird are called Rooster, including one made by Stangl Pottery. Those listed here are by Southern Potteries.

Box, Cover.................. 10.00
Cup & Saucer................ 5.00
Plate, 6 In..........1.00 To 7.00
Plate, 10 In.................. 6.00

Rose Parade

The Hall China Company, East Liverpool, Ohio, sometimes made surprising color- and decal-decorated wares. Rose Parade has a solid Cadet Blue body with contrasting Hi-white knobs and handles. A rose decal was added to the white spaces. Sometimes the flower is pink, sometimes blue. The pattern was made from 1941 through the 1950s. Serving pieces, not dinnerware sets, were made.

Casserole, Tab Handle...... 30.00
Coffeepot, Drip-O-Lator,
Tab Handle, Hall.......... 17.00
Jug, Sani-Grid,
7 1/2 In.................... 23.00
Pepper Shaker, Sani-Grid ... 8.50
Salt & Pepper................ 16.00
Saltshaker, Sani-Grid......... 8.00
Shaker, Flour, Sani-Grid..... 8.00

Rose White

Rose White, first made in 1941 by Hall China Company, is similar to Rose Parade. The same shapes were used, but the pieces were all white with a slightly different rose-decal decoration. There is silver trim on many pieces.

Casserole, Cover............ 25.00
Creamer 8.50
Jug, 6 1/2 In................ 18.00
Jug, 7 1/2 In................ 13.00
Pepper Shaker, Sani-Grid ... 7.50
Salt & Pepper............... 18.00
Saltshaker..................... 8.00
Teapot, Sani-Grid,
4-Cup 20.00

Rosebud

Rosebud was made by Coors Pottery, Golden, Colorado, from 1934 to 1942. It is a solid-colored ware with a stylized flower and leaves on the edge of plates or sides of cups. It was made in blue, green, ivory, maroon, turquoise, and yellow.

BLUE

Casserole, Cover, 8 In. 23.00
Plate, 7 In. 4.50
Plate, 10 In................... 7.50
Saucer......................... 3.50
Shaker, Tall 8.50

COORS
ROSEBUD
U.S.A.

GREEN

Plate, 10 In................... 8.50

Royal Rose

Royal Rose is a Hall China Company pattern that can confuse you. It is Cadet Blue with Hi-white handles and knobs. The floral decal is the one used on Rose White. Pieces have silver trim. The shapes are different from those used for Rose Parade.

Bowl, 9 In. 20.00
Casserole, Cover .... 25.00 To 34.00
Drip Jar, Cover 18.00
Drip Set 35.00
Mixing Bowl, 6 1/2 In. 10.00
Pepper Shaker, Handle 6.00
Saltshaker, Handle .... 8.50 To 10.00
Teapot, French ... 37.00 To 45.00

Rugosa

Rugosa is a hand-painted pattern by Blue Ridge. The large flowers are yellow with brown centers and green leaves.

Bowl, 5 1/2 In. 2.00
Bowl, 9 In. 7.50
Gravy Boat 7.00
Plate, 6 In. 2.00
Plate, 7 In. 3.25

Blue Ridge
Hand Painted
Underglaze
Southern Potteries, Inc.
MADE IN U. S. A.

Plate, 9 In. 4.25
Soup, Dish, Lug Handle 4.00

Russel Wright, see American Modern; Iroquois

Rustic Plaid

Rustic plaid was made on the Skyline shape by Blue Ridge in the 1950s. Black lines and rim decorate a sponged background.

Bowl, 6 In. 2.50
Cup & Saucer 3.50
Plate, 6 In. 1.25
Plate, 10 In. 6.00

Saf-Handle

Saf-Handle is a kitchenware line that had, as would be expected from the name, an unusual handle on some pieces. Most pieces are found in Chinese Red, but other colors were also used. The line was made from 1938 until the 1960s. Some pieces were made in several variations and there are three different styles of creamers.

CANARY

Creamer 10.00

CHINESE RED

Casserole, 8 In. 20.00
Syrup 45.00
Teapot, Individual 24.00

Sani-Grid

Sani-Grid is a colorful kitchenware line usually found in Cadet Blue or Chinese Red. It has white knobs and handles. The pattern was made by the Hall China Company, East Liverpool, Ohio, after 1941.

CHINESE RED

Creamer 7.00
Jug, 7 1/2 In. ..... 16.00 To 18.00
Pepper Shaker 7.00
Sugar 7.00
Teapot, 6-Cup ... 22.00 To 27.00

Serenade

There were two patterns named Serenade, one by Hall, the other by Homer Laughlin. The Homer Laughlin dishes listed here were plain, made in green, pink, blue, or yellow.

GREEN

Bowl, 6 In. 4.50
Bowl, 8 In. 8.00
Bowl, 9 In. 7.00
Gravy Boat........ 9.00 To 11.00
Platter, 6 In. 2.00
Platter, 13 In. 16.00

LIGHT BLUE

Platter, 13 In. 18.00

PINK

Bowl, 6 In. 4.50
Platter, 13 In. 9.00

YELLOW

Bowl, 6 In. 4.50

Serenade Hall

Hall China Company made a pattern on their D-shape dishes called Serenade. The dishes were decorated with sprigs of orange flowers.

Baker, French.... 10.00 To 12.00
Casserole, 8 1/2 In. 18.00
Coffeepot 25.00
Cup 3.50

SHELLWARE, see Cameo Shellware

Silhouette

Silhouette looks just like its name. The 1930s pattern shows a black silhouette of two people eating at a table and a dog begging for food in front of the table. The plates are trimmed in platinum. The pattern, made by Crooksville China Company, Crooksville, Ohio, is similar to Taverne, but Taverne has no dog. Matching metal pieces and glasswares were made.

Bowl, 5 5/8 In. 10.00
Cup & Saucer 12.00
Gravy Boat 18.00
Plate, 7 1/4 In. 7.00

Plate, 9 In. 11.00
Soup, Dish .... 6.00 To 8.50
Sugar & Creamer 38.00
Tray, Chrome & China Handle, 11 In. 20.00

Spiderweb

Spiderweb is a modern, plain pattern of dishes made on the Skyline shape. It was made by Southern Potteries. There was no design, just a solid pastel color with a flecked finish.

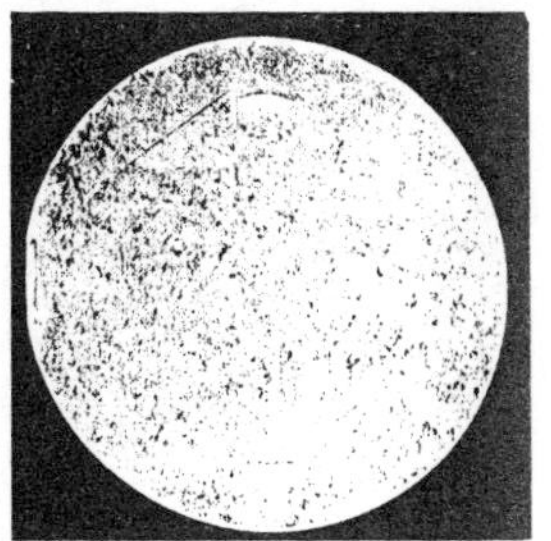

GRAY

Bowl, 5 In. 5.00
Creamer 6.00
Salt & Pepper 10.00
Saucer 2.00
Soup, Dish, Flared Rim...... 7.50
Sugar, Cover 10.00

PINK

Cup 5.00
Plate, 10 In. 7.00
Saucer 2.00

Blue Ridge
Hand Painted
Underglaze
Southern Potteries, Inc.
MADE IN U. S. A.

Spring Glory

A bright blue flower and bud with green leaves is hand painted on the center of the Spring Glory pattern dishes by Southern Potteries of Erwin, Tennessee.

Blue Ridge
Hand Painted
Underglaze
Southern Potteries, Inc.
MADE IN U. S. A.

Cup............................ 5.00
Plate, 9 In..................... 4.00
Saucer.......................... 1.00

Springtime

Springtime is a dinnerware made by Hall China Company, East Liverpool, Ohio. It has a pink floral arrangement.

Bowl, 5 1/2 In. ....2.00 To 4.00
Bowl, 9 In.....................15.00
Cake Plate..................... 7.50
Creamer 7.50
Cup............................ 5.00
Cup & Saucer ....5.00 To 8.50
Gravy Boat.......17.00 To 18.00
Plate, 6 In..................... 1.75
Plate, 8 1/4 In................ 3.50
Plate, 9 1/4 In......5.25 To 8.50
Platter, 13 In......9.00 To 12.00
Saucer.......................... 2.00
Soup, Dish, 8 1/2 In........10.00
Sugar, Open................... 6.00
Teapot, French...............40.00

Stanhome Ivy

Stanhome Ivy is a Blue Ridge pattern made on the Skyline shape after 1954. It is decorated with a stylized green ivy sprig.

Bowl, 5 1/4 In. 2.50
Bowl, Vegetable, Round,
9 In.......................... 7.00
Creamer 5.00
Cup & Saucer 5.00
Gravy Boat, Underplate 10.00
Plate, 6 In..................... 2.00
Plate, 9 1/2 In................ 5.00
Platter, Oval, 14 In........... 9.00
Sugar & Creamer, Cover 6.00

Blue Ridge
Hand Painted
Underglaze
Southern Potteries, Inc.
MADE IN U. S. A.

Star Flower

Star Flower is a pattern of dinnerware made by Stangl Pottery from 1952 to 1957.

Bowl, 10 In. 12.00
Creamer 4.00
Pitcher, 1 Qt. 10.00
Plate, 8 In..................... 4.00
Plate, 10 In...................12.00
Saucer.......................... 2.00

Sunflower

A bright yellow flower with an orange center is hand-painted on Sunflower, a dinnerware by Southern Potteries of Erwin, Tennessee. The flower is placed close to the edge, so it is only partly visible.

Blue Ridge
Hand Painted
Underglaze
Southern Potteries, Inc.
MADE IN U. S. A.

Bowl, Vegetable,
9 1/2 In.....................12.00
Cup............................ 4.00
Plate, 6 In..................... 1.50
Plate, 8 1/2 In................ 5.00
Plate, 9 1/2 In...............10.00
Plate, 10 In.................... 7.00
Saucer.......................... 1.00
Soup, Cream, 6 In............ 4.00
Soup, Dish, 8 In.............. 4.00

T

Tam O'Shanter

Tam O'Shanter is one of the many plaid patterns made by Vernon Kilns, Vernon, California. It is a forest green, lime, and reddish brown plaid with forest green border. Other related plaids are Calico (pink and blue), Coronation Organdy (gray and rose), Gingham (green and yellow), Homespun (cinnamon, yellow, and green), Organdie (brown and yellow), and Tweed (gray and blue).

Bowl, 5 1/2 In. 3.00
Bowl, 7 1/4 In. 5.00
Bowl, Chowder............... 9.00

Bowl, Vegetable,
8 3/4 In. 7.00
Butter Chip 9.00
Carafe, Coffee, Cover 23.00
Casserole, Cover 20.00
Coaster 8.00
Creamer 1.50
Cup 2.00
Cup & Saucer 6.00 To 8.00
Gravy Boat 9.00
Mug 10.00
Pitcher, 2 Qt. 15.00
Plate, 6 In. 1.50 To 2.00
Plate, 9 1/2 In. 3.50 To 6.00
Plate, 10 1/2 In. 9.00
Platter, 12 3/4 In. 7.00
Salt & Pepper 12.00
Saltshaker 4.00
Sugar, Cover 3.00
Syrup 30.00
Tidbit, 2 Tiers 14.00

Tampico

Tampico, a brown, green, and watermelon-colored pattern on a Futura shape, was made by Red Wing Pottery of Red Wing, Min-

nesota. This modern design was introduced in 1955. Many other patterns were also made on the Futura bodies.

Bowl, 7 In. 9.00
Bowl, Vegetable, 2 Sections,
10 In. 8.00
Creamer 3.00 To 4.50
Cup & Saucer 4.50 To 7.00
Gravy Boat 8.00 To 12.00
Plate, 6 1/2 In. 1.75
Plate, 7 1/4 In. 2.75
Plate, 10 1/2 In. 4.00 To 7.00
Platter, 13 In. 7.50
Relish, 2 Sections 12.00
Saucer 2.00
Sugar, Cover 7.00 To 9.00

Taverne

Taverne serving pieces were made by the Hall China Company of East Liverpool, Ohio, in the 1930s. Matching dinnerware was made by Taylor, Smith, and Taylor of Chester, West Virginia. A rolling pin was made by Harker Potteries. The silhouetted figures eating at a table are very similar to those seen on the pattern Silhouette, but there is no dog in this decal. In some of the literature, Taverne is called Silhouette.

Baker, French, Fluted 15.00
Bowl, 5 1/2 In. 3.00 To 4.50
Bowl, 6 1/4 In. 8.50

Bowl,
7 3/4 In. 11.00 To 13.00
Bowl, Salad, 9 In. 11.00
Bowl, Vegetable, Round,
9 In. 15.00 To 18.00

Casserole,
Cover 24.00 To 30.00
Coaster, Metal 4.00
Coffeepot, Banded 35.00
Coffeepot, Electric 65.00
Creamer 10.00 To 12.00

Cup & Saucer 5.50 To 7.50
Jar, Pretzel 75.00
Jug, Colonial, 5 In. 17.00
Mixing Bowl, No.3, 6 In. 8.00
Mixing Bowl, No.5,
8 1/2 In. 12.00
Mug 28.00 To 32.00
Plate, 6 In. 2.00
Plate, 9 1/4 In. 6.75
Rolling Pin, Harker 100.00
Salt & Pepper, Banded 16.00
Saucer 2.50
Soup, Dish, 8 1/2 In. 12.00
Sugar, Cover 12.00 To 15.00
Teapot, Colonial 40.00

Thistle

Thistle, or No. 3847, is a pattern made by Stangl Pottery, Trenton,

New Jersey. The hand-painted decoration is a purple thistle and green spiked thistle leaves. The dishes were made from 1951 to 1967.

Bowl, 5 In. 3.25
Bowl, 10 In. ..... 10.00 To 15.00
Bowl, 12 In. 15.00
Bowl, Vegetable,
2 Sections .... 12.00 To 18.00
Butter, Cover 18.00
Casserole, Cover,
8 In. .... 18.00 To 25.00
Celery .... 10.00 To 12.00
Creamer 6.00
Cruet, Stopper 15.00
Cup .... 3.50 To 5.50
Cup & Saucer 8.50
Eggcup 8.00
Pitcher, 9 In. 4.50
Plate, 6 In. .... 1.50 To 3.00
Plate, 8 In. 3.00
Plate, 10 In. .... 6.00 To 8.00
Plate, Chop, 12 1/2 In. 11.00
Plate, Chop, 14 1/2 In. 15.00
Salt & Pepper ..... 7.50 To 10.00

Sandwich Server,
Center Handle 12.00
Soup, Cream .... 5.00 To 6.00
Soup, Dish .... 5.00 To 6.50
Sugar & Creamer,
Cover .... 12.00 To 13.00
Sugar, Cover 8.00

Tom & Jerry

Tom & Jerry sets were made to serve the famous Christmas punch. A set was usually a punch bowl and six matching cups.

Bowl .... 45.00 To 125.00
Bowl, 6 Mugs, Hall 30.00
Cup 8.00

Town & Country

Stangl Pottery made Town & Country pattern in a variety of colors in the 1970s. The design looks like the sponged stoneware made in the nineteenth century, but the pattern was not made just in blue. Black, green, honey beige, and yellow were also used.

GREEN

Coffeepot 55.00
Jell-O Mold 55.00

HONEY

Soup, Ladle 55.00

YELLOW

Soup, Dish 15.00

Tulip

Tulip is a 1930s pattern made by Hall China Company, East Liverpool, Ohio. It remained popular until the 1950s. Most of the pieces were distributed by Cook Coffee of Cleveland, Ohio. Pale yellow and purple tulips were applied by decal. The ware is trimmed with silver. The same design is found on a Harker Pottery pattern called Pastel Tulip. Other patterns called Tulip were made by Stangl Pottery; Edwin H. Knowles; Paden City Pottery; Universal Pottery; Leigh Pottery and Crescent China Co.; and Royal Pottery. Other patterns called Tulips were made by Homer Laughlin Company; Pottery Guild; Taylor, Smith, and Taylor; and Blue Ridge.

Bowl, 5 1/2 In. 3.50
Coffeepot 20.00
Cup 4.50
Mixing Bowl, No.3, 6 In. ... 8.00
Plate, 9 In. 4.50
Plate, 10 In. 8.50

U

Ultra California

Ultra California is a Vernon Kilns' pattern made from 1937 to 1942 in carnation, aster, gardenia, and buttercup.

ASTER

Cup 6.00
Cup & Saucer, Demitasse ... 14.00
Eggcup 8.00
Mug 25.00

Good tips for Bauer pottery and Fiesta and any other heavy, color-glazed dishes of the 1930s. Bauer is oven safe for baking—up to 350 degrees. Do not use in a microwave. Do not use on a direct flame. Do not wash in an automatic dishwasher. The detergent may discolor the glaze. Do not scour. Store with felt between stacked plates to avoid scratching. Some early 1930 to 1942 dishes used a lead in the glazing, so do not use scratched dishes with acidic foods. Lead poisoning is possible with prolonged use.

BUTTERCUP

Coffeepot 30.00
Cup 6.00

CARNATION

Eggcup 8.00

GARDENIA

Cup & Saucer, Demitasse ... 20.00

V

Virginia Rose

Virginia Rose is the name of a shape of dishes made by Homer Laughlin Company, Newell, West Virginia. The shapes were decorated with a variety of decal decorations. The dishes with a design of a spray of roses and green leaves is the pattern most often called Virginia Rose by collectors.

Bowl, 5 1/2 In. .... 2.50 To 5.00
Bowl, Vegetable, 7 1/2 In. 4.50
Bowl, Vegetable, 8 1/2 In. 7.00
Bowl, Vegetable, Oval, 8 1/2 In. 6.50
Butter, Cover, 1/2 Lb. 45.00
Casserole, Cover 32.00
Creamer .... 3.00 To 4.00

HOMER LAUGHLIN
VIRGINIA ROSE
MADE IN U.S.A.
L 46 N 8

Cup & Saucer .... 3.75 To 8.00
Gravy Boat .... 6.00 To 8.00
Mixing Bowl, 5 In. 8.00
Mixing Bowl, 9 1/2 In. 12.00
Plate, 6 In. .... 1.00 To 2.00
Plate, 7 In. 1.75
Plate, 9 In. 3.50
Plate, 10 1/2 In. 7.00
Plate, Deep 5.00
Platter, 11 1/2 In. .... 6.50 To 8.00
Platter, 13 1/2 In. 8.00
Sugar, Open 3.00

Vistosa

Taylor, Smith, and Taylor of Chester, West Virginia, made a solid-colored dinnerware about 1938 called Vistosa. The plates had piecrust edges and the other pieces had some bands or ridges. The glaze colors were cobalt blue, deep yellow, light green, and mango red. Pieces were marked with the name Vistosa and the initials T.S. & T. Co. U.S.A.

BLUE

Plate, 6 1/4 In. 3.00
Saucer 1.50

GREEN

Saucer 1.50

YELLOW

Plate, Handle, 11 In. 12.00

W

White Clover

White Clover is a dinnerware that was designed by Russel Wright for Harker Pottery Company of East Liverpool, Ohio. It had the very sleek modern shapes inspired by his other design, American Modern, but a sprig of clover decoration was added. It was made in four colors, meadow green, coral sand, golden spice,

Russel Wright

and charcoal. The dinnerware was advertised as oven-proof, chip-resistant, and detergent-resistant. The pattern was discontinued in 1955.

CHARCOAL

Bowl, 5 In.	3.00
Cup & Saucer	6.00 To 8.00
Plate, 10 In.	5.00
Saucer	2.50

CORAL

Bowl, 5 In.	3.00
Cup & Saucer	7.00
Plate, 6 In.	2.50
Plate, 10 In.	5.00

White Rose

White Rose is a cameo ware made by Harker China Company of Chester, West Virginia, in the 1940s. The rose pattern is cut into the glaze. It has white leaves and an outline of a single rose. The background is blue, pink, or yellow. The pieces are marked White Rose, Carv-Kraft by Harker. Both dinnerware and kitchenware were made in this pattern for Montgomery Ward.

WHITE ROSE
carv-kraft
◆◆◆ BY HARKER

BLUE

Cup	5.00
Plate, 9 In.	5.00
Salt & Pepper	6.00
Sugar, Cover	4.00

YELLOW

Pitcher	10.00

Wildfire

Great American Tea Company gave Wildfire pattern as a premium. This Hall Pottery pattern of the 1950s has a Hi-white body and flower garland decal decoration.

Bowl, 5 1/2 In.	3.25
Bowl, 6 1/2 In.	5.00
Bowl, Salad, 9 In.	8.50
Bowl, Vegetable, Oval	12.00
Bowl, Vegetable, Round, 9 In.	15.00
Plate, 6 In.	2.50
Plate, 10 In.	5.00
Platter, 11 In.	11.00 To 12.00
Platter, 13 In.	10.00 To 14.00
Salt & Pepper, Teardrop	12.50
Saltshaker, Sani-Grid	5.00
Soup, Dish, 8 1/2 In.	7.00
Sugar, Open	3.25

Wildflower

Wildflower was made by Edwin M. Knowles, Newell, West Virginia.

Pie Plate	15.00
Plate, 9 In.	4.00
Vase, 6 1/2 In.	16.00

Windflower

Windflower was made by Blue Ridge in the 1940s. It is decorated with a fanciful red flower with green leaves.

Blue Ridge
Hand Painted
Underglaze
Southern Potteries, Inc.
MADE IN U. S. A.

Bowl, 5 1/2 In.	1.50
Plate, 6 In.	1.50
Plate, 9 In.	3.00
Sugar, Cover	5.00

Woodfield

Woodfield was a dinnerware made by the Steubenville Pottery, Steubenville, Ohio. The dishes were shaped like leaves and were colored in many of the shades used for American Modern dishes also made by the same pottery. Full dinner sets were made.

BLUE

Plate & Cup	4.00

CHARTREUSE

Cup	2.75
Cup & Saucer	3.00
Plate & Cup	4.00
Platter, 13 In.	7.00 To 9.00
Salt & Pepper	3.00

CORAL

Plate, 6 In.	2.00
Snack Plate	3.00

By
Steubenville
U. S. A.

GRAY

Cup & Saucer 3.00
Pitcher, 8 In.................. 4.00
Plate, 8 In. 3.00
Salt & Pepper ....3.00 To 5.00

GREEN

Cup............................. 2.75
Saucer.......................... 1.25
Snack Plate 3.00

PINK

Pitcher, 6 In.................. 3.50

Woodvine

Woodvine was made by Universal Pottery as a premium to be used in grocery stores. The design pictured small red flowers and large leaves.

Bowl, 5 3/8 In. 2.50
Bowl, Oval, 9 In.............. 7.00
Bowl, Round, 9 In. 7.00
Casserole, Cover.............18.00
Cup & Saucer 4.00
Gravy Boat.................... 7.00
Jug, 7 In....................... 9.00
Leftover, Cover, 5 In......... 7.00
Mixing Bowl, 6 1/2 In. 6.00
Mixing Bowl, 7 1/2 In. 7.00
Mixing Bowl, 8 1/2 In. 8.00
Pie Pan, 10 In. 9.00
Plate, 6 In. 1.75
Plate, 9 1/4 In................ 3.50
Plate, 10 1/2 In. 8.00

Yellow Carnation

Yellow Carnation is a Fiesta Casual design with yellow and brown flowers on a white background. The rim is edged with yellow. It was made from 1962 to 1968 by Homer Laughlin Company.

GENUINE
fiesta
H. L. Co. USA
CASUAL

Plate, 7 In. 6.00
Plate, 10 In................... 8.00
Saucer.......................... 4.00

Yorktown

E.M. Knowles, Newell, West Virginia, manufactured the Yorktown pattern in 1936. The solid-colored, Deco-shaped dishes were made in light yellow, maroon, periwinkle blue, and terra cotta.

BLUE

Plate, 9 1/4 In................ 4.00
Salt & Pepper 4.00

TERRA COTTA

Saltshaker...................... 2.50

YELLOW

Plate, 9 1/4 In................ 4.00
Plate, 10 In.................... 4.50

Zeisel

Eva Zeisel designed the Hallcraft shape for the Hall China Company in 1952. It remained popular until the 1960s. The solid white dinnerware is marked with her name.

HALLCRAFT
BY
Eva Zeisel

Ashtray......................... 5.50
Baker, 11 1/2 In. 9.00
Bowl, 8 3/4 In. 7.00
Bowl, Salad, Large 16.00
Casserole, Large 24.00
Celery........................... 9.00
Cookie Jar, Ivory Dot.......24.00
Jug, Vinegar...................16.00
Ladle 10.00
Plate, 6 In. 2.00
Platter, 15 In........7.00 To 8.00
Salt & Pepper 14.00
Sugar, After Dinner.......... 4.50

AMERICAN DINNERWARE
Factories

NAME	LOCATION	DATES
Abingdon Potteries	Abingdon, Illinois	1908–1951
American Pottery	Byesville, Ohio	1942–1965
Bauer Pottery Company	Los Angeles, California	1905–c.1958
Blair Ceramics	Ozark, Missouri	1946–1950s
Blue Ridge, see Southern Potteries		
Brusché Ceramics	Whittier, California	c.1950
Brush-McCoy	Roseville and Zanesville, Ohio	1911–1925 (Combined firm of Brush Pottery and J. W. McCoy Company)
Brush Pottery	Roseville and Zanesville, Ohio	1907—present (Brush-McCoy 1911–1925)
California Ceramics	Los Angeles, California	c.1948–1954
Caribe-Sterling	Vega Baja, Puerto Rice	early 1950s–1977
Catalina Pottery	Catalina Island, California	c.1927–1947 (name purchased by Gladding McBean Company in 1937; Catalina name remained in use until 1947)
Continental Kilns	East Liverpool, Ohio	1944–1954
H. F. Coors Company	Inglewood, California, and Golden, Colorado	1925–present
Crescent China Company	Alliance, Ohio	1920–1930 (Associated with Leigh Pottery after 1926)
Crooksville China Company	Crooksville, Ohio	1902–c.1960
Crown Pottery	Evansville, Indiana	1882–1962
Flintridge China Company	Pasadena, California	1945–present
Franciscan Ceramics	Los Angeles, California	1934–present (Wedgwood Group after 1979)
Frankoma Pottery	Sapulpa, Oklahoma	1936–present
French Saxon China Company	East Liverpool, Ohio	1935–present
W. S. George Company	Kittanig, Pennsylvania	1880–1959
Gladding, McBean & Co.	Los Angeles, California	1875–present (Wedgwood Group after 1979)
Gonder Ceramic Art Company	Zanesville, Ohio	1941–1957
Haeger Potteries	Dundee, Illinois	1914–present

NAME	LOCATION	DATES
Hall China Company	East Liverpool, Ohio	1903–present
Harker Pottery Company	Chester, West Virginia, and East Liverpool, Ohio	1890–1972
Harmony House	Mark used by Sears, Roebuck and Co.; various manufacturers	
Homer Laughlin China Company	Newell, West Virginia, and East Liverpool, Ohio	1877–present
A. E. Hull Pottery Company	Crooksville, Ohio	1905–present
Iroquois China Company	Syracuse, New York	1905–1969
James River Potteries	Hopewell, Virginia	1922–1938
Edwin M. Knowles China Company	Chester and Newell, West Virginia, and East Liverpool, Ohio	1900–1963, 1975–present
Leigh Pottery	Alliance, Ohio	1926–1938 (Crescent China Company before 1926)
J. W. McCoy Company	Zanesville, Ohio	1899–1925 (Brush-McCoy Pottery Company from 1911–1925)
Metlox Potteries	Manhattan Beach, California	1935–present
Montgomery Ward	Sold variety of patterns under own name, various manufacturers	
Paden City Pottery	Paden City, West Virginia	1914–1963
Pickard, Inc.	Chicago and Antioch, Illinois	1893–present
Pope-Gosser China Company	Coshocton, Ohio	1902–1958
Pottery Guild	New York, New York	1937–1946
Purinton Pottery	Shippenville, Pennsylvania	1941–1951
Red Wing Potteries	Red Wing, Minnesota	1878–1967
Roseville Pottery Company	Zanesville, Ohio	1892–1954
Royal China Company	Sebring, Ohio	1933–present
Sabin Industries	McKeesport, Pennsylvania	1946–present
Salem China Company	Salem, Ohio	1898–1967
Scio Pottery Company	Scio, Ohio	1932–1985
Sears, Roebuck and Company	Sold variety of patterns under their own name, various manufacturers	
Sebring-Limoges	Sebring, Ohio	1887–1955 (Sebring Pottery Company and Limoges China Company combined under same management c.1940)
Shawnee Pottery Company	Zanesville, Ohio	1936–1961
Southern Potteries (Blue Ridge)	Erwin, Tennessee	1917–1957
Standard Pottery Company	East Liverpool, Ohio	1886–1927
Stanford Pottery	Sebring, Ohio	1945–1961

NAME	LOCATION	DATES
Stangl Pottery	Flemington and Trenton, New Jersey	1930–1978
Stetson China Company	Lincoln, Illinois	1919–1965
Steubenville Pottery Company	Steubenville, Ohio	1879–c.1960
Syracuse China Corporation	Syracuse, New York	1871–present
Taylor, Smith, and Taylor	Chester, West Virginia, and East Liverpool, Ohio	1901–present
Terrace Ceramics	Marietta, Ohio	1961–1975
Universal Potteries	Cambridge, Ohio	1934–1956
Vernon Kilns	Los Angeles and Vernon, California	1912–1958 (name purchased by Metlox Potteries)
Watt Pottery Company	Crooksville, Ohio	1922–1965

AMERICAN DINNERWARE
Pattern List

Note: * = prices and paragraph in body of book

PATTERN	SHAPE	MAKER	DATE	DESCRIPTION
ABC	Kiddieware	Stangl	Mid-1940s–1974	Solid colors
Abingdon	Square	Abingdon	1935	
Abundance	Colonial	Blue Ridge		Pear and cherries; broken green rim
Abundance	Ultra	Vernon Kilns	1939	Maroon fruit and floral border
Acacia	Kitchenware	Hall		Pastel flowers; decal
Acacia Flowers	Shellcrest	Paden City		
Acorn		Harmony House		Blue, pink; cameoware
Adam	Antique	Steubenville		Rich ivory glaze; heavily embossed
Adobestone	Ceramastone	Red Wing	1967	
Adonis, see Prince				
Adrian		Stangl	1972–1974	
After Glow	Montecito	Vernon Kilns	1935–1937	Yellow with ivory bottom and interior
*Airflow	Teapot	Hall	1940	Canary, Chinese Red, cobalt, turquoise, and other colors
Al Fresco	Al Fresco	Franciscan	1952	Coffee Brown, Hemlock Green, Misty Gray, Olive Green
*Aladdin	Teapot	Hall	1939	Variety of colors; decals

PATTERN	SHAPE	MAKER	DATE	DESCRIPTION
*Albany	Teapot	Hall	1930	Solid colors; gold decorations
*Albert	Teapot	Hall	1940s	Celadon only; Victorian style
Alexandria	Candlewick	Blue Ridge		Red, yellow, and blue flowers; green leaves
Alia Jane	Round	Taylor, Smith, and Taylor	1933–1934	Decal
All Apple		Purinton		Hand painted; large apple
Alleghany	Colonial	Blue Ridge		Blue, red, yellow flowers; red rim
Allure	Classique	E. M. Knowles	1960	
Aloaha	Skyline	Blue Ridge	1950s	Gray, green, white; large leaves
Aloha		French Saxon		
Amapila	Amapila	Franciscan		Hand painted
Amarylis	Colonial	Blue Ridge		Red flowers, border, and rim
Ambassador	Regent	E. M. Knowles	1948	
Amber Glo		Stangl	1954–1962	
*Amberstone	Fiesta	Homer Laughlin	1967	Solids; brown designs
American Beauty	Minion	Paden City		Large pink rose
American Beauty		Stetson		
*American Modern	American	Steubenville (Russel Wright)	1939–1959	Bean Brown, Black Chutney, Cantelope, chartreuse, Clear Green, coral, Glacier Blue, Granite Gray, Seafoam Blue, white
American Provincial		Homer Laughlin		Pennsylvania Dutch designs
Americana pattern	A2000	Stangl		
Amhurst	Colonial	Blue Ridge		Pink flowers; center and line border
Amy		Harker		Gold trim; multicolored flowers
Anemone	Piecrust	Blue Ridge		Red flowers; two-tone green leaves
Anniversary		Salem China	1943	
Antiqua		Stangl	1972–1974	Stylized flower, gold background, brown and black border
Antique Gold		Stangl		
Antique Leaf	Lace Edge	Blue Ridge		Red, green, black leaf border

PATTERN	SHAPE	MAKER	DATE	DESCRIPTION
Anytime	Anytime	Vernon Kilns	1955–1958	Bands of gray, mocha, yellow
Appalachian Spring	Candlewick	Blue Ridge		Stylized red tulip and red border
*Apple	Apple	Franciscan	1940–present	
Apple		Purinton	1936–1959	Large center apple; scalloped rim
*Apple	Watt Ware	Watt	1930s–1965	Hand-painted red apple, green leaves
Apple and Pear	Woodcrest	Blue Ridge	1950s	
Apple Blossom		Crooksville		Pink flowers
Apple Blossom	Nautilus Eggshell	Homer Laughlin	1935–1955	Flowered border; gold trim
Apple Crisp	Skyline	Blue Ridge	1950s	Three red apples, red rim
Apple Crunch	Piecrust	Blue Ridge	1948	Red and white apple, green leaves and border
Apple Delight		Stangl	1965–1974	Red and yellow apples, dark border
Apple Jack	Skyline	Blue Ridge	1950s	Two apples; sponged yellow background
Apples		Pottery Guild		Apple tree branch
April		Homer Laughlin		Flowered border
Aquarium	Ultra	Vernon Kilns	1938	Tropical fish
Arabesque	Arabesque	Catalina	1935	Solids
Arabian Night		Paden City		
*Arcadia	Melinda	Vernon Kilns	1942; 1950–1955	Brown laurel wreath border
Ardennes	Provincial	Red Wing	1941	Laurel leaf band
Argosy		W. S. George	1930	Ivory body
*Aristocrat	Refrigerator ware	Hall	1940–1941	Westinghouse; Acrtic Blue, canary, Garden, Sunset; also called Hercules; Peasant Ware label
Aristocrat		Homer Laughlin		Flowered border
Aristocrat	Century	Salem		Delphinium blue; black and platinum band
Arlene	Trellis	Blue Ridge		Pink tulip, blue daisy, wide blue rim
Arlington Apple	Skyline	Blue Ridge	1950s	Two red apples
Art Deco	Art Deco	Catalina	Early 1930s	Solids
Asbury	Pegasus	Sebring	1940s	
Ashland	Colonial	Blue Ridge		Red, light blue flowers; green rim
Astor Fruit	Astor	Blue Ridge		Aqua fruit; aqua and orange rim
Atlanta	Skyline	Blue Ridge	1950s	
Aurora	Candlewick	Blue Ridge		Two large pink flowers
*Automobile	Teapot	Hall	1938	Canary, Chinese Red, maroon, common colors; sometimes with gold or silver trim

PATTERN	SHAPE	MAKER	DATE	DESCRIPTION
Autumn		Franciscan	1934	Leaves
Autumn Apple (No. 3735)	Colonial	Blue Ridge	1941	Apples border; broken red rim
Autumn Ballet	Ultra	Vernon Kilns	1940	Maroon floral and leaf
Autumn Breeze	Skyline	Blue Ridge	1950s	Stylized leaves, gray, green, and rust
Autumn Fancy		Universal		Decals
Autumn Harvest	Versatile	Taylor, Smith, and Taylor		
Autumn Laurel	Colonial	Blue Ridge		Yellow berries, green leaves, border
Autumn Leaf		Blair		Floral decals
Autumn Leaf		Crooksville China		Floral decals
Autumn Leaf		Crown		Floral decals
*Autumn Leaf		Hall	1936–present	For Jewel Tea Co.; floral decals of dark yellow and rust leaves
Autumn Leaf		Harker Potteries		Floral decals
Autumn Leaf		Paden City		Floral decals
Avenue	Coupe, LaGrande	Crooksville		Reddish-brown plant sprigs
Aztec		Stangl	1967–1968	
Aztec	Citation	Steubenville		
Aztec on Desert Sand	Citation	Steubenville		
Bachelor's Button		Stangl	1965	
*Ballerina	Ballerina	Universal Potteries	1947–1956	Solids; burgundy, charcoal, chartreuse, Dove Gray, Forest Green, Jade Green, Jonquil Yellow, Periwinkle Blue, pink; abstract designs
Baltimore	Teapot	Hall	1930s	Emerald and marine common colors
Bamboo		Blair		Stylistic bamboo design
Bamboo	Woodcrest	Blue Ridge	1950s	
Banana Tree	Montecito	Vernon Kilns	1937	Tree on ivory ground
*Banded	Kitchenware	Hall	1937	Kitchenware; floral decals; solid colors; Cadet, canary, Chinese Red, cobalt, Indian Red, ivory, marine, maroon; also called Five Band
Barbara	Colonial	Blue Ridge		Blue flowers and leaves
Bardstown	Skyline	Blue Ridge	1950s	Red flowers, outlined
Barkwood	San Marino	Vernon Kilns	1953–1958	Beige and brown; like tree bark
Basket	Decal	Hall	1932–1960	Small flower basket and diamond-shaped designs
*Basket	Teapot	Hall	1938	Embossed flower; canary, Chinese Red, marine common colors
Basket	Harker			Flower basket border

PATTERN	SHAPE	MAKER	DATE	DESCRIPTION
Basket		Leigh/Crescent		Flower Basket and individual small flowers
Basket		Salem		Center flower basket; border of leaves and individual flowers
Basket of Tulips	Bonjour	Salem		Various colored tulips; platinum rim
Basket Petit Point	Victory	Salem		Decals
Basketball	Teapot	Hall	1938	
Basketweave	Skyline	Blue Ridge	1950s	Black cross-hatch on beige background
Bauer, see Ring				
Beaded Apple	Colonial	Blue Ridge		Apple border, broken red rim
Beatrice	Skyline	Blue Ridge	1950s	Black-haired girl
Becky	Colonial	Blue Ridge		Large red flowers
Becky		Harker		Blue and red flowers
Beehive, see Ring				
Beige	Montecito	Vernon Kilns	1935–1937	Solid beige
Bel Air	San Marion	Vernon Kilns	1940; 1955	Three lines crossing three lines; green and brown on ivory
Bella Rosa		Stangl	1960–1962	Spray of roses and lily of the valley; pale gray background
Belle Haven	Woodcrest	Blue Ridge	1950s	Plaid tree, farm, rooster at sunrise; green rim
Bellemeade	Astor	Blue Ridge		Yellow flowers, blue and green leaves; brown line border
Bench	Deanna	E. M. Knowles		Mexican-styled jugs and cactus
Benjamin	Teapot	Hall	Early 1940s	Victorian style; see also Birch, Bowknot, Connie, Murphy, Plume
Berea Blossom	Colonial	Blue Ridge		Pastel flowers
Berkeley	Williamsburg	E. M. Knowles	1955	
Bermuda		Homer Laughlin	1977–1978	
Berry Patch	Skyline	Blue Ridge	1950s	Golden berries
Berryville	Colonial	Blue Ridge		Strawberry border; red rim
Bethany Berry	Moderne	Blue Ridge	1950s	Orange berries; gray, green, brown leaves
*Betty	Candlewick	Blue Ridge		Red and yellow flowers; green leaves
Beverly	Melinda	Vernon Kilns	1942	Rose blossom border
Big Apple	Colonial	Blue Ridge		
Big Boy	Coffeepot	Hall		Maroon with silver trim
Bimini		Homer Laughlin	1977–1978	
Bingo	Refrigerator ware	Hall	Late 1930s	Chinese Red; also called Zephyr

PATTERN	SHAPE	MAKER	DATE	DESCRIPTION
Birch	Teapot	Hall	Early 1940s	Victorian style; see also Benjamin, Bowknot, Connie, Murphy, Plume
Bird	Derwood	W. S. George		Red and brown bird on border
Bird		Blair		Sgraffito bird
Birdcage	Teapot	Hall	1939	Maroon most common color; embossed birds
Bird in the Heart		Universal Cambridge		
Bird Pottery		Vernon Kilns	Early 1930s	
Birds and Flowers		Harker		Multicolored flowers, small birds
Bird's Eye	Montecito	Vernon Kilns		Floral
Bit Series	Kiddieware	Stangl	Mid-1940s–1974	
Bittersweet		Hall		Flowers
Bittersweet	Skyline	Blue Ridge	1950s	Red berries
Bittersweet		Stangl		Sgraffito decoration
*Bittersweet		Universal Potteries	1949	Decals; orange and yellow
Black Beauty		Hall	1935	Red flowers and leaves, black shadows
Black-Eyed Susan	Forcast	E. M. Knowles	1959	
Black Ming	Skyline	Blue Ridge	1950s	Black tree
Black Tulip		Crooksville	1950s	Hand painted; black on pink
Blackberry Lily	Colonial	Blue Ridge		Dots on pink flowers
Bleeding Heart	Candlewick	Blue Ridge		Pink flowers; blue leaves, border, and rim
Blend No. 4	Montecito	Vernon Kilns	1938	Concentric rings in browns and greens
Blend No. 10	Montecito	Vernon Kilns	1938	Concentric rings in pinks and greens
Blossom Ring		Stangl	1967/68–1970	
Blossom Time	Coupe	Crooksville		Off-center decoration; branch of pink flowers
*Blossom Time	Concord	Red Wing	1947	Modern shapes; red flowers, green leaves, yellow and green accessory pieces
Blossom Time	Melinda	Vernon Kilns	1942	Blue blossoms
Blossom Tree	Skyline	Blue Ridge	1950s	Stylized tree; green leaves and yellow flowers
Blossoms	Shellcrest	Paden City		Large flower spray
Blossoms	Fruits	Crooksville		Red and pink flowers
Blossoms	Montecito	Vernon Kilns	1937	Blue blossom border on cream ground
Blossoms	Lido	W. S. George		Pink blossoms border
Blossomtime	Bolero	W. S. George		
Blossomtime	Accent	E. M. Knowles	1958	

PATTERN	SHAPE	MAKER	DATE	DESCRIPTION
Blue Bell		Stangl	c.1942	
Blue Belle	Accent	E. M. Knowles	c.1954	
Blue Bird		Crown	1941	Blue birds perched on pink apple blossoms; turquoise blue rim
Blue Blossom	Kitchenware	Hall	c.1939	Cobalt blue background, floral decals
Blue Blossoms		Crooksville		Flowers in shades of blue
Blue Bonnett	Accent	E. M. Knowles	1954	
Blue Bouquet	Candlewick	Blue Ridge		Red flowers
•Blue Bouquet	D-Line	Hall	1950–1960s	Premium for Standard Coffee; thin blue border with roses
Blue Carousel	Kiddieware	Stangl	Mid-1940s–1974	
Blue Daisy		Stangl	1963–1974	Blue daisies
Blue Dresden	Virginia Rose	Homer Laughlin	1949	
Blue Elf	Kiddieware	Stangl	Mid-1940s–1974	
Blue Flower	Colonial	Blue Ridge		Large blue off-center flower
•Blue Garden	Kitchenware	Hall	1939	Cobalt blue background, floral decals
Blue Heaven	Colonial	Blue Ridge		Blue flowers, gray leaves
Blue Medallion		Homer Laughlin	1920	Decals
Blue Moon	Candlewick	Blue Ridge		Blue flowers and leaves
Blue Parade, see Rose Parade				
Blue Rhythm		Harker	1959	Cameoware
Blue Shadows	True China	Red Wing	1964	
Blue Star	Montecito	Vernon Kilns	1938	Blue stars on blue ground
Blue Symphony		Homer Laughlin		
Blue Tango	Colonial	Blue Ridge		Floral design
Blue Tulip		Stangl		Terra Rose mark
Blue Willow	Trellis	Blue Ridge		Blue oriental scene, rim
•Blue Willow		Homer Laughlin	1942	Blue and pink
•Blue Willow	Cavalier	Royal	Late 1940s–1980s	Overall oriental design; pink, green
Blue Willow		Sebring-Limoges		
Bluebell		Paden City		Floral sprig
Bluebell Bouquet	Candlewick	Blue Ridge		
Blueberry		Sold by Montgomery Ward	1921	Decals
•Blueberry		Stangl	c.1940	Red with yellow border; blueberries in center
Blueberry Hill	Year 'Round	Vernon Kilns	1957–1958	Blue and brown floral abstract
Bluebird		Salem		Small bluebirds on border
Bluebird	Derwood	W. S. George		Bluebird on border; thin blue rim

PATTERN	SHAPE	MAKER	DATE	DESCRIPTION
Bluefield	Colonial	Blue Ridge		Blue flowers; red, green leaves
Blushing Rose, see Lido Dalyrymple				
Bo Peep	Kiddieware	Stangl	Mid-1940s–1974	
*Bob White		Red Wing	1956–1967	Hand painted; stylized bird; figurals
Bolero		Homer Laughlin	1977–1978	
Bonita		Caribe-Sterling	1950s–c.1963	Modernistic flowers
Bonita		Stangl		Della-Ware mark
Boncai	Skyline	Blue Ridge	1950s	Gnarled tree
Bouquet	Astor	Blue Ridge		Pink and yellow flowers, pink border
Border Bouquet	LaGrande	Crooksville		Border of small flowers
Border Rim		E. M. Knowles		Border design of flowers
Border Rose		Crooksville		Continuous border design
Bosc	Colonial	Blue Ridge		Red pear, blue leaves, broken red border
*Boston	Teapot	Hall	1920	Variety of colors; gold decorated line
Botanica	Esquire	E. M. Knowles	1957–1966	Abstract decal; Russel Wright
Bountiful	Colonial	Blue Ridge		Fruit; broken green rim
Bouquet		Crown		Multicolored flowers and bow
Bouquet	Hallcraft	Hall	1950s–1960s	Random flower sprays; designed by Eva Zeisel
Bouquet		Harker		
Bouquet	Ultra	Vernon Kilns	1938	Floral; yellow rim
Bourbon Rose	Colonial	Blue Ridge		Two roses, leaves allover design
Bow Knot	Piecrust	Blue Ridge		Chartreuse and brown variation of Whirligig
Bowknot	Teapot	Hall	Early 1940s	Victorian style; see also Benjamin, Birch, Connie, Murphy, Plume
Bowling Ball	Teapot	Hall	Late 1930s	Cobalt, turquoise
Boyce		Harker		Flowers in shades of pink
Bramwell	Colonial	Blue Ridge		Yellow, red, and blue flowers
Breakfast Nook		W. S. George		Open windows with flower trellis
Breath O'Spring	Classique	E. M. Knowles	1960	
Breckenridge	Colonial	Blue Ridge		Red flowers and leaves
Breeze	Bountiful	Salem China; French Saxon	1948	
Brentwood	Cavalier	Royal		Ironstone; bold flower center design
Briar Patch	Colonial	Blue Ridge		Red flowers, green leaves, allover pattern

PATTERN	SHAPE	MAKER	DATE	DESCRIPTION
Briar Rose	Century	Homer Laughlin	1933	Sprays of wild roses, platinum edge
Bridal Bouquet	Colonial	Blue Ridge		Pink flowers, yellow and green leaves
Bridal Flower		Taylor, Smith, and Taylor		
Bridge	Tricorne	Salem		Decals
Bridle Rose		W. S. George		
Brilliance	Coupe	Crooksville		Multisized pink flowers
Brim		Harker		Bold-colored flower border
Bristol Bouquet	Astor	Blue Ridge		Centered red, yellow, blue flowers; red border
Bristol Lily	Candlewick	Blue Ridge		Two yellow flowers and birds; red border
Brittany	Clinchfield	Blue Ridge		Centered woman and flowers; stylized red border
*Brittany	Provincial	Red Wing	1941	Yellow rose; yellow band on rim
Brocade	True China	Red Wing	1964	
*Brown-Eyed Susan	Montecito; Ultra	Vernon Kilns	c.1938–1958	Yellow daisies on ivory ground
Brown Leaf	Accent	E. M. Knowles	1954	Hand-painted leaf shapes
Brown Leaves		Watt		
Brown Satin		Stangl		
Brownie	Candlewick	Blue Ridge		Edge design of three stylized flowers with brown center
Brunswick	Candlewick	Blue Ridge		Red, yellow, and blue flowers; green rim
Brushes	Al Fresco	Bauer		
Bryn-Mawr	Symphony	Salem		Floral sprays in brown, lavender, and gray
Bud	Concord	Red Wing	1947	
Buddah	Corinthian	Sebring		
Bunny Lunch	Kiddieware	Stangl	Mid-1940s–1974	
Buttercup	Colonial	Blue Ridge		
Buttercup		E. M. Knowles	1948	
Butterfly and Leaves	Trellis	Blue Ridge		Red, yellow flowers; two-tone green leaves
Cabaret	Cabaret	Franciscan		
Cactus		Blue Ridge		
Cactus	Banded; Kitchenware	Hall	1937–1940s	Decal; cactus in flowerpots
Cactus and Cowboy, see Ranger				
Cactus Banded, see Cactus (Hall)				
Cadenza	Piecrust	Blue Ridge	1948	Red and yellow flowers
Cadet Series		Salem		Fluted edge; thin bands of color
Caladium	Skyline	Blue Ridge	1950s	Yellow flower; yellow and red leaf

PATTERN	SHAPE	MAKER	DATE	DESCRIPTION
Calais	Astor	Blue Ridge		Center pattern of male, female, and ducks; leaf and flower border
Cal-Art		Bauer		
Calico	Colonial	Blue Ridge		Red and yellow flowers; allover pattern
*Calico	Montecito	Vernon Kilns	1949–1955	Blue border; pink and blue plaid; see also Coronation Organdy; Gingham; Homespun; Organdie; Tam O'Shanter; Tweed
Calico Chick	Coupe	Crooksville		Calico-print chickens
Calico Farm	Skyline	Blue Ridge	1950s	Red and green plaid forming scene
Calico Flower		Pottery Guild		Red band; calico print flowers
Calico Flowers	Dartmouth	Crooksville		Calico-print tulips
Calico Fruit		Pottery Guild		Red band; calico-print fruits
*Calico Fruit		Universal	1940s	White background; bright red and blue fruits
Calico Tulip		Harker		
*Caliente		Paden City	1940s	Solids; blue, green, tangerine, yellow
California Heritage, see California Originals				
California James Poppy	LaGrande	Crooksville		Large sprays of pastel flowers
California Originals	San Marino	Vernon Kilns	1947; 1954	Drip glaze border; Almond Yellow, Raisin Purple, Redwood Brown, Vineyard Green
California Poppy	Candlewick,	Blue Ridge		Two large center flowers
California Pottery		Bauer		Solid Colors
*California Provincial	Poppytrail	Metlox	1965	Green, maroon, and yellow rooster in center; green and brown border
California Shadows	San Marino	Vernon Kilns	1953; 1955	Drip glaze border; Antique Gray, Cocoa Brown
California Strawberry	Poppytrail	Metlox		
Call Rose	Century	Homer Laughlin		Floral decal
Callaway	Piecrust	Blue Ridge	1948	Large blue and yellow and small pink flowers
Camelot	Piecrust	Blue Ridge	1948	Light blue, purple, red, and yellow flowers
*Cameo Rose	E-Shape	Hall	1970s	Gray and white leaf decorations
Cameo Rose		Harker	1940s	Solid white roses; blue, pink, gray, yellow background
*Cameo Shellware	Shell	Harker	1940s	White, blue, pink, gray, yellow background; same cameo flower design as Cameo Rose; fluted plate edge

PATTERN	SHAPE	MAKER	DATE	DESCRIPTION
Candied Fruit	Candlewick	Blue Ridge		Different fruits; two yellow bands
Cantata	Piecrust	Blue Ridge	1948	Red and blue flowers
Canton	Encanto	Franciscan	1953	
Capistrano	Anniversary	Red Wing	1953–1967	Swallow design
Capri		Paden City	1933	
Capri	Rhythm Coupe	Homer Laughlin		
Caprice	Hallcraft	Hall		Designed by Eva Zeisel
Caprice	Accent	E. M. Knowles	c.1954	
Caribe Casual		Caribe-Sterling	1950s–c.1963	
Carlise	Colonial	Blue Ridge		Blue leaves, tiny pink berries, blue rim
Carlton	Heritage	E. M. Knowles	1955	
Carmen	Accent	E. M. Knowles	1958	
Carnation Beauty		Homer Laughlin	1920	Decal
Carnival	Candlewick	Blue Ridge		Red, yellow, and blue flowered border
Carnival	Fruits	Crooksville		Abstract
*Carnival		Stangl	1954–1957	Pink, green and black abstract starlike pattern
Caroline	Skyline	Blue Ridge	1950s	Brown flowers
Carraway	Coffeepot	Hall		
Carretta Cattail	Woodcrest	Blue Ridge	1950s	Three cross-hatched cattails and leaves
Carriage		Crown		Coach and horses, manor
Casa California	Montecito	Vernon Kilns	1938	Blue; green leaves; pink flowers; yellow border
Casa del Sol	Cavalier	Royal		Indian-style design
Casablanca	Cavalier	Royal		Ironstone; large center sunflower design
Cascade		Sold by Montgomery Ward	1936	White with red lines; solids
Cashmere		Homer Laughlin		Border of small sprays of flowers
Cassandra	Waffle Edge	Blue Ridge		Wide blue and pink border; center flowers
Casual California	San Marion	Vernon Kilns	1947–1956	Acacia Yellow, Dawn Pink, Dusk Gray, Lime Green, Mahogany Brown, Mocha Brown, Pine Green, Snowhite, Turquoise Blue; solids
*Casualstone	Fiesta	Homer Laughlin	1970	Gold and yellow, plain or with design; marked Coventry
Cat and the Fiddle	Kiddieware	Stangl	Mid-1940s–1974	
Cathedral, see Arch				

PATTERN	SHAPE	MAKER	DATE	DESCRIPTION
*Cat-Tail	Camwood; Old Holland; Laurelle	Universal	1934–1956	For Sears, Roebuck and Co.; red and black decals
Cattail		Hall	1927	Stylized cattails
Cattails	Trailway	Blue Ridge	1950s	Brown cattails, light blue leaves and border, brown rim
Cattails	Accent	E. M. Knowles	1955	
Celeste	Tempo	E. M. Knowles	1961–1963	
Celestial	Criterion	E. M. Knowles	1955	
*Century		Homer Laughlin		Floral decals; ivory
Chalet	Accent	E. M. Knowles	1955	
Champagne Pinks	Colonial	Blue Ridge		Overall large floral
Chanticleer	Skyline	Blue Ridge	1950s	Rooster; green stylized border
Charstone Bleu	Ceramastone	Red Wing	1967	
Chartreuse		Sold by Montgomery Ward	1936	Decals; green; green border
Chateau		Homer Laughlin		
Chateau-France		Sebring-Limoges		
Chatelaine	Chatelaine	Vernon Kilns	1953	Bronze, jade, platinum, topaz
Cheerio	Skyline	Blue Ridge	1950s	Brown and green flowers; yellow dappled background
Cherokee Rose	Rope Handle	Blue Ridge	1950s	
Cherries Jubilee	Colonial	Blue Ridge		Bold cherries and leaves
Cherry		Harker		Brightly colored fruits
Cherry		Salem China	1951	
Cherry		Stangl	1940	Brown band with tan glaze and blue lines; blue band with tan glaze and yellow line, blue band with blue glaze and green lines; cherry stems in center
Cherry Blossom	Colonial	Blue Ridge		Red and yellow cherries; pink flower; border
Cherry Blossom		Harker		Sprig of cherries and flowers
Cherry Cobbler	Colonial	Blue Ridge		Pink cherries, rim
Cherry Coke	Colonial	Blue Ridge		Red cherries, border, green rim
Cherry Trim		Harker		Border of groups of cherries
Chesterton	Royal Gadroon	Harker	1945–1965	Gray, green, blue, pink, yellow
Chevron	Gypsy Trail	Red Wing	1935	Blue, ivory, orange, turquoise, yellow
Chicken Feed	Skyline	Blue Ridge	1950s	Girl feeding chickens; green rim
Chicken Pickins	Skyline	Blue Ridge	1950s	Hen and rooster; pink and green stylized border

PATTERN	SHAPE	MAKER	DATE	DESCRIPTION
Chickory	Colonial	Blue Ridge		Small yellow and blue flowers
Chicory		Stangl	1961	
Children's Plates		Harker		Blue and pink cameoware; duck, teddy bear, dog
*Chinese Red (color used by Hall), see also individual pattern names				
Chinling	Lotus	Vernon Kilns	1950	Oriental floral spray
Chintz	Colonial	Blue Ridge		Allover flower pattern
Chintz	Melinda	Vernon Kilns	1942; 1950	Floral design
Choreography	Criterion	E. M. Knowles	1955	
Christmas Doorway	Skyline	Blue Ridge	1950s	
Christmas Tree	Colonial	Blue Ridge		
Chrysanthemum	Colonial	Blue Ridge		Blue and red flowers
Chrysanthemum	Concord	Red Wing	1947	
Cinnabar	Colonial	Blue Ridge		Bold pink and yellow flowers, green leaves
Circus Clown	Kiddieware	Stangl	Mid-1940s–1974	
Clairborne	Colonial	Blue Ridge		Centered pink and black flowers; border
Classic	Essex	E. M. Knowles	1954–1955	
Clear Day	Cavalier	Royal		Ironstone
*Cleveland	Teapot	Hall	1930s	
Clio	Corinthian	Leigh		Floral
Clive	Brittany	Homer Laughlin		Border of maroon panels and floral sprays
Clover	Clinchfield	Blue Ridge	1947–1954	Pink flowers with green clover; blue and black rim
Clover	Kitchenware	Hall	1940–1960	Bright colors; Impressionistic design
Cloverleaf, see Clover				
Coastline	Montecito	Vernon Kilns	1937	Map of Pacific coast; blue, black on ivory ground
Cock-a-Doodle	Skyline	Blue Ridge	1950s	Rooster in center; blue rim
*Cock o' the Morn	Skyline	Blue Ridge	1950s	Crowing rooster
Cock-o-the-Morn (Harker), see Engraved Rooster				
Cock O' Walk	Candlewick	Blue Ridge	1948	Center rooster; red and cream flowered border; broken green rim
Cocky-Locky	Clinchfield	Blue Ridge		Rooster; red stylized border
Cocolo	Cocolo	Franciscan		
Coffee Queen	Coffeepot	Hall		Chinese red and olive green common colors
*Colonial	Kitchenware	Hall	1932	Chinese Red, Daffodil, Dephinium, Golden Glo, Hi-white, ivory, Lettuce Green; decals; also called Medallion
Colonial		Salem		Red and green stencil-like decorations

PATTERN	SHAPE	MAKER	DATE	DESCRIPTION
*Colonial		Stangl	1926	Aqua, Colonial Blue, brown, Persian Yellow, rust, silver-green, Surf White, tangerine
Colonial Birds No. 1	Colonial	Blue Ridge		Centered bird
Colonial Birds No. 2	Colonial	Blue Ridge		Centered bird
Colonial Dogwood		Stangl		Marked Prestige
*Colonial Homestead		Royal	1940s–1950s	
Colonial Lady		Harker		
Colonial Rose	Colonial	Blue Ridge		Red rose, green leaves, red border, green rim
Colonial Rose		Stangl	1970–1974	
Colonial Silver		Stangl	c.1970	
Colonnes	Futura	Red Wing	1960	Pillars
Color Stitch	Colonial	Blue Ridge		Red, blue, gray border
Colorado				Brown
Columbia	Teapot	Hall		
Columbia	Williamsburg	E. M. Knowles	1948	
Columbine	Skyline	Blue Ridge	1950s	Red and white flowers; red line border
Columbine	Century	Homer Laughlin		Floral decal; off-center
Commodore		Salem		Gold medallions and trim
*Conchita	Century	Homer Laughlin	1938	Mexican-inspired decal
*Conchita Kitchen Kraft		Homer Laughlin	1930s	Ovenwares; Mexican-inspired decal
Concord		Continental Kilns	1944–1957	
Concord		Stangl	1957	
Concorde	Astor	Blue Ridge		Centered grapes; blue line border; brown edge
Confetti	Candlewick	Blue Ridge		Red, yellow, and blue flower border; gray rim
Connie	Teapot	Hall	Early 1940s	Victorian style; see also Benjamin, Birch, Bowknot, Murphy, Plume
Constance	Colonial	Blue Ridge		Centered red and yellow flowers; small flowers on border; pink rim
Contempo	Al Fresco	Bauer	1950s	
Contemps		Brusche	1952	Champagne White, Desert Beige, Indigo Brown, Pumpkin, Slate, Spicy Green
Cookie Twins	Kiddieware	Stangl	Mid-1940s-1971	
Coors, see Rosebud				
Coral Pine	Criterion	E. M. Knowles	1954	
Coral Reef	Ultra	Vernon Kilns	1938	Tropical fish in blue, mustard, maroon on cream ground

PATTERN	SHAPE	MAKER	DATE	DESCRIPTION
Coreopsis	Colonial	Blue Ridge		Yellow flowers; thin yellow border
Corn		American Pottery		
Corn		Brush-McCoy		
Corn		Paden City		
Corn		Standard Pottery		
Corn		Stanford Pottery	1946–1961	
Corn Gold		Sold by Montgomery Ward	1921	Decals
Corn Is Green		Paden City		Cornstalk center design
*Corn King	Corn King	Shawnee	c.1950	Yellow and green; three-dimensional
*Corn Queen	Corn Queen	Shawnee	1954–1961	Three-dimensional; lighter kernel than Corn King; dark foliage
Cornflower Blue		E. M. Knowles	1930s	Decals
*Coronado	50 different shapes	Franciscan	1935–1942	Fifteen solid colors
Coronado		E. M. Knowles	1948	
Coronado	Coronado, Montecito	Vernon Kilns (grocery promotion)	1935–1939	Blue, brown, dark blue, light green, orange, pink, turquoise, yellow
Coronado Swirl		Franciscan	1936–1956	
Coronation Organdy	Montecito	Vernon Kilns	1937	Gray and rose plaid; see also Calico; Gingham; Homespun; Organdie; Tam O'Shanter; Tweed
Corsage	Astor	Blue Ridge		Pastel flowers, blue leaf border
Corsage	Lyric	E. M. Knowles	1954	
Cosmos	Skyline	Blue Ridge	1950s	Large yellow flowers
Cosmos		Stangl		Marked Prestige, cosmos flower border
Cosmos	Melinda	Vernon Kilns	1942	Red allover floral
Cosomi	Skyline	Blue Ridge	1950s	Large red and blue flowers
Cottage		Harker		Flowered path leading to red-roofed cottage
Cottage Window	Montecito	Vernon Kilns	1937	Window with curtain
Country Classics		Haeger		
Country Cousin	Year 'Round	Vernon Kilns	1957–1958	People and flowers with geometric border
Country Fair	Colonial	Blue Ridge		Fruit; green rim
Country Fair	Criterion	E. M. Knowles	1955	
Country Fruit	Trailway	Blue Ridge	1950s	Plaid fruit, wide yellow border
Country Garden	Candlewick	Blue Ridge		Pink and purple flowers
Country Garden	Anniversary	Red Wing	1953	Floral

PATTERN	SHAPE	MAKER	DATE	DESCRIPTION
*Country Garden		Stangl	1956–1974	Three realistic flowers
Country Garden	Anniversary	Red Wing	1953	
Country Gentleman		W. S. George		Fruit
Country Home	Fruits	Crooksville		Cottage with mountains in background
Country Life		Stangl	1956–1967	
Country Road	Colonial	Blue Ridge		Yellow flowers; orange rim
Country Road		Homer Laughlin	1977–1978	
Countryside		Harker		Cottage with smoking chimney
Country Side	Montecito	Vernon Kilns	1950	Rural farm scene; marked "da Bron"
County Fair	Colonial	Blue Ridge		
Coverlet, see Cozy Cover				
Cowboys and Cactus, see Ranger				
Cowslip	Colonial	Blue Ridge		Yellow flowers
Cozy Cover	Teapot	Hall		Fleece-lined aluminum cozy to fit pot
*Crab Apple	Colonial	Blue Ridge	c.1930–1957	Hand painted red apples with green leaves; red spatter border
Crab Orchard	Candlewick	Blue Ridge		Two apples; green rim
Cradle	Square	Blue Ridge		Blue flowers and leaves
Cranberry		Stangl		
Crazy Quilt		Homer Laughlin	1977–1978	
Crazy Rhythm	Futura	Red Wing	1960	Abstract; hand painted
Crestone		Hull		Turquoise
Crocus	Colonial	Blue Ridge		
*Crocus	D-Line	Hall	1930s	Floral decals; black, green, lavender, pink, red; platinum trim
Crocus	True China	Red Wing	1960	Floral
Crocus		Stangl		
Cross Stitch		Blue Ridge		Black x's and dots; red and green leaves
Croydon	Sovereign	Crown	1941	Black trellis border with multicolored flowers
Cube	Teapot	Hall		Also coffeepot, creamer, and tea tile
*Cumberland		Blue Ridge	1948	Hand painted blue and white flowers
Curiosity Shop, see Old Curiosity Shop				
Currier & Ives		Homer Laughlin	Present	Blue decal on white
*Currier & Ives	Cavalier	Royal	1940s–1980s	Ironstone; scenic center design in blue and white
Currier & Ives	Coupe	Scio		
Cut-A-Way		Hall	1930	Multicolored flowers
Cynthia		Blue Ridge	1949	

PATTERN	SHAPE	MAKER	DATE	DESCRIPTION
Cynthia	Lido	W. S. George		Sprigs of small pink flowers (Peach Blossom has same decal on Bolero shape)
*Daffodil	Piecrust	Blue Ridge	1948	Single flower
Dahlia	Candlewick	Blue Ridge	1948	Large red flower
Dahlia		Stangl	1970–1974	Blue flowered border; marked Prestige
Dainty	Montecito	Vernon Kilns	1935–1947	Dark pink leaves and flowers
Daisies	Deanna	E. M. Knowles		Field of flowers
*Daisy	Fiesta	Homer Laughlin	1962–1968	Turquoise band; turquoise and brown daisies; Casual pattern; see also Yellow Carnation
Daisy		Stangl	1936–1942	
Daisy	Versatile	Taylor, Smith, and Taylor		
Daisy	True China	Red Wing	1960	Floral
Daisy Wreath	Daisy Wreath	Franciscan		
Damask	True China	Red Wing	1964	
Damask Rose	Accent	E. M. Knowles	1954	
Dandridge Dogwood	Skyline	Blue Ridge	1950s	Single flower
Dawn Rose	Americana	E. M. Knowles	1958	
Daydream	Colonial	Blue Ridge		Gray flowers
Deanna		E. M. Knowles		
Debussy	Tempo	E. M. Knowles	1961–1963	
Deca-Flip	Coffeepot	Hall		
Deco-Dahlia		Harker		Stylized red flowers
Deco-Delight		Stangl		Deco shaped; Colonial Blue, silver green
Deep Purple		Blue Ridge		Purple flower and leaves
Del Mar	Del Mar	Franciscan		
Delft	Americana	E. M. Knowles	1957	Purple flower; wide yellow rim
Delft Rose	Colonial	Blue Ridge		
*Delicious	Candlewick	Blue Ridge		Two painted apples with green and yellow leaves
Delight	Ultra	Vernon Kilns	1938	Blue and yellow peonies and gardenias
Della Robbia	Piecrust	Blue Ridge	1948	Border of variety of fruit
Della Robbia	Vernonware	Metlox	1965	
Delmar		Stangl	1972–1974	Gold background; brown and blue border
Delores		Vernon Kilns		
Delta Blue	Village Green	Red Wing	1954	Light blue with flowers
Desert Bloom	San Fernando	Vernon Kilns	1944; 1955	Small flowers on wide border
Desert Flower	Skyline	Blue Ridge	1950s	One yellow and one brown flower
Desert Mallow	Montecito	Vernon Kilns		Yellow and orange flowers

PATTERN	SHAPE	MAKER	DATE	DESCRIPTION
*Desert Rose	Desert Rose	Franciscan	1941	
Desert Sun	New Shape	Red Wing	1962	Geometric
Design 69		Taylor, Smith, and Taylor		Pale blue and brown
Dewberry	Colonial	Blue Ridge		Green leaves; white berry border
Dewdrop Fairies	Ultra	Vernon Kilns	1940	Blue print border on cream ground
Diana		Stangl	1972–1974	Light blue flowers and rim
Dick Tracy	Century	Homer Laughlin	1950	Decal; child's set
Dinner Rose, see Queen Rose				
Dis 'N Dot	Anytime	Vernon Kilns	1957–1958	Blue, green, and mustard off-center lines and dots
Disney		Vernon Kilns	1940s	
*Disraeli	Teapot	Hall	1940s	Pink only; Victorian style
Dixie Harvest (No. 3913)	Piecrust	Blue Ridge	1949	
D-Line		Hall	1936	Plain; round; floral decals
Dogwood	Skyline	Blue Ridge	1950s	Large yellow flowers
Dogwood	Dogwood	Franciscan		
Dogwood	Bolero	W. S. George		
*Dogwood	Century	Homer Laughlin	1960s	Pink and white floral decals
Dogwood		Stangl	1965	Della-Ware mark; raised border of pink flowers and pale green leaves
Dogwood		Taylor, Smith, and Taylor	1942	Underglaze pattern; overall flowers
*Dolores	Melinda	Vernon Kilns	1942–1947	Floral border
Dominion	Victory	Salem		Poppies, wheat, blue flowers; decal
Dorset		Scio		
*Doughnut	Teapot	Hall	1938	Ivory with orange poppy decal common; Chinese Red, cobalt, Delphinium
Dragon Flower		California Ceramics		Stylized brown plant
Drape, see Parade				
Dream Flower	Colonial	Blue Ridge		Red, blue, and yellow flowers; dot border
Dreambirds	Colonial	Blue Ridge		Birds kissing; red rim
Dresden		Crown	1941	Sprays of assorted flowers; gold rim
Dresden Doll	Colonial	Blue Ridge		
Driftwood	Anniversary	Red Wing	1953	Tree branch design
Dubarry	Regent	E. M. Knowles	1948	
Duchess, see Coffee Queen				
Duchess		Paden City	1942	Small flowers and scrolls
Ducky Dinners	Kiddieware	Stangl	Mid-1940s-1974	
Duet	Tempo	E. M. Knowles	1961–1963	
Dubonnet	Criterion	E. M. Knowles	1955	

PATTERN	SHAPE	MAKER	DATE	DESCRIPTION
Duff	Candlewick	Blue Ridge		Eight different fruits; gray and rust stylized background
Dutch Bouquet	Candlewick	Blue Ridge		Red tulip decoration
Dutch Iris	Candlewick	Blue Ridge		Two red and blue iris; red border
Dutch Petit Point	Tricorne; Bonjour	Salem		Decals; Dutch boy and girl
Dutch Tulip	Candlewick	Blue Ridge		Centered yellow-orange tulip, green leaves
Dynasty	Cavalier	Royal		Ironstone
Early American		Homer Laughlin	1960s	Floral
Early California	Montecito	Vernon Kilns	1935–1947	Blue, dark blue, brown, green, ivory, maroon, orange, peach, pink, turquoise, yellow
Early Days	San Fernando	Vernon Kilns	1944; 1950–1955	1860s scene with wide floral border
Ebonite	Criterion	E. M. Knowles	c.1954	
Ecstasy	Ultra	Vernon Kilns	1938	Light brown peonies and gardenias
Edgemont	Colonial	Blue Ridge		Yellow and red flowers
Edmonton		Syracuse		
Eggshell Nautilis		Homer Laughlin	1935–1955	Floral decals
Eggshell Polka Dot		Hall	1934	Matte white; ivory glaze; blue, green, red dots; floral decals
Eggshell Theme		Homer Laughlin	1940s	English look; decals; floral border
Eglantine	Clinchfield	Blue Ridge		Pink flower, red border
El-Chico		Bauer		
Eldorado		E. M. Knowles	1948	
*El Patio		Franciscan	1934–1954	20 different solid colors
El Rosa				Della-Ware mark; pink rose and lavender flowers; border of dark green, white and yellow
El Vuelo		Caribe-Sterling	1950s–c.1963	Modernistic swirls
Elegant Modern		Homer Laughlin		Hotel dinnerware; decals on white
Emerald		Sold by Montgomery Ward	1921	Decals
Emma Susan	Washington Square	Taylor, Smith, and Taylor	1933–1934	Decals
*Emperor	Refrigerator ware	Hall	1939	Westinghouse; Canary, Delphinium, Garden, Sunset; also called General
Enchantment		Harker		
Enchantment	Ultra	Vernon Kilns	1940	Blue print border
English Countryside		Hall		

PATTERN	SHAPE	MAKER	DATE	DESCRIPTION
English Garden	Century	Homer Laughlin	1933	Landscape design
Engraved Rooster		Harker		Cameoware
Epicure		Homer Laughlin	1955	Solid; Charcoal Gray, Dawn Pink, Snow White, turquoise blue; highly sculptured
Equation	Criterion Antiques	E. M. Knowles	1955	
Eureka Homewood		Hall (made for Eureka Co.)		Decal
Evening Flower	Skyline	Blue Ridge	1950s	
Evening Song	Classique	E. M. Knowles	1960	
Evening Star	Montecito	Vernon Kilns	1935–1937	Blue and ivory
Eventide	Woodcrest	Blue Ridge	1950s	Log cabin and tree in center; brown rim
Fairlawn		Stangl	1959–1962	
Fairmede Fruits	Clinchfield	Blue Ridge		Centered fruit, four-line border
Fairmount	Skyline	Blue Ridge	1950s	Brown and green leaves on partially brown background
Fairy Bells	Colonial	Blue Ridge		Red and purple flower bells, tan ground
Fairy Tale	Astor	Blue Ridge		Pink flowers, blue leaves, pink border
Fairyland	Ultra	Vernon Kilns	1940	Blue floral and leaf design
Falling Leaves	Colonial	Blue Ridge		Multicolored leaves; orange rim
Falmouth	Skyline	Blue Ridge	1950s	Blue and red outlined flowers; yellow swirled background
*Fantasia	Skyline	Blue Ridge	1950s	Abstract leaf pattern; brown, blue, yellow
Fantasia	Ultra	Vernon Kilns	1940	Brown floral and leaf pattern
Fantasy	Kitchenware	Hall	1930s–1940s	Decal; Swedish modern bright flowers on ivory
Fantasy	Accent	E. M. Knowles	1955	
Fantasy	Concord	Red Wing	1947	Abstract
Fantasy Apple	Skyline	Blue Ridge	1950s	Stylized apples; gray rim
Far East	Shellcrest	Paden City		Oriental design
Farmer Takes a Wife	Colonial	Blue Ridge		Figures in center; yellow flowers border; green rim
Farmhouse	Woodcrest	Blue Ridge	1950s	Large scenic design
Farmyard	Skyline	Blue Ridge	1950s	Barn, farmer, tree
Fashion White		Sold by Montgomery Ward	1936	Decals
Fayette Fruit	Candlewick	Blue Ridge		Apple, pear; series of three slashes on border
Feather Fantasy	Criterion	E. M. Knowles	1955	
Feathered Friends	Skyline	Blue Ridge	1950s	Cardinal, bluejay; gray background

PATTERN	SHAPE	MAKER	DATE	DESCRIPTION
Federal		Sebring-Limoges	1942	
Festival	Williamsburg; Forcast	E. M. Knowles	1955; 1957	
Festival		Stangl	1961–1967	Della-Ware mark
Festive	Skyline	Blue Ridge	1950s	Black and yellow crepe paper
Festive Fruit, see Fruit (Stangl)				
Field Daisy	Colonial	Blue Ridge		Red and yellow flowers, brown leaves; broken rim
Field Daisy		Stangl	1941–1942	White daisies on blue; yellow background
*Fiesta	Fiesta	Homer Laughlin	1936–1972	Antique Gold, Bright Green, Chartreuse, Dark Blue, Forest Green, Gray, Light Green, Mango Red, Old Ivory, Red, Rose, Turf Green, Turquoise, Yellow; see also Amberstone; Casualstone; Daisy; Fiesta Ironstone; Fiesta Kitchen Kraft; Yellow Carnation
Fiesta Casual, see Daisy; Yellow Carnation				
*Fiesta Ironstone	Fiesta	Homer Laughlin	1970–1972	Antique Gold, Mango Red, Turf Green
*Fiesta Kitchen Kraft		Homer Laughlin	1939–early 1940s	Bake and serve line; red, yellow, green, blue
Fiesta Wood	Fiesta	Homer Laughlin		Colored border stripes; sleeping Mexican
Fireside	Skyline	Blue Ridge	1950s	Hearth and rocker; brown rim
First Love		Stangl	1968–1973	
Fisherman	Square	Blue Ridge		Man fishing; broken black rim
Five Band, see Banded				
Five Fingers	Ultra	Vernon Kilns	1938	Autumn leaves on ivory
Five Little Pigs	Kiddieware	Stangl	Mid-1940s–1974	
Fjord	Americana	E. M. Knowles	1959	
Flaming Rose		Paden City		Brightly colored floral design
Flamingo	Gray Lure	Crooksville		Sprig of delicate flowers
Flamingo		Hall		
Flare Ware Gold Lace		Hall	1960s	Overall stars and scalloped border
Fleur de Lis	Kitchen Kraft	Homer Laughlin		
Fleur de Lis		Vernon Kilns		Large pastel center design
Fleur de Lis	Criterion	E. M. Knowles	1955	
Fleur de Lis Iris, see Iris (Universal)				
Fleurette	Tempo	E. M. Knowles	1959	
Flight	Skyline	Blue Ridge	1950s	Centered flying birds
Flight	Forcast	E. M. Knowles	1957	
Flight	New Shape	Red Wing	1962	Birds

PATTERN	SHAPE	MAKER	DATE	DESCRIPTION
Flight of the Swallows	New Art	Homer Laughlin	1930s	Foliage spray and group of flying birds
Flirt	Piecrust	Blue Ridge	1950s	Red flowers; green leaves and rim
Flora	Williamsburg	E. M. Knowles	1948–1955	
*Flora		Stangl	1941	Yellow band with pink, blue, and yellow flowers; Terra Rose mark
Flora	Ultra	Vernon Kilns	1938	Floral spray
Floral	Floral	Franciscan		
Floral	Lido	W. S. George		Decal of multicolored small flowers
Floral		Paden City		
Floral		Stangl	1941–1942	
Floral		Watt		Charcoal, pinkish-blue floral
Floral Bird-song	Sabina II	Sabin	c.1946	
Floral Border		Sold by Mont-gomery Ward	1936	Decals
Floral Bouquet	Fairway	Taylor, Smith, and Taylor	Early 1930s	
Floral Lattice	Five Band	Hall		
Floral Plaid		Stangl	1940–1942	
Florence	Squared-Off Edges	E. M. Knowles	1933–1934	Decals
Florence		Pope-Gosser	1940s	Border of small flowers
Florentine		Stangl	1958	
Floret	Ultra	Vernon Kilns	1939	Red floral
Florette		Stangl	1961–1962	
Florida	Williamsburg	E. M. Knowles	1948	
Flounce	Colonial	Blue Ridge		Red, pink, and blue cut-off flowers around edge
Flower Ballet	Ultra	Vernon Kilns	1940	Maroon border print
Flower Basket	Yorktown	E. M. Knowles		
Flower Bowl	Colonial	Blue Ridge		Flowers in bowl; green and yellow border
Flower Fair	Coupe	Crooksville		Muted flowers
Flower Fantasy		Blue Ridge	1954	
Flower Power		Homer Laughlin	1977–1978	
Flower Rim	Lido	W. S. George		Bands of small flowers
*Flower Ring	Colonial	Blue Ridge		Red, blue, and yellow flow-ers; green leaves and rim
Flower Wreath	Candlewick	Blue Ridge		Purple and pink flowers and border
Floweret	Skyline	Blue Ridge	1950s	Red flowers, black rim
Flowering Berry	Candlewick	Blue Ridge		Pink and red flower border
*Flowerpot	Banded	Hall		Early decal
Flowers of the Dell	New Art	Homer Laughlin	1930s	Two floral sprays
Fluffy Ruffles	Astor	Blue Ridge		Large blue flowers

PATTERN	SHAPE	MAKER	DATE	DESCRIPTION
Flute	Kitchenware	Hall	1935	Kitchenware; Chinese Red, Hi-white Marine, Russet; also called Ribbed
Flying Bluebird	Empress	Homer Laughlin	1920	Decal
Foliage	Tempo	E. M. Knowles	1961–1963	
Fondoso	Gypsy Trail	Red Wing	1938	Pastels; blue, turquoise, yellow
*Football	Teapot	Hall	1938–1940	
Forest Flower	Shellridge	Harker		Light brown and yellow
Forest Fruits	Skyline	Blue Ridge	1950s	Yellow fruit, dark border
Forever Yours	Shellridge	Harker		Rosebud garland
Formal		Salem		Rust and gold rim; gold border design
Forman		Hall		
Fountain	Ballerina	Universal	1950	Abstract
Four Seasons White	Four Seasons	E. M. Knowles	1959–1963	
Four Winds	Melinda	Vernon Kilns	1950	Yacht; maroon and blue border
Fox Grape	Colonial	Blue Ridge		Green leaves, dark grapes, broken rim
Foxfire	Skyline	Blue Ridge	1950s	Red leaf-shaped flowers
Frageria	Skyline	Blue Ridge	1950s	Red strawberries; green border
*French	Teapot	Hall	1920	Gold decorated line
French Peasant	Colonial	Blue Ridge		
French Provincial				Silhouette decal
Frolic	Anytime	Vernon Kilns	1955	Aqua, gold, and purple abstract floral
*Frontenac	Futura	Red Wing	1960	Abstract flowers
Frontier Days	Montecito	Vernon Kilns	1950; 1954	Western scene
Frosted Fruit		Stangl	1957	
Frosted Leaves	Mayfair	E. M. Knowles	1955	
Fruit		Purinton	1936–1959	Four fruits; brown X
Fruit	Concord	Red Wing	1947	
*Fruit		Stangl	1942–1974	Center designs of fruit
*Fruit & Flowers		Stangl	1957–1974	Center design; colored border
Fruit & Flowers		Universal		Subdued colors; large center design
Fruit Basket		Homer Laughlin	1977–1978	
Fruit Basket		Salem		Narrow checkerboard band; border of fruit baskets
Fruit Cocktail	Astor	Blue Ridge		Different fruits; black and yellow border
Fruit Fantasy	Colonial	Blue Ridge		Painted fruits, green rim
Fruit Punch	Colonial	Blue Ridge		Various fruits; allover pattern
Fruit Ring	Clinchfield	Blue Ridge		Fruit border
Fruit Salad	Colonial	Blue Ridge		Yellow pear, red apple, blueberries; red rim

PATTERN	SHAPE	MAKER	DATE	DESCRIPTION
Fruit Sherbet	Colonial	Blue Ridge		Pastel fruit; broken blue rim
Fruitdale	Melinda	Vernon Kilns	1942–1947	Flower and fruit center
Fruitful	Colonial	Blue Ridge		Painted fruit
Fruits	Utility ware	Harker		Large stem of fruit—apple and pear
Fruits		E. M. Knowles		Brightly colored individual fruit
Fuchsia	Colonial	Blue Ridge		
Fuchsia		Leigh/Crescent		Predominately orange and green floral spray
Fuji		Hall		Oriental-styled flower
Full Bloom	Candlewick	Blue Ridge		Two large purple and red center flowers
Futura		Red Wing	1961	Hand painted
Fuzz Ball		Hall	1930s	Pink and green
Gaity	Skyline	Blue Ridge		Red flowers
Galaxy		Stangl	1963–1970	
Garden Design		Salem China	1940s	
Garden Flower		Stangl	1947–1957	
Garden Flowers	Colonial	Blue Ridge		Eight different flowers
Garden Lane	Colonial	Blue Ridge		Hand painted tulips, daisies, and roses
Garden Magic	Classique	E. M. Knowles	1960	
Garden Party	Garden Party	Franciscan		
Garden Pinks	Skyline	Blue Ridge	1950s	Pink flower
Garden Trail	Shellridge	Harker		Center bouquet; floral border
Garland	Colonial	Blue Ridge		Black leaves; pastel flower border
Garland	Monarch	Crown	1941	Garland of small roses
Garland	Williamsburg	E. M. Knowles	1948	
Garland		Pickard		
Garland		Stangl	1957–1967	
Gascon		W. S. George		Bright blue flowers, gray leaves; sold by Sears, Roebuck and Co.
*Gay Plaid		Blair		Yellow, green and brown; large plaid
Gayety	San Marion	Vernon Kilns	1948; 1954	Green and rose stripes on ivory
General, see Emperor				
*General Electric	Refrigerator ware	Hall		G.E. logo on lid; Addison (blue) and yellow
Ginger Boy	Kiddieware	Stangl	Mid-1940s–1974	
Ginger Cat	Kiddieware	Stangl	Mid-1940s–1974	
Ginger Girl	Kiddieware	Stangl	Mid-1940s–1974	

PATTERN	SHAPE	MAKER	DATE	DESCRIPTION
Gingersnap	Gingersnap	Franciscan		
*Gingham	Montecito	Vernon Kilns	1949–1958	Green and yellow plaid; dark green border; see also Calico; Coronation Organdy; Homespun; Organdie; Tam O'Shanter; Tweed
Gingham Fruit	Trailway	Blue Ridge	1950s	Fruit with plaid leaves; gray swirled border
Gladstone	Teapot	Hall	1940	Pink/gold only; Victorian style
Glamour	Ultra	Vernon Kilns	c.1938	Blue, maroon peonies and gardenias
Glencoe	Thermal Porcelain	Coors	1920s	Brown, green, yellow, and other colors
Glenedon		Leigh		
Glenwood	Cavalier	Homer Laughlin	1961–1968	
*Globe	Teapot	Hall	Early 1940s	
Gloria		Blue Ridge	1949	
Gloriosa	Skyline	Blue Ridge	1950s	Yellow flowers
Glorious	Candlewick	Blue Ridge		One red and two blue morning glories centered
Gloucester Fisherman	Ballerina	Universal Potteries	1950	
Godey Ladies		Salem		
Godney Prints	Victory	Salem		Decals; service plates
Gold & Cobalt	Empress	Homer Laughlin	1920	Decal
Gold Band		Sold by Montgomery Ward	1920–1936	Decals
Gold decorated line of Hall teapots, see Airflow; Aladdin; Albany; Automobile; Baltimore; Basket; Basketball; Birdcage; Boston; Cleveland; Doughnut; Football; French; Globe; Hollywood; Hook Cover; Illinois; Los Angeles; Manhattan; Melody; Moderne; Nautilus; New York; Parade; Philadelphia; Rhythm; Saf-Handle; Sani-Grid; Star; Streamline; Surfside; Windshield; World's Fair				
Gold Drape		Crooksville		Floral design; gold border, draped effect
Gold Floral Band		Homer Laughlin	1920	Decal
Gold Garland		Homer Laughlin	1920	Decal
Gold Initial		Sold by Montgomery Ward	1921	Decal
Gold Label	Kitchenware	Hall	1950s	Gold stamped decorations
Gold Lace over Cobalt Blue		Homer Laughlin	1920	Decal
Gold Stripe		Sold by Montgomery Ward	1936	Decals
Golden		Coors	1930s	Blue, green, ivory, orange, rose, yellow
Golden Blossom		Stangl	1964–1974	Brown blossoms, orange leaves
Golden Crown	Queen Anne	Sabin		
Golden Foliage	Four Seasons	E. M. Knowles	1960–1963	
Golden Grape		Stangl	1963–1972	
*Golden Harvest	Coupe	Stangl	1953–1973	Yellow flowers, gray background

PATTERN	SHAPE	MAKER	DATE	DESCRIPTION
Golden Laurel		E. M. Knowles	1930	Decals
Golden Maple	Montecito	Vernon Kilns	1935–1937	Pumpkin and ivory
Golden Viking	Futura	Red Wing	1960	Geometric; gold
Golden Wheat	Rhythm Coupe	Homer Laughlin	1953–1958	
Golden Wheat	Yorktown	E. M. Knowles	1936	Decals
Golden Wreath	Accent	E. M. Knowles	1960	
Goldtrim	Briar Rose	Salem	1952	Gold rim; gold border design
Gooseberry	Candlewick	Blue Ridge		Yellow fruit and rim
Gourmet	Accent	E. M. Knowles	1956	
Granada		French Saxon	1939–1940	Solids; blue, green, tangerine, yellow
Granada	True China	Red Wing	1960	Floral
Grandfather's Clock	Square	Blue Ridge		Clock in hallway; broken black rim
Grandiose	Coupe	Paden City	1952	Muted large flowers
Grandmother's Garden	Colonial	Blue Ridge		
Granny Smith Apple	Skyline	Blue Ridge	1950s	Two red apples on yellow center
Grape	Teapot	Hall		Grape clusters in relief; decal decorations and/or embedded rhinestones
Grape		Stangl	1973–1974	
Grape Salad	Candlewick	Blue Ridge		Grapes with large green leaves; border and rim
Grass	Esquire	E. M. Knowles	1957–1962	Abstract decal; Russel Wright
Grass Flower	Moderne	Blue Ridge	1950s	Black and yellow flowers; green leaves and rim
Greenbriar	Forcast	E. M. Knowles	1959	
Green Briar	Piecrust	Blue Ridge	1948	
Green Dots	Avona	Taylor, Smith, and Taylor	Early 1930s	Wide border of dots
Green Eyes	Skyline	Blue Ridge	1950s	
Green Grapes		Stangl		
Green Valley		Homer Laughlin	1977–1978	
Green Wheat	Yorktown	E. M. Knowles		Decals
Green Wheat		Leigh/Crescent		Separate wheat stalks
Greensville	Skyline	Blue Ridge	1950s	Cream and brown flower
Greenwich-stone	Ceramastone	Red Wing	1967	
Gumdrop Trees	Candlewick	Blue Ridge		Red, yellow, and red with green leaves
Gypsy	Colonial	Blue Ridge		Red, orange, and yellow flowers
Gypsy Dancer	Colonial	Blue Ridge		Red and yellow flowers; red and green border
Gypsy Trail		Red Wing	1930s	
Hacienda	Hacienda	Franciscan		Hacienda green
*Hacienda	Century	Homer Laughlin	1938	Decal; cactus, bench, side of Mexican house; red trim

PATTERN	SHAPE	MAKER	DATE	DESCRIPTION
Hall teapots, see individual names				
Hallcraft, see Boquet; Caprice; Harlequin; Peach Blossom; Zeisel				
Ham 'N Eggs	Candlewick	Blue Ridge		Pig, hen; wide green and thin red border
Happy Days	Forcast	E. M. Knowles	1957	
Harlequin	Fantasy/ Hallcraft	Hall		Designed by Eva Zeisel
*Harlequin	Harlequin	Homer Laughlin	1938–1964, 1979	Ironstone; chartreuse, cobalt blue, dark blue, forest green, gray, ivory, light green, maroon, mauve blue, rose, spruce green, tangerine, turquoise; 1979—deep coral, green, turquoise, yellow,
Harvest	Concord	Red Wing	1947	
Harvest		Stangl		
Harvest	Ultra	Vernon Kilns	1938	Fruits in center: pears, green apples, plum, cherries, and a peach
Harvestime	Skyline	Blue Ridge	1950s	Wheat tied with bow
Hawaii	Melinda	Vernon Kilns	1942	Maroon lotus flower
Hawaiian Coral	San Marion	Vernon Kilns	1952; 1956	Spatter edge; brown, yellow, and green on cream
Hawaiian Daisy, see Daisy				
*Hawaiian Flowers	Ultra	Vernon Kilns	1938	Lotus in blue, maroon, mustard, pink
*Hawaiian Fruit	Cinchfield; Piecrust	Blue Ridge	1948	Hand painted pineapple and two other fruits in blue, yellow, and brown; colors repeated in border
Hawaiian 12 Point Daisy, see Daisy				
Hawthorne	Qena	Crown		Pastel pink and blue flowers; gold rim
Hawthorne	Hawthorne	Franciscan		
Hazel	Ranson	Scio		
Hazelnut		Universal		Decals
Hearthstone	Casual	Red Wing	1961	Solids; beige, orange
*Heather Rose	E-Style	Hall		Pale pinkish-purple rose on a stem with many leaves
Heavenly Days	Anytime	Vernon Kilns	1956–1958	Aqua, mocha, and pink geometric designs
Heirloom	Candlewick	Blue Ridge		Blue, yellow and red flowers; green rim
Heirloom	Corinthian	Sebring		Wide gold floral border; garland and bouquet in center
Hen Party	Lyric	E. M. Knowles	1954	Green
Hercules, see Aristocrat				
Heritage		Stangl		
Heritance		Harker		
Heyday	San Marion	Vernon Kilns	1954–1958	Geometric circles in green and brown
Hibiscus, Crooksville, see Flamingo				

PATTERN	SHAPE	MAKER	DATE	DESCRIPTION
Hibiscus	San Fernando	Vernon Kilns	1944; 1954	Yellow flowers and brown print
Hidden Valley	Cavalier	Royal		Ironstone; colored band and large center stencil-like flowers
Hi-Fire		Bauer	1930s	
High Serria	Accent	E. M. Knowles	1955	
High Stepper	Square	Blue Ridge		Rooster stepping
Highland Ivy	Piecrust	Blue Ridge	1949	Dark and light green ivy
Highlands	Criterion	E. M. Knowles	1957	
Highlight		Paden City	1948	Heavy quality oven- and craze-proof colors; Blueberry, Citron, dark green, Nutmeg, Pepper, white; Russel Wright; distributed by Justin Tharaud and Son
*Hilda	Candlewick	Blue Ridge		Large red flower and smaller blue and yellow flowers
Hilo	Ultra	Vernon Kilns	1938	Light brown lotus flower
Holland, see Crocus (Hall)				
Holly		Stangl	1967–1972	
Hollyberry	Colonial	Blue Ridge		Traditional Christmas plant; green rim
Hollyhock	Colonial	Blue Ridge		Pink flowers; yellow line border
Hollyhock	New Art	Homer Laughlin		Decal; pink flowers on stem
Hollyhock		Universal		Multicolored flowers
*Hollywood	Teapot	Hall	Late 1920s	Variety of colors; three sizes
Homesplace	Skyline	Blue Ridge	1950s	Tree, fence, and house
*Homespun	Montecito	Vernon Kilns	1949–1958	Brown, green, and yellow plaid; see also Calico; Coronation Organdy; Gingham; Organdie; Tam O'Shanter; Tweed
*Homestead	Skyline	Blue Ridge	1950s	Farm scene
*Homestead	Iva-Lure	Crooksville		Winter scene
Homestead in Winter, see Homestead (Crooksville)				
Honolulu	Candlewick	Blue Ridge		Different fruits; green rim
Honolulu	Ultra	Vernon Kilns	1938	Yellow and blue lotus flower
*Hook Cover	Teapot	Hall	1940	Cadet, Chinese Red, Delphinium, emerald common colors
Hopscotch	Astor	Blue Ridge		Centered yellow and orange flower; cross-hatched border
Hors-d'oeuvres	Accent	E. M. Knowles	1955	
Hostess Pantry Ware		Pottery Guild	1954	Hand painted
Hotpoint	Refrigerator ware	Hall		Addison, Chinese Red, Dresden, Green Lustre, Indian Red, maroon, Sandust, Warm Yellow Daffodil

PATTERN	SHAPE	MAKER	DATE	DESCRIPTION
Housetops		Leigh/Crescent		Variety of buildings
Humpty Dumpty	Kiddieware	Stangl	Mid-1940s–1974	
Hunting	Iva-Lure	Crooksville		Scenic
Illinois	Teapot	Hall	1920s–early 1930s	Cobalt and emerald common colors
Imperial	Anytime	Vernon Kilns	1955–1956	Sgraffito; white lines on black ground
Indian Campfire	Kiddieware	Stangl	Mid-1940s–1974	
Indian Tree		Leigh/Crescent		Large floral spray; pink and blue
Indian Tree	Victory	Salem		Decals; Minton-style floral
Indiana	Teapot	Hall		Warm yellow
Ingrid	Regent	E. M. Knowles	1954	
Inspiration		Stangl	1967–1968	Marked Prestige
Intaglio		Purinton	1936–1959	Dark swirling background; white etched flower
*Iris	Concord	Red Wing	1947	Brown, turquoise-green
Iris		Universal		Pastel pinks
Iris Bouquet		Leigh/Crescent		Brightly colored flowers
Irongate	Teapot	Hall		Made for Irongate Products Co. of New York; black
*Iroquois	Casual	Iroquois China	1959–mid-1960s	Aqua, Avocado Yellow, Brick Red, Cantelope, Charcoal, Forest Green, Grayed-blue, Ice Blue, Lemon Yellow, Lettuce Green, Nutmeg Brown, Oyster Gray, Parsley Green, Pink Sherbet, Ripe Apricot, Sugar White
Iroquois Red	Ranchero	W. S. George		Red banded design
Isle of Palms	Commonwealth	James River Pottery		
Isobella		E. M. Knowles	1948	
*Ivy	Ivy	Franciscan	1948	Hand painted
Ivy	Regal	Harker		Fall colors
Ivy		Paden City		
Ivy Vine	Coupe	Crooksville		Pastel greens
Ivy Vine		Harker		Border of ivy
Jack in the Box	Kiddieware	Stangl	Mid-1940s–1974	
Jacobean	Queen Anne	Sabin	c.1946	
Jade Ware		Sebring	1940s	
Jamestown	Tempo	E. M. Knowles	1961–1963	
Jamoca	Jamoca	Franciscan		
Jan	Candlewick	Blue Ridge		Red, yellow, purple, and pink flower border
Jane Adams	Victory	Salem	1950s	Yellow and green floral sprays
Jean	Nancy	Steubenville		
Jeanette	New Yorker	Salem		Flowerpot center design

PATTERN	SHAPE	MAKER	DATE	DESCRIPTION
Jellico	Skyline	Blue Ridge	1950s	Two-tone red and yellow flowers
Jessamine	Piecrust	Blue Ridge	1948	Red flowers, multi-colored leaves, green border
Jessica	Colonial	Blue Ridge		Red, pink, and blue flowers; pink line border
Jessica		Harker		Brightly colored flowers
Jessie		Crooksville		Pastel pink; floral sprays on border and center
Jigsaw	Skyline	Blue Ridge	1950s	Rooster
Joan of Arc	Diana	Sebring-Limoges		
Joanna	Colonial	Blue Ridge		Red and yellow flowers
Jonquil	Astor	Blue Ridge		Yellow flowers, red border
Jonquil		Paden City		Pastel flowers, border of yellow sprays
Jonquil	Tricorne	Salem		Decals
Jonquil		Stangl		
Joy	Ultra	Vernon Kilns	1938	Yellow peonies and gardenias on brown
Joyce	Colonial	Blue Ridge		Red, light blue, and dark blue flowers
J-Sunshine		Hall		Floral decals
Jubilee		Homer Laughlin	c.1948; 1977–1978	Pastel; Celadon Green, Cream Beige, Mist Gray, Shell Pink; solids
June Apple	Woodcrest	Blue Ridge	1950s	Broken line outlining red apples and leaves
June Bouquet	Colonial	Blue Ridge		Pink, purple, and yellow flowers
June Bride	Colonial	Blue Ridge		Pink and yellow flowers; yellow centered border
June Rose	Colonial	Blue Ridge		Pink flowers, dark leaves
Kaleidoscope	Birds	Crooksville		Floral pattern with green divider
Karen	Colonial	Blue Ridge		Pink, purple, and red flowers
Karen		Sebring-Limoges	1940	
Kashmir	True China	Red Wing	1964	
Kate	Colonial	Blue Ridge		Red flower and rim
Kimberly	Moderne	Blue Ridge	1950s	
King	Refrigerator ware	Hall		Westinghouse ovenware; canary
Kingsport	Astor	Blue Ridge		Centered pink flower; inner and outer leaf border
Kitchen Bouquet	Century-Kitchen Kraft	Homer Laughlin		Floral decals
*Kitchen Kraft	Kitchen Kraft	Homer Laughlin	1930s	Red, blue; also decals under pattern name
Kitchen Shelf	Astor	Blue Ridge		Kitchenware; centered light blue and yellow borders

Kitchenware, see Acacia; Banded; Blue Blossom; Blue Garden; Cactus; Clover; Colonial; Fantasy; Flute; Gold Label; Meadow Flower; Morning Glory; No. 488; Plum Pudding; Provincial; Radiant Ware; Red Dot; Rose Parade; Royal Rose; Saf-Handle; Sani-Grid; Shaggy Tulip; Sunshine; Thorley

PATTERN	SHAPE	MAKER	DATE	DESCRIPTION
Kitten Capers	Kiddieware	Stangl	Mid-1940s–1974	
Kitty	Harker			Blue and pink cameoware
Knowles	Esquire	E. M. Knowles	1955	Russel Wright
Kumquat		Stangl		
La Gonda		Gonder	1950s	Modern shapes; aqua, pink, yellow
Lacquer Blossom	Accent	E. M. Knowles	1957	
Lady Alice	Brittany	Homer Laughlin		Maroon border; bluebells and roses
Lady Greenbriar	Liberty	Homer Laughlin		Green border
Lady Stafford	Liberty	Homer Laughlin		Maroon border
La-Linda		Bauer		Solid colors; smooth (no ridges)
Landscape		Salem China	1940s	
Language of Flowers	Candlewick	Blue Ridge		Blue basket, red flowers, blue rim, writing
Lanterns	Concord	Red Wing	1947	Abstract
Largo		Universal		Border of fall leaves; small center decal
Laura	Colonial	Blue Ridge		Red flowers, red and yellow leaves
Laurel	Monarch	Crown	1941	Black and gold wreath border
Laurel		Stangl	c.1942	
Laurelton		Harker		Green, beige
Laurie	Colonial	Blue Ridge		Large pink flowers, small blue flowers
Laurita		Stangl		Della-Ware mark
Lavalette	Moderne	Blue Ridge	1950s	Pink flower; green border
Lavender Fruit	Colonial	Blue Ridge		
Lazybone		Frankoma	1953	Solids
Leaf		Taylor, Smith, and Taylor		Coral
Leaf and Flower		Harker		Cameo-type design
Leaf Ballet	Accent	E. M. Knowles	1953–54	
Leaf Dane	Four Seasons	E. M. Knowles	1960–1963	
Leaf Spray		E. M. Knowles		Muted colors
Leaf Swirl	Shellridge	Harker		Fall colors
Leaves of Fall	Trailway	Blue Ridge	1950s	Centered leaves with outline; wide yellow border
Ledford	Candlewick	Blue Ridge		Mostly pink flowers
Lei Lani	Ultra; San Marion	Vernon Kilns	1938–1942; 1947–1955	Maroon lotus flower
Lenore	Candlewick	Blue Ridge		Pink and red tulip; red border
Lenore	Monticello; Olivia	Steubenville		
Lexington	Colonial	Blue Ridge		Gray flowers; blue leaves and rim

PATTERN	SHAPE	MAKER	DATE	DESCRIPTION
Lexington	Concord	Red Wing	1947	Rose
Lexington		Homer Laughlin		Wide solid-colored border
Lexington Rose		Red Wing		Large flowers
Lido		Homer Laughlin	1977–1978	
Lido	Regent	Knowles	1948	
Lido Dalyrymple		W. S. George		Tiny buds
Lime		Stangl	1950	
Linda	Montecito	Vernon Kilns	1940	Burgundy border; pink and blue flowers
*Lipton	French; Boston	Hall		Teapots, sugars and creamers; marked Lipton Tea; maroon and warm yellow most common colors
Little Bo Peep, see Bo Peep				
Little Bouquet	LaGrande	Crooksville		Small flower grouping
Little Boy Blue	Kiddieware	Stangl	Mid-1940s–1974	
Little Mission	Montecito	Vernon Kilns	1937	Mission house
Little Quackers	Kiddieware	Stangl	Mid-1940s–1974	
Little Violet	Astor	Blue Ridge		Centered bunch of violets; border
Liz	Colonial	Blue Ridge		Pink and yellow flowers; red rim
Lollipop Tree	Year 'Round	Vernon Kilns	1957–1958	Abstract pastel lollipops
Los Angeles		Bauer		
*Los Angeles	Teapot	Hall	1926	Variety of colors; three sizes
Lotus		Harker	1960s	Cameoware
Lotus	Concord	Red Wing	1947	
Lotus	Lotus	Vernon Kilns	1950	Red and yellow lotus flower
Louise	Virginia Rose	Homer Laughlin		
Louisiana Lace	Candlewick	Blue Ridge		
Love Song	Astor	Blue Ridge		Centered male, female, and leaves; yellow and double black border
Lucerne	Classique	E. M. Knowles	1960	
Lupine	Futura	Red Wing	1960	Floral
*Lu-Ray	Laurel, (1932); Empire (1936)	Taylor, Smith, and Taylor	1930s–1950s	Pastel; Chatham Gray, Persian Cream, Sharon Pink, Surf Green, Windsor Blue
Lute Song	True China	Red Wing	1960	Musical instruments
Lyric		Stangl	1954–1957	Black and brown freeform shapes; white background
Madison		Leigh		
Madras	Square	Blue Ridge		Bold geometric
Madrid		Homer Laughlin	1977–1978	
Magic Flower	Candlewick	Blue Ridge		Red and blue flower; green border
Magnolia	Piecrust	Blue Ridge	1948	White and red flowers; green leaves; dark stems

PATTERN	SHAPE	MAKER	DATE	DESCRIPTION
Magnolia	Liberty	Homer Laughlin		Decal
*Magnolia	Concord	Red Wing	1947	
*Magnolia		Stangl	1952–1962	Red border
Majestic	True China	Red Wing	1960	White
Mallow		Harker		Pastel flower arrangements
Manassas	Colonial	Blue Ridge		Red leaves; green leaf border
Mandarin Red		Salem		Solid colored; bright red and white
Mandarin Tricorne	Tricorne	Salem		Red borders, white interiors
Mango	Mango	Franciscan		
Manhattan	Teapot	Hall		Stock Brown; side handle
Manhattan		Leigh/Crescent		Bordered with rings of gold
Mantilla	Tempo	E. M. Knowles	1961–1963	
Maple Leaf	Woodcrest	Blue Ridge	1950s	Stylized leaves with outlines
Maple Leaf		Salem		Fall leaf design
Maple Whirl		Stangl	1965–1967	
Mar-Crest				Many different designs; wholesaled by Marshall Burns
*Mardi Gras	Colonial	Blue Ridge	1943	Blue daisy and pink flower; flowers cut off on plates
Mardi Gras Variant	Colonial	Blue Ridge		Red cut-off flowers
Margaret Rose		Homer Laughlin		Thick colored border; floral center
Mariner	Candlewick	Blue Ridge		Center sailboat; blue rope border; Mariner written on plate
Marines	Montecito	Vernon Kilns	1937	Anchor and ships
Mariposa Tulip	Montecito	Vernon Kilns		Yellow flowers
Mary	Astor	Blue Ridge		Fruit and flowers, border
Mary Quite	Kiddieware	Stangl	Mid-1940s–1974	
Marylou		Hall		Floral decals; creamer and sugar
*Max-i-cana	Yellowstone	Homer Laughlin	1930s	Mexican decal; man, cactus, pots; octagonal plates
May and Vieve Hamilton		Vernon Kilns		
May Flower	Melinda	Vernon Kilns	1942–1955	Large floral spray
Mayan Aztec		Frankoma		Solids
Mayfair	Esquire	E. M. Knowles	1957	
Mayfair		Leigh/Crescent		Bold flower decal
*Mayflower	Skyline	Blue Ridge	1950s	Two bold pink flowers; off-center
Mayflower		E. M. Knowles	1957–1963	
Mayflower		Vernon Kilns	1940s–late 1950s	Fully covered center; floral
Maypole	Maypole	Franciscan	1977	
Maywood		Purinton	1936–1959	Gray-blue background; white flower

PATTERN	SHAPE	MAKER	DATE	DESCRIPTION
*McCormick	Teapot	Hall	1907	Golden brown oldest color; made for McCormick Tea Co.
Meadow Beauty	Colonial	Blue Ridge		Brightly colored floral border
Meadow Bloom	Montecito	Vernon Kilns	1947	Blue flowers and rose; brown border
Meadow Flowers	Kitchenware	Hall	1938	Flowers in meadow on ivory; teapot
Meadow Flowers	Coupe	Crooksville		Brightly colored floral border
Meadow Gold	Criterion	E. M. Knowles	1954	
Meadow Rose	Meadow Rose	Franciscan	1977	
Meadowlea	Skyline	Blue Ridge	1950s	White flowers, brown leaves, outlined
Mealtime Special	Kiddieware	Stangl	Mid-1940s–1974	
Medallion, see Colonial				
Medallion		Crooksville		Small floral border
Medici	Cavalier	Royal		Ironstone; wide, elaborate scroll border
Mediterranean	True China	Red Wing	1960	Floral
Mediterranean		Stangl	1965–1974	Dark blue and black
Medley	Colonial	Blue Ridge		Blue flower and rim
Melinda	Melinda	Vernon Kilns	1942	Solid colors
Mello-Tone		Coors	Late 1930s	Pastels; aqua blue, canary yellow, coral pink, spring green
*Melody	Teapot	Hall	1939	Canary, cobalt common colors
Memory Lane	Astor	Blue Ridge		Pink, deep red, and yellow flowers
Memphis	Colonial	Blue Ridge		Pastel flowers, brown and black leaves, hatch-mark border
Mermaid	Ballerina	Universal	1950	Abstract
Merrileaf	True China	Red Wing	1960	Floral
Mesa	Encanto	Franciscan		
Metlox Poppy Trail, see Poppy Trail				
*Mexicana	Century	Homer Laughlin	1930s	Decal; orange and yellow pots of cacti
Mexicana	Montecito	Vernon Kilns	1950; 1954	Dark brown, rust, and yellow bands on border
Mexicana		W. S. George		Colored rim
*Mexicana Kitchen Kraft		Homer Laughlin	1938	Mexican decals, scenes with different colored bands
*Mexi-Gren		W. S. George	1930s	Mexican-style archway, pots, blanket; green rim
Mexi-Lido		W. S. George		Mexican-style pots
Meylinda	Colonial	Blue Ridge		Red, yellow, and blue flowers; gray leaves
Michigan Coastline	Montecito	Vernon Kilns	1937	Lake Michigan coast; blue and black on ivory ground

PATTERN	SHAPE	MAKER	DATE	DESCRIPTION
Mickey	Colonial	Blue Ridge		Red and pink flowers; green and gold leaves
Middlebury	Cavalier	Royal		Ironstone; large flower-burst center design
Midnight Rose	Anniversary	Red Wing	1953	Rose
Midsummer	Victory	Salem		Decals
Midsummer		Sebring-Limoges	1940	
Milkweed Dance	Montecito; Ultra	Vernon Kilns	1940	Floral pattern in blue, maroon
Ming Blossom	Woodcrest	Blue Ridge	1950s	Oriental motif; pink flowers, brown rim
Ming Tree (No. 4387)	Woodcrest	Blue Ridge	1950s	Gnarled tree; yellow dappled background
Ming Tree	Accent	E. M. Knowles	c.1954	
Mini Flowers	Deanna	E. M. Knowles		Small red flowers
Mirador		Homer Laughlin	1977–1978	
Mirasol	Mirasol	Franciscan		
Miss Terry	Teapot	Hall		H/3 mark; gold dots
Moby Dick	Ultra	Vernon Kilns	1939	Blue, brown, maroon, and orange; whaling scene
*Mod Tulip	Colonial	Blue Ridge		Two red and yellow striped tulips with green leaves
Modern		J. A. Bauer	1935	Solids
*Modern California	Montecito	Vernon Kilns	1937–1947	Azure, gray, ivory, orchid, Pistachio, Sand, Straw
Modern Classic	Four Seasons	E. M. Knowles	1960–1963	
Modern Orchid	Round; Trend	Paden City		Large center orchid; gold border
Modern Tulip	Plymouth	Harker	1930s	Stencil-type tulip design; muted colors
Moderne		J. A. Bauer	1948	Black, brown, burgundy, chartreuse, gray, olive green, pink, yellow
*Moderne	Teapot	Hall	1930s	Gold foot, knob, and inside of spout
Mojave	San Marion	Vernon Kilns	1955	Brown, green, yellow bands on rim
Monk's Head	Tankard/ flagon	Hall		Decal of friar's head
Monogram		Salem		Gold-initialed
Montecito	Montecito	Vernon Kilns	1935	
Monterey		Stangl	1967–1968; 1970	
Monterey	Melinda	Vernon Kilns	1942; 1950–1954	Red and blue leaf border
Montgomery Ward	Refrigerator ware	Hall	Early 1940s	Delphinium, Mid-white
Monticello	E-Shape	Hall	1941	Border; small, individual, pale flowers
Monticello		Steubenville		
Montmarte	Futura	Red Wing	1960	French street scene
Moon Flower		Salem		
Moon Song		J. A. Bauer		

PATTERN	SHAPE	MAKER	DATE	DESCRIPTION
Morning	Teapot	Hall		Solid colors or decals; sets with matching sugar and creamer
Morning Blue		Stangl	1970	
*Morning Glory	Kitchenware	Hall	1942–1949	Cadet Blue with Hi-white features and morning glory; decal
Morning Glory	Concord	Red Wing	1947	
Morning Glory	Shenandoah	Paden City		Floral sprays
Morning Glory	Montecito	Vernon Kilns		Turquoise and blue flowers
Morningside	Delphian	Taylor, Smith, and Taylor	Late 1920s	Flower garden scene
*Moss Rose (No. 4486)	Trailway	Blue Ridge	1950s	Hand painted
Moss Rose	Criterion	E. M. Knowles	1954	
Moss Rose		Universal Potteries	1953–1955	Decals
Mother Hubbard	Kiddieware	Stangl	Mid-1940s–1974	
Mountain Aster	Colonial	Blue Ridge		Pink and blue flowers
Mountain Bells	Colonial	Blue Ridge		Pink flowers
Mountain Cherry		Blue Ridge	1951	
Mountain Flower		Hall	1940	Cobalt; floral design; red line treatment
Mountain Ivy	Candlewick	Blue Ridge	1951	Two-tone green leaves, border
Mountain Laurel		Stangl	1947–1957	
Mountain Nosegay	Candlewick	Blue Ridge		Blue tulip and multicolored flowers
Mountain Sweetbriar	Skyline	Blue Ridge	1950s	Pink flowers
*Mt. Vernon	E-Line	Hall	1941	Wreath with center decal of pink and green flowers; Granitetone; for Sears, Roebuck, and Co.
Multi Flori California	Montecito	Vernon Kilns	1935–1937	Petal outlined in blue, brown, green, rose, yellow; ivory ground
Mums		Hall	1930s	Pink mums
*Mums		Taylor, Smith, and Taylor		Pink flowers; black and blue leaves
Muriel	Square; Colonial	Blue Ridge		Yellow and pink floral
Murphy	Teapot	Hall	Early 1940s	Victorian style; see also Benjamin, Birch, Bowknot, Connie, Plume
Nadine	Colonial	Blue Ridge		Floral
Nassau		Homer Laughlin		Border of large roses
Nassau	Concord	Red Wing	1947	
Nasturtium	Shell-Crest; Shenandoah	Paden City	1940s	Bright orange flower

PATTERN	SHAPE	MAKER	DATE	DESCRIPTION
Native American		Vernon Kilns	1930s	Mexican scenes; soft pastel colors
*Native California	Melinda	Vernon Kilns	1942–1947	Pastels; aqua, blue, green, pink, yellow
Nautical	Candlewick	Blue Ridge		
*Nautilus	Century	Homer Laughlin		Floral decals
*Nautilus	Teapot	Hall	1939	Seashell design
Navajo		Crown		Mexican design; red banded rim
Navarra	Williamsburg	E. M. Knowles	1955	
Neville		W. S. George		Small rosebuds interspersed on colored border; sold by Sears, Roebuck
New Art	New Art	Homer Laughlin	1930s	Solid colors
New Princess		Sebring-Limoges		
*New York	Teapot	Hall	1920	Gold decorated line; many sizes
Newport	Teapot	Hall	Early 1930s	Solid colors, gold decoration, or black decal
Newport		Stangl	1940–1942	Blue shading from dark to pale; matte finish; sailboat
Night Flower	Skyline	Blue Ridge	1952	White flowers on dark background
Night Song	Cavalier	Royal		Ironstone; bold patterned border
No. 488	Kitchenware	Hall	1930s	Flower decal
Nocturne	Colonial	Blue Ridge		Rose-red flower; red brushed edge
Nora, see Norris				
Nordic		Homer Laughlin	1977–1978	
Nordic Flower	Americana	E. M. Knowles	1959	
Norma	Colonial	Blue Ridge		Pink and blue flower border, green rim
*Norma		Stangl		Della-Ware mark; pear branch in center; rings of color on rim
Normandy	Skyline	Blue Ridge	1950s	Two designs—one man, one woman, on sponged willow background; brown rim
*Normandy	Provincial	Red Wing	1941	Blue and maroon bands, later apple blossoms added
Normandy Plaid		Purinton	1936–1959	Red plaid
Norris	Refrigerator ware	Hall	1950s	Water server in blue, canary, green lustre; also called Nora
North Star Cherry	Colonial	Blue Ridge		Cherries on border; red rim
North Wind	Montecito	Vernon Kilns	1948	Dark green and lime
Northern Lights	Futura	Red Wing	1960	Geometric blue
Norway Rose		Homer Laughlin		Floral decal
Nut Tree	Nut Tree	Franciscan		

PATTERN	SHAPE	MAKER	DATE	DESCRIPTION
Nutcracker	Ultra	Vernon Kilns	1940	Brown print border
Oakleaf	Criterion	E. M. Knowles	1955	
Obion	Candlewick	Blue Ridge		Red and yellow flower; red border
Octagon	Octagon	Catalina	1930s	Solids
October	October	Franciscan	1977	
Ohio, see Miss Terry				
Oklahoma, see Plainsman				
*Old Curiosity Shop	Cavalier	Royal China	1940s	Scenic center design; elaborate border
Old Dutch		Sebring-Limoges		
Old English		Homer Laughlin		Decal scene with castle
Old Mexico	Alara	Limoges		
Old Orchard		Stangl	1941–1942	
Old Provincial		Red Wing	1943	Aqua, brown bottom
Olena-Aztec	Montecito	Vernon Kilns	1937	Floral and geometric Aztec design; blue, green, rose, yellow; ivory ground
Olivia		Stangl		Della-Ware mark
Orange Blossom	Regina	Paden City		
Orange Poppy, see Poppy (Hall)				
Orange Tree	Orange Tree	Homer Laughlin		Raised design on outside of nested bowls
Orbit		Homer Laughlin	1960s	Streamlined design; avocado, brown, and other colors
Orchard	Ultra	Vernon Kilns	1937; 1939	Hand painted fruit design
Orchard Glory	Colonial	Blue Ridge		Yellow pear and red apple; broken green rim
*Orchard Song		Stangl	1962–1974	Green and orange stylized fruit
*Organdie	Montecito	Vernon Kilns	1940–1958	Overall brown pattern; yellow and brown plaid border; see also Calico; Coronation Organdy; Gingham; Homespun; Tam O'Shanter; Tweed
*Organdy		Homer Laughlin		Pastel border on eggshell; green handles
Oriental Poppy	Colonial	Blue Ridge		Three red poppies; red border
Orion	Colonial	Blue Ridge		Blue flowers; blue and black leaves
Orleans	Provincial	Red Wing	1941	Red rose
Oslo	Mayfair	E. M. Knowles	1954	
Our America		Vernon Kilns	1939	Dark blue, maroon, and walnut brown on cream ground
Our Barnyard Friends	Kiddieware	Stangl		
Overtrue	Cavalier	Royal		Ironstone; bold center design
Paden Rose		Paden City		Large, pale rose and bud

PATTERN	SHAPE	MAKER	DATE	DESCRIPTION
*Painted Daisy	Colonial	Blue Ridge		Red, blue, yellow and green flowers; broken green rim
Painted Desert	Ballerina	Universal	1950	Abstract
Paisley		Stangl	1963–1967	
Palm Tree	New Art	E. M. Knowles		
Palm Tree		Purinton	1936–1959	Two palm trees
Palo Alto	Encanto	Franciscan		
Pan American Lei	Lotus	Vernon Kilns	1950	Lei design on pink ground
Pandora	Colonial	Blue Ridge		Floral design
Pansy		Harker		Pastel flowers
Pantry Shelf	Yorktown	E. M. Knowles		
Paper Roses	Colonial	Blue Ridge		
*Parade	Teapot	Hall	1942	Canary common color
Paradise	Coupe	Homer Laughlin		
Park Lane	Heritage	E. M. Knowles	1955	
Parsley	Salem	Salem		
Partridge Berry	Skyline	Blue Ridge	1950s	Yellow pear-like flower, red berry border
Passy	Ballerina	Universal	1950	Abstract
Pastel Garden	Sabina	Sabin		
Pastel Morning Glory	D-Style	Hall	1930s	Pink flowers
Pastel Poppy	Astor	Blue Ridge		Pink flowers and border
Pastel Tulip		Harker		Floral decals
Patchwork Posy	Colonial	Blue Ridge		Red plaid; blue plaid flowers
Pate Sur Pate		Harker		Scalloped border; solid colors
Pate-Sur-Pate	Shalimar	Steubenville		
*Patio	Shell-Crest	Paden City	1907–1950s	Mexican decal decorated
Patricia	Skyline	Blue Ridge	1950s	Brown and gray flowers
Patrician	Refrigerator ware	Hall	1938	Westinghouse; Delphinium, Lettuce
Pauda (Freesia)	Pauda	Franciscan		Hand painted
Pauline	Astor	Blue Ridge		Yellow flowers; wide yellow and thin brown border
Peach		Pottery Guild		Peaches and lavender flowers
Peach Blossom	Bolero	W. S. George		Sprigs of small pink flowers (Cynthia has same decal on Lido shape)
Peach Blossom	Hallcraft	Hall		Designed by Eva Zeisel
Peach Blossom	Accent	E. M. Knowles	1955	
Pear		Pottery Guild		Fruit grouping
Pear Turnpike		Vernon Kilns		Brown
Peasant Ware, see Hercules				
Pebble Beach	Pebble Beach	Franciscan		
Pedro & Conchita	Montecito	Vernon Kilns	1937	Indian man and woman

PATTERN	SHAPE	MAKER	DATE	DESCRIPTION
Pembrooke	Colonial	Blue Ridge		Yellow flowers; pink dot border
Pennsylvania Dutch		Purinton	1936–1959	Red and blue plaid tulips around border
Penny Serenade	Colonial	Blue Ridge		Red and blue flowers, green leaves, border
Penthouse	Yorktown	E. M. Knowles		Flowerpots
Peony	Colonial	Blue Ridge		Centered large pink flower; pink and green line border
Peony Bouquet	Candlewick	Blue Ridge		One pink and 3 blue flowers
*Pepe	New Shape	Red Wing	1963	Geometric; Bittersweet, dark bluish-purple, and green
Periwinkle	Astor	Blue Ridge		Two-tone blue flower and leaves
Petalware		W. S. George	Late 1930s	Solid colors
Peter Rabbit	Kiddieware	Stangl		
Petit Point		Crown	1941	Flower bouquet; cross-stitch effect
Petit Point		Leigh/Crescent		Floral border
Petit Point		Sold by Montgomery Ward	1936	Decals
Petit Point		Taylor, Smith, and Taylor		
Petit Point Basket		Salem		Flower basket; sampler effect
Petit Point Bouquet	Delphian	Taylor, Smith, and Taylor	Late 1920s	
Petit Point House		Crooksville		Decal of houses, trees; sometimes called "House"
Petit Point Leaf		Crooksville		Decals
Petit Point Rose		Harker		Rose border
Petit Point Rose	Fleurette	W. S. George		Cross-stitch, floral
Petite Flowers		Stangl	1970–1974	
Petitpoint		Homer Laughlin	1960s	Floral decal like stitched petit point
Petunia	Colonial	Blue Ridge		Red and blue flowers, border
Petunia		Hall	1932–1969	Pink floral decal
Phacelia	Montecito	Vernon Kilns		Pink flowers
Pheasant	LaGrande	Crooksville		Flying birds; scenic
*Philadelphia	Teapot	Hall	1923	Variety of colors, decals, or gold trim; many sizes
Philodendron	Melinda	Vernon Kilns	1942; 1950–1954	Green and yellow leaf border
Phoenix, see Patrician				
Picardy	Clinchfield	Blue Ridge		Centered man, woman, and ducks; pink border
Picardy	Village Green	Red Wing	1960	Yellow rose

PATTERN	SHAPE	MAKER	DATE	DESCRIPTION
Picket Fence	Yorktown	E. M. Knowles		Brightly colored floral and fence
Picnic	Picnic	Franciscan		
Pie Crust		Stangl	1969	
Piedmont Plaid	Square	Blue Ridge		Brown plaid on yellow swirled background
Pilgrims	Skyline	Blue Ridge	1950s	Figures in center; flowered border
Pine Cone		Harker		Wispy, brown design
Pinecone	Skyline	Blue Ridge	1950s	Pinecones with gray swirled background
Pinecone Spray	Fiesta	Homer Laughlin	Decal	
Pink Border	LaGrande	Crooksville		Tiny pink flora border
Pink Carousel	Kiddieware	Stangl	Mid-1940s–1974	
Pink Cosmos		Stangl	1966	Marked Prestige
Pink Dogwood	Moderne	Blue Ridge	1950s	Stylized
Pink Dogwood	Classique	E. M. Knowles	1960	
Pink Dogwood		Stangl		
Pink Fairy	Kiddieware	Stangl	Mid-1940s–1974	
Pink Lady	Vernon Ware	Metlox	1965	
Pink Lily		Stangl	1953–1957	
Pink Morning Glory		Hall		Early decal
Pink Moss Rose		Homer Laughlin	1920	Decal
Pink Mums		Hall	1930s	Floral decals
Pink Pastel		E. M. Knowles		Pale pink and white with pink flowers
Pink Petticoat	Colonial	Blue Ridge		Pink flowers; rim
Pink Print		Sold by Montgomery Ward	1936	Decals
Pink Rose		Homer Laughlin	1920	Decals
Pink Rose & Daisy	Plain Edge	Homer Laughlin	1920	Decals
Pink Spice	Anniversary	Red Wing	1953	Butterfly design
Pinkie	Skyline	Blue Ridge	1950s	Pink flowers; sponged center; green rim
Pintoria		Metlox	c.1939	
Pippin	Skyline	Blue Ridge	1950s	Three red apples; green rim
Plaid, see Calico; Gay Plaid; Gingham; Homespun; Organdie; Tam O'Shanter; Tweed				
Plain (Hall), see Queen				
Plain	Gypsy Trail	Red Wing	1935	Blue, ivory, orange, turquoise, yellow
Plain-Jane	Lido	W. S. George		
Plainsman		Frankoma		
Plantation Ivy	Skyline	Blue Ridge	1950s	Yellow and green ivy
Playful Pups	Kiddieware	Stangl	Mid-1940s–1974	
Plaza	Regrigerator ware	Hall	1930s–1960s	Water server

PATTERN	SHAPE	MAKER	DATE	DESCRIPTION
Plum	Candlewick	Blue Ridge		
Plum		Stangl	1940	Blue, green, tan
Plum Blossom	Dynasty	Red Wing	1947	Green, pink, and yellow oriental motif; six-sided
Plum Duff	Candlewick	Blue Ridge		Two plums; gray and gold swirled background
Plum Pudding	Kitchenware	Hall		White bowls with holly decals
Plume	Astor	Blue Ridge		Three rose plums; rose border; light blue rim
Plume	Teapot	Hall	Early 1940s	Victorian style; see also Benjamin, Birch, Bowknot, Connie, Murphy, Plume
Pocahontas	Common-wealth	James River Pottery		
Poinsettia	Colonial	Blue Ridge	1950	Hand painted red flowers, gray leaves
Polka Dot	Colonial	Blue Ridge		Flowers, center, random dots
Polka Dot		Hall	1942	
Polo	Tricone	Salem		Decals
Polychrome A	Montecito	Vernon Kilns	1935–1937	Rims decorated with brightly colored blocks
Pom Pom	Candlewick	Blue Ridge		Red and blue flower; red border
Pomegranate	Montecito	Vernon Kilns	1935–1937	Pink with ivory
Pompadour	Sabina	Sabin	c.1946	
Pompeii	New Shape	Red Wing	1962	Geometric
Pony Tail	Kiddieware	Stangl		
Poppy		Crown		Floral center; pastel vinelike border
Poppy	Rainbow	W. S. George		Center design of three flowers
*Poppy	C-Line	Hall	1933–1950s	Floral decals; orange poppies
Poppy	Deanna	E. M. Knowles	1948	Orange floral spray
Poppy	Shenandoah	Paden City		Floral border
*Poppy & Wheat		Hall	1933-c.1939	Orange flowers and wheat heads
*Poppy Trail		Metlox	c.1939	Solids; Delphinium Blue, Canary Yellow, ivory, Old Rose, Poppy Orange, rust, turquoise blue
Posey Shop	Triumph	Sebring-Limoges	1944–1945	
Posies	LaGrande	Crooksville		Pastel flowers
Posies	Coupe	Paden City		Abstract flowers
Posies		Stangl	1973	
Potpourri	Colonial	Blue Ridge		Off-centered floral; black line border
*Prelude		Stangl	1949–1957	Stylized flower design
Pretty Pinks	Accent	Knowles	1957	
Pricilla	Clinchfield	Blue Ridge		
Primitive Bird, see Bird				

PATTERN	SHAPE	MAKER	DATE	DESCRIPTION
Primrose Path	Astor	Blue Ridge		Red, yellow, and blue flower border
*Prince	Refrigerator ware	Hall	c.1952	Westinghouse; Turk Blue and Daffodil; also called Adonis
Priscilla	Clinchfield	Blue Ridge		Red and blue flowers, center and border
*Priscilla	Kitchen Kraft	Homer Laughlin	1940s–1950s	Pale pink roses and sprigs of flowers
Pristine	Colonial	Blue Ridge		Blue flowers and leaves, border
Provincial	Kitchenware	Hall	1938	Clay-colored with American Indian
*Provincial		Stangl	1957–1967	Floral center; border
Provincial Blue	Poppytrail	Metlox	1951	
Provincial Bouquet	Tempo	Knowles	1961–1963	
Provincial Fruit	Poppytrail	Metlox	1965	
Provincial Tulip		Harker	1959	Cameoware
Provincial Wreath		Harker		Stoneware; Pennsylvania Dutch design
Puppy-Flower	Floral edge	E. M. Knowles	1933–1934	Decals
Puritan	Royal Gadroon	Harker		Plain white
Pussy Willow		W. S. George		
Quaker Maid		Harker	1960s	Dark brown, drips of lighter color
Quartette	Concord	Red Wing	1947	Four solid colors
Queen	Refrigerator ware	Hall		Westinghouse ovenware; Delphinium
Queen Anne's Lace	Skyline	Blue Ridge	1950s	Dark flowers; brown, gray, and green leaves
Queen Anne's Lace	Esquire	E. M. Knowles	1955–1962	Russel Wright; abstract decal
Queen Rose	Coupe	Crooksville		Pastel rose stem
*Quilted Fruit		Blue Ridge	1950s	Fruit design, printed calicos
Quilted Ivy	Woodcrest	Blue Ridge	1950s	Red plaid, black, and yellow ivy
R.F.D.	San Fernando	Vernon Kilns	1953–1954	Brown rooster; green plaid border
Radiance, see Sunshine				
Radiant Ware	Kitchenware	Hall	1940s	Bowls; blue, green, red, yellow
Raffia	San Marino	Vernon Kilns	1953–1954	Green and brown; like tree bark
Rainbow		Hall		Hall's Radiant ware
Rainbow		Stangl	1935	Aqua, Colonial Blue, brown, Persian Yellow, Rust, Silver Green, Surf White, Tangerine

PATTERN	SHAPE	MAKER	DATE	DESCRIPTION
Rainbow	Rainbow	W. S. George	Late 1930s	Solid colors
Rainelle	Colonial	Blue Ridge		Bold pastel flowers
Raisin	Ring	Vernon Kilns		Drip glaze; solids
Rambler Rose	Aristocrat	E. M. Knowles	1930s	Decals
Rambler Rose		Universal		Rose medallions
Rancho		French Saxon		Solid colors
*Random Harvest		Red Wing	1961	Hand painted brown, copper, coral, green, and turquoise on flecked dish
Ranger		Stangl		Cowboy and cactus
Ranger Boy	Kiddieware	Stangl	Mid-1940s–1974	
Rawhide		Harker	1960s	Stoneware; dark brown
Raymond	Yellowstone	Homer Laughlin	1926	Floral decal
Raymor		Roseville (Ben Siebel)	1952	Blue, brown, dark green, mottled green, rust, white; modern
Raymore	Contempora	Steubenville (Ben Siebel)		Three-dimensional rippling; charcoal, Fawn, Mist gray, Sand white
Razzle Dazzle	Skyline	Blue Ridge	1950s	Black, gray, and red leaves; sponged background
Red & Gold		Sold by Montgomery Ward	1936	Decals
Red Apple		Blue Ridge		Center apple; green rim
Red Apple		Franciscan		
Red Apple 1		Harker		Small, continuous apple decal
Red Apple 2		Harker		Large, individual apple decal
Red Bank		Blue Ridge		Red and blue flowers; green leaves border
Red Barn	Skyline	Blue Ridge	1950s	Red barn and fence; yellow sponged background; brown rim
Red Berry	Victory	Salem		Decals
Red Cone Flower	Clinchfield	Blue Ridge		Large red flower and bud; green, blue, and yellow leaves
Red Dot	Kitchenware	Hall		Red dot on Eggshell white
Red Ivy		Stangl	1957	
*Red Poppy	D-Line	Hall	1930–1950	Made for Grand Union Tea Company; red flowers, black leaves
*Red Riding Hood	Figural	Hull	1943–1957	Three-dimensional little girl
Red Rooster Provincial	Poppytrail	Metlox	1965	
Red Rose		Paden City		Red rose decal, rosebud decal
Red Starflower		Watt		Stylized fresh and flowery
Red Tulip	Candlewick	Blue Ridge		Red tulip border

PATTERN	SHAPE	MAKER	DATE	DESCRIPTION
Red Tulip	Kitchen Kraft	Homer Laughlin		Decals
Red Willow	Colonial	Blue Ridge		Red oriental scene; rim
Red Wing Rose	Futura	Red Wing	1960	Rose
Reed	Gypsytrail	Red Wing	1935	Blue, ivory, orange, turquoise, yellow
Reflection	Four Seasons	Knowles	1960–1963	
Refrigerator ware, see Aristocrat; Bingo; Emperor; General Electric; Hotpoint; King; Montgomery Ward; Norris; Patrician; Plaza; Prince; Queen; Sears, Roebuck and Co.				
Regal	Teapot	Hall		by J. Palin Thorley
Regal Rings	Queen Anne	Sabin	c.1946	
Remembrance	Citation	Steubenville		
Rhapsody	Colonial	Blue Ridge		Blue, pink, and yellow flowers; yellow border
Rhea	Trend	Steubenville		
Rhonda	Americana	E. M. Knowles	1958	
*Rhythm	Teapot	Hall	1939	Cadet, Canary, Chinese Red common colors
*Rhythm		Homer Laughlin	1951–1958	Harlequin colors; simple, modern shapes
Rhythm		Paden City	1936	
*Rhythm Rose	Century	Homer Laughlin	Mid-1940s–1950s	Large center rose
Rialto		Stangl		Della-Ware mark; yellow flowers on blue background
Ribbed, see Flute				
Ribbon	Criterion	E. M. Knowles	1954	
Ribbon Plaid	Skyline	Blue Ridge	1950s	Green and yellow
Richmond	E-Style	Hall	1941	Granitetone; yellow daisies and other flowers
Rick-Rack		Blair		Yellow and brown
Ridge, see King				
Ridge Rose	Colonial	Blue Ridge		Pink flowers; broken pink border
Ring-A-Round	Four Seasons	E. M. Knowles	1959–1963	
Ring-O-Roses	Piecrust	Blue Ridge	1948	Red rosebud border
*Ring		J. A. Bauer	1932–1962	Solids: black, burnt orange, dark blue, green, ivory, maroon, yellow; pastels: chartreuse, gray, green, light yellow, olive, pale blue, pink, turquoise, white
Ringles		Stangl	1973–1974	
Rio		Salem	1943	
Rio Chico	Ultra	Vernon Kilns	1938	Pink border; central floral design
Rio Verda	Ultra	Vernon Kilns	1938	Green border; center floral design
Rio Vista	Ultra	Vernon Kilns	1938	Blue border; central floral design
Rite of Spring		Paden City		

PATTERN	SHAPE	MAKER	DATE	DESCRIPTION
*Riviera	Century	Homer Laughlin	1938–1950	Made for Murphy Co.; solids; blue, dark blue, ivory, light green, mauve, red, yellow
Roan Mountain Rose	Colonial	Blue Ridge		Pink flowers; bold green leaves; pink line border
Roanoke	Astor	Blue Ridge		Red, blue, and yellow flowers
Rock Garden	Skyline	Blue Ridge	1950s	Small blue and gray flowers; gray rim
Rock-Mount		Coors	Late 1930s	Colored tableware and ovenware; blue, green, ivory, orange, rose, yellow
Rock Castle	Skyline	Blue Ridge	1950s	Gray and brown leaves
Rock Rose	Colonial	Blue Ridge		Hand painted; pink flowers and green leaves
Rockport Rooster	Candlewick	Blue Ridge		Stylized rooster center
Rococo	Princess	Paden City	1933	
Rodelay	Tempo	Knowles	1961–1963	
Romance	Cavalier	Homer Laughlin		
Romance	Regent	E. M. Knowles	1955	
Ronald Reagan	Teapot	Hall	1970s	Three-dimensional caricature resembling Ronald Reagan
*Rooster		Blue Ridge	1950s	Red rooster
Rooster		Harker		Blue, pink; cameoware
Rooster	Poppytrail	Metlox		Rust yellow; black rooster in center; zigzag border
Rooster		Stangl	1970–1974	Gold background; rooster center
Rooster Motto	Candlewick	Blue Ridge		Rooster center; "My love will stop when this rooster crows" on border
Rope Edge	Rope Edge	Catalina	1936	Solids
Rosalinde	Colonial	Blue Ridge		Pink, purple, and yellow flowers
Rose	Deanna	E. M. Knowles		Pale rose and buds
Rose & Lattice	Plain edge	Homer Laughlin	1920	Decals
Rose-A-Day	Anytime	Vernon Kilns	1956–1958	Pink rose, pastel leaves, ivory ground
Rose Bouquet	Floral edge	E. M. Knowles	1933–1934	
Rose Bud	Horizon	Steubenville		
Rose Garden	Gray Lure	Crooksville		Rose spray
Rose Garland		Crooksville	1920s	Border of tiny roses
Rose Garland Border		Homer Laughlin	1920	Decals
Rose Hill	Colonial	Blue Ridge		Pink, purple, and rose flowers
Rose Leaf		Syracuse		
Rose-Marie		Salem		Large cluster of rosebuds; platinum edge
Rose Marie		Sebring-Limoges		

PATTERN	SHAPE	MAKER	DATE	DESCRIPTION
Rose O'Day		Vernon Kilns		
Rose Parade		Hall	1941–1950s	Cadet Blue body, Hi-white knobs and handles; rose decals
Rose Point	Stafford Rose	Pope-Gosser		Embossed roses
Rose Red	Candlewick	Blue Ridge		Red flowers; green leaves border
Rose Spray		Harker		Allover pattern; tiny pink and yellow flowers
Rose Tree	Criterion	E. M. Knowles	1955	
Rose White	Kitchenware	Hall	1941	Hi-white body; trimmed in silver with a pink floral decal
Rose I		Harker		
Rose II		Harker		
Rosebud		Coors	1920–1939	Blue, green, ivory, maroon, turquoise, yellow; raised rosebud and leaf design
Rosebud	Horizon	Steubenville		
Rosemont	Victoria	E. M. Knowles	1948	
Roses	Birds; Bolero	Crooksville		Multicolored flowers
Rosetta		Homer Laughlin		Bird hovering over flowers
Rosette	Colonial	Blue Ridge		Blue and yellow flowers; broken pink rim
Rosettes		Harker		Thin sprays of flowers on border and in center
Rosey	Moderne	Blue Ridge	1950s	
Rosita	Ranchero	W. S. George		Rose blossoms
Roundelay (No. 4499)	Trailway	Blue Ridge		
Round-up	Casual	Red Wing	1958	
Roxanna		Universal		Decals
Roxanne		Stangl	1972–1974	Blue flowers and rim
Royal	Teapot	Hall		White; some with gold
Royal Brocade	Forcast	E. M. Knowles	1957	
Royal Harvest	Coupe	Homer Laughlin		
Royal Marina	Sebring	Sebring-Limoges	1944–1945	
Royal Rose	Kitchenware	Hall		Cadet Blue exterior; Hi-white handles and knobs; silver trim; floral decals
Royal Rose		Harker		Bright single rose decal
Royal Windsor		Salem	1950s	
Ruby	Clinchfield	Blue Ridge		Blue; large red flowers with blue centers border
Ruffled Tulip		Harker		Bright flowers
*Rugosa	Colonial	Blue Ridge		Large yellow flowers with brown centers and green leaves
Russel Wright, see also American Modern; Botanica; Grass; Highlight; Iroquois; Queen Anne's Lace; Seeds; Solar				
Russel Wright		Bauer	1945	Art pottery

PATTERN	SHAPE	MAKER	DATE	DESCRIPTION
Russel Wright	Vitreous restaurant ware	Sterling	1948	Cedar brown, ivy green, straw yellow, suede gray
Rust Bouquet	LaGrande	Crooksville		Fall shades
Rust Floral	Lido	W. S. George		Predominantly orange flowers
Rust Tulip	Shell-Crest	Padan City		Assorted flowers
Rust Tulip	Victory	Salem		Assorted pastel flowers
Rustic		Stangl	1965–1974	
Rustic Garden		Stangl	1972–1974	Orange flowers; green border
Rustic Plaid	Skyline	Blue Ridge	1950s	Black plaid and rim; sponged background
Rutledge	Colonial	Blue Ridge		Blue bow, red tulips
*Saf-Handle	Refrigerator ware	Hall	1938–1960s	Chinese Red most common color
Saf-Handle	Teapot	Hall	1938	Canary most common color
Sailing	Georgette	W. S. George		Variety of boats on border
Sailing	Tricorne	Salem		Decals, coral and black sailboats
Salamina	Ultra	Vernon Kilns	1939	Scene of Greenland with girl
Sampler	Piecrust	Blue Ridge	1948	Red flower; green border
Sampler	Victory	Salem		Decals
Sandra		Salem	1950s	
*Sani-Grid	Kitchenware	Hall	1941	Decal; Chinese Red, Cadet; Hi-white handle and knobs
*Sani-Grid	Teapot	Hall	1941	Contrasting Hi-white handle and knob
Santa Anita	Melinda	Vernon Kilns	1942	Pink blossoms on border
Santa Barbara	Melinda	Vernon Kilns	1939	Brown print; blue and yellow flowers
Santa Maria	Melinda	Vernon Kilns	1939	Purple print; blue and yellow flowers
Santa Paula	Melinda	Vernon Kilns	1939	Pink print; blue and yellow flowers
Saratoga	Skyline	Blue Ridge	1952	
Sarepta	Colonial	Blue Ridge		Multicolored flowers; yellow border
Scandia	Accent	E. M. Knowles	1954	
Scotch Plaid	Coupe	Crooksville		Plaid center design
Scroll	Accent	E. M. Knowles	1955	
Sculptured Daisy	Poppytrail	Metlox	1965	
Sculptured Fruit		Stangl	1966–1974	Marked Prestige; fruit border
Sculptured Grape	Poppytrail	Metlox	1975	
Sculptured Zinnia	Poppytrail	Metlox	1965	
Sea Fare	Forcast	E. M. Knowles	1957	
Sea Shell		Paden City		

PATTERN	SHAPE	MAKER	DATE	DESCRIPTION
Sears, Roebuck and Co.	Refrigerator ware	Hall		Cadet, Hi-white
Seeds	Esquire	E. M. Knowles	1956–1962	Russel Wright; abstract decal
September Song	Forcast	E. M. Knowles	1959	
Sequoia		E. M. Knowles	Late 1930s	Bright floral bouquet
*Serenade	D-Shape	Hall		Sprigs of orange flowers
*Serenade		Homer Laughlin	1940s	Solid pastels; blue, green, pink
Serenade	Classique	E. M. Knowles	1960	
Sesame		Stangl	1972–1974	Brown stylized flower and rim
Seven Seas	San Marino	Vernon Kilns	1954	Brown and blue sailboats
Sevilla				Solids, similar to Harlequin
Shadow Fruit	Skyline; Moderne	Blue Ridge	1950s	Stylized line drawing of fruit; green rim
Shadow Leaf	San Marion	Vernon Kilns	1954–1955	Red and green flowers on green swirled background
Shaggy Tulip	Kitchenware	Hall	Mid-1930s–mid-1940s	
Shalimar	Shalimar	Steubenville		
Shantung	San Marion	Vernon Kilns	1953	Cloth-like texture; brown and green
Sheffield		Salem China	1943	
Shellridge		Harker		Gold decal design
Shellware, see Cameo Shellware				
Sherry	Colonial	Blue Ridge		Red and blue flower, border
Sherwood	Anytime	Vernon Kilns	1955–1958	Brown, bronze, and gold leaves on beige background
Shoo Fly	Colonial	Blue Ridge		Yellow and pink flowers
Shortcake	Lido	W. S. George		Strawberry decal
Showgirl	Candlewick	Blue Ridge		Red and yellow flowers; broken green rim
Sierra		Stangl	1976/ 1968–1970	Marked Prestige
Sierra Madre	Ultra	Vernon Kilns	1938	Pink, green, blue border
Signal Flags	Piecrust	Blue Ridge	1948	Red and black squares
*Silhouette		Crooksville	1930s	Silhouette decal; dog included
Silhouette	Skyline	Blue Ridge	1950s	Clothlike appearance; various colors
Silhouette		Hall	1930s	Black decal
Silhouette		Harker		
Silhouette		Taylor, Smith, and Taylor		
Silver Rose		Homer Laughlin	1960s	Floral decals
Silver Spray	Accent	E. M. Knowles	1954	
Simplicity	Accent	E. M. Knowles	1955	
Skiffs	Yorktown	E. M. Knowles		
Skyblue		Homer Laughlin	1977–1978	

PATTERN	SHAPE	MAKER	DATE	DESCRIPTION
Skylark	Americana	E. M. Knowles	1959	
Skyline Songbirds	Skyline	Blue Ridge	1950s	Eight different birds
Skytone		Homer Laughlin		Light blue
Sleeping Mexican	Deanna	E. M. Knowles		Mexican style; man sleeping under palm tree
Slender Leaf		Harker		Gray border; graceful leaf design
Smart Set	Casual	Red Wing	1955	
Smoky Mountain Laurel	Candlewick	Blue Ridge		Solid light blue with dark blue border
Smooth		J. A. Bauer	1936–1937	Solids
Snappy	Colonial	Blue Ridge		Red and blue flower
Snowflake		Homer Laughlin	1920	Decals
Snowflake		Sold by Montgomery Ward	1936	Decals
Snowflower		E. M. Knowles	1956	Russel Wright
Soddy-Daisy	Skyline	Blue Ridge	1950s	Small brown and cream flowers; red and green leaves; allover pattern
Solar	Esquire	E. M. Knowles	1957–1966	Russel Wright; abstract decal
Sombrero		Pottery Guild		Brightly colored fruit in straw basket
Sonata	Skyline	Blue Ridge	1950s	Blue flowers; pink buds
Sonesta		Homer Laughlin	1977–1978	
Songbirds	Astor	Blue Ridge		Eight different bird designs
Sorrento		Homer Laughlin	1977–1978	
Southern Belle	Coupe; Iva-Lure	Crooksville		Large single rosebud
Southern Camelia	Piecrust	Blue Ridge	1948	Pink flower, blue leaves, broken blue rim
Southern Dogwood	Skyline	Blue Ridge	1950s	Hand painted cream dogwood
Southern Rose	Melinda	Vernon Kilns	1942	Floral bouquet
Southwind	Forcast	E. M. Knowles	1959	
Sowing Seed	Square	Blue Ridge		Farmer; broken blue border
Speck Ware		J. A. Bauer	1946	Gray, pink, tan, white
Spice Islands	Montecito	Vernon Kilns	1950	Map of East and West Indies; sailing ships; marked "de Bron"
Spider, see Spring Blossom				
*Spiderweb	Skyline	Blue Ridge	1950s	Various solid colors, flecked finish
Spindrift	Candlewick	Blue Ridge		Center circle of small blue, red, and yellow flowers; thin red border
Spray	Piecrust	Blue Ridge	1950s	Small black and yellow flowers; green leaves
Spray	Coupe	Crooksville		Pink ground; gray and black decal

PATTERN	SHAPE	MAKER	DATE	DESCRIPTION
Sprig Crocus		Hall		Several sprigs on border
Spring	Trend	Steubenville		
Spring Blossom	LaGrande	Crooksville	1940s	Delicate floral sprays
Spring Bouquet		Sold for Montgomery Ward	1936	Decals
*Spring Glory	Candlewick	Blue Ridge		Hand painted blue flower and band
Spring Hill Tulip	Colonial	Blue Ridge		Center plaid tulips
Spring Song	Cavalier	Homer Laughlin		
Spring Song	Concord	Red Wing	1947	Birds
Springblossom	Regina	Paden City		Large multicolored pastel flowers
Springtime		W. S. George	1940s	Open window with flower trellis
*Springtime		Hall		Pink flowers on Hi-white body
Springtime		Harker		Large single budding flower
Spun Gold		Stangl	1965–1967	
Square Dance	Colonial	Blue Ridge		Party set of square dancers
Squares	Skyline	Blue Ridge	1950s	Three squares and ribbon
Standard		Salem		Narrow floral sprays; blue edge
*Stanhome Ivy	Skyline	Blue Ridge	1950s	Stylized green ivy sprig
Star	Teapot	Hall	1940	Turquoise or cobalt with gold stars
Star Bright	Accent	E. M. Knowles	1957	
*Star Flower		Stangl	1952–1957	Large center flower
Starburst		Franciscan		
Stardancer	Colonial	Blue Ridge		Two-handled vase with pink flowers
Stardust		Stangl	1967	
Stardust	Skytone	Homer Laughlin	1940s–1950s	Light blue background; stylized flowers
Starlight	Teapot	Hall		Band of stars; some with rhinestones
Step-Down	Coffeepot	Hall		Sugar and creamer; large and small sizes; different handles
Step-Round	Coffeepot	Hall		Large and small sizes; same handles
Sterling, see Russel Wright				
Still Life	Colonial	Blue Ridge		Bowl of fruit
Strathmoor	Colonial	Blue Ridge		Big dark and yellow flowers; broken rim
Stratosphere	Forcast	E. M. Knowles	1955	
Strawberry	Shenandoah	Paden City		Strawberry plant border
Strawberry Patch	Colonial	Blue Ridge		Strawberries; green and blue leaves
Strawberry Sundae	Skyline	Blue Ridge	1950s	Red strawberries; broken green rim

PATTERN	SHAPE	MAKER	DATE	DESCRIPTION
Streamers	Skyline	Blue Ridge	1950s	Ribbons
*Streamline	Teapot	Hall	1937	Canary and Delphinium most common colors; often silver trim
Style	Ultra	Vernon Kilns	1939	Fruits and floral border
Suburbia	Forcast	E. M. Knowles	1956	
Summer Day		Salem		Blue and white flowerpot with floral sprays
Sun Drops	Astor	Blue Ridge		Yellow and orange flowers, centered; miniature flowers border
Sun Garden	San Marion	Vernon Kilns	1953	Butterflies and flowers on green ground
Sun-Glo	Olympic	Harker	c.1955	Harmony House mark
Sun Glow	Forcast	E. M. Knowles	1958	
Sun Porch	Fiesta	Homer Laughlin		Decals; striped umbrella, table scene
Sunbright	Colonial	Blue Ridge		Yellow flowers, border; green line rim
Sunburst	Tempo	E. M. Knowles	1959	
Sundance	Candlewick	Blue Ridge		Large yellow flowers; border design
Sundial, see Saf-Handle				
Sunfire	Colonial	Blue Ridge		Yellow flowers, gray leaves
*Sunflower		Blue Ridge	c.1947	Large flowers
Sundowner	Candlewick	Blue Ridge		Two blue and two yellow flowers around plate
Sungold	Candlewick	Blue Ridge		
Sunny	Colonial	Blue Ridge		Yellow flowers
Sunny Day	Cavalier	Royal		Ironstone; large flower branch
Sunnybrook Farm	Accent	E. M. Knowles	1957	
Sunrise	Woodcrest	Blue Ridge	1950s	Sun rising behind a log cabin
Sunshine	Candlewick	Blue Ridge		Yellow flowers center; thin red border
Sunshine	Kitchenware	Hall	1933	Kitchenware; decals, lettering, solids; blue, Canary, Cadet, Chinese Red, Delphinium, Dresden Emerald, Indian Red, ivory, Lettuce, Marine, maroon, pink, rose, turquoise, yellow
Sunshine		Stangl		
*Surfside	Teapot	Hall	1939	Seashell-type pot
Susan	Skyline	Blue Ridge	1950s	Rust flowers
Susan		Stangl	1972–1974	Gold daisies and rim
Susan	Trend	Steubenville		
Susannah	Colonial	Blue Ridge		Pink and red flowers; thin red border; pink rim
Swedish		Crown		Modern flowers

PATTERN	SHAPE	MAKER	DATE	DESCRIPTION
Sweet Clover	Candlewick	Blue Ridge		
Sweet Pea	Colonial	Blue Ridge		Pastel blue and pink flowers on border; pink rim
Sweet Pea	Empire	Taylor, Smith, and Taylor		Pink decal
Sweet Rocket	Woodcrest	Blue Ridge	1950s	Brown and pink thistles; green rim
Swirl	Coupe	Crooksville		Flower sprigs on border pointing to center
Symmetry	Tempo	E. M. Knowles	1959	
Symphony	Colonial	Blue Ridge		Red flowers; blue leaves
T-Ball	Teapot	Hall	1948	Square or round; silver; marked Made for Bacharach, Inc. of New York
Tahiti	Triumph	Sebring-Limoges	1938	
Tahitian Gold	New Shape	Red Wing	1962	Gold
*Tam O'Shanter	Montecito	Vernon Kilns	1939	Green, lime, and reddish-brown plaid; green border; see also Calico; Coronation Organdy; Gingham; Home-spun; Organdie; Tweed
*Tampico	Futura	Red Wing	1955	Modernistic design
Tanglewood	Colonial	Blue Ridge		Pink flowers, green leaves, allover pattern
Tango		Homer Laughlin	1930s	Blue, green, yellow and red solids
Taste	Ultra	Vernon Kilns	1939	Maroon fruit and floral border
*Taverne		Hall	1930s	Silhouette decal; serving pieces
*Taverne	Laurel	Taylor, Smith, and Taylor		Silhouette decal; no dog; dinnerware
Tazewell Tulips	Colonial	Blue Ridge		Striped tulips
Tea for Two/ Tea for Four	Teapot	Hall		Angled top; no decoration
Tea Rose	Accent	E. M. Knowles	c.1954	
Tea Rose		Purinton	1936–1959	Two red rosebuds and broken dark rim
Teal Rose	Aladdin	Harker	1952	Wide border, large rose
Teataster	Teapot	Hall	Late 1940s	For Teamaster; oval; two compartments
Tempo	Piecrust	Blue Ridge	1948	Red and yellow flowers; green rim
Terra Rose		Stangl	1941–1942	
Terrace Ceramics	Corn Shape	Terrace Ceramics		
Texas Rose	Candlewick	Blue Ridge		Yellow flower
Thanksgiving Turkey	Skyline	Blue Ridge	1950s	Turkey in center
Thermo-Porcelain		Coors		Canary-tone glaze with decal, white glaze with chrysanthemums

PATTERN	SHAPE	MAKER	DATE	DESCRIPTION
Think Pink	Candlewick	Blue Ridge		Two pink flowers centered; dark pink border
Thistle	Trailway	Blue Ridge	1954	Thistle in center; wide gray border
Thistle		Hall		Muted floral
Thistle		French Saxon		
*Thistle		Stangl	1951–1967	Hand painted; purple and green decoration
Thistle		Universal		Decals
Thorley	Kitchenware	Hall		Small starbursts
Thorley	Teapot	Hall		
Tia Juana	Deanna	E. M. Knowles		Ivory, white background; Mexican decal
Tic Tack	Piecrust	Blue Ridge	1948	Apple, pear, cross-hatched center; broken green rim
Tickled Pink	Colonial	Blue Ridge		Pink leaves and rim; gray dots
Tickled Pink	Anytime	Vernon Kilns	1955–1958	Pink and gray geometric designs
Tiffany	Accent	E. M. Knowles	1955	
Tiger Flower	Tiger Flower	Franciscan		Pink
Tiger Lily	Colonial	Blue Ridge		Red, yellow flowers
Tiger Lily		Stangl	1957–1962	Decal
Tiny Rose	Casual	Red Wing	1958	
Toledo Delight	Trojan	Sebring	1941–1942	
*Tom & Jerry		Hall	1930s	Tom & Jerry printed on punch bowl, mug
Tom Thumb & the Butterfly		Homer Laughlin		Child's set; decal
Touch of Black	Regina	Paden City		Pastel flower sprays with occasional black leaves
Touch of Brown		Taylor, Smith, and Taylor		Brown and white flowered decal
Tower		Leigh		
Town & Country		Red Wing	1946	Blue, chartreuse, Forest Green, Metallic Brown, rust, Sandy Peach
*Town & Country		Stangl	1970s	Black, blue, green, honey, yellow; graniteware look
Trade Winds	San Marino	Vernon Kilns	1954–1956	Rust and chartreuse flowers on swirled ground
Tradition	Regent	E. M. Knowles	1948	
Trailing Rose	Montecito	Vernon Kilns	1939	Blue and red flowers and leaves on ivory ground
Traveler		Syracuse		Railroad china
Trellis	Duckbill	Crooksville	1929	Bright flowers on black trellis
Tricorne		Salem	1934	Red-orange; stripes; modern
Trinidad		Stangl	1972–1974	White background; aqua and brown flower burst; wide borders
Triple Treat	Cavalier	Royal		Ironstone; three modernistic flowers

PATTERN	SHAPE	MAKER	DATE	DESCRIPTION
Tritone	Teapot	Hall	1950s	Diagonal triangular sections of colors
Trojan	Trojan	Catalina Gladding, McBean and Co.	1930–1940s	Solids
Tropical	Skyline	Blue Ridge	1920–1957	Brown bamboo with green leaves
Trotter	Coupe	Crooksville		Racing horse
True Blue	Vernonware	Metlox	1965	
Tudor Rose	Sabina	Sabin		
*Tulip	D-Line	Hall	1930–1950s	Decals; yellow and purple tulips
Tulip		Universal		Decals
Tulip		Stangl	1942–1973	Blue and yellow; Terra Rose mark
Tulip		Salem		Tulip and bud
Tulip		E. M. Knowles		Bright orange tulip
Tulip		Paden City		Floral bouquet
Tulip		Leigh/Crescent		Vivid tulips
Tulip Tree		Homer Laughlin	1977–1978	
Tulip Trio	Candlewick	Blue Ridge		Three red tulips
Tulip Wreath	Coupe	Homer Laughlin		
Tulips	Kitchen Kraft	Homer Laughlin	1930s	Decals on ovenware
Tulips		Pottery Guild		
Tulips		Taylor, Smith, and Taylor		
Tuliptime	Tempo	E. M. Knowles	1961–1963	Ruffled tulips
Tuliptime	Candlewick	Blue Ridge		Red, yellow, and purple tulips; green border
Tuna Salad	Skyline	Blue Ridge	1950s	Blue and brown fish
Turkey with Acorns	Skyline	Blue Ridge	1950s	
Turtle Dove	New Shape	Red Wing	1962	Two Doves
Tweed	Montecito	Vernon Kilns	1950–1955	Gray, blue plaid; see also Calico; Coronation Organdy; Gingham; Homespun; Organdie; Tam O'Shanter
Tweed Tex	Anniversary	Red Wing	1953	White
Twilight		Flintridge China Co.		
Twin Oaks	Accent	E. M. Knowles	c.1954	
*Twinspout	Teapot	Hall	Late 1940s	For Teamaster; round; two compartments
Twin-Tee	Teapot	Hall		Flat top; decorated in gold or decal
Two-Some	Montecito	Vernon Kilns	1938	Brown bands on cream ground
Two Step	Village Green	Red Wing	1960	Geometric design
Two-Tone	Ultra	Vernon Kilns	c.1938	Wide border in blue, green, pink
Tyrol	Olivia	Steubenville		Aster, buttercup, carnation, gardenia

PATTERN	SHAPE	MAKER	DATE	DESCRIPTION
*Ultra California	Ultra	Vernon Kilns	1937–1942	Blue, ivory, light green, maroon, pink, yellow
Unicoi	Clinchfield	Blue Ridge		Red and blue flowered border
Valley Violet	Astor	Blue Ridge		Small flowers
Vegetable Patch	Skyline	Blue Ridge	1950s	Corn and tomato on black sponged background
Veggie	Skyline	Blue Ridge	1950s	Vegetables
Veggies		Crooksville		
Vera	Ultra	Vernon Kilns	1938	Floral
Vermillion Rose	Triumph	Sebring-Limoges		
Vernon 1860	San Fernando	Vernon Kilns	1944; 1955	Scene of 1860s America in brown; floral border
Vernon Rose	San Fernando	Vernon Kilns	1944; 1950–1954	Yellow rose, blossoms; cream ground
Verona	Colonial	Blue Ridge		Large blue flowers, border
Veronica	Clinchfield	Blue Ridge		Yellow and red flowers and borders in center; wide green outer border
Vestal Rose		E. M. Knowles	1930s	Decals
Victoria	Colonial	Blue Ridge		Pink and yellow flowers; red rim
Victoria	Teapot	Hall	Early 1940s	Celadon only; Victorian style
Victoria	Americana	E. M. Knowles	1959	
Victoria	Montecito	Vernon Kilns	1939	Green flowers and leaves
Victory		Salem		Fluted border
Vienna	Victory	Salem	1940s	
Viking, see Bell				
Village Brown	Village Green	Red Wing	1955	Brown
Village Green	Village Green	Red Wing	1953	Green
Vine		Harker		Cameoware
Vine Yard	Vernonware	Metlox	1965	
Vine Wreath	Laurel	Taylor, Smith, and Taylor	1933–1934	Decals
Vintage	Colonial	Blue Ridge		Bold grapes, vine, and leaves
Vintage	Royal Gadroon	Harker	1947–1949	Red and green ivy
Vintage	Accent	E. M. Knowles	1953–1954	
Vintage	Lotus	Vernon Kilns	1950	Purple grapes, brown leaves
Vintage	True China	Red Wing	1960	Floral
Vintage Pink	Poppytrail	Metlox	1965	
Violet	Trend	Steubenville		
Violet Spray	Skyline	Blue Ridge	1950s	Off-centered large and small violet sprays
Violet Spray		Homer Laughlin	1920	Decals
*Virginia Rose	Virginia Rose	Homer Laughlin	1935–1960	Decal; spray of roses, leaves
*Vistosa		Taylor, Smith, and Taylor	1938	Solids; cobalt blue, deep yellow, light green, mango red

PATTERN	SHAPE	MAKER	DATE	DESCRIPTION
Vistosa		E. M. Knowles	1936	Solids; cadet blue, burgundy, red, russet, yellow
Vogue		Syracuse		
Wagon Wheels		Frankoma	1942	Solids; Clay Blue, Desert Gold, Onyx Black, Prairie Green, Red Bud
Waldorf		Sebring-Limoges	1939	
Waltz Time	Colonial	Blue Ridge		Pastel flowers, broken blue border
Wampum	Ranchero	W. S. George		Floral
Ward's Garland		Sold by Montgomery Ward	1936	Decals
Water Lily	Yorktown	E. M. Knowles		
Water Lily		Stangl	1949–1957	
Waterlily	Astor	Blue Ridge		Multicolored pastel flower; blue rim
Waverly		Homer Laughlin	1977–1978	
Weather Bloom	Squared-Off Edges	E. M. Knowles	1933–1934	Decals
Weathervane (No. 4277)	Skyline	Blue Ridge	1950s	House and tree; sponged yellow background; green rim
Weathervane	Forcast	E. M. Knowles	1957	
Westinghouse, See Aristocrat; Emperor; King; Patrician; Prince; Queen				
Westwind		Frankoma	1962	Solids
Wheat	Skyline	Blue Ridge	1950s	Three golden wheat stalks
Wheat		Harker	1961	Cameoware
Wheat	Deanna; Accent	E. M. Knowles	1954	Wheat stalks
Wheat	Melinda	Vernon Kilns	1942	Sheaths of wheat and blossom sprays; Harmony House mark and "Exclusively for Sears, Roebuck and Co."
Wheat		W. S. George		Brightly colored wheat stalks
Wheat (Hall), see Poppy & Wheat				
Wheat Sheaf	Criterion	E. M. Knowles	1955	
Wheatfield		Sebring-Limoges		
Whirligig	Piecrust; Colonial	Blue Ridge	1950s	Red and light blue flowers; green leaves and rim
White and Embossed		Sold by Montgomery Ward	1920	Decals
White & Gold		Homer Laughlin	1920	Decals
White & Gold Carnation		Homer Laughlin	1920	Decals
White & Green Persian		Homer Laughlin	1920	Decals
*White Clover		Harker		Russel Wright; engraved design; Charcoal, Coral Sand, Golden Spice, Meadow Green

PATTERN	SHAPE	MAKER	DATE	DESCRIPTION
White Dogwood		Stangl	1965–1974	Marked Prestige; white flowered border
White Gold Ware		Sebring	1940s	
White Grape		Stangl	1967	
*White Rose		Harker Potteries	1940s	Cameoware; blue or pink; outlined flowers in center
Wild Bouquet		Homer Laughlin	1977–1978	Corn-Kraft; made for Montgomery Ward
Wild Cherry #1	Skyline	Blue Ridge	1950s	Rust leaves; yellow cherries; broken green rim
Wild Cherry #2	Skyline	Blue Ridge	1950s	Pink and gray leaves; black rim
Wild Cherry #3	Piecrust	Blue Ridge	1950s	Cherries; yellow and brown leaves; broken green rim
Wild Irish Rose	Colonial	Blue Ridge		Red flowers border
Wild Oats		E. M. Knowles	1955	
Wild Poppy	Radiance; Kitchenware	Hall	1930s	Orange poppies; green leaves
Wild Rose		Crown	1941	Wild flowers and wheat sheaths
Wild Rose		Hall		
Wild Rose	Regent	Knowles	1948	
Wild Rose	Princess	Paden City		
Wild Rose	Colonial	Blue Ridge		Pink flowers
Wild Rose	Floral Edge	E. M. Knowles	1933–1934	Decals
Wild Rose		Homer Laughlin		Floral decals
Wild Rose		Stangl	1955–1973	
Wild Rose & Flower	Empress	Homer Laughlin	1920	Decals
Wild Straw-berry	Colonial	Blue Ridge		Two strawberries; green rim
*Wildfire	D-Line	Hall	1950s	Hi-white body; floral garland decals
*Wildflower	Floral Edge	E. M. Knowles	1933–1934	Decals
Wildwood	Colonial	Blue Ridge		Red, pink, and yellow flowers, center, border
Wildwood		Stangl		
Williamsburg	Tempo	E. M. Knowles	1961–1963	
Willow	Coupe	Crooksville		Pussy willow stalks
Willow	Willow	Franciscan		
Willow Wind	Concord	Red Wing	1947	Abstract
Winchester '73	Montecito	Vernon Kilns	1950	Western scene on cream ground
Windcrest	Teapot	Hall	1940s	Canary and sponged gold; fluted; high lip
Windfall		Stangl	1955–1957	Canary
*Windflower	Colonial	Blue Ridge		Fanciful red flower with green leaves
Windjammer	Clinchfield	Blue Ridge		Center sailboat; wide blue border; black rim

PATTERN	SHAPE	MAKER	DATE	DESCRIPTION
Windmill		Crown		
Windmill		Universal		
Windmill	Victory	Salem		Decals
*Windshield	Teapot	Hall	1941	Maroon and camellia most common colors
Winesap	Skyline	Blue Ridge	1950s	Three red apples
Winged Streamliner		Homer Laughlin		Railroad china
Winnie	Skyline	Blue Ridge	1950s	Off-centered red flowers
Wishing Well	Skyline	Blue Ridge	1950s	Well, tree, and fence
Wizard of Oz	Kiddieware	Stangl	Mid-1940s–1974	
Woman in the Shoe	Kiddieware	Stangl	Mid-1940s–1974	
Wood Echo	Forcast	E. M. Knowles	1957	
Wood Rose		Stangl	1973–1974	
Wood Song		Harker		
Wood Violets	Accent	E. M. Knowles	c.1954	
*Woodfield		Steubenville		Leaf shapes; American Modern shades: Dove Gray, Golden Fawn, Salmon Pink, Tropic Rust
Woodhue	Flair	Salem		
Woodland	Round Coupe	Salem		
Woodland Gold		Metlox		Marked Poppytrail
*Woodvine		Universal		Small red flowers, large leaves
*World's Fair	Teapot	Hall		Cobalt and gold; trylon and perisphere embossed on side
Wren	Square	Blue Ridge		Bird; broken black rim
Wrightwood	Rainbow	E. M. Knowles	1930s	Decals
Wrinkled Rose	Colonial	Blue Ridge		Pink flower; yellow rim
Year 'Round	Year 'Round	Vernon Kilns	1957–1958	Gray, mocha, and yellow circles
*Yellow Carnation	Fiesta	Homer Laughlin	1962–1968	Yellow and brown flowers on white background; yellow rim; Casual pattern; see also Daisy
Yellow Flower		Stangl	1970	
Yellow Matte Gold		Homer Laughlin	1920	Decals
Yellow Matte Gold Band	Plain Edge	Homer Laughlin	1920	Decals
Yellow Plaid		Blair		
Yellow Poppy	Candlewick	Blue Ridge		Off-centered pattern
Yellow Rose	D-Style	Hall		
Yellow Rose	Minion	Paden City	1952	
Yellow Trim Poppy	Deanna	E. M. Knowles		

PATTERN	SHAPE	MAKER	DATE	DESCRIPTION
Yellow Tulip		Stangl		Terra Rose mark
Yellowridge		Salem		Multicolored flowers
Yorkshire	Swirled Edge	Metlox	c.1939	Solids; pastels; Delphinium Blue, Canary Yellow, Old Rose, Opal Green, Peach, Poppy Orange, Satin Ivory, Satin Turquoise, turquoise blue, yellow
Yorktown	Colonial	Blue Ridge		Centered bird, apple, and leaves; dark line border
*Yorktown	Yorktown	E. M. Knowles	1936	Concentric Deco shape; solid colors; light yellow, maroon, periwinkle blue, terra cotta
Young in Heart	Year 'Round	Vernon Kilns	1956–1958	Flowers in aqua, charcoal, mocha, and yellow
*Zeisel	Hallcraft	Hall	1950–1960s	Solid white; designed by Eva Zeisel
Zephyr, see Bingo				
Zinnia	Colonial	Blue Ridge		Red, blue, and orange flowers
Zinnia		Homer Laughlin	1977–1978	
Zinnia	Concord	Red Wing	1947	

We welcome any additions or corrections to this chart. Please write to us c/o Crown Publishers, 225 Park Avenue South, New York, NY 10003.

KOVELS

SEND ORDERS & INQUIRIES TO: **Crown Publishers, Inc.**
225 Park Avenue South, New York, N.Y. 10003
ATT: SALES DEPT.

SALES & TITLE INFORMATION
1-800-526-4264

NAME ______

ADDRESS ______

CITY & STATE ______ ZIP ______

PLEASE SEND ME THE FOLLOWING BOOKS:

ITEM NO.	QTY.	TITLE		PRICE	TOTAL
56579X	______	Kovels' Antiques & Collectibles Price List 20th Edition	PAPER	$10.95	______
566133	______	Kovels' Bottles Price List Eighth Edition	PAPER	$12.95	______
566966	______	Kovels' Guide to Selling Your Antiques & Collectibles	PAPER	$9.95	______
558718	______	Kovels' Advertising Collectibles Price List 1st Edition	PAPER	$11.95	______
549808	______	Kovels' Collector's Guide to American Art Pottery	PAPER	$13.95	______
001411	______	Dictionary of Marks – Pottery and Porcelain	HARDCOVER	$10.95	______
559145	______	Kovels' New Dictionary of Marks	HARDCOVER	$17.95	______
568659	______	Kovels' Depression Glass & American Dinnerware Price List 3rd Edition	PAPER	$12.95	______
55044X	______	Kovels' Illustrated Price Guide to Royal Doulton 2nd Edition	PAPER	$10.95	______
545012	______	Kovels' Know Your Antiques Revised and Updated	HARDCOVER	$15.95	______
536080	______	Kovels' Know Your Collectibles	HARDCOVER	$18.95	______
54668X	______	American Country Furniture 1780 – 1875	PAPER	$14.95	______

______ TOTAL ITEMS

TOTAL RETAIL VALUE ______

CHECK OR MONEY ORDER ENCLOSED MADE PAYABLE TO CROWN PUBLISHERS, INC., 225 Park Avenue South, New York, N.Y. 10003 or telephone 1-800-526-4264 (No cash or stamps, please)

Shipping & Handling
Charge $1.40 for one book;
60¢ for each additional book ______

TOTAL AMOUNT DUE ______

Charge: ☐ MasterCard ☐ Visa ☐ American Express
Account Number (include all digits) Expires MO. YR.

______

______

nature ______

Thank you for your order.

PRICES SUBJECT TO CHANGE WITHOUT NOTICE. If a more recent edition of a price list has been published at the same price, it will be sent instead of the old edition.